VALUABLE WORKS.

Diary and Correspondence OF THE LATE AMOS LAWRENCE. Edited by his son, WM. R. LAWRENCE, M. D. Octavo, cloth, $1.25; also, royal 12mo. ed., cl., $1.00.

Kitto's Popular Cyclopædia OF BIBLICAL LITERATURE. 500 illustrations. One vol., octavo. 812 pages. Cloth, $3.

Intended for ministers, theological students, parents, Sabbath-school teachers, and the great body of the religious public.

Analytical Concordance of the Holy SCRIPTURES; or, The Bible presented under Classified Heads or Topics. By JOHN EADIE, D. D. Octavo, 836 pp. $3.

Dr. Williams' Works.

Lectures on the Lord's Prayer — Religious Progress — Miscellanies.

☞ Dr. Williams is a profound scholar and a brilliant writer. — *New York Evangelist.*

Modern Atheism. Considered under its forms of Pantheism, Materialism, Secularism, Development and Natural Laws. By JAMES BUCHANAN, D. D., LL. D. 12mo. Cloth, $1.25.

The Hallig: or the Sheepfold in the Waters. A Tale of Humble Life on the Coast of Schleswig. From the German, by Mrs. GEORGE P. MARSH. 12mo. Cl., $1.

The Suffering Saviour. By Dr. KRUMMACHER. 12mo. Cloth, $1.25.

Heaven. By JAMES WM. KIMBALL. 12mo.

Christian's Daily Treasury. Religious Exercise for every Day in the Year. By Rev. E. TEMPLE. 12mo. Cloth, $1.

Wayland's Sermons. Delivered in the Chapel of Brown Univ. 12mo. Cl., $1.00.

Entertaining and Instructive Works FOR THE YOUNG. Elegantly illustrated. 16mo. Cloth, gilt backs.

The American Statesman. Life and Character of Daniel Webster. — *Young Americans Abroad;* or Vacation in Europe. — *The Island Home;* or the Young Cast-aways. — *Pleasant Pages for Young People.* — *The Guiding Star.* — *The Poor Boy and Merchant Prince.*

THE AIMWELL STORIES. Resembling and quite equal to the "Rollo Stories." — *Christian Register.* By WALTER AIMWELL. *Oscar;* or the Boy who had his own way. — *Clinton;* or Boy-Life in the Country. — *Ella;* or Turning over a New Leaf. — *Whistler;* or The Manly Boy. — *Marcus;* or the Boy Tamer.

WORKS BY Rev. HARVEY NEWCOMB. *How to be a Lady.* — *How to be a Man.* — *Anecdotes for Boys.* — *Anecdotes for Girls.*

BANVARD'S SERIES OF AMERICAN HISTORIES. *Plymouth and the Pilgrims.* — *Romance of American History.* — *Novelties of the New World, and Tragic Scenes in the History of Maryland and the old French War.*

God Revealed in Nature and in CHRIST. By Rev. JAMES B. WALKER. Author of "The Philosophy of the Plan of Salvation." 12mo. Cloth, $1.

Philosophy of the Plan of Salvation. New enlarged edition. 12mo. Cloth, 75 c.

Christian Life; SOCIAL AND INDIVIDUAL. By PETER BAYNE. 12mo. Cloth, $1.25.

All agree in pronouncing it one of the most admirable works of the age.

Yahveh Christ; or the Memorial Name. By ALEX. MACWHORTER. With an Introductory Letter, by NATH'L W. TAYLOR, D. D., in Yale Theol. Sem. 16mo. Cloth, 60 c.

The Signet Ring, AND ITS HEAVENLY MOTTO. From the German. 16mo. Cl., 31 c.

The Marriage Ring; or How to Make Home Happy. 18mo. Cloth, gilt, 75 c.

Mothers of the Wise and Good. By JABEZ BURNS, D. D. 16mo, Cloth, 75 c.

☞ A sketch of the mothers of many of the most eminent men of the world.

My Mother; or Recollections of Maternal Influence. 12mo. Cloth, 75c.

The Excellent Woman, with an Introduction, by Rev. W. B. SPRAGUE, D. D. Splendid Illustrations. 12mo. Cloth, $1.

The Progress of Baptist Principles IN THE LAST HUNDRED YEARS. By T. F. CURTIS, Prof. of Theology in the Lewisburg University. 12mo. Cloth, $1.25.

Dr. Harris' Works.

The Great Teacher. — The Great Commission. — The Pre-Adamite Earth. — Man Primeval. — Patriarchy. — Posthumous Works, 4 volumes.

The Better Land; OR THE BELIEVER'S JOURNEY AND FUTURE HOME. By Rev. A. C. THOMPSON. 12mo. Cloth, 85 c.

Kitto's History of Palestine, from the Patriarchal Age to the Present Time. With 200 Illustrations. 12mo. Cloth, $1.25.

An admirable work for the Family, the Sabbath and week-day School Library.

The Priest and the Huguenot; or, PERSECUTION IN THE AGE OF LOUIS XV. From the French of L. F. BUNGENER. Two vols., 12mo. Cloth, $2.25.

This is not only a work of thrilling interest, but is a masterly Protestant production.

The Psalmist. A Collection of Hymns for the Use of Baptist Churches. By BARON STOW and S. F. SMITH. With a SUPPLEMENT, containing an Additional Selection of Hymns, by RICHARD FULLER, D. D., and J. B. JETER, D. D. Published in various sizes, and styles of binding.

This is unquestionably the best collection of Hymns in the English language.

☞ In addition to works published by themselves, they keep an extensive assortment of works in all departments of trade, which they supply at publishers' prices. ☞ They particularly invite the attention of Booksellers, Travelling Agents, Teachers, School Committees, Librarians, Clergymen, and professional men generally (to whom a liberal discount is uniformly made), to their extensive stock. ☞ To persons wishing copies of Text-books, for examination, they will be forwarded, per mail or otherwise, on the reception of *one half* the price of the work desired. ☞ Orders from any part of the country attended to with faithfulness and dispatch.

POSTHUMOUS WORKS

OF THE

REV. JOHN HARRIS, D.D.

EDITED BY THE

REV. PHILLIP SMITH, B. A.,

LATE COLLEAGUE OF DR. HARRIS IN CHESHUNT COLLEGE, AND IN NEW COLLEGE, LONDON.

SERMONS

AND

ADDRESSES

DELIVERED ON

SPECIAL OCCASIONS.

BY

JOHN HARRIS, D. D.,

LATE PRESIDENT OF NEW COLLEGE, LONDON; AUTHOR OF "THE GREAT TEACHER," "THE GREAT COMMISSION," "PRE-ADAMITE EARTH," "MAN PRIMEVAL," "PATRIARCHY," ETC. ETC.

SECOND SERIES.

BOSTON:
GOULD AND LINCOLN,
59 WASHINGTON STREET.
NEW YORK: SHELDON, BLAKEMAN & CO.
CINCINNATI: GEORGE S. BLANCHARD.
1858.

PREFACE.

THE former volume contained those Sermons which had for their theme the everlasting being and perfections of God, and their manifestation by Him to man; the incarnation, the work, and the sacrifice of Christ, and the nature, progress, and final establishment of His kingdom upon earth.

The present series begins with man, viewed first as God created him, then as fallen and again redeemed; and, in this character, as made the servant of his Saviour in a new course of inward life and outward duties. These Sermons are, however, naturally more miscellaneous as to their subjects than those in the former volume; and the Editor's chief object has been to give a specimen of the Author's manner of treating each great topic of discourse. The two Sermons on the Christian Ministry and

Ministerial Education (Nos. XII. and XIII.), which are of peculiar interest on account of their connection with our lamented Friend's labours as a Tutor, presented a difficulty from their close resemblance in some parts; but the Editor could not make up his mind to omit, or mutilate, that comprehensive view of the whole subject which is given in the twelfth Sermon, and much less that masterly defence of Ministerial Education which is made in the thirteenth. Repetitions of less consequence, in other discourses, have been dealt with on the principles stated in the Preface to the first volume.

The final decision as to those Sermons which could not be included in these two volumes, has been made with reference partly to the resemblance in subject to those now printed, and partly to the fact of previous publication. It is on the latter ground that the well-known Discourses on "The Witnessing Church," the "Christian Citizen," and the "Conversion of the Jews," and the Funeral Sermon for Dr Pye Smith, are not reprinted in this collection.

CONTENTS.

SERMON V.

SERMON VI.

SERMON VII.

SERMON VIII.

SERMON IX.

SERMON X.

THE WORDS OF LIFE SPOKEN IN GOD'S TEMPLE.

SERMON XI.

THE CHRISTIAN MINISTRY.

SERMON XII.

THE IMPORTANCE OF AN EDUCATED MINISTRY.

SERMON XIII.

RELIGIOUS EDUCATION.

SERMON XIV.

CHRIST PRECIOUS TO THE BELIEVER.

SERMON XV.

JACOB'S DREAM.

CHARGES.

CHARGE I.

THE SERVANT OF JESUS CHRIST.

CHARGE II.

THE IDEA AND AIM OF THE CHRISTIAN MINISTRY.

CHARGE III.

THE CAPABILITIES OF THE CHRISTIAN MINISTRY.

CHARGE IV.

THE GOOD SOLDIER OF JESUS CHRIST.—HIS LAST DISCOURSE.

SERMON I.

GOD'S REGARD FOR MAN.

JOB vii. 17.—"What is man that thou shouldest magnify him? and that thou shouldest set thine heart upon him?"

THIS sentiment is to be found, in a slightly different form, in several parts of the Word of God: in this passage of Job, which is the earliest instance of its occurrence; in the 8th and 144th Psalms; and in the 2d chapter of the Epistle to the Hebrews, where it is applied to Christ as the representative of the human race.

In every instance in which this sentiment is uttered, the inspired writer will be found to be contemplating man from a somewhat different point of view. Here, he is regarded chiefly as the subject of that moral discipline, by which he is shewn to be the object of God's incessant care. Elsewhere—in the 8th Psalm—the same sentiment is uttered in reference to man's wonderful constitution, his high rank in the scale of creation, and his dominion over the inferior creatures; especially, when his insignificant appearance is placed in contrast with the amplitude and magnificence of the starry heavens. And as this view takes us back to the starting-point of man's historical career—back to his very introduction upon earth—and prepares us to take affecting views of the Divine condescension towards him in every subsequent stage—with this we propose to begin.

I.

Now, in specifying some of the proofs that God has magnified man, and set His heart upon him, let me inquire, first, if it should appear that all the original arrangements of nature were but one vast provision for the arrival of man upon earth, would not this demonstrate the Divine regard for his wellbeing? Now, such is actually the fact.

And here let me avow my conviction that the Adamic creation was only the last of a long series of creations which at far distant intervals had taken place. Often, I believe, since the material of the earth had been first called into existence,—often had it been "without form, and void, and darkness had hung on the face of the deep." And as often had the great Creator arisen out of His place to recall it from chaos, and to restore it to order and beauty. But even each of these successive wrecks of the earth had looked on beyond itself, and had a respect to the coming of man; and each of these new creations which followed had formed part of a system of means of which man was to be the subordinate end. For him volcanic fires had fused and crystallized the granite, and piled it up into lofty table-lands. For him the never-wearied water had worn and washed it down into extensive valleys, and plains of vegetable soil. For him the earth had often vibrated with electrical shocks, and had become interlaced with rich metallic veins. Ages of quiet had succeeded each revolution of nature, during which the long-accumulating vegetables of preceding periods were, for him, transmuted into stores of fuel—some of the deposits of primeval waters were becoming iron—and successive races of destroyed animals were changed into masses of useful material. For him the interior of the earth had become a storehouse in which everything necessary had been laid up for his use; that when the time should come for him to open and gaze on its treasures—"on the blessings of the deep that lieth under," on "the chief things of the ancient mountains, and the precious things of the lasting hills"—he might recognize the benevolent foresight of the Being who had prepared, selected, and placed them there, and might exclaim, "The whole earth is full of His goodness!"

But long as the earth had been solemnly marching from stage to stage in obedient fulfilment of its great destiny—and often as its anarchy had been hushed and the morning of a new creation had dawned on it—never till now, perhaps, when man was about to be formed, had angel witnesses looked on, nor such vast and stately preparations been made for the event. Long years of the life of the king of Israel were spent in collecting materials for the erection of a temple on Zion; and, when, at length, he was obliged to devolve the work on his son, and when he had informed him, in the midst of his assembled nobles, of all the great and costly preparations which he had made, what heart did not swell with the grandeur of the design, and, at the same time, tremble at its solemnity and magnitude? But here were materials which had been collecting and preparing under the eye of the Great Designer, for a period, perhaps, never to be dated; out of these a temple-world is to be made, of which every part is to be an altar of memorial—a symbol of the Godhead;—and now, as soon as it is completed, the new-made worshipper is to enter and adore. What seraph did not burn with unwonted ardour for the issue! For now the hour was at hand.

Already, and only five days before, in preparation for his coming, the anarchy of chaos had been suddenly reduced to order; and the laws of nature, resuming their operation, had received their new commission to be to him "for signs, and for seasons, and for days, and years," till time itself shall be no more. Already the earth has received its appropriate geographical distribution, as the theatre in which the great drama of humanity is to be performed. Power, already, has reared its hills, and smoothed its valleys, and directed the course of its rivers; and has established all its chains of causes and effects. Wisdom has clothed the earth with verdure, and has completed its arrangements of means and ends. Goodness has filled all the channels of animal enjoyment from its own overflowing fountain. And as the great work has advanced from stage to stage, the Mighty Maker has paused, and surveyed, and pronounced it good.

But still it is only a relative good—good, that is, in relation to the addition about to be made to it in the coming of man. Viewed in this relation, it is good as compared with what it has ever yet been. Hitherto, though the Divine Power, and Wisdom, and Goodness, have for ages been here, where was the eye intelligently to behold them? Where, when the Divine Benignity smiled—where was the countenance to reflect and return the smile? But now the Divine Creator knew that His work would be read with an intelligent eye. To these mountains His Faithfulness will be able to point for an image of its own stability, and say, "It is like the great mountains, and it reacheth to the heavens." In that glorious sun, the new-made eye of man will soon recognize an emblem of a purity too bright to be gazed on, and of an omniscience from which nothing is hid. The boundless magnificence of night will call forth the admiring burst, "The heavens declare the glory of God, and the firmament sheweth his handy work." Day after day will be uttering speech to man's listening ear; and night after night will be shewing knowledge to man's intelligent eye. That "great and wide sea, wherein are things moving innumerable," will come to be regarded as a vast treasury of solemn thoughts. Over its dim, and restless, and apparently shoreless waters, the Spirit of God will still, in a sense, continue to brood; impregnating and making it prolific of sublime conceptions. Thence lofty motives will come, and solemn imaginations, and dark but ennobling hints of the infinite and the eternal. And so overpowering a conception of the Creator's excellence will be derived from a survey of the boundless fulness of terrestrial life and being, that the enraptured beholder will be heard to call out on all created things to join him in a hymn of lofty praise. Viewed in this relation, too, creation was good as compared with what it might have been. For He to whom all *possibilities* are foreknown, as well as all *realities*, knew what the most distant result to man would be, of a single change in the arrangements and laws of creation; knew, for example, how injuriously a slight alteration in the constitution of the atmosphere would affect the wellbeing of man; knew how a change in the direction of the course of a river would impede for ages the march of civilization; and how the introduction of even another race of animal existence might prevent the spread of colonization, and even endanger the continuance of man upon the earth. Now He that "seeth the end from the beginning" knew that no such element of evil had been admitted into His new creation. Everything had been prepared, and selected, and exquisitely adjusted to the constitution of the coming man.

And could we have had all this mighty preparation to pass before us—could we have known that every thought of the projected creature man would find an image in external nature, and that every object in nature would find a responsive emotion in the mind of man—could we have seen that for him the Creator had weighed the very mountains in scales and the hills in a balance—that in him the laws of matter would find their interpreter, the vegetable kingdom its uses, the animal tribes their sovereign, and all creation its subordinate completion and its end—could we have forborne exclaiming, "Lord, what is man that thou shouldest thus magnify him, and that thou shouldest set thine heart upon him!"

II.

But, secondly, if it shall appear that the constitution of man is made answerable to all this rich provision for his arrival, this would still further prove the depth of the Divine regard for his wellbeing. I need not remind you that there was much that was special in the provision made for the first man. "A garden did the Lord God plant eastward in Eden" for his happy abode. Here was the mansion; but as yet the inhabitant was not. Here was the temple complete; the worshipper is now to be created. Did not all nature hold in its breath, and await his coming, with suspense? Did not a universal silence reign to hear the fiat for his creation issued. But mark, the form of the creative command is changed. He who hath said, "Let there be light," saith not, "Let there be man." The Creator himself, as if to mark the importance of the crisis, hath paused. To denote the new style and excellence of the work which He is now to perform, the Creator is represented as proceeding to it deliberately, and as the result of self-consultation. To indicate the God-like character and destiny of the creature, the Elohim said, "Let us make man in our image, after our likeness, and let them have dominion over all the earth." And to denote man's direct and peculiar derivation from God, he is described as formed by the immediate hand, and inspired by the inbreathing of the Godhead.

And could we have marked that bodily organization, as it still lay under its Maker's hand, prostrate on the earth—could we have seen how every part of it was related to every other part, and the whole adapted for the reception of the indwelling soul, and for the relations of that soul to all the external universe—should we not have recognized an argument for the divinity of its Maker in every part of the structure, and, with the Psalmist, have deeply felt, that it was "fearfully and wonderfully made!"

But even this wonderful structure was only to be the servant of the more wonderful soul which was to actuate and employ it. Glance at the capacities and powers of that soul. One of its most recent and surprising discoveries is, that light falling on certain substances, under particular circumstances, actually produces the likenesses of objects. Yet what is this but the type of another and a more wonderful process, by which all the objects of nature are constantly leaving their image on the mind—all the events of providence writing their history and leaving their impress on the tablet of the heart;—a process by which, at every step through life, the soul is filling with recollections and impressions for evil or for good, all of which it will take away with it, as subjects for remorse or for gratitude, throughout eternity.

Think of his intellectual powers. Are all creation and providence constructed and conducted on a mighty plan? *His* mind is capable of tracing the relations of things; of classifying and distributing a world, a universe, of objects and events; of reproducing, in his own mind, parts of the great plan of the Infinite mind itself;—capable of seeking after the Author of that plan; of ascending the pyramid of creation, whose head towers away into the invisible, till he finds the Creator himself enthroned on the summit.

As a being capable of affection and emotion, he asks for objects of pity, compassion, and benevolence; for in the relief of their necessities, or in communion with their excellences, he sympathizes with God himself, and finds his purest enjoyment. But these alone are not equal to his desires. Bring them all before him, and he would still ask for more—still sigh for excellence unlimited, and for a sphere of activity infinite. After taking all created excellence to his heart, and lavishing his affections on it, he would still have affection to spare, capacities unoccupied, boundless love unemployed; and the loftiest height of *created* excellence would only furnish him with a point from which to soar away in quest of Him who challenges all the love of which he is capable.

As a creature influenced by motives, he is capable of being moved by every class of objects. While his appetites stoop to gather up their objects from the dust, a sense of duty can bear him away in homage to the throne of the Invisible. Yes, though he is here upon earth, the same motive can impel him to action which at the same moment is impelling an archangel as he speeds his way on some high and heavenly mission. And as a creature capable of moral government, he is made, not only to find happiness in obeying the very laws to which God himself conforms—he is capable of sympathizing with the Divine character, of reflecting the Divine excellence, and of even aspiring to live for the very same end as that for which God himself lives and reigns—for the manifestation of the Divine glory.

Tell us not, then, of man's insignificance as contrasted with the vastness of the material universe. You are comparing mind with matter—things in their nature essentially different. Imagine not that because, to the eye of sense, man is only a speck in the universe, he is therefore overlooked. His importance depends not on his physical dimensions. Far other is the standard of the Divine measurement. Reckon up the number of the stars if you please, measure their masses, and shew us that earth itself is but an atom in the all but boundless system;—the very process by which you prove this, serves to shew the superiority of the mind which can thus survey, and measure, and make the whole its own. Imagine, if you please, that the limits of the universe should yet be indefinitely extended—that worlds and systems should be added to it beyond all calculation—and in tracts of space beyond the sweep of the strongest created wing—your very power to imagine this proves your superiority to the whole. That sun—those stars—see not their own light, feel not their own heat, know not even of their own existence; while you, receiving the impression of the whole, can refer their existence to the hand that made them, and fall down in adoration at His feet.

Tell us not, either, of the faint and flickering indications of animal understanding. Intellect, in its true definition, is denied to it. In the brightening ascent of mind, man leaves behind him whole tribes of animals at every step; till, having reached the sphere of the true reason, he finds himself entirely alone. He alone is conscious of the power to will. The sacred domain of conscience, too, is all his own. God himself has led him to a throne which overlooks and commands all earthly things; and, placing him upon it as His own representative, has empowered him to occupy it in

His name; and to remember that there is but one throne to which he is finally amenable—the throne of Him who ruleth over all. "Lord, what is man that thou art mindful of him? and the son of man that thou visitest him? For thou hast made him a little lower than the angels, and hast crowned him with glory and honour. Thou madest him to have dominion over the works of thine hands; thou hast put all things under his feet." How lofty his endowments; how glorious his prospects! For know, that they are not bounded by the visible and the present;—they stretch away into eternity—they embrace the throne of God! Oh, had but one of all the human race been endowed with immortality—if, with one solitary exception, all mankind were doomed to annihilation—would not that one be deemed the wonder, the envy, the admiration of all the rest? In the presence of that heir of immortality, would not all earthly crowns be eclipsed, all human distinctions be forgotten? But this great inheritance belongs to all! And more than this—immortality with constant progression—progression in excellence, progression in happiness, progression for ever—the mind ever augmenting its stores of happiness, and enlarging only to augment them more—ever ascending, and attaining the loftiest throne it can behold, only to see others loftier still, and to rise to them—in a word, all the resources of God thrown open, and an infinity of duration in which to enjoy them. For all this was man created. Lord, what is man that Thou shouldest thus magnify him; thus set Thine heart upon him!

III.

For all this, we have said, man was created. But what if he forfeit the whole by transgression! If then it shall appear, in the third place, that the means employed for his recovery are equal to the magnitude of his wants, this will still further shew the intenseness of the Divine regard for him. You need not be reminded that this forfeiture actually occurred; that, with infinite obligations to obey the will of God, man transgressed it; that, in proportion to the height of his original position, was the depth of his subsequent degradation and ruin.

"But my thoughts are not your thoughts, saith the Lord, neither are your ways my ways." Behold that cross—and Him who hangs upon it. Survey that bleeding form—*there* is the depth of condescension! He is *dying*—dying for *us*—dying for us *the accursed death of the cross.* Herein is love! "He was in the form of God, and thought it not robbery to be equal with God; but he made himself of no reputation, and took upon him the form of a servant, and was made in the likeness of man; and being found in fashion as a man, he humbled himself, and became obedient unto death, even the death of the cross." Herein is love! The universe is crowded with proofs of the Divine regard for man—but here is a proof which outweighs them all. Take us, if you please, through the ample walks of nature, and point us to all its rich and varied provisions—we admit and admire the whole; but arrest not our progress till we have reached the cross. Throw a veil, if you please, over every other object; only leave the cross unveiled; only stand aside from that; let us contemplate that. "Herein is love; not that we loved God, but that he loved us, and sent his Son to be the propitiation for our sins." "Here," says the Apostle, after quoting the sentiment of the text, "here we see Jesus made lower than the angels for the suffering of death; that he by the grace of God should taste death for every man." For "God so loved the world"—how much He loved us we can never compute; we have no line with which to fathom, no standard with which to compare it—but he *so* loved man, "that he gave his only begotten Son, that whosoever believeth in him might not perish, but have everlasting life."

Nor is this all; the vicarious sacrifice of Christ, while providing a complete satisfaction for human guilt, provides that which you equally require—means for the renovation of your sinful nature, and motives to a constant progress in holiness. You cannot approach the cross of Christ—cannot enter into its mediatorial design—without feeling that a virtue comes out of it—that the Holy Spirit is honouring and employing it as the means of your renovation. Yes, so wonderfully adapted—so exquisitely adjusted to all the springs of our nature, is the cross of Christ, that, in the hand of the Spirit, it relieves our fears while it quickens our sensibility; gives peace to the conscience, while it increases its activity and power; inspires hope, and yet produces humility by the very magnitude and splendour of the objects which inspire it; demands perfection by presenting the heart with an object calculated to produce it.

Nor is even this all; "what is man," exclaims the patriarch, "that thou shouldest set thine heart upon him? And that thou shouldest visit him every morning and try him every moment?"—that thou shouldest never lose sight of him—never for a moment cease to aim at his welfare. Yes, the Bible draws aside the veil which hides the spiritual world from our view; and, behold, a vast scheme of providence administered by God himself—in which every want of His people is noticed, every object numbered, every being moving in the direct gaze of omniscience. Would the assurance of sympathy lighten the sufferer's griefs? The Bible assures him that there is a sense in which his every pang vibrates to the throne of God—thrills the very heart of Divine compassion. Hence the Bible contains a promise for every pang that rends—a solace for every throb that beats in the human breast. Hence it brings the most afflicted the nearest to the throne of grace; reserves for him there the favoured place. And hence too the Son of God himself became a man of sorrows, that He might be able to succour them that are tempted. Should it sustain the Christian to know that his trials conduce to his moral improvement here; and, more than that, to his blessedness hereafter? Let him know that there *are* lines of relation between every sanctified trial on earth, and the highest throne in heaven. Would he see the men who once had the world against them for their attachment to Christ? He must look for them now before the throne of God. He will find them now, with a number which no man can number, clad in robes of royalty, and having palms of triumph in their hands. Oh blessed arrangement, and worthy of a God, by which our light afflictions, and but for a moment, can thus be made to work out for us a far more exceeding and eternal weight of glory. "Lord, what is man that thou shouldest thus magnify him!"

IV.

And this leads us to think of the end of the whole. For, fourthly, if this result shall prove to correspond with the costly means employed for our recovery, the proof of the infinite condescension and love of God to man will be completed. And here I might remind you of the amazing honour conferred on His people in taking them into His service. This is one of the fruits of His love. From being the slaves of sin, He advances us into His high and holy service. He has no need of our services, for He is self-sufficient, and could accomplish every thing by the word of His power; or, if He chose to surround Himself with obedient servants as a thing becoming His majesty and state, He might have taken them all from the heavenly world. *They* have never revolted from Him, as we have done; never abused His goodness, nor renounced his authority, as we have done; but have ever counted it their highest honour to adore and serve Him. How astonishing is it, then, that He should come to seek for servants in this sinful world! that He should call any into His service from among our apostate race! And yet He does this. And He does it in a manner as though He were really dependent on our services—unable to conduct the affairs of His government without us; for He not only calls us, He urges, and entreats, and even offers to reward us—though we can never be otherwise than unprofitable servants. If we neglect His first invitations, He repeats them; if we faint in His service, He supports and encourages us; if we decline from His service, He actually follows and brings us back to it again; He stoops to do that which we should count it a degradation to do to a fellow-man. He reminds us that angels are our fellow-servants; He calls us co-workers together with himself; He even engages to applaud us at last in the face of the universe, by saying, "Well done, good and faithful servants, enter ye into the joy of your Lord."

And, oh, that joy of our Lord! "Beloved," says an apostle, "now are we the sons of God; and it doth not yet appear what we shall be." Now are we the sons of God; and when we look down to the depth from which He has raised us, we may well be astonished at the height of our present elevation. But when we look up towards the summits which we are yet destined to attain, we feel that it doth not yet appear what we shall be. Great as the honour is which He has already conferred on His people, it is only the beginning, the pledge of what He purposes to bestow on them in heaven. High as is the exaltation to which He has already raised them, they are still rising and shall continue to ascend, till they have left sin, and death, and hell, at an infinite depth below them, and find themselves placed at the right hand of God. And think you that even then they will have reached the limits of His glory? That glory is an ocean; and they will only then be just launched forth on its shoreless expanse. Even then, as they survey the interminable prospect of blessedness which stretches before them, they will be heard saying, "It doth not yet appear what we shall be; but this we know, that we *are* like him, for now we see him as he is." Brethren, were the operation of the grace of God to terminate at this moment—were the affairs of His kingdom to be wound up at once—how astonishing the effects which His condescension has already produced! How many has it raised to the enjoyment of eternal life! What a tide of happiness has it poured through the world, bearing on its bosom to the haven of rest an innumerable multitude, every one of whom would else have perished in the blackness of darkness for ever! But it shall not cease to operate till it has compassed the salvation of all His people; and then, and not till then, will it be adequately appreciated and adored. But then, when all the objects of His love—the fruits of His condescension—shall stand upon the mount of God; when they shall look up and gaze upon the glories of Him who sits upon the throne; and then look back and down upon the cross, and remember that He once hung upon it, and trace the various stages through which He passed till He reached it—what an amazing impression of His condescension will they have, and what a theme for praise. And when they shall contrast their high exaltation with their former depression—when they shall find that they are without fault before the throne of God, that they are walking in the society of angels, are raised to the enjoyment of all that heaven contains—and shall then look down upon that state in which His condescension found them—and, still lower, on that state of perdition from which His grace has saved them, what a view will they obtain of their sublime exaltation, and what cause for gratitude to Him who hath so magnified them—so set His heart upon them!

1. Now, if this be a true and scriptural account of the manner in which God has shewn His infinite regard for man, one of the first reflections which the subject suggests relates to man's own voluntary degradation. *How great must be the folly and guilt of man in setting his heart supremely on any object less than God!* And yet this is the condition of mankind generally, and this the secret of their spiritual debasement. The scriptural account of them is, that they "forget God." Whatever else they may remember, they forget Him! Whatever other knowledge they may like to retain, they do "not like to retain him in their knowledge." Idols they have—idols of the mind, and idols of the sense; but they are "without God in the world"—in His own world they are without Him! Objects they have to which they are

looking for happiness; but they are "without Christ," without the only Being who could make them truly happy. His *name* they *may* have, but Himself they have not. Although His kingdom has come nigh unto them, they are not in it. In the very presence of the Cross, they are without Christ. What but degradation and guilt can ensue? They were made for God, constituted to engage in the pursuit of an infinite object, and to find in that pursuit an ever-enlarging capacity for enjoyment, ever-increasing excellence and happiness. To engage in the pursuit of any other object, then, is to set their hearts on that which is infinitely less than they were meant for. So that, even if there were no guilt in this conduct, it could not be otherwise than ruinous to themselves. For, as the object of their pursuit was less than God—and, therefore, an object infinitely less than they were made for—the time would infallibly arrive when they would have overtaken that object, have comprehended and exhausted it. From that moment their progress would be at an end, their souls would be lost—for from that moment their misery would begin. To arouse them to a sense of this danger, the Saviour himself has drawn near to them, and has put the startling enquiry, "What shall it profit a man though he could gain the whole world, and yet lose his own soul?" Answer this, my unconverted hearers. The gain of the world, even if that were possible, would still involve the loss of your soul. Even if the pursuit should for awhile engross your attention and enlarge your mind, the time would come when you would have exhausted all its powers to please, and when, instead of enlarging and filling your capacities, you would have to contract, and let yourself down, and reduce yourself to its meagre dimensions; and from that moment your soul would be lost. You would be carrying about within you powers undeveloped, faculties unused, capacities unfilled; for of the only object which could employ and fill them without end, you would have defrauded them.

But are not some of you engaged in this process of self-degradation—setting your hearts, not on a world, but upon some of its smallest, meanest fractions? And have you not almost succeeded in reducing your souls to the littleness of the object you are striving to embrace? And are you not doing this in the very presence of God?—putting Him aside, that you may give yourself up to trifles—asking Him to withdraw His light, that you may live on in darkness—asking Him to hide from your view that throne to which He is offering to raise you, in order that you may be left undisturbed to embrace the dust? "Lord, what is man that Thou still magnifiest him"—that Thou art not wearied out with his provocations—that Thou shouldest still be saying, "How shall I give thee up?"—that Thou shouldest still set thine heart upon him, following him, calling, correcting, urging him to repentance; assuring him that Thou art ready to forgive, waiting to save him!

2. Again, how superior is the *estimate* which the Gospel forms of man, compared with that of every other system; and how sacred and lofty the *claims* which it gives him on our best efforts for his welfare! Ask any other system, "What is man?" and it either gives you, in so many words, a degrading view of the whole species, or else, by trying to monopolize what it believes to be dignity for its own party, and by degrading the rest of mankind, it unwittingly debases the whole race. Ask a selfish philosophy, *What is man?* and it replies, that whatever some tribes and classes may be, the poor are the better for being left in ignorance; that the negro is made to be enslaved, and the uncivilized to be destroyed, as so many beasts of prey, by the civilized. Ask the question in China, and the reply is to be gathered in relation to woman—one-half of the species—by the seal of degradation impressed on her brow; and, in relation to man, by the absence of everything ennobling in his hopes and pursuits. Ask the question alike of Hindooism and of Mohammedanism, *What is man?* and they both reply, only a

sensual being—for the former has painted his image in its licentious gods, and the latter in the sensual heaven which it promises to its votaries. Ask a worldly scepticism, *What is man?* and it replies, "An object not worth a sacrifice. Guilt! he has none; he is the victim of necessity. A soul! he has none. Let him eat, and drink, and animalize, for to-morrow he dies. And let him die!" And, alas, could we take an enlarged survey of the actual condition of mankind, what a humiliating illustration of all this should we behold! How successfully has man laboured to make himself in appearance the degraded being which he believes himselt to be!

But on repairing to the holy oracle, and asking, *What is man?* the answer is "Come, and see;" and, oh, how different the estimate given! I see a world created, and beautified, and enriched, in a manner which calls forth the complacency of even the Divine Creator; and I am told that, glorious as it is, it is designed expressly for the home of man. I hear the Triune Deity, in awful consultation—and I learn that it relates to the creation of man. I hear the voice of God in accents of wrath—the windows of heaven are opened—the fountains of the great deep broken up—and the world is swept by a destructive deluge; and the reason is, *man has sinned*—the magnitude of the punishment denoting the terrible importance of the sinner. I see Sinai in flames, and I learn that God is there legislating for man. Deity descends to assume a created nature; but I see that "he taketh not on him the nature of angels"—descending through their ranks, He takes on him the nature of man. Tracking His steps, following Him to Calvary, pressing near to the cross—there, with the heavens darkened and the earth trembling—there, amidst a throng of invisible and astonished angels, and the triumphs of the powers of darkness, I behold Him die as the sacrifice and Saviour of man. Oh, had we never beheld a human being—had we belonged to some other race of beings—and if, knowing the dignity of the

Son of God, we had gazed on His agony and death for man, should we not have panted, next, to look upon man? Would not our language have been,—How astonishing must the nature and the destiny of that creature be for whom God has thus become manifest in the flesh, for whom the only begotten of the Father has thus died the ignominious death of the cross! And when we first beheld a human being, should we not have approached and gazed on him with reverence!

Do we still press the question, *What is man?* The Bible refers me to far other scenes. I see worlds in conflict; and it tells me they are conflicting for the soul of man. Passing the gates of the heavenly state, I hear strains of unwonted joy burst from the seraphim before the throne; and I learn that it is because "one sinner hath repented"—because a human soul is coming back to God. I see vacant thrones around the mediatorial throne; and my look of inquiry as to who shall be the occupants is met by the language of the Mediator himself, "to him that overcometh will I grant to sit down with me on my throne, even as I also overcame, and am set down with my Father on his throne." Loud strains of triumph are suddenly heard from all the harps of heaven; and I learn that they celebrate the arrival of a human soul, victorious over sin and death; that a welcome and "an entrance is ministered to him abundantly into the everlasting kingdom of our Lord and Saviour Jesus Christ." Do I need any other proof of God's estimate of man? I might be pointed to the scene of the general resurrection, and the final judgment. But let me rather look beyond. When these events shall have transpired—when the pillars of earth shall have given way—when the vast wheels of Providence shall have completed their mighty rounds—and Time itself shall be no longer; the human soul, defying all earthly change, gazing unmoved on the destruction of everything by which it was once surrounded, shall be still seen the sole, the immortal survivor of the whole. Yes, when these heavens and this earth shall have passed away, and no vestige of them, as they now are, shall be left, man shall be found in other worlds, rising to heights of glory in heaven, or sinking to depths of woe in perdition. This, this is man; a being ennobled by the love of God; destined for immortality; capable of enjoying God for ever; yet in danger of being for ever banished from His presence.

And can we ask, after this, how we should estimate man? Why God hath magnified him?—hath magnified him by setting His heart upon him? Let it be known that the merest trifle was once an object of interest to some celebrated human being; and all the world feel an interest in it also. But here is an object on which God hath set His heart; and the very fact that He hath done so demonstrates its intrinsic importance. And not satisfied with shewing us our duty by His own acts, He enjoins it in so many words. "Honour all men," saith He. Honour man as man. True, his nature is in ruins; but reverence him—they are the ruins of a temple in which God once dwelt, and may dwell again. True, his earthly lot may be obscure, his outward form repulsive; but honour him, he is more than a prince in disguise; and he is on his way to more joy than time has ever known, or to more suffering than eternity will be able to exhaust. Take him to your heart, then, as the most magnificent object of compassionate regard with which God himself can present you. Set *your* heart upon him.

And do you now ask what you shall do for him? Live and labour to save him. Whatever you can do for such a being, even short of saving him, is highly important. Is he suffering from bodily want? Relieve his necessities, and remove, if you can, the causes which led to them. Is he the victim of ignorance and improvidence? Do what you can to enlighten his mind and improve his condition. Is he enslaved? Break his fetters, and let him walk forth a man. But, oh, his soul! Concentrate your chief regards upon that. It is your relation to that which stamps infinite importance on every moment of your time—every action of your life.

Be ready to become all things to all men, if by any means you can save some. Be unhappy—count yourself to have lived comparatively in vain, unless you have been the means of assisting to save a soul. For, "brethren," saith the apostle, "if any of you do err from the truth, and one convert him, let him know"—let it go forth as a proclamation from the throne of God—let it be told to every member of the Church—let it be resounded through the world—"that he which converteth the sinner from the error of his ways, shall save a soul from death, and shall hide a multitude of sins."

3. And then, finally, the subject furnishes us with a scriptural test of the worth of our religious professions. Are we magnifying the same objects as those on which God hath set His heart, and for the same reasons? There is a monarch in regal splendour on his throne, and there, in an obscure corner, is a little child in earnest prayer to God; which, in your eyes, is the nobler object of the two? There is the rich man, surrounded with all the luxuries which wealth can procure; and there, in that poverty-stricken cottage, is one musing in silence over the Word of God: disturb not his thoughts, for they are far away in the heavenly world, expatiating on glories which eye hath not seen; with which of these two would you rather exchange? There is one at the head of an army, marching from region to region in triumph; and there is another going forth alone, his only weapon the sword of the Spirit, his only object the recovery of the human soul; which of the two is clothed, in your eyes, with the truer sublimity? There rises a stately palace, the home of royalty; and there, hard by, stands the humble house, where "prayer is wont to be made"—where all the higher elements of man's nature are developed—all his nobler concerns recognized; which of the two wears the loftier interest in your sober judgment? There is the boundless magnificence of the midnight heavens; and there is a dying man—a departing saint—his body is falling into the dust—his soul is on

the wing for the invisible world; which do you deem the nobler object of the two?

Need I remind you on which of the two classes of objects the heart of God is set? That little child in prayer is an object of interest to angelic eyes. That lowly man is on his way to an unfading crown. That humble agent of mercy is accompanied by more than angels, by the Holy Spirit himself. That unpretending house of prayer is the house of God—an earthly palace of the King of kings—occupies a distinguished place in the map of the Divine dominions—stands in close relation to the heavenly world—often have its worshippers to exclaim (as they enjoy times of refreshing from the presence of the Lord), "Lord, what are we that thou shouldst thus magnify us, thus set thine heart upon us!" And then, that departing saint—do you ask, what is he compared with the material heavens, the moon and the stars which God hath created? The Word of God itself replies that those visible heavens are too limited for his range—that that sun itself is but an emblem of the glory which awaits him—that one reason why it has been lighted up is to give him an idea of that glory; for, when the fires of that sun shall have burnt out, he, saith Christ, "shall shine forth as the sun in the kingdom of my Father for ever."

Ask not, then, for a sphere adapted to your activity; complain not of the want of objects worthy of your regards. *That* sphere lies immediately around you; *those* objects throng and press you on every side. Withdrawing your attention from the tinsel and the glare of outward show, and concentrating your regards on that which constitutes the man, you will find in the work of his recovery to God claims on your tenderest sympathies, and scope for enterprise so vast, that the greatest powers, and the noblest ambition, will never be able to fill it. Parents, pretend not to piety if you are setting your heart on any thing for your children more intently than you are to behold them the sons and daughters of the Lord God Almighty. Abandon your claims to be considered pious professors of religion if *any* knowledge is greater in your estimation, either for yourselves or for others, than the knowledge which maketh wise unto salvation—any title nobler than that of the children of God—any end more exalted than that of living to the glory of God.

Come, then, and revisit the cross, and there let us aim at a higher order of Christian devotedness than we have ever yet exhibited—there, while we feel amazed that God should have so magnified us, let us give ourselves up to penitence that we have done so little for His cause.

My young friends, come, I entreat you, and make this the season of your dedication to God. Room is yet left you to commence a glorious era in His Church. Only give yourselves up to the absorbing sentiment of the text, and throw your hearts into the great work of man's recovery,—and Heaven itself shall join you, and the Spirit anoint you to your work, and the world be given unto your hands. Only "thus judge, that if one died for all, then were all dead; and that he died for all, that they which live should not henceforth live unto themselves, but unto him which died for them, and rose again."

SERMON II.

THE WORTH OF THE SOUL.

MATTHEW xvi. 26—"For what is a man profited, if he shall gain the whole world, and lose his own soul? or what shall a man give in exchange for his soul?"

OUR Lord's teaching was eminently practical. And if the practical portion of His teaching were to be distributed into two parts, one part might be said to be directed to the conduct necessary *in order* to become His disciples; and the other, to the conduct necessary *in consequence* of becoming His disciples. For obvious reasons, however, the former part—that which related to the *conditions* of discipleship—predominated. As He addressed men before they had become Christians—before Christianity itself had become a fact—His practical public teaching was naturally directed rather to the *conditions* of discipleship than to its *consequences.*

Of course His teaching, in this relation, took its complexion from what He found man thinking, and feeling, and doing—from the actual necessities of the case. He did not warn men against impracticable sins, and impossible dangers. He saw things as they were, and spoke of them as they should be. If, therefore, He warned men against worldliness, it was because He saw himself surrounded by its victims. Or if He warned them against attempting a compromise of sin with holiness, or of His own high and spiritual claims with the claims of self-indulgence and earthly distinction, it was because He saw men actually perishing in the attempt.

Now, so much of our Lord's discourses *was* occupied in teaching of this kind—in readjusting the claims between heaven and earth—that it may be said to be one of their characteristic features. He finds men mistaking phantoms for realities, and realities for phantoms—calling an atom a world, and a world an atom—absorbed in providing for the temporal future—and He urges them, as they respect their own rationality, not to omit eternity from their reckoning. Approaching the toiling multitude, exhausting themselves in efforts for the bread which perisheth, He reminds them that there is angels' food—bread of life—and urges them to put forth their soul's endeavour after that. Glancing at the devotee of wealth, and contrasting the burden of thick clay which he carries, with the narrowness of the entrance to the way of life, He exclaims, in accents of deep commiseration, "How hardly shall they that have riches enter into the kingdom of heaven!" Penetrating into the inmost circle of domestic life, and arresting the inmates in the midst of their household cares, He calls them to His side, and turns on them a look of pity, as He reminds them, that while they are careful and troubled about many things, "one thing is needful." Taking his stand on the world's highway, and surveying the busy crowds as they pass and repass, each one as eager as if he had just discovered the secret of happiness after a thousand failures, and were about to give it an instant trial, He points them upwards, and reminds them that the good they seek is *there*—that there is one thing to which everything else desirable is appended—and *that* He exhorts them to "seek first." Some of them pause, admit the validity of His claims, and—if they may but bring the world with them—profess a readiness to fall into His train. But such a compromise is impossible. The experiment has been made and repeated, in effect, in every form and in every age; and He solemnly avers, with the confidence of one who knows that it has failed as often as it has been made, that it is inherently and eternally impracticable. "Ye cannot serve

God and mammon." "If any man will come after me, let him deny himself, and take up his cross and follow me. For whosoever will save his life shall lose it, and whosoever will lose his life for my sake shall find it." The question is one of life and death. Both neutrality and compromise are impossible. It is a conflict, and sides must be taken. On each side a sacrifice is involved. On the side of Christ, the sacrifice of the world; on the side of the world, the sacrifice of the soul—of the man himself. Here, therefore, there is no comparison. "For what is a man profited, if he shall gain the whole world, and lose his own soul?"—lose that which alone is capable of enjoyment—"or what shall a man give in exchange for his soul?" Let us, then, attempt to impress our minds with the nature of the risk we run of losing it—with the infinitude of the loss—and with the remedilessness of the ruin. Brethren, this is a subject which will be resumed—should we never look at it on earth again—resumed after every other question of time has been dismissed—on the final day. Whatever the interest we may feel in it now, be it great or little, *then* it will be all-absorbing. God help us to consider it *now* as in the view of *that* day!

I.

What then, firstly, is the nature of the risk we run of losing our souls? Whatever it be, it must be of a nature corresponding with the nature of the soul. We are not to picture any violent seizure and hurrying away of the soul into darkness by a visible foe. No fatal wounds inflicted on its substance are to be thought of. These are not necessary for the destruction even of the body. The wellbeing of the body requires constant communication with certain external objects and agents. Let it be deprived of these, and it perishes; and so of the soul. The wellbeing of the body requires the attainment of certain ends; defrauded of these, it is conscious only of unrest and suffering; and so of the soul. Supply the body as liberally as you please with means not congenial with its wants, you not only frustrate the ends of its being, you incapacitate and disqualify it for ever attaining those ends; and so of the soul.

1. But that which we have here to remember is, that in speaking of the soul, we are speaking of that which, in a sense, is already lost. By an act of his own, man has cut himself off from communion with his proper good. Having lost from his heart the love of God, the love of the world has rushed into and filled the vacuum. The *mind* which, with one sweep of its pinions, should have reached the stars, settles down in the dust; the *affections*, which were meant to rise and be diffused over an infinite circumference, of which God is the centre, let themselves down, and labour to accommodate themselves to an indivisible point, a fugitive atom. The *soul*, which was meant for a life whose highest law is the love of God—whose supports were to come direct from intercourse with Him—whose ultimate home was to be in the light of His immediate presence—that soul is laboriously training itself to do without Him, to forget Him. And will not this account for that feeling, of which the soul is often conscious, of a dignity departed, of a happiness blighted, and of moral conflicts ending in defeat? Will it not account for the consciousness often felt of a constitution violated, a conscience dethroned, a nature not answering its highest ends, ill at ease, and full of forebodings for the future? Yet this is the condition of mankind generally.

2. But though the soul, as sinful, may be said to be already lost, "the Son of Man hath come to seek and to save that which was lost;" salvation is possible; and there is the further risk *of not being saved*—of thus being doubly lost. The first loss is incurred by doing something—immersing the soul in destructive influences; the second loss is incurred by declining to do something—declining to detach the soul from these evil influences, and to bring it within the means of its recovery.

And here, again, the nature of the risk corresponds with the nature of the soul. It is not necessary that the man should avow *disbelief* of the Gospel, or even *unbelief*. It is not necessary that he should live in open defiance of its claims. All that he may be conscious of may be merely a distaste for it. He may think of its requirements only as too self-denying and severe. He may speak of its doctrines only as attended with difficulty. He may flatter himself with the delusion that he is only postponing the requisite attention to it for a time. But, meanwhile, he is keeping aloof from the only means of his soul's recovery. His health may not suffer in consequence. His worldly prosperity may not decline—may go on increasing. But his *soul*—the noblest part of his nature—is wronged. This entire system of Gospel-truth was meant for his soul's life—the soul and it were meant for each other—so that as long as he stands aloof from it he is wronging his own soul. Here is the rich inheritance—pardon, purity, immortal life—his soul is the only part of him capable of enjoying it—and he is wronging the immortal heir of the immortal inheritance. And dying thus the wrong will be irretrievable. He will ever carry about with him a wronged, lost, soul; for he will ever carry about with him guilt which might have been forgiven, pollution which might have been washed away, a sense of loss never to be relieved; for of the only thing which could have renewed, and saved, and satisfied his soul, he wronged it. The full extent of the wrong he will never know. Though his sense of it will go on perpetually increasing, ten thousand ages will have only partially revealed to him its untold extent.

The nature of the risk in question is even more easy, and therefore more imminent than this. It may arise not merely, as in the first instance I have named, from doing something wrong; or, as in the second, from declining to do something right; but from too readily taking it for granted that the first has been avoided or repented of, and the second performed. This is pre-eminently the danger of the day. Our chapels are thronged with those who number themselves among the followers of Christ, although self-denial is to them an untried duty, and the bearing of the Cross a burden unknown. They admit that there are forms of worldliness destructive of the soul; but because they have never committed themselves to such excessive forms, they assume that everything *less* is allowable and safe. They admit that to postpone attention to religion is fraught with danger; but because they are attending to its outward *decencies*, they assume that they are already yielding themselves up to its *spirit*. They have a religious history; but repentance, faith, progressive holiness form no part of it; it consists chiefly in the number of religious services attended, and in acts in which the soul took no part. Objects they have to which they are looking for happiness; but they are, in reality "without Christ"—without the only being who could make them truly happy. His *name* they have, but himself they have not. Although His kingdom has come nigh unto them, they are not in it. In the very presence of the Cross, they are without Christ.

Are not some of you engaged in this slow but certain suicide of the soul? Are not some of you proficients in this art of "destruction made easy?"—setting your hearts, not on a world, but on some of its smallest, meanest fractions? And have you not almost succeeded in reducing your souls to the littleness of the object you are striving to embrace? And are you not doing this in the very presence of Christ—accepting the withering crown which the world offers you, and declining his Cross—bartering your soul away for self-indulgence and trifles?

II.

Then, let us think, secondly, of the infinitude of the loss, even on the supposition of the highest possible gain.

1. The hypothesis in the text is, that a man should be able to gain the whole world. This is plainly impracticable.

But even admitting its possibility, how small a proportion of the world could you enjoy at any one time! Your horizon would not be larger than it is now. Your capacity for pleasure would be of the same limits as now. Thousands of your fellow-men would be extracting more satisfaction from your world than you. It would be more their world than yours, after all. In the only sense in which you can ever gain the world, you have it already. You have been the possessor of ten thousand worlds already. You have had a new world every day of your conscious life. To the full extent of your use and experience of it, it was yours. The probability is, that, could you have called more of it your own on any one day, you would have enjoyed less; that could the twenty or thirty of the most unhappy men on the face of the earth at this moment be selected, they would be found to be among those who have most of the world at their command. So that we might well ask, "What shall it profit a man if," at his soul's peril, "he could gain the whole world," when he can only enjoy so small a portion of it?

2. But, further:—"If two men," (says a celebrated writer, Buffon,) "if two men were to determine to play for their whole property (supposed equal, and with equal risks,) what would be the effect of the agreement? The one would only double his fortune, and the other would reduce his to nought. What proportion is there between the loss and the gain? The same that there is between all and nothing. The gain of the one is but a moderate sum; the loss of the other is numerically infinite." But in the case before us, the point to be remarked is, that the two parties opposed to each other are not *two* men, but one—the man himself; the lower part of his nature against the higher; the passing and the perishable, against the spiritual and immortal; the soul staking its unfading crown and celestial birthright for a mess of pottage. The odds, indeed, are so vast, that the barter is commonly regarded as the greatest triumph of Satanic temptation. Almost every language in Christendom has its fearful tale,

or tragedy, representing how the Tempter appeared to a certain man, and promised him his heart's desire, on condition of his soul's surrender at a certain time; how the covenant was sealed with blood; and how, at the appointed moment, the Fiend returned and claimed his trembling victim. And the tale inspires wonder at the amazing guilt and folly which could thus barter away being and blessedness for the gratification of a few fleeting hours. And yet, who does not see the moral of the tale? How many present are exemplifying it in their own history! The blood, and the formal stipulation, and the visible fiend, are not necessary to give it reality. You are your own tempters. Your worldly tastes are more binding than blood. Your propensities and purposes are stronger than any covenant. Your passions are mightier than a host of fiends. Remember that your ruin is self-inflicted. It is your own soul you are bartering away for a few hours of the world. The earthly side of your nature craves, and to allay its vile cravings for a few short days, you sign away your interest in everlasting life. Well, then, might we carry this question further, and ask, "What shall it profit a man if," at his soul's loss, "he shall gain the whole world," when he can enjoy so *small* a portion of it, and for so *short* a time?

3. But even this is not the worst. You are *losing* your soul. In the very act of gaining your little momentary modicum of the world, you are losing—parting with your capacity for happiness—qualifying yourself for misery ever after. What would you think of an offer to regale you with the most ravishing music, on one condition—that you consented to forfeit your sense of hearing? or to conduct you to a view of a sublime landscape, provided you assented to the loss of your sight? What would you think of a party who should offer to initiate you in the art of reasoning, on condition that you surrendered your reason? What would you think of the man who should *accept* the offer? Yet his folly would be incomparably less than is that of the man who, for the

sake of a little worldly enjoyment for a little time, consents to part with the very faculty of enjoyment—consents to have his eyes put out, and all his spiritual senses incapacitated for ever.

Were the offer formally made him to barter away all the future for the present, he would perceive and resent the insult. "No," (he would say,) "for the longer I exist, the greater will be my capacity for happiness or for misery. And the future is infinite." Were he the only being on earth endowed with immortality, who would think of offering him the world in exchange for his immortality? "No," (he would say,) "you surely cannot know what is meant by immortality. You are asking me to give up my power of the *highest* enjoyment *for ever,* as the price of the *lowest* enjoyment for a *moment.* There is no proportion, nothing commensurate between the two." And yet, *practically,* he is chargeable with the enormous folly. No offer would induce him to part with *one* of the faculties of his soul. He would spurn with resentment an offer of wealth in exchange for his *memory,* to have all the past of his life become an utter blank, involving even an oblivion of the very wealth for which he had exchanged it; and yet he is spending life in storing memory with the materials of self-reproach. He would be amazed at the folly which should propose to traffic for his *judgment,* yet he is hardly less impatient at being warned that he is arming his judgment against him for eternity. Part with his *reason!* The very proposal, in his eyes, betrays insanity. Yet he thinks little of losing his *soul*—of acting a part which shall convert his memory, judgment, reason, all his spiritual and immortal nature, into one vast capacity of wretchedness for ever. What will this profit him?

III.

And then mark, thirdly, the remedilessness of the ruin. The text consists of two questions, often confounded, but essentially distinct. The first describes the folly of a man who should aim to enjoy life by means which could not fail to incur the penalty of death; and the second denotes his willingness to resign every thing in order to accomplish the impossibility of purchasing back again his forfeited life. The first, therefore, contemplates the soul before it is lost—while it is yet in the process of being lost; the second contemplates it when the irretrievable loss has actually taken place. The first appeals to the judgment on this side death; the second appeals to the imagination, places us on the other side death, and would have us picture our condition there, looking back on the period when we were losing our souls as a period never, never to be regained.

Dear brethren, I am not about to attempt the scene. Some of you may have seen a modern artistic sketch—an engraving—representing the arch-fiend and a human being playing a fearful game, in which the soul of the man is staked. The game is far advanced. The man has already lost several of the pawns, denoting his truth, his peace, his purity, &c. His hope is just going. There can be no doubt that the game will terminate against him. His soul will be lost. The very prospect is dreadful. But the reality—the reality—no pencil can reach it. It is beyond the power of words. It belongs to silent imagination.

This is implied in the *form* of the text—a question. No answer is given. What shall a man give in exchange for his lost soul? What? Summon such a soul—call for an answer from one of the lost; and what *could* you receive in reply, but a look of upbraiding despair? Imagine *yourself* in the abode of the lost; visit and question your future self there. You have been lost; you can look back to the very moment your probation closed; the throne of grace, the offers of mercy, the means of salvation—you looked, and saw that you had left them all behind; and now—the mediation of Christ, the consciousness of hope—you have to look back on them as things long, long passed; you are in a region beyond, where you have no peace; you belong to another order of things. What would you give in exchange for your soul? The question only awakens you afresh to the consciousness, not only that the period of exchange has passed; but that, even if it had not, you have nothing to give—absolutely nothing; that in losing your soul, you lost everything. What would you give in exchange for your soul? You will feel that that is a question which admits of no reply. You will remember that the Saviour himself left it unanswered. And the unanswered question shall remain—a barbed arrow—in the self-convicted breast of the sinner for ever.

Such, brethren, is the incomparable value of the soul—such the nature of the risk we run of losing it—the absolute infinitude of the loss, and the remedilessness of the ruin. And is it true that some of us reckon ourselves among the saved? And are there those amongst us, and around us, who are still lost? And can we doubt or question our duty respecting them? Why, Christ hath died for them. God hath so loved a world of such, as to give his only-begotten Son for their redemption. Save a soul from death—and think what you have done. You have done more than extinguished all the miseries of all the beings who have lived up to the present time. Take them in their nations and generations, and unnumbered myriads of individuals, and cast up the sum of the whole. Vast as is the total of their years and their sufferings, after all it is finite. But that soul has before it a history which is infinite. Give it time, and it will overtake the entire amount of emotion which the human race has hitherto known. It will pass beyond that amount. It will immeasurably exceed it. It will have a larger history than the entire world up to the present moment. Is it not true, then, that "he that winneth souls is wise"? He proposes to himself a loftier aim than that of the conquest of a world. He wins a larger tract of spiritual life than all the territories of spiritual death, at this moment, added together. He rescues from suffering a longer period, and a larger amount of human capacity and emotion, than would be the sum-total of all that man has experienced up to the present time.

Conceive, if you can, that up to the present day you had belonged to a world inhabited by beings in every sense mortal—beings who, after threescore years and ten, ceased, entirely and in every sense ceased, to exist; and that there, in that world, your efforts had all necessarily related to that little span of life. And conceive that, as the reward of your activity there, you had been divinely apprised that you should be promoted to a world inhabited by beings who would never die, and that everything you did to them, and for them, would influence the whole futurity of their being—with what trembling anxiety would you anticipate and assume your momentous charge! But with what additional solemnity would it invest your office, to be told that all these deathless beings were in danger of destruction—on their way to it—hastening to it! And still more, to find that you were to be posted somewhere between them and the place of destruction, to arrest their steps, and to turn them back! Dear brethren, this is almost literally the actual post of every follower of Christ. This is why the ministry of the Gospel is appointed—to warn men to flee from the wrath to come. It is this which gives so much importance to all our great religious societies—for they are societies for saving souls from death—holy confederations for plucking brands from the burning. It is this which at once inspires the faithful preacher with his ardour, and which amply justifies it. "Knowing the terrors of the Lord, we persuade men." "We beseech men, in Christ's stead, be ye reconciled to God." We see their danger; we hear, by anticipation, their coming doom; and "we cannot but speak the things which we have seen and heard."

Then what, we may ask, what shall it profit the Christian Church if it should gain the whole world, and lose one soul, which it might have been the means of saving? If it should gain the friendship of all the worldly, and alliance with all the powerful, and the riches of all the wealthy, and could place the whole at its Master's feet, would He regard it as a compensation for that soul; and would not they, when confronted with that lost soul, willingly give it all back again in exchange for that soul's recovery?

Who that ever thought on the subject but must be struck with the *high* estimate which the Gospel forms of man compared with that of every other system. Even pantheism, the most pretentious of the whole—which talks largely of the human soul as a diffused portion of the Deity—robs man of his proper immortality, by teaching that at death that diffused portion is resumed—absorbed back again into the Deity, leaving man no personality, no individual existence, and pointing to a period when all souls shall have lost their separate being, and God alone shall exist, as far as we are concerned, in solitary state.

Far different is the teaching of the Gospel on the subject. It treats man as a personal, accountable, and immortal being, destined to retain his personality for ever. He is in danger, and it unveils a cross on which the Son of God is dying for his redemption. He is giving himself to the pursuit of trifles, but it weighs his soul against the world, and calls us to mark how inappreciably light the world is in the comparison. His earthly lot may be obscure, and even his form repulsive; but it tells us that he is more than a prince in disguise, and is on his way to more joy than time has ever known, or to more suffering than eternity will be able to exhaust. It assures us that worlds are conflicting for the soul of man; that the tear of penitence excites the rapture and feeds the adoration of heaven; that the humblest house of prayer—the place where all the higher elements of man's nature are developed, all his nobler interests recognized—stands in close relation to the heavenly world—is the very "gate of heaven."

Let us ask then, does our practical estimate of the worth of the soul harmonize with that of the Word of God? If the souls of men are endangered by the *world*, our fitness to save them will depend on our *unworldliness*. The measure of our spirituality will be the exact measure of our fitness to detach them from the world. To be apathetic about their highest interests, self-indulgent, half worldly ourselves, can only tend to rivet their chains, and to render them satisfied with their state.

My young friends, come, I entreat you, and make this the season of your dedication to God. Christ and the world invite and divide *your* regards. Could we actually put you in possession of the entire world, and make your life commensurate with the world's existence, do you not see that the lapse of every moment would diminish your interest in your possessions, and bring you nearer to the period when the whole would vanish? On the other hand, what shall it *not* profit you if, in parting with the world, you save your own soul? What? You find life! Not merely existence, but all that can enrich, expand, and make existence infinitely desirable—motives for all its actions, and objects for its noblest affections. You gain a world in which to enjoy it; this world is too confined for it.; it asks the scope of infinity for its expansion. You find yourselves surrounded with the means of saving others. Only give yourselves up to the absorbing sentiment of the text, and throw your heart into the great work of man's recovery, and Heaven itself shall join you, and the Holy Spirit anoint you to your work.

SERMON III.

THE CONSECRATION OF MAN'S WHOLE NATURE.

1 COR. vi. 19, 20—"What! know ye not that your body is the temple of the Holy Ghost which is in you, which ye have of God, and ye are not your own? for ye are bought with a price: therefore glorify God in your body, and in your spirit, which are God's."

SOME ages hence, when an intelligent descendant of the liberated negroes shall read, "your release was bought with £20,000,000," what visions of the past we may suppose the expression to call up before the eye of his mind—a vision of Africa as it was before the first slave-ship touched its shores, peopled with myriads of freemen—"noble shapes, kings of the desert, men whose stately tread brought from the dust the sound of liberty"—a vision of those same men changed into shapes of deformity, by degradation, madness, and despair, scorning the iron which gnawed into their hearts—recollections of the tears, the travels, the entreaties, the heart-wearing labours, the multiform struggle maintained year after year by the Christian apostles of freedom against the inhuman abettors of slavery, till the hand of God smote and shivered the system; and all its fiendish apparatus, manacles, scourges, and chains, were brought as spoil to the feet of divine Christianity—the clouds which for ages had hung over Africa and her children in the west rolled away, and a voice was heard, saying, as from heaven, "Arise, shine, for thy light is come, and the glory of the Lord hath arisen upon thee!" And with these visions of the past before his view, what sentiments of veneration and gratitude for those who instrumentally achieved the grand consummation may we suppose expanding his soul—what a devoted champion may we picture him for the freedom of the world!

We, brethren, as Christians, occupy a spiritual position very analogous to the civil position of the individual supposed. On opening this ancient and sacred book, we find a document addressed nearly eighteen hundred years ago to certain Christians, and containing this remarkable expression, "Ye are bought, or bought off—that is, redeemed—with a price." What a hint to the imagination is here! what a world of truth condensed into an atom! Who does not think at once of primeval Eden—of man walking there in his Maker's image, with perfect liberty for his birthright, the world for his free domain, and God, and the angels of God, for his companions? But soon the vision changes—another party appears on the stage of action in the person of the Tempter, and Eden vanishes, and happiness departs. Man is seen in a wilderness moving among thorns and briars. The creatures have shaken off his yoke, and revolted from his dominion. His own passions rebel, each one asserting its right to reign, and he is the slave of them all. Two thousand years roll on, and the entire race, sworn as one man to the service of Satan, and in love with his chains, is swept from the earth by a universal flood. Another long and dreary period succeeds; and behold a whole nation in civil captivity one day, and the next at liberty, and marching to take possession of a distant land—the greatest providential event in the history of the world. But great as it is, it is only a type of that spiritual redemption which, in the fulness of time, awaits the entire race. Another cycle of ages, and behold on Calvary a scene with which all nature sympathizes. The veil of the temple rent in twain—the convulsions of the earth—the darkened sun, proclaim some unparalleled occurrence. The Son of God is there paying the price of human redemption. For the ransom of a world in bondage to sin, and sold to destruction, He is there presenting a moral compensation—a compensation consisting not of corruptible things, such as silver and gold, but of blood—His own most precious blood. Angels pressed in to see that sight. God himself was there to ratify the transaction, and, when it was concluded, a voice from the excellent glory may be regarded as saying to the world, "Ye are now bought—redeemed with a price—glorify God in your bodies, and in your spirits, which are his." And who does not know the effect? Thousands did thus glorify him. So effectually were they wrought on by that display of Divine compassion, that they thus judged, "that if One died for all, then were all dead; and that He died for all, that they who live should not henceforth live unto themselves, but unto Him that died for them, and rose again"—they judged, that instead of living as if they were under little or no obligation to Him, they should henceforth act as if the duty of living to Him were the only obligation they were under, and that the best way of doing that would be by conveying the knowledge of His redemption to others, and thus working out the grand purposes of His atoning death.

But were none of them in danger of losing sight of this obligation, and of relapsing into their original selfishness and sin? This was precisely the fact with the persons addressed in the text. To rescue them from this danger it was that we here see the apostle rushing into their presence with the Cross—bringing the blood of Christ before their eyes as the price of their redemption. As if he had said, "Even in the Roman civil law it is a maxim, that a person whose life has been forfeited, but ransomed and preserved by another, is bound to devote all his future life for the benefit of his deliverer. You were the slaves of Satan—your lives were forfeited to the justice of God—soon, very soon would you have eternally perished—but you have been bought off with a price! what a price I will not attempt to say, language would only impoverish the idea. Oh! let the recollection of its value, of the infinite love which it displays, and the infinite blessings which it procures, reclaim you to a sense of your obligation to glorify God in your bodies, and in your spirits, which are His."

Brethren, though nearly two thousand years have elapsed since the apostle wrote thus to the Church at Corinth, do we not all recognize its applicability to us? Are we less prone than they to forget our obligation to live unto Christ? Do we need less than they to be reminded of the price by which we have been redeemed? to have Christ "evidently set forth crucified amongst us?" Oh, as if the scenes of Calvary had but just transpired—as if the ransom-blood had just been shed—and Paul were still visiting the Churches—and the epistle containing the remonstrance in the text had been addressed by name to the Christians of this assembly, and had only reached us this day fresh from his inspired pen—let it impress us with the universality and entireness of Christian consecration, and with the great Gospel motive or obligation to it.

I.

First, when the apostle enjoins us to glorify God *in our body and in our spirit,* he would teach us that our consecration is to be universal, including every thing in us and belonging to us. As the property of Christ, every part and faculty of our nature, and everything by which we can influence others, is converted into a talent of which He may be regarded as saying "Occupy till I come—employ it for me." Now, in order that we may see the *extent* of our obligation, let us glance at a few of the various means we possess of serving Him.

1. The knowledge of His Gospel is a talent—the first *Christian* talent we are supposed to possess—and that which is to induce us to consecrate every other talent to His glory. Knowledge of every kind is proverbially said to be *power.* "There is no power on earth," said the great man who originated that proverb—"there is no power on earth which setteth up a throne or chair of state in the spirits and souls

of men, but knowledge." He who is the discoverer, or sole possessor, of a moral truth, has it in his power to exercise a sovereignty which approaches nearer than any other to the likeness of the Divine rule. Not only is he stronger than any other man, than any given number of men, but stronger than all the race together. Now the Christian has had disclosed to *him* the doctrine of the Cross! His hand is on a lever which can move the world! on *the* lever which *shall* move it! and his hand is there that instrumentally he may attempt to move it! Moses descending radiant from Divine communion in the Mount—the High Priest reappearing from within the mysterious veil—Isaiah fresh from the visions of the Lord, never returned to the waiting and breathless people with a burden so precious, a truth so great, as that which the Christian holds! It is that from which all other truths derive their force—it comes, not in word only, but *in power* —it is emphatically *the power of God* unto salvation! It enables the Christian to give back to the world a God—and, by unveiling the great Propitiation, to contribute towards giving back to God a world. To propagate this knowledge is to take for our motto, "Glory to God in the highest"—it is to honour Him in our body and spirit, which are His.

2. The power of speech is a talent. It is the great instrument for the interchange of thought and feeling. The thoughts of a community are by this means kept in perpetual circulation; and the long-cherished sentiment of a private individual is propagated till it acquires the force and universality of a law, and "sets on fire the whole course of nature." To say nothing of the power of public oratory, the simplest conversation has an effect on the minds of those who engage in it, regulated by laws as certain as those which direct and determine the course of the lightning. So that never do we come out from such intercourse the same persons as we entered. The most casual remark lives for ever in its effects. There is not a word which has not a moral

history. And hence it is that every "idle word" which men utter assumes a character so important that an inquest will be held on it in the general judgment. But the Christian is taught to regard the faculty of speech as a means of grace. If the highest use of his reason be to know God—the highest employment of his speech must be to make Him known—and the highest knowledge of Him he can impart is surely that for which Christ himself assumed the power of human speech, and to the announcement of which He devoted it. Whoever his audience may be, the Christian is to "*minister grace* to the hearers." Even when he is not conversing *on* grace, his speech is to be "always *with* grace"—in harmony with his religious character, and favourable to a hallowed impression. Like the narrative and incidental parts of Scripture, it is to illustrate and subserve the saving tendency of the whole. In the salvation of the Cross, the Gospel has supplied him with a theme of which his heart is supposed to be full; and he "cannot but speak the things which he has heard and seen." Every man he meets is interested in it as deeply as himself. Every individual he addresses is perishing through want of it. Every conversation he holds affords him an opportunity of introducing it. Every word he has to utter concerning it is gospel. Unless he speaks, they may die in ignorance of it; and he is held responsible for every truth he might have uttered, but omitted, and for every soul that perished through that neglect. "He believes, and therefore speaks." As if his lips had been touched with sacred fire, or sprinkled with consecrating blood, he is to stand in the midst of his social circle as the oracle of the Cross. His words are no longer his own. As if his were the tongue of Christ himself, or the only tongue on earth that could testify of the wonders of the Cross, he is to regard himself as set apart to bear witness of Christ. And as it is his office, so it is to be his holy ambition, so to announce and make Him known, that at the close of life, and even of each day of life, he may be able to say, though in an inferior sense, as Christ himself appealed to the Father, and said, "I have declared unto them thy name, and will declare it."

3. The influence arising from relationship, whether natural or acquired, is a talent. The parent, for instance, possesses an influence over his offspring more powerful than the mightiest monarch ever swayed over his subjects. His voice is the first music they hear—his smiles their bliss—his authority, the image and substitute of the Divine. So absolute is the law which impels them to believe his every word—to imitate his every tone, gesture, and action—and to receive the ineffaceable impressions of his character, that his every movement drops a seed into the virgin soil of their hearts to germinate for eternity. His influence, by blending itself with their earliest conceptions, and incorporating with the very elements of their constitution, and by the constancy, subtlety, variety, and power of its operation, gives him a command over their character and destiny, which renders it the most appropriate emblem on earth of the influence of God himself.

Now, there is not a member of the human family who does not sustain *some* relation, original or acquired, public or private, permanent or temporary—nor is there *any* relation which does not invest the person sustaining it with some degree of influence. Not only does his relation place him in some points of moral contact with others; it gives him the power of exerting an influence there which no other being on earth possesses.

Here, then, is an important talent which the Christian is to "occupy" for Christ. As if the relations which he sustains had been appointed now for the first time, and appointed expressly to afford *him* a sphere of Christian influence, he is to hold them chiefly for Christ. And, indeed, for what but holy purposes were the primary and principal relations of life designed at first? For "did he not make one?" asks the prophet, "yet had he the residue of the Spirit. And wherefore one? That he might seek a godly seed." So that, in holding his relationships for Christ, the renewed man is but restoring them to the purpose from which sin has divorced them. Is he a parent?—"the promise is unto him and to his children." He is to look on himself as a first man, and on his children, who are the mirrors to reflect his character, as belonging to a new regenerated race. As if they had been sent to him from heaven, with a Divine command to train them for Christ, he is to radiate on them nothing but hallowed influence. Their first lispings are to be of Christ—their first imaginings of His love—their first steps to His footstool. The influence of *his* Christian character is to surround them like the atmosphere of a temple; that, by being breathed and mingled with their earliest being, it may become an elementary part of *their* character. But, indeed, whatever the relation which he sustains to others, he is to regard the influence with which it invests him as a golden chain for drawing them to Christ. There is a sense, indeed, in which he stands related to the whole race. But there is also *an order* in which he is to seek their welfare. By filling with Christian instrumentality the sphere immediately around him first, he is multiplying his agencies for a wider and still wider range of influence. It is by entering into cohesive union with the particles immediately around it, that the atom becomes a component part of the rock, contributes something towards the stability of the everlasting hills, and towards the gravity of the great globe itself;—and, by erecting the cross in his own house, and converting his own house into a church, and that church into a centre of usefulness to the neighbourhood, he is preparing to subserve most effectually the interests of the race at large.

4. Property is a talent. The material itself, indeed, of which money is made, is intrinsically worthless, yet having, by the general consent of society, been constituted the representative of all property, and as such the key to all the avenues of worldly enjoyment, it excites some of the strongest

desires, and reflects some of the deepest emotions of the human breast. Its fluctuations are the tides of national fortune. It sways the heart of the world. Every piece of coin that passes through our hand belongs to the moral history of the world. Industry has toiled for it—enterprise has hazarded life for it—speculation has gambled for it—licentiousness has sinned for it—childhood has eyed it—poverty rejoiced over it — covetousness worshipped it — it has passed through the hands of profligacy, intemperance, and all the vices — how often has it been carried past the temple of God on its way to some shrine of Satan — how seldom been diverted from the service of sin! Oh, could the wealth of antiquity be all recovered, collected together, and its history correctly given, what should we hear, but, substantially, the history of the ancient world itself—of its sensual pleasures, its projects of ambition, its sanguinary wars, polluting temples, and national oppressions! Think of all the wealth which Christendom has possessed — of the familiarity and frequency with which history speaks of its millions in every age—and then reflect what might have been done with it as contrasted with what has been done. Think of the wealth still in its possession, and remembering how the great bulk of it is employed, see what an opportunity the Christian has of glorifying God in this single department. While they are consuming life in the pursuit of wealth, he, by visibly subordinating whatever he possesses to the service of God, is to attract their notice, and awaken their inquiries concerning the divinity of that Gospel which can lead to such results. While they are sullenly appropriating everything to themselves as if God had ceased to reign, and even to exist, he is to consecrate and offer up his substance before their eyes as an oblation to His glory, and thus daily vindicate His claims. While they are idolizing money, and making it the common object of their trust, he is to strike at its very throne, and to awaken them from the dream of its omnipotence, by shewing that it highest value arises from its subserviency to the purposes of the Gospel. "He knows the grace of our Lord Jesus Christ;" and by asking himself how *he* would have employed such property, he proposes to himself an example which condemns the selfishness of the world. He may not possess much—but the influence of what he does possess depends, not on its *amount,* but on the *way* in which he employs it; for, if he be poor, by casting only two mites into the temple-treasury, he may, at once, be publicly vindicating the outraged supremacy of the blessed God, and asserting the claims of the glorious Gospel, and constraining the world, more than by a thousand arguments, to bow down to its divinity.

5. Self-denial is another means of glorifying God. So unearthly a quality is this, that no man can fully and consistently practise it without exposing himself, perhaps for years, to the suspicion of assuming it for some sinister object in the distance. But does not this very incredulity, arising from the extreme rareness of self-denial, hold out to him the promise of proportionate influence hereafter should he live long enough to vanquish it, and to enjoy the reaction of opinion in his favour. His self-denial, indeed, is meantime furnishing him with all those means of benevolence which self-indulgence would have lavished on itself; and these, by increasing his usefulness, are increasing his influence. But the influence which he acquires by this *increase of means* is as nothing compared with that which he obtains by the fact—when it comes to be known—that he *denies himself* in order to obtain it. The *amount* which he saves may be only an additional mite, but the *fact* that he denies himself in order to obtain it as a means of doing good, will ultimately invest him with a greater moral influence than the stranger to self-denial, though the giver of thousands, can ever possess. Now, Christianity is a system of self-denial. Its centre is a cross. This is at once the secret of its influence to attract, and the means of its power to save. Having felt that attraction, and experienced that

power, the Christian is to extend its influence by exhibiting in his own life the image of the cross. Were it possible for him to live in worldly self-indulgence, he would be doing all in his power, not only to stop the influence of the cross from extending beyond himself, but to efface from the memory of a world—too willing to forget—that Christianity ever had a Cross. The only evidence on which the world will believe that Christ was crucified for its redemption is, that the Christian may be seen, in the true spirit of the Cross, voluntarily and vicariously denying himself in the work of diffusing the blessings of that redemption. If the Cross of Christ inculcates a single lesson, it is this—that self-denial is an essential condition of practical benevolence—that in proportion to the amount of wretchedness to be remedied, must be the degree of self-denial in him who remedies it—that as the *redemption* of the world required the vicarious sufferings of Christ, the instrumental diffusion of that redemption requires that the same principle of self-denial pervade that instrumentality, and become the law of Christian beneficence. As a representative of the Cross, the Christian is charged with a responsibility which requires a willingness to do and to bear the utmost of which humanity is capable. And as an appointed agent for diffusing its blessings, he is bound, by the very nature of his office, and the momentous interests placed in his hand, to withhold no power of exertion, no faculty of endurance, to surrender whatever he may possess that has in it a tendency, under God's blessing, to obtain success.

6. Persevering activity in a course of religious benevolence is another means of glorifying God. It is by perseverance that the small stream of the mountain, a thousand leagues from the parent sea, conquers intervening obstacles, wears itself a channel, swells to a river, traverses continents, gives names to countries, assigns boundaries to empires, and becomes celebrated in history. And by patiently persevering with his face and step always direct towards his object, a

single individual will acquire an amount of influence and success in reference to that object, which a multitude, pursuing it only by convulsive starts, would fail to obtain. The multitude itself, gradually awed into respect for his steady onward course, will come, at length, to clear a space, and make way for his advance. And though for years his course may not appear to be attended with any success, an event, unexpected perhaps, will at length disclose that there never was a moment in which he was not exciting the silent admiration of some, and preparing numbers to fall into his train, and yield themselves entirely to his influence. Now, the Christian has motives to patient perseverance in promoting the knowledge of Christ, which no other object *can* inspire, no other man can know. The persisting energy which built the mountain pyramids of Egypt—which reared the Chinese wall—by which Alexander conquered the old world—Columbus discovered the new—and Newton elaborated the system of the universe—the persisting energy which did all this had trifles for its object compared with the aim of Christian instrumentality *to save the world.* But besides the infinite importance of his object, engaging as it has the Divine perseverance from eternity, there never was a moment in the life of Christ, his great Exemplar, which was not, directly or indirectly, made subordinate to it—there is not a moment in which the command is suspended, "Be not weary in well-doing"—"be always abounding in the work of the Lord." So that, unless it can be shewn that the perishing world ever pauses in its cry for deliverance, or that the Destroyer ever pauses in working the great system of destruction, the Christian can know no moment in which it is permitted him to pause in his peculiar vocation. The termination of one duty is only to be a signal for the commencement of another—his life is to be one continuous act of obedience. Every day returns charged with an amount of obligation proportioned to his *utmost means* of usefulness. His utmost powers are to be constrained into the service, till, by the force of habit, his perseverance becomes invincible. He is to live under the ever-present conviction that he has *one thing to do,* and that he is in danger of dying before he has done it. He is to make the grand experiment *how much* a Christian may effect in the cause of Christ, cheered on by the conviction that every act adds a ray to the radiance of that crown which he hopes to cast at his Saviour's feet, and tends to secure the perseverance of others when he himself shall have ascended to receive it.

7. The privilege of prayer is a talent—a transcendent means of honouring God. It has well been said that "it is by prayer we master our own spirits, and it is by prayer we can best influence the spirits of other men. A life of prayer is a life of power. Prayer has power with God, and prayer imparts energy to our own character; for the man that prays must plead, he that pleads must believe, and he that believes feels confident of success—confident that God will fulfil His own promise." Prayer, while it tends to annihilate self, renders appropriate homage to His greatness, and thus keeps us in active and constant communication with the fountain of grace. To pray for the kingdom of Christ is to say, in effect, that we ourselves have made proof of His cross—that we believe there is no hope for the world but through that cross—and that so satisfied are we of its healing efficacy, that were all the world to feel its power, all the world would be saved, and heaven begin on earth. To the success of the Gospel, God has pledged every perfection of His nature—so that, in praying for it, the Christian is taking His stand on the immutable covenant of God—moving the arm of God—pleading with all the force of an Almighty decree—bringing Omnipotence itself to his aid. What an abundant variety of means do we possess for glorifying God!

II.

But not only is the consecration of the Christian to be thus universal, it is to be constant, exclusive, and in the highest degree. In other words, it is, secondly, to be eminent—*entire*—having all the characteristic devotedness of a temple. His fitness for glorifying God will of course depend on the moral state of the world, and on the perfection of his contrast to it. If that contrast be not very apparent, the world cannot be expected to take pains and look after it. If it be not very considerable, it will, in effect, be nothing, but will itself be neutralized and borne down by the counter-influences of the world. If it exists only in some particulars, the world will be quick to detect the inconsistency between those particulars and the rest of his character; and will quote him against himself, and in confirmation of itself. If he still approaches the world, and places himself in friendly contact with it where he ought not, for the cause of Christ he exists comparatively in vain. *Say* what he will for the Gospel, the world will judge of it by his *example*. *Refer* them as he may to the inspired Record itself, *his life* is the Bible which they read—an epistle known and read of all. His usefulness, we repeat, will depend, under God, on the breadth and distinctness of the line of demarcation which separates him from the world, and on the perfection of contrast to the world which he exhibits.

For instance; the world is selfish—acts without reference to a Supreme will—and constitutes itself the end of all it does. How important, then, that he should embody the self-sacrificing spirit of Christ. To do this by halves only—to study his own aggrandisement—or to live in comparative indolence and luxury—would be to symbolize with the world, and to confirm it in its besetting sin. But he is to exhibit that fiction of the world—a life of self-denial. By casting loose all delights, all passions, all pursuits by which the world is engrossed and enslaved; and by going out of himself, abandoning himself, evincing a readiness to sacrifice life itself in the cause of Christ, he is to stand out in vivid contrast with the selfishness of the world—silently to condemn it—to proclaim a will higher than human—the responsibility of men to that will, and the supreme happiness of absolute conformity to it. And thus he is to prepare them to hear with effect of that sacrifice, compared with which there is nothing else deserves the name.

The world is sensual—supremely influenced by the visible and the present. The constancy and force with which the bodies of men gravitate to the earth, is only an emblem of the manner in which the universal heart of man tends to the concerns and objects of the world. But the Christian is to "come out from them, and to be separate"—"to love not the world, nor the things of the world"—to "set his affections on things above." The cross is to him the perpetual memorial of another world—the representative of the most glorious Being there, and the medium of constant communication with Him. As if he were daily standing in the open portal of that celestial state, and surveying the glories within, he is to evince a perfect superiority to all the objects of worldly pursuit. And, as if he were empowered to take others with him there, and were only waiting here till he had succeeded, he is to move among them as one not of this world—an angel partly on the wing.

Now, this twofold principle of worldly selfishness, or selfish sensuality, is the ruling principle of man, and the essence of his guilt. How important, then, that the Christian should stand out in bold and bright relief as the representative of the Cross—the living personification of holy, spiritual, unworldly benevolence. And well may the Christian regard himself with all the sacredness of a temple, since he cannot yield himself to any other claimant than Christ, even for a moment, without yielding himself, during that moment, to a hostile party; so that, in truth, his only escape from partial hostility to Christ is that of unreserved devotedness to His service.

III.

Thus have we shewn that every part and property of the

Christian is to be devoted to Christ—and that he is to be thus devoted, at all times and in the highest degree, both in order to his more striking contrast with the world, and because it is his only alternative from partial hostility to Christ. We would now remark, thirdly, that the great Gospel inducement to such consecration is that we are actually the property of Christ, and that He has made us His property *for the specific object of our devotedness to Him.*

" What, know ye not that your body is the temple of the Holy Ghost, which is in you?" What, can you have allowed an analogy so obvious as that which exists between a temple and a believer to escape your notice? Angels mark it—and that is one reason why they rejoice over the sinner when he repents—they know that God is consecrating another living temple—is advancing another step towards the completion of that universal temple destined to resound through eternity with the echoes of His praise. God himself *designs* it—designs that the consecrated character of the temple on Zion shall be copied and repeated in the devoted character of every living temple. If, then, you would see the pattern of your Christian devotedness, go, and survey the temple and its service. Are you not conscious of a holy awe stealing over your mind as you approach it?—such should be the feeling which the presence of the Christian inspires—that he is a man set apart for God. Enter the sacred precincts—cross the threshold, and look around—all its priests are the anointed servants of God—all its vessels, holiness to the Lord—all its parts, sprinkled with blood. Can you imagine anything which you see in it taken and applied to any other than temple purposes without a sense of profanation?—that priest, for instance, just offering the victim, polluted with licentiousness?—that sacred vessel, taken away and turned into a cup of intemperance—that altar, transferred for a time to the temple of Moloch—or the temple itself lent during the interval of God's worship to celebrate the orgies of some idol-god? The very thought seems profanation!—blasphemy! And why, but because we feel that the place is sacred to God throughout, and should be entirely and exclusively devoted to His service? Well, know ye not that the Christian is now the temple of God—that even while the ancient temple stood, when looking round on all the scenes and objects of the universe, and inquiring, "Where is the house that ye built unto me, and where is the place of my rest?"—the reply of His own lips was, that the heart of the contrite was the place of His abode? Know ye not that He whose glory then dwelt between the cherubim, has now transferred His residence to the hearts of His people, "as he hath said, I will dwell in them, and walk in them"—and know ye not that He has claims on your devotedness which He could never have on a material temple—the great claim that you are bought with a price—that everything you are and have belongs by purchase to the God of the temple—and that, by your voluntarily and cordially devoting the whole to Him, He counts himself glorified? Yes, the apostle intimates that not only is every individual believer, but every particular church, a living temple. Its members, "as living stones, are built up a spiritual house, an holy priesthood, to offer up spiritual sacrifices, acceptable to God by Jesus Christ." And may we not suppose, must we not believe, that as often as they meet in this capacity, and for this object, the great Lord of the temple himself comes among them? Are we not to conclude that He has come here this day, and that as He marks the character of your service, and the degree of your devotedness, His eyes are as a flame of fire? Are we prepared for the inspection? Are we aware that we are now undergoing it? Does He find the first talent we spoke of—our knowledge of salvation—kept bright and burnished, like a vessel of the sanctuary, by constant use? Our speech—do the lips of the priest keep knowledge, and the people order their conversation aright? Are their tongues like living censers for offering the incense of praise? The influence arising from our relationship—has it been made to serve like a golden cord to draw others with us into the Divine presence? Does He find none of His property abstracted from the treasury, and lavished on worldly objects? or is it all ready to meet His claims? Is self-denial here bearing its cross, and presenting its precious oblations?—and Christian activity and zeal flaming like an altar of sacrifice, and ready to say, "the zeal of thine house hath consumed me?"—and prayer, wrestling with God for a universal blessing? Does He behold in *this* Christian Church the consecration of a temple?

Brethren, you have met to-day to collect a sum sufficient to complete the purchase of the place in which you assemble as the Church of Christ. Shall it continue after to-day under the stigma of a debt? Is there not a grave inconsistency in the fact of a Church which He hath bought with a price, assembling in a house the price of which remains unpaid? Church of Christ, "which He hath purchased with His own blood," will you not evince your sense of obligation so far as to complete the purchase of this house for His service? Suppose the price of your redemption were still unpaid—imagine that Christ had withheld a particle of His Divine resources from completing your ransom—how appalling the bare idea! But, no, He withheld nothing—withdrew nothing. He became the sole, the entire property of His Church—and all He asks is that we become His property in return—that we glorify Him in our body, and in our spirit, which are His. And, oh, what a dignity and a destiny is this! Serve Him, and you reign. Wear His yoke, and you assume a crown. Glorify Him, and you catch His radiance, and are glorified by Him.

SERMON IV.

GOD'S GLORY THE END OF LIFE.

1 Cor. x. 31.—"Whether therefore ye eat, or drink, or whatsoever ye do, do all to the glory of God."

Everything in the government of God is regulated—not by the uncertain and shifting expedients of human policy—but by universal and eternal principles. Within the scope of one or other of these principles, the Christian is to consider himself moving, through every moment, and in every act of his life. And one of the characteristic excellences of the Bible is, that it never loses a suitable occasion, when speaking of any of the particulars of life, of referring to the general principle under which they range, and to which they belong; or else, if the specific principle be not named, of referring them to that ultimate and all-comprehending law, for which all other laws exist—the glory of God.

In the context, we find the apostle adjudicating between two parties on a point concerning which no distinct law existed. With the skill of a master—or rather, with the wisdom of inspiration—he reminds them of the great first principle, which stands in the stead of a thousand particular laws—and living under the guidance of which they would not feel the want of such particular laws—that they are to do good on the largest possible scale—that in the absence of positive enactments on any particular subject, their grand rule should be the welfare and salvation of others—"seeking the profit of the many, that they may be saved;" that they never need be at a loss for an end at which to aim, since there is an end so great that every thing else stands to it only in the relation of means—the glory of God. So that even if there were a separate law enacted for every separate action of life, these laws would be all subordinate to that ultimate end. Instead of waiting, then, like children, for particular directions, let them aim at once at that great end. Whether they ate, or drank, or whatever they did—from the least act of life to the greatest—let them do all to the glory of God.

Not that they were to indulge in a mean-spirited and gloomy asceticism in trifles; nor to suppose that they would be bringing honour to God by the frequent repetition of His mere name; but by gratefully receiving, and moderately enjoying, even their ordinary mercies, and by avoiding everything likely to impair their usefulness, they would be serving Him. Even while here on earth, they would be thus placing themselves in harmony with the adoring cherubim before the throne; even while eating and drinking—some of man's lowest acts—they would be falling in with the great movements of the universe. For, by regarding life as a united and continuous system of means—an organized whole, in which every part, even the smallest, is to have its place, and to work out the main end, they would be effectually promoting the glory of God.

We will not here stop to point out how advantageously Christianity contrasts in this respect with every false religion, and even with the abrogated economy of Judaism—how generously it discharges us from the cares and vexations of an elaborate ceremonial—how few, simple, and comprehensive are its laws—how it dignifies that which is comparatively little in our earthly lot, by linking it on to all that is heavenly and Divine—how the object at which it directs us to aim is one in which we find angels are our associates and competitors, and for which the Son of God himself occupies the mediatorial throne. We will proceed at once to enlarge on some of the particulars suggested by the text, and appropriate to the present occasion. And whether we speak or hear, whether we worship, or contribute of our property, or whatever we do for the furtherance of the object which has brought us together, may we do all to the glory of God.

I.

And, first, what is it to glorify God? A clear and definite idea on this point is indispensable. Now, I think the answer may be thus stated—to glorify God is to be consciously moved, chiefly, and on the whole, by an intelligent and affectionate regard for the will and character of God.

This, you will perceive, makes it ultimately an affair of the *motives*. And do you not see how it enables us to correct that fatal and prevalent error, that to obey natural and social law is to obey God?—that to obey the law, is to obey the Lawgiver? whereas I may obey the law in one respect, only that I may resist the Lawgiver in every other respect. The *morality* of conduct depends entirely on the motives which lead to it. These motives are of different classes. There are those of the appetites and passions—those of self-love—those of the affections and dispositions towards others—and those derived from a regard to the will and character of God. These motives range in an ascending scale—our obligation to God being paramount. Now, as there is no duty which we owe to ourselves, or to our fellow-men, which we do not owe partly and chiefly because God has willed it, to omit all reference to Him in the performance of it is to lay ourselves open to the charge of *ungodliness*. A man may spend life in the performance of acts outwardly right—and he may even perform many of his social duties (not merely from a *native* kindliness, in which there may be no more morality than in the innocence of the dove, or the gentleness of the lamb), he may perform them because he deems the performance socially right. Yet these very acts may be wanting in a whole order of motives, and that the highest order—a regard to the will of God. These acts are right as arising out of relations which God has appointed;

to perform them, therefore, irrespective of His will on the subject—from no conscious regard to Him—is to be found wanting in the highest obligation. You would not say that the man who regulated his appetites was therefore at liberty to be as selfish as he pleased. You would not say that the man who, besides regulating his appetites, regulated also his self-love, was therefore discharged from all duties to society. So neither can you say that his attention to these three classes of duties discharges him from all regard to the fourth —namely, to the will of God on the subject. This would be to arm the laws against the Lawgiver; to make obedience to inferior duties the occasion for shutting out God—a moral vacuum this of the most fearful description—that God should not be "in all his thoughts."

To glorify God, then, is not merely to obey certain laws, because they are laws of nature, but to obey them *consciously* as laws of God. This conscious reference to God cannot, indeed, attend every act—the demands of duty are often too sudden for it—the man has often to *act* rather than to think —and therefore, I say that he must be consciously actuated by a regard to the will of God *on the whole.* It is not to be supposed that he is to be thus actuated to the exclusion of all the other classes of motives—motives of appetite, of self-interest, and of benevolence, for all these are motives of Divine appointment, as well as those which arise from a regard to the will of God; but this last is supreme, and therefore, I say, that he is to be moved by this *chiefly.* It is not to be supposed that his being thus moved blindly—without any light as to the direction in which he ought to move—can glorify God. It may dishonour God, for the man may imagine, in his ignorance and bigotry, that by persecuting the faithful he is doing God service—that he is proving his *piety* when he is only proving his sincerity—and a man may be sincerely wrong as well as sincerely right —and therefore, I say, that his regard for the will of God must be *intelligent,* enlightened. Nor is it to be supposed that even this can be acceptable to God if separated from the consciousness of holy *love.* Morality, rightly understood, is the discharge of *every* obligation arising from *every* relation we sustain. But to obey God from any motive less than love to Him, is to ignore *His* highest claim, and to fail in *our* highest obligation. It is to yield to His *will* what we withhold from His *character.* It is to give to His *authority* that which is due to His infinite *excellence.* His highest command, the summary and essence of all His laws, is, "Thou shalt *love* Me supremely. Thou art made to love *most* that which is *best;* and thou shalt not violate the law of thy being. Thou shalt not live in the presence of infinite perfection without sympathizing with it. Thou art created to share My happiness by sharing My excellence; and to share My excellence is to reflect My glory." I repeat, then, to glorify God is to be consciously moved chiefly, and on the whole, by an intelligent and *affectionate* regard for the will and character of God.

II.

But, secondly, if this be to glorify God, what is the change or state of mind which it presupposes? Evidently this is not man's prevailing condition. The vast majority of the race are living in utter forgetfulness of God, not merely as the Source of *moral* law, but even as the Giver of the laws of nature. A large proportion of the race, besides ignoring the Lawgiver, live in the habitual violation of nearly all His laws. And even of those that obey His laws—the laws, I mean, of temperance and chastity, honesty, justice, and humanity—even of those, a very large proportion regard their obedience of these *laws* as a substitute for their obedience of *Him.* They obey them as the laws of *their* own nature, and not as the expressions of *His* nature, or the laws of *His* appointment. And thus the very laws which were meant to teach them their dependence upon God, and to bring them into His presence, are built up into a wall of separation from Him—into a fortress for keeping Him out. And the very health, and ease, and reputation which accrue to them, owing to their obedience to these laws, like provisions taken into a fortress, are perverted into the occasions for forgetting Him and all His sovereign claims. And who does not see that a very thin partition separates this mere thoughtlessness of God from a feeling of alienation and aversion from Him? Who does not feel that it would be easy to convert this indifference into hostility? Who cannot imagine what would take place were God himself to summon that fortress—how their worldliness would revolt from His spirituality and holiness—how, throwing off every disguise, their self-sufficiency would proclaim their independence of God,—in other words, how certainly it would appear that the most smooth and smiling surface of mere ungodliness conceals the seeds of that carnal mind which is enmity against God? And hence the magnitude of our present inquiry—whence the change or state of mind presupposed in the directly opposite duty of glorifying God?

Whence comes it? "Not of blood, nor of the will of the flesh, nor of the will of man, but of God." By what instrumentality? "By the word of God, which liveth and abideth for ever." By whose agency? "By the washing of regeneration, and renewing of the Holy Ghost." The change itself is nothing less than the restoration of God to the soul. It may not be a sudden or abrupt change. Commencing early in life, and proceeding so quietly as to resemble the regular development of natural character, rather than the result of a direct agency from without, it *may* not be marked by any moral convulsions—may exhibit nothing startling or strange; and yet does it involve in reality nothing less than the setting up in the heart of a new kingdom—the very throne of God. For mark how, in relation to that scale of motives to which I just now referred—mark how certainly the man ascends from the lowest to the highest—from that which identifies him with the animal to that which joins him to the angel. As a being abandoned to the darkness and distance of nature—one on whom sin had worked out all its worst effects—the gospel finds him, it may be, a creature of mere instincts and appetites—moved only by his animal passions; but from the moment the cry issues from his lips, "What must I do to be saved?" it is clear that he has risen in the scale of motive—he is moved by *self-love.* Besides the *present,* about which he has been hitherto engrossed, he is now filled with apprehensions for the future. Ascending above the mere gratification of his passions, he now stands on a point which reveals him to himself—responsible, but guilty—in danger, but helpless—immortal, but entirely dependent on the mercy of God. But now, again, from the moment he finds himself in the arms of that mercy—saved by the grand expedient of the Cross—and begins to desire the salvation of others, it is clear he has risen another step in the scale of motive—he is now moved by the *benevolent affections*—by a tender regard for the everlasting welfare of others. From living in a state in which he thought only of himself—only of a *part* of himself—and that the *lowest*—he has come to care for every part of his nature, and for the immortal most; he has come even to extend his regards to the salvation of others. But *this* is not all; for, from the moment he traced this change to its source in the love of God, a higher motive still affected him. From the moment the sense of his vast obligations to Christ dawned on his mind, he came to be moved by the highest power—the "love of Christ constrained him." He has now reached the loftiest order of motives. From stooping to take his pleasures from the dust, he now erects himself, and reaches for them to the throne of God. He has emerged and emerged, till He has come forth on a height radiant with the glory of God.

Mighty transformation this! So great that, by the lips of Inspiration itself, he is pronounced to be "a new creature!" Yes, a new creature! The doctrine of the transmutation of species, false in the natural kingdom, is true in the spiritual.

For here is a being that, without losing his identity, has passed over into a new nature. The animal has emerged into the man. The man has acquired a whole order of life unknown to him before. A new world stretches its horizon around him. New objects attract him. The functions of a new life devolve upon him. New motives impel him. He has awoke to find that there is an end which all things are destined to subserve—that he has been called into being expressly to promote it—and that the means by which he has been recalled from deserved destruction have laid him under new and peculiar obligations to live for this end supremely.

III.

And this prepares the way for a third inquiry, Why *is the glory of God* to be the great end of life? To which I might reply in brief, because it is the only end which is infinitely excellent. Other ends, doubtless, are aimed at, and are attained; but this end includes them all. Other ends are designed; but in relation to this end they are all subordinated as means. No objection can be alleged against the view that the glory of God is to be the end of all things in the eternity to come, which would not equally lie against the view that He has been His own end in the eternity past; and yet no one *can* raise a question on this point, for during the eternity past He alone existed. Besides which, the only alternative to God being the great end of creation is, that the creature itself be that end; but the only reason which *could* be assigned for this view is that it would seem to be more worthy of God, which would be only saying, in other words, that that must be the end of creation which is most worthy *of Him*—most glorious *to Him*—thus, in reality, affirming the doctrine in the very act of denying it—the doctrine that the glory of God is the great end of life and of creation.

But this seems hardly a subject for argument. It commends itself to the mind independently of proof. In the same moment in which it is understood, it is felt to be self-evident. It runs through the Scripture like a line of light. The only sense of dissatisfaction the mind feels in connexion with it, arises from the haunting conviction of the utter inadequacy of all creation to reflect the glory of God in its purity and fulness. Wing your way, in imagination, to some far distant sphere—and make that the starting point for another flight as far beyond—and repeat the flight to a number that baffles all calculation—still the line which bounds the space devoted to His glory lies immeasurably beyond. You have been moving only at its centre. Yet vast as this theatre is, it is less by infinity than the glory which it proclaims. Imagine if you will that each of the worlds which people these amplitudes of space is itself peopled with its own order of holy beings; and then try to estimate the excellences of the whole. But while you are trying to make the estimate, you are to suppose that all that excellence goes on increasing, and that it will go on for ever, and yet that, at the remotest point of futurity, it will still be infinitely short of *His* excellence. Count up, if you can, the number of all the objects included in this vast circumference, and all the combinations of which they admit; yet you are to bear in mind that, after they have gone on multiplying, and combining, and illustrating His resources for ages, what will then be known of His resources will be as nothing compared with what will remain to be known. Would you know what *one* thought on the subject who had been rapt into a vision of the third heavens—who saw the departure of one economy, and was himself the apostle of another—who was permitted to occupy a point from which he could take a wide survey of the Divine plans?—"O the depth (said he) of the riches both of the wisdom and knowledge of God; how unsearchable are his judgments, and his ways past finding out. . . . For of him, and through him, and to him, are all things; to him be glory for ever." Would you know the verdict of beings who have looked at the subject in the light of unnumbered worlds, and who have lived in the Divine presence for unknown ages? Listen, and with one voice you hear them exclaim, "Thou art worthy, O Lord, to receive glory, and honour, and power; for thou hast created all things; and for thy pleasure they are and were created." But, more than all, would you know the estimate of Christ himself on the subject—of Him who came forth from the very bosom of God—of Him who had shared uncreated glory with the Father before the world was? You know that He signified *His* estimate not so much by words as by deeds; and you know the vastness of the occasion which led to those deeds. Did I say just now that the only sense of dissatisfaction we feel in connexion with this subject arises from the felt and utter inadequacy of all creation to reflect the glory of the Infinite? Alas, we have now reached a point where a reason for more than dissatisfaction comes to light—for personal sorrow and profound humiliation. For need I remind you that the great occasion which brought forth the Son of God in a visible manifestation, was no less than that we—a race of creatures destined to find our happiness in perpetual approaches to God—had dared to revolt, and to set up another course, and another end? Need I remind you that He came down to earth expressly to vindicate the claims of that glory, and to restore that revolted race to obedience. Tell me, then, if you can, the might—the *all*mightiness—of the force which brought Him from heaven to earth, and which incessantly acted on Him while here—and I will tell you the value which He attached to the glory of God. Weigh, if you can, the amount of holy and agonizing emotion of which He had been conscious by the time He uttered the language, "Father, I have glorified thee on the earth." Measure, if you can, the value of the influences He had shed, of the truths He had taught, the miracles He had wrought, and the anguish He had endured, when He summed up His earthly course in the mysterious utterance, "It is finished!" —and I will tell you His estimate of the glory of God as the end of creation. Nay, tell me, if you can, the value which

He attaches to His mediatorial exaltation—the worth of all the blessings which, since His exaltation, He has dispensed, and of all the richer blessings which He has yet to dispense, and I may then be in a condition to tell you of the importance which He attaches to the glory of God. For He *must* reign—it is a moral necessity with Him that He should reign—till He hath put all the enemies to that glory under His feet—that He may then restore the kingdom to the Father, and God be all in all. Yes, much as He may delight in the *favour* of the Deity, He rates *the glory* of God higher still; for it is that which gives even to His *favour* all its value; so that to be the means of manifesting it to the universe is the crown of His mediatorial happiness, as it is the end of creation.

2. But in thus answering the question, Why is the glory of God to be the great end of life? we have found a new reason for glorifying Him—a second answer. Here is the great Gospel inducement—that we are actually the property of Christ, and that He has made us His property for this specific end.

"What! know ye not that ye are not your own? for ye are bought with a price: therefore glorify God in your body, and in your spirit, which are his." The fact that He is our *Creator*, gives Him a right in us which nothing can ever alienate; but on this right, absolute and inalienable as it is, He does not here insist. The fact that we have ever been cared for by His providence—that we have never been out of the arms of Infinite tenderness—gives Him a claim on us which nothing can ever cancel; but on this claim, strong and subduing as it is, He does not insist. He has a claim more powerful and affecting still—the fact that He has *bought* us—bought us with *a price*. He waives every other ground of claim, and trusts to this alone. And what a claim it is—the claim of redemption! the last and strongest plea which Infinite love itself can employ! Alas, that our familiarity with it should ever diminish its freshness and its force!—that we do not always feel as if the ransom-blood had only just been shed—the mystery of the Cross just concluded! To think that there should ever have been a period in our history when we were legally and morally *lost ;* lost to *ourselves*—all our capacity for happiness being turned into a felt capacity for suffering; lost to the *society of heaven*—the place which might have awaited us there to remain eternally vacant; the part we should have taken in the chorus of the blessed to be for ever unfilled; heaven itself, as far as in us lay, turned into a place of mourning and desolation; lost to *God*—to the disposition of serving Him—to the right of beholding and enjoying Him—and therefore lost to the very end for which He had given us existence! To think that in point of law we were thus lost as truly as if the hand of justice had actually led us down to our place in woe—had drawn on us the bolts of the dreadful prison—and as if years of wretchedness and ages of darkness had rolled over us there. Well may we ask ourselves again and again—how is it that we are here? here, in the blessed light of day—here, in the still more blessed light of God's countenance? Why is this? and how has it come to pass? Has justice relaxed its demands? Have the penal flames become extinct? "What! know ye not that ye are bought with a price?" It is the theme of the universe. Know ye not that your ransom-price is "the precious blood of Christ" —that in virtue of that grand moral compensation, your sentence can be remitted, your heart renewed, your soul be saved! Feel you not the power of this love constraining you once more to live unto God? "How much owest thou unto thy Lord?" Try to compute it. He asks not for a greater surrender than He deserves. He asks only for His due. So that if there *be* any part of your nature which He has not redeemed—any portion of your time on which He has not any claim—or any thing in your possession for which you are not indebted to Him—keep it back, and apply it to some other purpose. But does not the bare suggestion do violence to your new nature? does not every part of that nature resent the idea as robbery, and find a voice to exclaim, "O Lord, I am *not* my own; in body, soul, and spirit I am thine!"

IV.

If now it be asked, fourthly, Why God is to be glorified *in the particular manner which is here specified*—"whether we eat, or drink, or whatever we do"—we are prepared with a reply.

1. For do you not see, first, that inasmuch as life is made up principally of what men account small things, an opportunity is thus, and only thus, secured to all for constantly glorifying God? I say, *life* is made up chiefly of what men account small things. Indeed, what is not so made up? The works of the God of nature;—the globe consists of atoms; the greatest material whole consists of parts, and may be analyzed to particles indefinitely divisible. And thus we find God glorifying *himself* in the little as well as in the great; indeed honouring himself in the little, as the only way of honouring himself in the great—clothing the grass of the field, painting the lily, succouring the sparrow's wing, counting the hairs of our head. Descend from one degree of minuteness to another, and you will find the atom polished, and the members of the living mote articulated in a manner too delicate for your eye to trace. Take the microscope, and you will find that in that moving point—too small for the naked eye to notice—God has built up, with what seems to us an infinite patience of detail, a little world as perfect as the great one. Multiply your power of vision to the utmost, and you will find that "the last discernible particle passes out of your sight with the same glory resting on it as on the last star which faintly glimmers in the skirt of the universe." Whatever the Creator does—whether He make an atom or an angel—He does all so as to reflect His own glory.

What impressive illustrations of the same principle are to be found in the life of Christ! "For this cause He died, and rose, and revived, that He might be Lord of the dead and of the living." How unparalleled the magnitude of His object! But was He therefore inattentive to things apparently small? Though armed with omnipotence, the portion of time which He occupied in the performance of miracles was comparatively small; while the wide intervals were occupied in the quiet of devotional retirement, the patient journeyings on foot, and the conversational instruction of His disciples. Though He died to inherit the throne of supremacy, yet, when only a step from the cross, he washed His disciples' feet; when in the very crisis of the cross, He tenderly provided for a mother's comfort; and though He arose to burst the bars of death, and to take the keys of the invisible world, He came not forth from the sepulchre till He had folded the linen clothes, and had laid the napkin that was about His head in a place by itself; and though He revived to be Lord of the universe, "it came to pass as He sat at meat with his disciples, when He took bread, He blessed, and gave thanks, before he gave it to them." And thus, whether *He* "ate, or drank, or whatever he did, He did all to the glory of God."

Now, in harmony with these facts, He may be regarded as drawing a circle around each of His followers, and as claiming all within it as sacred to himself. That circle will be found to include, not those objects and duties merely which are more immediately religious, but the minor affairs of the street and the shop, the hearth and the table. And why? Partly, we repeat, because life is almost entirely made up of such minor affairs. Great occasions are only of rare occurrence. Recal the history of yesterday, or of any average day of your life—the objects you saw, the words you uttered, the purposes you framed—your thoughts, desires, gratifications, and trials—how ordinary, and apparently unimportant the whole! And yet each of them all has affected your character for eternity. Numbers are at this moment passing to the bar of God whose life, with a few trifling exceptions, has been made up of such days—and yet, think, to what a result it has brought them! Is it not important that there should be some principle which should gather up all these particles of life, and turn them to account for eternity? Such a principle is that contained in the text; like the law of attraction, which makes a globe of material atoms, and carries the whole through boundless space, so this spiritual law—this law of love to Christ—gathering up all the particles of life, unites and employs them to catch and to reflect the glory of the throne of God—that throne to which it carries them.

This, it is to be feared, is not the general opinion on the subject. The prevailing notion is, that to glorify God is entirely an affair of religion—that it is a thing of times and places—that it recurs only at intervals—that it requires an ample space to be done in—that its works are all efforts and loud explosions—that it should have the presence of a multitude to witness them—and that, being ended, it allows a season of relaxation, a Carnival for the exhaustion of Lent. And the consequence of this erroneous impression is that religion, with numbers, is restricted to small and separate portions of life—is fenced off within little enclosures of time; —that, instead of consisting of habits, it consists only of occasional acts—and that, instead of living *with* the man, and leavening him, and becoming one with him, he and it come together only at set times, and on great occasions, and by particular appointment.

Now this false and pernicious view arises, partly, from the want of observing that every thing is connected with every other thing—the near with the distant, the mean with the momentous—so that nothing is absolutely unimportant, because nothing is isolated and alone. A whisper, it is said, may bring down an Alpine avalanche, and a word may revolutionize our character and condition for ever. A look may disturb an everlasting principle, and affect the eternal destiny of others. A thought may give birth to an institution. We know but little of the relative importance of duties and events; so that if we call them great or little according to their outward appearance, we are in danger of falling into grievous error. The mightiest forces in nature are not the thunder and the tempest, but those which we never see nor hear. Were an unreflecting man to take his stand to-night on some mountain top, and to look forth and listen, he might fancy, from the absence of all sights and sounds, that the pulse of nature had stopped. But no, throughout the spacious plains around him mysterious processes are going on—every herb is a chemical centre in which the great elements are noiselessly at work—and, in the beautiful language of the prophet, the heavens are calling to the earth, and the earth is calling to the seed deposited in her bosom. And the things which most permanently affect the character of man are not the influences of set times, expressing themselves in violent efforts, and attracting general attention, but the still small voice—and the moment of reflection—and the view which he takes of ordinary duties—and the influences of the common means of providence and of grace which are ever falling on him softly as the dew—these are the things which penetrate, which interpenetrate, his nature, and take the deepest hold of his being. And it is this wise and gracious arrangement which invests him with power over others. He stands the centre of, it may be, a *small* circle, but let him live unto God, and it will be more than a charmed circle to all that enter it. His day of life may be a day of small things, but let it be a day of grace, and whether he eat, or drink, or whatever he do, he will do all to the glory of God.

2. The injunction in the text supplies the most searching and satisfactory test of Christian character. It does so, partly, by applying a rule to us in those things in which, owing to their apparent littleness, we are most likely to be off our guard; and, partly, by applying it to those things in

which our fellow-men have no right to judge us—for in all *these* things a regard for the will of God alone can rightly influence and determine us. Tell me not how a man deports himself on some great occasion, when all eyes are upon him; but let me know his conduct in the private and obscure performances of ordinary duty. There is a sense in which common piety—piety about common things—is much rarer and greater than uncommon piety. Tell me not of his regularity and activity in the public sanctuary; if I am to judge of his character, let me hear the testimony of his closet. Tell me not of his heroism on some grand and foreseen emergency; let me know how he meets the trifling occurrences which take him by surprise, which give him no time to reflect or to prepare, but which yet incessantly flatter his selfishness, or else enter into conflict with it. As a test of character, it matters little how splendid a man's contribution may be to benevolent objects, it matters every thing whether he practises self-denial or sacrifice in order to make it. As a test of character, it *may* amount to little to say that he *appears* to be in earnest for the salvation of the world—is he quietly, regularly, and unostentatiously seeking, in addition, the salvation of his own family?

Brethren, besides the sphere definitely marked out by duty, there is a large outlying sphere left open to the operation of Christian motive; and it is in this higher and outer region that character proclaims itself—there, where the eye of man cannot pierce, where the judgment of man has no right to intrude, and where the Christian himself has nothing to guide his course by but the consideration of what is most likely to benefit man and to glorify God. Here piety luxuriates without restraint, and feels itself (if I may say so) "put on its honour." Here Christian heroism forms its noblest plans, and devises its most liberal things. Here a large-hearted Paul, leaving other and lesser souls to contend about their rights in meats and drinks, thinks only of what will be best for his weaker brethren; takes for his generous motto, "not seeking mine own profit, but the profit of many, that they may be saved." And here Christian gratitude, deeply conscious that its best efforts fall far below its sense of obligation, aims to gather up all the fragments of life, that nothing be lost, and to lay the whole as an oblation on the altar of God; instead of looking on verbal prayer and praise as sufficient, regards them only as momentary and passing indications of what should be an habitual state of mind; instead of supposing that God is worshipped only on the knees, aims to convert daily labour into an act of devotion, and eating and drinking into a means of honouring God, and life itself into a hymn of praise.

3. Reminding us, next, of the *dignity* of the Christian life—since everything the Christian does, *as a Christian*, is related to the glory of God. Complain not of the humiliations of life; occasion is given you to associate its lowliest acts with all that is grand and imperishable in the kingdom of Christ. As if *He* were the nerve—the great sympathetic nerve—over which all the sufferings of His people pass, He assures them that they cannot receive the slightest wound of which He does not instantly feel the smart. In His description of the final judgment, He represents himself as applauding the least act of holy benevolence as an act performed to himself, and as resenting every slight offered to His people as a violence done to His own nature. There is not a single voluntary act concerning which He will not say, "Ye did it unto *Me*," or "Ye did it *not* unto *Me*." So that, as He sits on the throne of judgment—the centre of the congregated world—every act will be seen like a line pointing directly to Him, in homage or in enmity, and terminating upon Him. Thus, nothing terminates on itself—nothing terminates short of the throne of God—everything travels on till it reaches that point, and there it waits for judgment. And yet how little do we think of this! How prone are we to think and speak of our actions as if they existed just so long as we happen to think of them, and no longer—as if

they operated only just as far as we can easily and visibly trace their effects, and no farther—as if they concerned only the persons, the human beings, immediately interested, and no others—as if, forsooth, God were not interested more than all other beings in the universe put together. For in every action we perform, there is one or other of His universal laws to which that action renders homage, or which it tramples under foot—yes, one of the great laws on which His government rests—one of the pillars of His throne.

A poor widow casts two mites into the temple-treasury; and if the Saviour had not graciously noticed it, man would have accounted it the merest trifle. But his noticing the act did not *make* it important. He noticed it because it *was* important. It would have been quite *as* important, had he never so noticed it. And one of His objects in noticing it was to teach us this—to assure us that *every* such act, whether noticed or not on earth, is both noticed and recorded in heaven—that He receives it as a tribute of affection to himself—accounts himself enriched by it—and will certainly distinguish and applaud it before an assembled world. A grateful penitent anoints His head with precious ointment; and by His arrangement, the deed has ever since filled the Church with its rich perfume. A persecutor goes forth to punish only, as he thinks, a few insignificant Christians at Damascus; but "to smite a saint on earth is, as it has been said, to create a sensation in heaven;" and, accordingly, a voice from the excellent glory inquires, "Saul, Saul, why persecutest thou *me?*" Penitence drops its first tear in some obscure nook; and "I say unto you, there is joy in heaven"—joy which thrills through entire principalities and powers—joy which, beginning at the heart of God, the centre of all benevolence, circulates through all ranks of existences to the utmost circumference of the spiritual creation. An humble man goes forth to proclaim to a people the Gospel of Christ, and is refused a hearing; and no sooner has he vanished from their sight than his visit is forgotten. But while they were yet chasing him from their presence, a hand was recording in heaven, "it shall be more tolerable for Sodom and Gomorrah in the day of judgment than for that people." He proceeds to another people, and His message is received; but all that appears to have taken place is, that a man believing himself to be the bearer of a message from heaven, has found an attentive audience. But, saith Christ, in receiving him as my messenger, "they have received me, and in receiving me, they have received Him that sent me." A willing people erect a house for the worship of God—and though the world may pass it unnoticed by—it becomes in His eye another point of friendly communication between earth and heaven—another place for His throne—another gate of heaven. See, brethren, how every object, action, and event in the Christian Church is complicated with all that is great in the universe—bound up with the glory of God—see how, whether you eat, or drink, or whatever you do, you *may* do all to the glory of God.

SERMON V.

EXHORTATION TO CHRISTIAN EXCELLENCE.

PHIL. iv. 8.—"Finally, brethren, whatsoever things are true—honest (or venerable)—just—pure—lovely—of good report; if there be any virtue, and if there be any praise, think on these things."

ON reading this remarkable language, one is almost unconsciously led to exclaim, "how noble and ennobling a system is the Gospel of Christ—how tranquilly does it sustain a comparison with every other system—how effectually does it eclipse—how gloriously transcend them all!"

For poor humanity has had its systems—systems of philosophy, morality, and religion—systems which, for a time, resounded through the world—systems which were to bring heaven down to earth, or to raise earth to an equality with heaven—it has had them by hundreds, if not by thousands.

Of all these, however, the system of Plato, I suppose, by aiming at what it called the true, the beautiful, and the good, is to be regarded as approaching the nearest to the surpassing excellence of the Gospel. To that system the apostle is supposed, by some, to refer in the text—for it professed to be composed chiefly of whatsoever things were true and valuable in the various systems which had preceded it. But this character he claims in an infinitely higher sense for Christianity. For even if that human system had ascertained the true, the beautiful, and the good, how could it have demonstrated that the true was not the false? how could it have embodied the beautiful, and made it visible? how could it have induced mankind to aim at the good, or to practise the useful? Where were its motives? what were its solemn sanctions? And, accordingly, where were its churches or societies of men embodying and propagating its principles? But ask you for the motives which the *Gospel* supplies? The apostle never enforces its duties apart from its motives. Before uttering the practical appeal in the text, he takes us, in the second chapter, to the cross—takes us there to behold an event, which whoever considers feels that it contains motives for all duties, and incentives equal to all sacrifices—takes us to behold *Him*, who was in the form of God, making himself of no reputation, taking upon Him the form of a servant—still humbling himself—still passing from one depth of ignominy to a lower still—till a cross receives Him—and death arrests His further descent.

Ask you, then, for the practical results of the Gospel?—for its churches and active societies? Oh, what miracles of moral transformation had it not accomplished! Was not the apostle—was not Philippi itself, an instance? There, its first triumph was to change the very jail into a church—the receptacle of a city's depravity into a sanctuary for God. And there already it had begun to leaven and to assimilate into its own glorious nature the mass of depraved humanity around. Nor was it yet satisfied. It calls them, in the text, to higher attainments and greater usefulness yet. Perfect itself, it labours to produce, and is impatient to behold perfection in all who embrace it.

Christian friends, the application of this subject to yourselves is obvious and inevitable. If the character of Christianity be so lofty, your character as its professors must be proportionally excellent. If it actually produced in the Philippians an amount of Christian excellence which called forth apostolic exultation—and if it still remains what it ever was—it comes into the midst of this church, and makes inquisition for the same excellence. It calls over—if I may say so—the muster roll of all the Christian graces; nor allows even one to be absent. Taking you to a mount of vision which commands a view of all the moral greatness and goodness the world—the universe—has ever known, it says to you—"Aspire to imitate the whole—whatever you behold in the wide horizon, true or venerable, just or pure, lovely or of good report, take them all to your heart, and make them your own." It does not specify, you perceive, what things these are. It seems to say—"Aim at *universal* excellence. Cherish the ennobling sentiment that there is nothing too good for Christian humility to hope—nothing too great for Christian devotedness to attempt. Propose to yourselves the loftiest standard of Christian piety, and resolve devoutly to reach it—devise some exalted end, and determine in the strength of God to attain it. Vow to live for the Cross of Christ. Do this—and it will not be necessary to particularize and prescribe. For, remember, he who dedicates himself to a great object is a law to himself—he who acts on a lofty principle lifts his whole nature at once—he who aims at an exalted end is more than resolving on good acts or even good habits, he is necessitating and producing them—he who lives for a noble purpose is keeping all laws at once without feeling that he is subjected to any."

In order to render this call intelligible and impressive, allow me to enforce, at least, *the spirit of the text* by shewing that whatever there is attractive in Christian morality, you are to exemplify it—whatever there is exalted and mature in Scriptural piety, you are to aim to attain it—whatever is useful in Christian activity, you should labour to accomplish it—whatever there is tender in solicitude for the salvation of others, you should cherish it—whatever lofty in Christian enterprise, you are to sympathize with it—and whatever there is sublime and animating in Christian motive, you are to live under its ever-present influence.

I.

Addressing myself especially to the professed disciples of Christ, permit me to remark, first, that *whatever is lovely in the practice of Christian morality you are to exemplify it.*

The Christian life, indeed, is associated in many minds with the idea of abstraction from secular pursuits, and constant occupation in the visible exercises of piety and benevolence. According to their notion, it involves little less than ministerial consecration, and would convert the Church into a society of devotees. But Christianity, while "it gave some to be apostles and some prophets, and some evangelists, and some pastors and teachers,"[1] yet so far from withdrawing us generally from the ordinary and active duties of life, instructs and prepares us to discharge them. According to the Scripture theory, the Christian Church should be the nursery and school of all practical excellence; capable of supplying the world with the noblest specimens of wisdom and virtue for filling offices of utility and trust. Like a city set upon a hill, it should be conspicuous from afar—that all might know where to look for whatsoever things are just, and lovely, and of good report. Here the irreligious master should always be able to find the most faithful servants—and the unchristian servant to find the most considerate and kind of masters. Here the city should find its most useful citizens—the country its most disinterested patriots—the state its wisest legislators and most incorruptible magistrates—and public liberty its ablest champions.

Not only is Christian piety *compatible* with the discharge of social duties; it will not absolve us from them, will not allow us to be idle spectators on the great theatre of life. It enters the domestic circle, and addresses an appropriate word to the husband and the wife, the parent and the child. It takes the servant by the hand, and daily leads him to his appointed task, and thus invests his station with a dignity beside which the most splendid idleness is eclipsed and disgraced. It accompanies the tradesman to the place of business, takes its seat by the judge, and establishes the throne in righteousness. And thus, while it seems to be intent only on the happiness of eternity, it overlooks nothing connected with the wellbeing of time. It even seeks to prepare us for the duties and immunities of that higher state, partly by exercising us in the duties of our earthly condition.

And the reason of all this is obvious—that the object of the Gospel is, not to repeal our *original and natural relations*, but to remedy and restore our *moral* constitution, and to do this through the medium of those relations. It is the tendency of *sin* to destroy them—the object of the Gospel is to *employ* them, and to restore and sanctify, that it *may* employ them. Hence, it not only republishes the duties of the second table, but adds tenderness and power to their sanctions. However exhausted its treasury may be, it will not allow the undutiful son to enrich it by saying "Corban," and casting into it that which the wants of his parents require. However naked its altar, it scorns to accept "robbery for burnt offering." However deserted its shrine, it will not allow the angry suppliant to approach it till first he has gone and become reconciled to his brother. And however long any of its offices in the house of God may have stood vacant, the only condition on which it will allow them to be filled is, that the occupants first "rule well their own house," and "have a good report of them that are without."

And the *advantage* of all this is as obvious as the *reason* in which it originates. At all events, the evil resulting from the want of it is obvious enough. Could the Gospel overlook these proprieties without arming against itself all that is most deep and central in human nature? Can a Church neglect them without soon becoming a proverb and a reproach? Is not the want of honesty, integrity, natural affection—of any of the domestic or of the social virtues—in two or three of its members only, sufficient to blast its reputation, and to impair its usefulness for years, if not for ever?

On the other hand, can the members of a Church honour these relations and cultivate these virtues without augmenting their influence and their means of usefulness? Why is it that the sinner, though he loves his sin, yet hates its effects, and often loathes himself on account of them?—because he feels that it is violating the first principles and original relations of his nature. And why is it that, while he hates the holiness of the Gospel, he is yet constrained to admire its effects?—because he feels that it is employing those first principles, and honouring those original relations. Oh, my friends, if you would adorn the doctrine of God your Saviour in all things, if you would win for it the secret admiration of the unconverted, and acquire for it an influence over their hearts, exemplify the attractions of Christian morality. Think what prodigious effect it would give to the Gospel if all its professors did this! If they took whatsoever things are true, and just, and pure, and lovely, and formed them into a bright and beauteous diadem, what a halo of glory would it shed over the whole of their earthly course! What a kind of emblazonment would be thrown over the very *name* of Christianity! How impossible it would be to pronounce that name, without calling up in the heart feelings of homage and love! And is not this what the Gospel actually requires? Can it consistently be satisfied with less? Does it not seek to enlist into its service all the relations which bind us together, and all the natural means by which we influence each other? It cannot do without them—consistently with the Divine appointments, it cannot do without them. They are the only instruments which it has to work with. It seeks to win the infant heart, by looking at it through the eyes, and caressing it in the tones, of maternal love. The father's authority, the sister's entreaty, the brother's warning, the persuasion of friendship, the active attentions of neighbourly kindness, the tradesman's integrity and weight of character, the disinterested beneficence of public life—it wants them all—has work for them all. And even if it had them, the kindest tones cannot equal the tenderness of its entreaties—the hottest tears cannot equal its anguish over human misery—the most throbbing heart cannot beat quick enough to satisfy its eager longing for human salvation—all the influence which the church can wield in its behalf cannot do justice to its free, and full, and gushing benevolence—cannot furnish channels wide and deep enough to pour forth the ocean fulness of its grace.

II.

But Christian morality supposes piety. The holier a church is, the more is it likely to excel in the practice of the virtues —for the more will it live under the influence of those motives which produce them. Then, secondly, *whatsoever things are exalted and mature in Christian piety, aim to attain them.* If the holiness of the individual Christian be progressive, then should the piety of a church be progressive also—for what is the piety of the whole, but the collective piety of all its parts? And if the individual believer should say, "Brethren, I count not myself to have apprehended"—the language of a church should also be, "this one thing we do; forgetting those things which are behind, and reaching forth unto those which are before, we press toward the mark, for the prize of the high calling of God in Christ Jesus."

And yet, how few the churches whose conduct would justify the adoption of this language! How many a church is seen to languish on from year to year, content with a bare existence! How many a church which not only exists, but wears the general aspect of health, is yet content to remain at a stand for years together! As if it had reached the standard of a perfect church, it never exhibits a single sign of self-dissatisfaction, or makes an additional onward move in the path of Christian activity. And how many a church, it is to be feared, that does exhibit some of these signs—signs of increase in wealth, in numbers, and even in Christian activity—signs like those which led an ancient church to say, "I am rich, and increased in goods, and have need of nothing" —is yet wanting, like that church, in a proportional increase of scriptural piety! Indeed, where is the church that aims as high, in this respect, or advances as rapidly, as it ought?

Where is the church which if it "does run well" for a time, does not soon begin to indulge in that self-complacency which is the sure precursor of a pause? Where is the church which thinks of making that grandest of all experiments, how much it may enjoy of God, and how much—even to the highest possible amount—it may achieve of Christian usefulness? And, consequently, where is the church which, if He who walks in the midst of the churches were to pronounce on its character, might not expect Him to say, "I have somewhat against thee?"

Christian brethren, is it true that you might expect Him to say this of *you?* And will you not anxiously examine what that "somewhat against you" would prove to be? And will you not pray for grace to discover and remedy the defect? and will you not henceforth aim at whatever is exalted and mature in Christian piety? What, know ye not that ye are the temple of the Holy Ghost? and what is a temple without piety? Know ye not that your only glory in the eye of Christ, and your only distinction from the world around, consist in the spirituality of your character, and your devotedness to His service? Know ye not that there is a something, the want of which alone can account for the comparative inefficiency of our churches, and the slow progress of the Gospel? Is it the want of that holiness of character which is essential to give it weight with the world—then will you not cast out from the midst of you everything evil as soon as it shews itself—and faithfully administer that Christian discipline appointed on purpose to promote your holiness—and attach supreme importance to everything calculated to increase your spirituality? Is it the want of that Christian devotedness which counts nothing that it has its own? then will you not act as those who feel that you are bought with a price—that all you have and are is the property of Christ? Is it the want of that Christian union for which Christ prayed when He entreated that they all might be one; and will you not join Him in that lofty supplication? shall He offer it alone? will you not take the entire Church into the ample embrace of your Christian affection?

Remember, however, that when you have given all diligence—and have added to your faith virtue, and to your virtue knowledge, and to your knowledge temperance, patience, and godliness, brotherly kindness and charity—that even then you will not have reached the limit of your progress. Never can you reach *that*, till you have entirely exhausted the power of prayer—or till the Holy Spirit has no more quickening and ennobling influence to impart. And when shall that be? As long then as the throne of grace continues to be accessible, and you continue to approach it in an earnest and united supplication—and as long as the Spirit of all grace is able to replenish your hearts with His influence—so long should you continue to advance in whatsoever is exalted and mature in Christian piety.

III.

But such piety is diffusive. It cannot exist without making itself be felt by all around. And the promise of God is, that it shall be felt so as to issue in His glory. Then, thirdly, *whatever is useful in personal Christian activity, aim to accomplish it.* As a church, remember, the very relative design of your formation is the increase of your usefulness. Everything in nature exists for a purpose. Even the atom of the rock has its appointed place and its definite end. Surely, then, man, and of all men the Christian, is not exempt from this law. He has not been created anew in Christ Jesus for mere self-enjoyment or show. And if not the individual Christian, still less a number of these combined. *As a church,* the mere circumstance of your *separation from the world* is designed of itself to attract attention. Your *number* is to invest you with comparative importance. Your formation and existence *as a visible society complete in itself,* is to raise you into the rank of a distinct power. *As a church,* you are entrusted with means either exclusively adapted, or eminently calculated to affect and benefit the world around. You possess, for instance, the ministry of reconciliation, and of what use is that but to beseech men to be reconciled to God? *As a church,* you have a special sphere of labour. However small the circle of Christian influence which each one separately filled before, from the moment you constitute a church, the hand which so forms you draws around you a circle which includes "the region round about." *As a church,* you are now charged with a collective responsibility—all the souls within that circle are, in a sense, given into your hands. All its sick are to be visited—all its ignorant instructed—all its children trained in the way they should go—its widows, and fatherless, and destitute visited in the time of their affliction—the whole of its area filled with appropriate works of faith and labours of love. Hence all your means—the mite of the widow, and the wealth of the affluent—the leisure of one, and the influence of another—the ardour of the young, the wisdom of the aged, the resources of all, are to be combined, surrendered, and actually employed. Here the motto of each is to be, "None of us liveth to himself;" each one is to be assigned a post of labour—the influence of each, by union with all, is made to be felt—and as often as others are added to you, you are to regard your circle as proportionally enlarged, and are again to fill it to the circumference with the influence of the Cross.

But all this, I say, supposes that every individual member is prepared to take his post as an agent for Christ. It does not allow the *indolent* to fold his arms, and devolve his duty on another. It does not permit the *fashionable professor* to wait till Christian labour becomes genteel. It will not permit the *wealthy* to buy off his personal services by the bribe of large donations. It requires both his activity and his donations too. Whether it contains a man for every post or not, it is certain that it contains a post for every man;—and hence the first inquiry which some churches make of a newly admitted member is, "What shall your post be?"

Christian friends, were I to be asked to what it was owing chiefly that the early triumphs of the Gospel were arrested—how it was that Christian usefulness died out of the world, and piety out of the Church?—I should say that it was to be ascribed chiefly to that master-device of Satan by which the Christian professor was led to suppose that he could do everything by proxy—that there was an order of men on whom, for a certain consideration, he could devolve his duties both to God and man. By this means it was that the requirements of God came to be lost sight of, and the claims of the world to be utterly neglected. Now this I need not remind you is substantial Popery. The very essence of that system consists in undertaking to exempt its votaries from their personal responsibility—in finding a price for every duty, and a discharge from every claim of individual accountableness. Brethren, we pride ourselves in our Protestantism, but from how much of that enormous system have we been rescued? For just as much of it as still cleaves to us, just so much are we effectually disabled from doing the first works, and emulating the first days of the Christian Church. Now, judging from the past, we should say that the Reformation rescued us only from one-half of the evil—from that part which blinded men to a sense of their personal concern in the affairs of their *own* salvation. But while the Protestant wonders at the infatuation of the Papist in imagining that anything can exempt him from the necessity of personal diligence in seeking his own salvation, are not we objects of equal wonder in acting so generally as if we thought anything could exempt us from the duty of personal activity in seeking the salvation of others. If the one is Popery, equally so is the other also. And, oh, glorious as the Reformation was *for the Church*, in rescuing its members from the grasp of a spiritual despotism, and making each one feel the necessity of personal *faith* and *personal* holiness —as glorious will that reformation be for the world, which shall complete the work of deliverance, by rescuing them also from the grasp of selfishness, and making each one feel his accountableness to God for personal activity in the work of human salvation. Never till every Christian feels himself as much ordained to *diffuse* the Gospel, as the minister is ordained to *preach* it—never till every church regards itself as a society organized expressly for that diffusion, will it be aware of its vast capabilities in the hand of God for blessing the world. What but this feeling in the hearts of a few has originated all the Christian instrumentality which is at this moment at work? And if a sense of responsibility for personal activity in only a few instances has led to so much, what might we not hope, under God, from the individual and united activity of the universal Church. Whatsoever things are useful, then, in personal Christian activity, aim to accomplish them.

IV.

But all this supposes a deep solicitude for human salvation. He who sympathizes with Christ in actively seeking the salvation of men, must have sympathized with Him first in His compassion for human misery. Then, fourthly, *whatever is tender in Christian solicitude for the salvation of others, cherish it.* The Cross is the utterance of Divine compassion, and the Church collected around it is the proof of its power. The compassion which bled on the cross is supposed to beat in the hearts of all its members. They know the wretchedness of sin into which the sinner is sunk—they look forwards, in imagination, to the end of his course—hear already his doom pronounced—see the pit open to receive him—and hear, by anticipation, his hopeless cries for deliverance; and the deep anxiety they should feel to "snatch the firebrands from the flames," and to quench them in the blood of the cross, should impart a depth of tenderness to their tones, an earnestness of solicitude to their manners, and a combination and energy to their efforts, which, by the blessing of God, nothing should be able to resist. But who feels this? Who sympathizes with Christ in His travail for souls? How little do we feel with God on that particular point on which, if on no other, the strongest bond of union might be supposed to exist—compassion for depraved, guilty, perishing men! Who is there that makes the burthen of a dying world his own?—that goes about with great heaviness and continual sorrow of heart—oppressed, and borne down by the weight of its woes? Jesus wept over the guilt and obduracy of Jerusalem—who is there prepared to mingle their tears with His over this city?—over the guilt and impending destruction of a thousand cities—of a world? Abraham and Moses, David and Jeremiah, and Paul, evinced the tenderness and depth of their compassion for men by tears, entreaties, and restless anguish of soul;—who is there now that can say, "Rivers of waters run down mine eyes because they keep not thy law." Who now is heard exclaiming. "Oh, that my head were waters, and mine eyes a fountain of tears, that I might weep day and night for the slain of the daughter of my people?" Who now asseverates, "I could wish myself accursed from Christ, for my brethren's sake?"

Christians, are there not souls perishing in the very midst of you? Do they not meet with you every Sabbath? sit by your side every service? Have they not done so for years?—are they not yet unsaved? Have not the very sermons which have proved to you a savour of life unto life, proved to them a savour of death unto death? Has not mercy wept over them in vain? Has not Jesus Christ been evidently set forth crucified before them in vain? Can you conceive any beings more deserving your deep commiseration? You will have to appear as witnesses against them. Can you conceive of any prospect more appalling? Oh, look at them, in imagination, till your eyes fill with tears—till your hearts fill with pity and yearn over them. Pray for them—your Lord has *died* for them—will *you* not pray for them? It is your *interest* to do so. At present, they constitute your weakness—your obstacles to enlarged prosperity. They impair the effect of every sermon delivered—of every prayer offered; whereas, if converted, they might constitute your strength. Pray for them—it is your *office.* You are to be intercessors for *them,* as Christ is for you. Pray for them—it shall be your *triumph;* for your prayers offered in faith shall avail much. Hold meetings of prayer for them—in that act alone, angels would see occasion to rejoice in the presence of God; and in its glorious results, Christ would "see of the travail of his soul and be satisfied."

V.

But it is impossible to feel and act thus for *some,* without being conscious of similar solicitude for *others.* Christian compassion knows nothing of geographical limits. The cross vibrates to the sounds of human misery in every part of the earth—and the heart of the Christian is to thrill in sympathy with it. Then, fifthly, *Whatever is lofty in Christian enterprize, aim to sympathize with and promote it.* After what we have said, we cannot be supposed to mean that the duties of the family are to be neglected, or the duties of the particular church to which we belong overlooked, for any other objects, however magnificent. Nor need they. Our duty is, in this respect, coincident with our most enlarged desires; for, by filling the sphere immediately around us first, we are multiplying our agencies for wider and still wider influence. And not only so;—such are the gracious arrangements of the scheme of mercy, that by earnest supplications at the throne of grace, the obscurest believer can touch and set in motion an almighty agency for the good of the world—such the facilities which exist, at present, for the operations of Christian beneficence, that, by contributing his mite, the poorest Christian can become an instrument of good to the ends of the earth, and to nations yet unborn;—and such the vast and varied machinery which that beneficence has put into action, that the humblest church is summoned to take part, and invited to share the honour of restoring a ruined world. And will not you aspire to partake of it? Can you ascend that mount of vision which takes in the field of the world, without marking how vast the multitudes? how urgent and awful their condition? and how momentous the results depending on our hastening to save them? Can you mark how uniformly God enlarges the successes of His people in proportion as they enlarge the sphere of their activity, without feeling a holy determination that no man shall take your crown? Can you remember the magnitude of the work to be accomplished, and the claims which the Saviour has upon you, without feeling the strong necessity of entire consecration to His service, and wishing that you could multiply your means a thousandfold? Oh, whatever there is ennobling in Christian enterprize, be ambitious to mingle in, and practically to serve it.

VI.

But all this supposes adequate motives; and accordingly, if the text does not *contain*, it, at least, *suggests* them: "If there be any *virtue*, and if there be any *praise*, think of these things;" in other words, *whatever there is sublime and animating in Christian motive, live under its ever-present influence.* Are we not apt to act from the lowest allowable, rather than from the highest possible, motives to Christian devotedness? And is not this one reason why our instrumentality is so feeble and inefficient? Whereas the apostle here seems to invoke all that is inspiring and noble from every part of the universe. If there be *any* virtue, and if there be *any* praise, he intimates that the Church has heard of it—has had it—and that we are to live as in its presence—that whatever the world has known of great and good has belonged to the Church—that its influence goes on accumulating from age to age, and is devolved on each successive generation in the Church, so that we of the present day are living under the collected influences of all the past, and moving under an impulsive power greater than that of any preceding age. "Ye are come," says the apostle, "to Mount Zion, and unto the city of the living God, the heavenly Jerusalem, and to an innumerable company of angels—to the general assembly and church of the first-born who are written in heaven." Your union with the Christian Church brings you into connexion with all that was great, and under the influence of all that was good, in the Jewish Church. True, the temple is gone, and the economy abolished, but all its proper and mighty influence exists still. Nothing that belonged to it existed for itself. Every judgment that made it awful looked on beyond its own time, and is frowning still. "All these things happened unto them for ensamples; and they are written for our admonition, upon whom the ends of the world are come." Each of its prophets spoke less for his own time than for ours; so that for us, in effect, he is prophesying still. "Not unto themselves, but unto us they did minister the things which are now reported to us by the Gospel." Every event which distinguished it is still in actual operation, diffusing the elements of other events, and propagating its influence somewhere. And where shall we look for it, but within the limits of the Christian Church?

The Bible is the true conductor of all the holy influences the Church has ever known. From *it*, the Jewish Church received "whatsoever things were true, and lovely, and of good report," in the preceding economies. In that Church, it may be truly said, Abel, though dead, was ever speaking; and Enoch, the seventh from Adam, was ever prophesying of the coming of the Lord. There the patriarchs came, and lived again for their posterity. There the rod of Aaron was ever blooming—the manna ever fresh—the rod of Moses ever working and repeating its wonders. There Sinai reared its awful head, and from its thundering top its law was ever demanding for God the heart of the world, and demanding for every man the love of all the rest.

In the same sense, the Bible has now discharged all the accumulated moral influence of the last economy into the present. The Christian Church has received the whole. There, in effect, the temple still stands. Though, in a *literal* respect, not one stone of that sacred pile remains upon another—in the hallowed influence which it sheds over the Church of God, it still lifts up its awful front—its fires still burn—its victims still bleed—its day of atonement still returns. We behold them now, we shall see them in eternity. All the great events and solemn transactions of the Old Testament may be regarded as having taken place in the Christian Church. Here, in the ministry of the Gospel, they do come, and occur again. Here, its miracles are still convincing, and its angelic messengers still appearing. Here Moses is still teaching self-renunciation, by wishing himself blotted out from the book of life for the good of others—and David leading the intercessions of the Church for the salvation of the ends of the earth—and the prophets still testifying the sufferings of Christ, and the glory that should follow.

And, what is more, here they are all present at once. Truths and events, which for the Jewish Church were scattered thinly over a long tract of time, are here collected to a point, and made operative at once. Ages, with the men who made them memorable, and dispensations, with all the miraculous facts and sublime disclosures which distinguished them, pass in quick and close succession before us, and we feel ourselves standing under the eye and influence of the whole. And, more still, great as was the influence which that economy was calculated to exercise during its actual existence; that influence has gone on gathering strength with each successive age, and is incomparably mightier for us than for those who lived in its immediate presence. All that was evangelical and immortal in its principles was far in advance of the time then present, and was destined to act chiefly on the future. Who does not feel, for instance, that the lofty aspirations of the Psalmist for the universal diffusion of the truth, and the splendid visions of prophecy in which those aspirations were seen realized, are only as yet beginning to produce their legitimate effect; and that, with every year, that effect, under God, is likely to increase!

But together with all this influence from the former economy there comes a mightier influence peculiar to the present—a power so irresistible, that wherever it has had free course, it has swept away the thrones of idolatry—changed the aspect of society—and left its sacred impress on every object it has touched. Ours is the cross—the great power of God—not only absorbing and concentrating all the influences of the past—but charged with a new power direct from God—containing in its bosom all the springs of benevolence the world will ever know—an energy of expansive goodness capable of replenishing the universe with light and love. Here God is seen enriching the world with a gift which leaves us nothing to ask for more. Here Christ is seen taking the world to his heart—seizing our nature as it trembles over the bottomless gulf—assuming it into union with His own—taking our place under the descending stroke of justice, and suffering in our stead. Here angels, drawn from heaven, bend to gaze, and labour to comprehend the mystery of incarnate love. Here the infinite Spirit himself, drawn from the heights of His everlasting dwelling-place, descends as a rushing mighty wind—and the cries of penitence are heard around. Apostles come to lose themselves in wonder, and exclaim, "Herein is love!"—and to surcharge their hearts with a benevolence which impels them to the ends of the earth, "testifying that the Father sent the Son to be the Saviour of the world."

And what do we behold in this result but the appropriate answer to the prayer of Christ, "Sanctify them through thy truth, thy word is truth?" The sanctification He prayed for was not their personal holiness—though that was indispensable—but their *relative* or *official consecration.* "As thou hast sent me into the world," He adds, "even so have I also sent them into the world. And for their sakes I sanctify or devote myself, that they also might, in the same sense, be sanctified or devoted through the truth,"—that, standing under the action of my cross, feeling the full influence of that mystery of compassion, beholding how I—thy Son—the brightness of Thy glory—there devote and set myself apart as a sacrifice for the manifestation of Thine infinite love—they may feel impelled to devote themselves with a similar entireness of consecration to the proclamation of that love to the world.

Oh, if the influence of promises comparatively vague in their meaning, and indefinitely distant in their fulfilment, could produce, under God, the martyr piety of Abel, the dauntless fidelity of Enoch, the persevering obedience of Noah, the missionary pilgrimage of Abraham, and the self-sacrificing zeal of Moses—if the comparatively feeble influences of the Jewish dispensation could create, under God, those splendid constellations of excellence which glow and burn in the Epistle to the Hebrews—who shall set limits to that moral greatness and Christian devotedness which the mightier influences of the Gospel should produce? To know that a whole economy has existed for us—that is, for the Church of which we are members—that for us its heroes lived and its martyrs died—to know that for us that economy of a thousand years was at last dismissed, as for us it had at first been called into being, leaving to us all its rich accumulations of inspired wisdom, godlike example, and moral wealth—this alone should surely be sufficient to teach us the greatness of living for the future, and to kindle in our hearts the unquenchable desire of transmitting the great inheritance to those who succeed us, not merely unimpaired, but augmented by the influence of our own devotedness. But to know that that which displaced that economy was the personal advent, the visible humiliation, the actual sacrifice of the Son of

God—that the eternal Father should have so loved us as to give from His bosom "the express image of His person" —should surely come on us with an effect which should leave us no power but that of obedience, no wish but that of multiplying our means of serving Him ten-thousandfold. Before that gift could have been bestowed, the ocean of the Divine benevolence must have been stirred in all its unfathomable depths—should the shallow stream of our gratitude be only rippled on the surface? Of all His infinite resources He freely gave the *sum*—of the mite-like penury of our nature shall we return him only a part? To know that He who was rich should for our sakes have become poor—that the second Person in the mysterious Godhead should have personally descended to our rescue—descended from one depth of humiliation to another, till He had reached a depth which made it impossible for Divine condescension itself to stoop lower—this is knowledge which, as it has moved all heaven, should surely be sufficient to move and agitate all earth. To hear that event succeeded by the signs and sounds of another advent—the advent of the Holy Spirit—to find that thus each of the three Persons in the awful and mysterious Godhead is infinitely interested in our recovery—that there has actually been disclosed in consequence a new bond of their ineffable union in the fact of their co-operation for that recovery—and that so intently is the compassion of the Triune God set on the object, that no truth is left untaught, no miracle of mercy unperformed—no angel or agency unemployed—no part of the universe unmoved—no perfection of the Divine nature unconcerned—no aspect of the Divine character unexhibited which is in the least essential to its accomplishment—surely this should leave no portion of the Church at rest, no means within its farthest reach untaxed, for the attainment of the same end. To find that this is clearly the Divine design—that Christ, as the head of the Church on earth, authoritatively requires that each individual Christian surrender himself and live supremely for the conversion of others—that these unite into particular societies for the conversion of greater numbers still—that all these societies in every land combine in sympathy and purpose for the salvation of the entire race—to find that, as the President of the universe, having "all power in heaven and on earth," He commands and combines the sympathies and instrumentality of the Church in heaven with that of the Church on earth—assigning to angels the time and the place for *their* agency in Providence, concurring with the movements of His kingdom of grace—and to find that, in the same mediatorial capacity, He even adds the presence and the power of the Holy Spirit himself—surely this should leave no Christian unemployed, no Church unrelated, no agency we could invoke in earth or heaven to be absent from our combined endeavour to carry it into effect. And to find that this design is as *practicable* as it is *obligatory*—to hear other Christians avowing *their* readiness to be messengers or martyrs, honoured or "accursed," anything or nothing, so that they might be instrumental in promoting it—to see churches selecting and sending out such men to carry the Gospel onwards—other churches emulating *their* example—to find that each convert as he comes into the Church, is expected to proceed to his post, and to commence his service—and that each church, as it comes into being, is expected to enter into the general fellowship, and to help forward the common object of the whole—to see that the success of one church is rejoiced in as the triumph of all, and that if they suspend their song of praise for a while, it is only to read over again the command which first sent them forth, "Go into all the world and preach the gospel to every creature"—only to prostrate themselves in prayer for that aid which the Spirit alone can impart, and which furnishes them with renewed occasion for louder triumphs still—this is a spectacle which should surely leave no other question on the lips of the individual Christian than "where is my post, and what shall I do?" and no other law for the Church universal than that of entire consecration.

Now this was the prayer of Christ, not for the apostles only, "but for them also," he adds, "who shall believe on me through their word; that they all may be one—that the world may believe that thou has sent me." Finding themselves acted on by the presence of whatsoever things are pure, and lovely, and of good report—by hallowed and benevolent influences from every quarter, and from the remotest period of the Church—finding themselves surrounded by lofty examples of Christian devotedness—and ever standing in the presence of His wondrous cross, He prayed that they might feel themselves impelled to make His consecration the model and motive of their own, that God might be glorified, and man be saved.

Be it remembered also, that there is a sense in which we of the present day sustain the accumulated responsibility of the eighteen centuries which have revolved since that prayer was uttered. In each succeeding age, "the truth" to which that prayer referred, has been exercising its consecrating influence, and instrumentally creating eminent examples of moral power—examples of conscientiousness which treated no duty as unwelcome, and which evaded no obligation—of fidelity, which spared no sin, nor allowed any iniquity, however splendid and powerful, to pass unrebuked—of courage, which cowered before no opposition, and shrank from no conflict—of enlarged benevolence, which knew no limits to its plans and toils and travails for the welfare of man—of Christian self-abandonment, which swore eternal devotedness to Christ, though in the presence of the flames which were kindled for its martyrdom—and of love for man, which even in those flames wept over the misery of the world, and agonized in prayer for its recovery. These examples are not lost. Though their memory is not embalmed in the volume of inspiration, their influence has been really added to that of patriarchs and prophets, of apostles and primitive saints. Whether we are conscious of its stimulating power or not, we are all at this moment reaping its advantages, and are consequently standing under the weight of an increased responsibility. And to this is also to be added the influence acting on us from the prophetic disclosures of the future. The torch which the hand of prophecy holds up throws its beams onward to the consummation of all things. By this light we catch glimpses of noble examples yet to arise, and of glories yet to dawn. Many are seen running to and fro with the message of salvation—multitudes flocking to embrace it—angels pouring destruction on its foes—mountainous obstacles rolled from its path—nations walking in its light—heaven and earth celebrating its triumphs—and Christ encircled by His redeemed myriads and receiving the homage of the universe. One of the obvious intentions of these disclosures is, that by the certain prospect they afford of ultimate success the Church may be encouraged to act out its Divine design, and to throw all its sanctified energies into the object of the world's recovery. This is the effect which they *have* had on many of its members in every age. "Having seen them afar off," and caught their inspiration, the martyr for Christ has embraced the block—the minister has startled the slumbering Church—the missionary has gone forth to awake the sleeping world—the saint, like David, has exclaimed in death, "let the whole earth be filled with his glory"—and the Church has echoed with the response of thousands, adding, "Amen and amen." And for us the light of prophecy still burns, that on us it may produce the same effects.

And shall it not produce them? *If* there be any virtue—here there is nothing else—and shall we not copy it? *If* there be any praise—here nothing but praise awaits the devoted Christian—and shall we not aspire to win it? Oh, if there existed a certain method of extinguishing all human misery, and replenishing the world with joy, would you not desire to promote it? Such a method there is—all the treasures of eternity have been lavished on it—all creation is groaning and travailing in pain together for want of it—and all the voices of heaven and earth are urging you to take part in it. If you knew of a scheme so vast in its sweep as to subordinate all other plans to its own design—so varied in its workings as to demand the strenuous activity of every agent in the universe—and yet so self-sufficient as absolutely to stand in need of none, would you not count it the highest honour to take part in it? Need I remind you that such a plan there is?—that in the arrangements of that plan a post of activity is assigned to each of you—and that in that post which awaited your coming into the world, the whole of your consecrated influence was bespoken from eternity? If we could tell you of an end so great that all other ends stand to it only in the relation of means—so lofty that there is nothing higher—so glorious that everything else is honoured by serving it—would you not pant to be identified with it? Need I remind you that such an end there is?—that the one point, the sole end, to which everything in the universe of God is tending, is to the praise of the glory of His grace—that apart from that end nothing is great or good; that connected with it nothing is mean or little—that it hallows whatever it touches, and ennobles whatever it employs—that, consequently, it is our highest wisdom to form such a plan, each one for himself, as shall link us on to that infinite ultimate end as its humble willing agents, as shall appropriate all our moments and all our powers to its grand designs? If we could tell you of a day when all the virtue and holy excellence in the universe shall be collected together in the presence of God, and all the holy beings in the universe shall be convened together to admire and to praise it, and when God himself shall applaud it in language with which eternity shall never cease to resound—would you not cheerfully give all the world, were it yours, to share in the transports of that day? Need I remind you that such a day there will be?—that Christ himself will preside over its transactions—and that inconceivable eternal blessedness will be His certain award to every one present devoted to His service? If, in the revolutions of time, there should come a period when events should thicken—when all the agencies of Providence should seem urged into unusual activity, and all things seem rushing to that final issue—would you not long to live at that time, and take part in its eventful scenes? Need I remind you that that time has come—that that period is the present? Brethren, we stand in the midst of a scheme which unites us with all the past, and is in progress for all the future. "Upon us the ends of the world are come"—upon our heads the relations, influences, and consequent responsibilities of all the past meet and rest; and to us the ends of the earth, the remotest generations of time, and all the holy beings and interests in the universe are looking for corresponding fidelity and zeal. Whoever may deem it necessary to form plans of independent action, we are surely exempted from that necessity, for we ourselves form part of a plan in which every being, from the loftiest archangel to the lowliest saint, has his course assigned, and every holy act its appointed effect—so that the only solicitude left for us is, how best we may satisfy its high requirements. Boast who may of extensive relations and influences, this plan connects us with every being and agency the past has known, and places in our hand lines of interminable relation and influence with all the universal and endless future. Tremble who may under a sense of responsibility, "Upon us the ends of the world are come." Our very position consecrates us to the loftiest service, loads us with the weightiest obligation, surrounds us with anxious eyes and cries of solicitude from every quarter of the Divine dominions. For the Church to be faithful now, is to save the world. Now, if ever, the weak should be "as David, and David as an angel of the Lord." Now, if ever, prayer should wrestle, liberality should bring forth its richest offering—its last mite; the Church should unite, and clothe itself with zeal. For now, if ever, crowns may be gained, and kingdoms won, and a world, in the crisis of its danger, be saved—crowns to be cast at the feet of Christ, kingdoms of which Christ is rightful Lord, and a world from which He is destined to derive His richest revenues of praise for ever.

SERMON VI.

THE INTERCESSION OF CHRIST.

1 JOHN ii. 1.—"My little children, these things write I unto you that ye sin not; and if any man sin we have an advocate with the Father, Jesus Christ the righteous."

THIS is temple-language, derived from the act of the High Priest on the great day of atonement. On that day the entire economy was summed up within the veil. He who had not been present at that intercessory scene had not seen the heart of the Jewish dispensation. We too have an Advocate with the Father; and in His advocacy, within the heavenly veil, the Christian economy, as a system of mediation, reaches its loftiest point.

But why is this advocacy here referred to? A man is supposed to have sinned; a fact which loses none of its tremendous significance by its frequency; a fact which, familiar as it may be to us, can never become ordinary or indifferent to the government of God;—every sin having all the freshness and enormity of a first sin to *it*—a sin containing a possible universe of evil. But here is a sin of peculiar turpitude. "There is, indeed, a sin unto death" (says the apostle), including, I suppose, the rejection of atonement, intercession, Christianity itself. And the sin before us is supposed to be only one step short of that; yet even for this there is mercy. Here is guilt so great that it is made hypothetical, yet confronted by an actual provision of mercy —the last conceivable aggravation of guilt met by the highest conceivable reach and arrangement of forgiveness;—a man who has exhausted all the ordinary resources of grace, but whose last effort at sin brings to light, and puts in stress, an expedient of mercy which leaves even *his* fears nothing to desire.

This, then, is our subject—Guilt of the deepest aggravation, met by Mediation of transcendent efficacy.

I.

First, *here is supposed to be guilt of the deepest aggravation.* To imagine that the apostle merely means that *sin admits of forgiveness,* is to ignore all that goes before, and much that comes after. He has despatched the subject of ordinary sin and its forgiveness. "If we confess our sins, he is *faithful and just* to forgive us our sins, and to cleanse us from all unrighteousness." He has conducted his readers through the grand temple of Christian truth, where God is seen to be light, and where Christ is seen reflecting that light, as the light of life, on the great brotherhood of Christian souls—and they are seen in the calm ecstacy of fellowship, pressing in, getting nearer, opening their souls that God might flow through them, that their joy might be full. But *why* does he take them into this temple, and lift this veil, and lead them into this radiance, and point them to this Divine communion, and thrill them with this delight? That they "sin not"—"These things write I unto you that ye sin not." This is to be the great practical result of the whole—the extinction of sin in the heart. Christianity, indeed, has higher and ulterior ends. But its first great aim is the extinction of sin. Till this is done, nothing is done. When this is done, the way is open for all that God can bestow, or man receive. Beyond, all is blessedness and eternal life. But for man — the *sinner* — the extinction of sin is its primary tendency and terminus. In forgiving the penitent at first, it says to him, "Go, and sin no more." It takes him to the cross that he may hear a voice, never to be forgotten, say, "that ye sin not." It offers him the highest aid—God's own Holy Spirit—that he sin not. Its angels rejoice over one sinner that repenteth, because in his first tear over sin they see the earnest of the coming day when he will sin no more. The sum of all its commands and promises—the moral and meaning of the entire system of Christianity—is, that ye sin not. And the apostle even adds, "he that is born of God doth not sin—*cannot* sin—because he *is* born of God." As a *Christian*, he cannot sin. In proportion as Christianity has taken effect on him, he cannot sin—he acquires a moral incapacity for sin—loathes, resents, and resists it.

Now it is, I apprehend, of such a one, conscious of sin, that the apostle speaks in the text. It is not of a David *before* he has agonized in penitence, and has tasted the sweets of forgiveness—but suppose him to have repeated his sin after he had written the 51st psalm. It is not of the prodigal before he had said, "I will arise and go to my father;" but suppose that after his father had run to him, and yearned over him, and adorned him, he had again wandered off, and wasted his substance in riotous living. It is not of Thomas before he had seen the print of the nails—but suppose that he had returned to his scepticism afterwards. It is not of Peter before the heart-probing question, "Lovest thou me?"—but suppose that he had afterwards "denied the Lord that bought him." If any man should sin under such circumstances—it matters not under what tempting influences, nor what the special form of his sin—the case is supposed to be possible—and the question is, does the Gospel provide for it? The man is supposed to have agonized at the strait gate—to have made some progress in the narrow way—to have wept at the cross—to have broken bread at the table of the Lord—to have felt happy and at home at the throne of grace—to have had many a successful struggle with sin—to have had light from the face of God fall upon his own—to have felt the most tender and melting influences which Christianity supplies;—and yet he is conscious of subsequent sins leaving behind a deep stain of guilt;

—and the question is, what provision does the Gospel make for such a man?

The time was, perhaps, when, in the first flush of Christian confidence, he deemed such guilt as he is now conscious of impossible; and, therefore, would have rejected such a question as I am now asking as *unnecessary*, or, as the text puts it, as merely *hypothetical*. And yet I have no doubt that in all our congregations there are those for whom this is *the* question; those who are carrying about in their bosom the festering sore of a wounded conscience—the burden of unpardoned sin—a gloomy sense of insecurity which enervates their best efforts at recovery—who wonder how it will be with them when they come to die—who see clouds rising and settling over the valley of the shadow of death—and feel, at times, as if they had exhausted all the ordinary means of mercy.

I do not intend by this that they who are the most conscious of guilt, and the most prone to despair of mercy, are commonly the most guilty. On the contrary, the more guilty a man is, the less *conscious* of guilt he may be. He may have felt more concern at his first conscious transgression than at all the subsequent sins of his life added together. A pure spirit falling into *one* sin would probably be conscious of greater agony than any one present has ever felt at all his sins combined. But suppose a man to be both chargeable with the aggravated form of guilt we have described, and to be proportionally *conscious* of that aggravation, does the Gospel contain an adequate remedy?

II.

Now, secondly, *the text meets this surpassing guilt by mediation of transcendent efficacy.* "If any man *so* sin, we have an advocate with the Father, Jesus Christ the righteous." Other aspects of our Lord's mediation, besides that of His advocacy, might have been pointed to for this purpose, His atoning death, His resurrection, and His exaltation. But we have Divine authority for saying, that His intercession sums up and transcends them all. Not that either of these facts is to be viewed as standing apart from the others. The last presupposes the first, and the first looks forward to the last. But regarding them as a series—parts of one whole—we have, I repeat, Divine authority for affirming that the *intercession* of Christ is the sum and application of the whole. For "Who"—asks the apostle Paul—"who is he that condemneth? It is Christ that died; yea, rather, that is risen again; who is even at the right hand of God; who also maketh intercession for us?" "*It is Christ that died.*" The atoning *death* of Christ, then, lies at the foundation of the whole. Hence the language immediately following our *text*, "He is the propitiation for our sins, and not for ours only, but also for the sins of the whole world." *Atonement—propitiation*—is the broad, deep, world-wide basis of that pyramid which climbs the skies, and of which *intercession* is the topstone. And the death of Christ alone—whether it be regarded as a sacrifice for us, or as an exhibition of the love of God, ought to be sufficient to satisfy the fears of the guiltiest, as it is sufficient to satisfy the demands of the violated law.

The great want of the penitent is, the means of restoration to God; and, taking him into the presence of the cross, the Gospel tells him, "it is Christ that died." As if it had said, "Here is an answer to every objection; for here is a being who unites in himself all the conditions of a perfect sacrifice, and He dies for you." You say He should be *sinless;* for *He* only can pay the debt who owes none. And such was Christ; "He did no sin." "He was the Lamb without blemish and without spot;" one on whom the law had no previous claim, and to whom it could point as the embodiment and exemplar of all its demands. You say, it should be One who has the right of *self-disposal.* Only *He* can become responsible to God for us, who himself knows no responsibility or superior. And such was Christ. "Being in the form of God, he *made himself* of no reputation; he *took upon him* the form of a servant." "He *gave* himself for us." You say that He must be *one able to vindicate the interests of the being whose government He represents;* otherwise, he might be degrading law in the very act of professedly honouring it, and deceiving man, though dying with the intention of saving him. But such was Christ. "He thought it not robbery to be equal with God." "He *was* God manifest in the flesh." "And how much more shall the blood of Christ, who through the eternal Spirit—through his Divine nature—offered himself up without spot, purge your conscience from dead works?" Do you ask the *extent* of His self-devotement? The cross speaks for itself. It was "obedience unto death, even the death of the cross." No part or property of His Person was withheld. All that could be imparted was given. In every *previous* step of His earthly course He had been the will of God incarnated. But the highest possible act of obedience was yet to come. It was on the threshold of that act He said, "Now is the Son of man glorified"—the very ideal of sacrifice was about to be realized in His atoning death. "Father, glorify thy name." All the feelings and desires of His life were collected and concentrated in that grand sacrificial act, which was the embodiment of all law, and the expression of all love. "He gave HIMSELF for us." And here, too, is the highest conceivable illustration of the love of God. "He *so* loved the world." He might have so loved it as to clothe the heavens in sackcloth on account of its impending doom. He might have so loved it as to delay, for ages, the execution of its doom—despatching embassies of mourning, lamentation, and woe, from heaven to earth. But "He so loved us as to give his only begotten Son, that whosoever believeth on him might not perish but have everlasting life." If the cross does not embody and express the heart of God, what can? It is infinite love labouring to expound, agonizing to utter, the fulness of infinite love. Beyond this He *cannot* go, even

He cannot go. It leaves nothing further for the heart of God to desire, nothing greater to bestow.

Now, should not the penitent himself be satisfied with that which satisfies the heart of God? By the death of Christ, the law of God is more gloriously maintained than ever it had been foully resisted. Here is more than equivalence. The reparation made is infinite. Moral government gains by it—is infinitely enriched. To say that it merely *vindicates government*, is to disparage it. "Herein is love"—love so vast that no inferior arrangement could satisfy and give utterance to it. And never, till we behold in the propitiatory sacrifice of Christ an expression of the infinitude of God's holy love, can we see it in its true light, or estimate its higher design as an illustration of the character of God. But this seen, fear is banished, and hope inspired; and the penitent feels that he has an adequate answer to every accusation, in the simple but grand declaration. "It is *Christ* that died."

2. Granted, you say—granted that He "died the just for the unjust," what proof have I that his sacrifice was accepted? The unsatisfied and inflexible law may have detained Him in the tomb. Thus reasoned an apostle, "If Christ be *not* raised, your faith is vain, ye are yet in your sins." But why should they be yet in their sins? They—the parties addressed—had practically forsaken their sins. If men are saved by repentance, *they* had repented. If men are saved by a return to obedience, they had so returned. If men are saved by faith, they had believed. If men are saved when repentance, obedience, and faith are united, they were entitled to salvation, for all the three were exemplified in them. Yet the apostle affirms that they were still in their sins, if Christ be not raised. The atonement contains the explanation. If Christ be not raised, there is no proof of its acceptance. And the absence of all proof of its acceptance could only be accounted for on the supposition of its inadequacy. And if the atonement be inadequate—that is, if there be no atone-

ment—our tears of repentance are vain—our confidence has been misplaced—we are yet in the grasp of justice, and under the condemnation of our sins. But "now *is* Christ raised;" and the converse consequences follow. The seal gave way; the stone receded before Him. He stood at the mouth of the sepulchre radiant with immortality. "He is not there, he is risen, as he said." It was not possible that *He* "should be holden of death." And His resurrection demonstrates the acceptance of His atonement, as the acceptance of His atonement demonstrates its sufficiency. "Who is he that condemneth? It is Christ that died; yea, rather that is risen again."

3. But granted, it may be said—granted that He thus "died for our sins, and that He rose again the third day according to the Scriptures," what warrant have I for believing that He is invested with any power to aid me? "God also hath highly exalted him." As His death was a grand compensative arrangement in the government of God, so His exaltation is the reward of His obedience unto death. All power is His in heaven and on earth. Yes, one spot there is in the universe where centre all authority, dignity, and power;—that spot is at the right hand of God;—and the sole occupant of that spot is He who wears our nature;—and all the resources He holds, He holds not for himself but for us. "Who, then, is he that condemneth? It is Christ that died; yea, rather, that is risen again; who is even at the right hand of God."

4. But granted that He is there (it may be said), how know we that His state there is not one of mere grand repose; that He retains the condescension and sympathy which distinguished Him when on earth? What, know you not, "it is Christ that died, that is risen, that is exalted, and that he also maketh intercession for us." This is a climax to which nothing can be added—a climax which, by leading us upward step by step, conducts us up to the very throne of God—places us there by the side of Jesus Christ the

righteous—calls on us to listen to His intercession for us—and to say, if we can, what more *could* be done to allay our fears, and to secure our acceptance.

But how is the intercession of Christ carried on? This is a question more curious than important, one which the anxious penitent would hardly stop to ask. I answer it, therefore, as briefly as possible. In favour of the view which regards the intercession of Christ not as verbal, but as practical, it is to be remembered that that which constitutes its essence—that which forms the ground on which pardon is bestowed on the penitent is, the infinite and unchanging value of the atonement. A verbal reference to its value would be a mere adjunct of intercession; it is not the thing itself. That which really intercedes is His love and His life expressed in the blood which was shed upon the cross. Hence *it* is represented as speaking—"speaking better things than the blood of Abel." Not that any audible sound actually emanated from Abel's corpse—no articulate remonstrance arose from the spot saturated with his blood, yet there was an appeal which God could hear. "Thy brother's blood crieth to me from the ground." In that murdered form there was an appeal to God, as the righteous Governor of the world, that He would avenge His outraged image. Hence, also, the high priest—when on the great day of atonement he entered within the veil to intercede for Israel—uttered no verbal petition. It was the blood sprinkled in solemn silence which really pleaded with God. So Christ "*appears* in the presence of God for us." His appearance there is a perpetual appeal in our behalf. His presence there in our nature—as the Being who made expiation for sin—is a visible memorial of the fact that atonement has been made; and a perpetual appeal to the justice and mercy, the truth and compassion of God on behalf of the penitent.

Now, all the encouragement which the intercession of Christ is calculated to afford is intended to descend and alight on the head of the earthly suppliant as he bends at the footstool of mercy. And what richer encouragement could the avarice of human fear desire? What stronger warrant could God himself supply? Let me point to a parallel case—a faint illustration of the subject—drawn from the former dispensation:—No part of the temple-service was so impressive—so calculated to fill the imagination—as the scene in which, on the great day of atonement, the high priest entered within the veil. In that act (as I have already said) the whole round of temple services was summed up. Every attendant circumstance—the sanctity of the veil, which the people dared not approach, nor even the priests to touch; the fact that only one man of all the human race was permitted to lift that veil, and to pass within; the rareness of *that* occurrence, for even to him it was accessible only once a year; and the awful being, the ineffable mystery that resided there—all conspired to fill the mind with the profoundest awe, and to set forth the sacred nature of drawing near to God in prayer. Now suppose, among the thousands that came up to Jerusalem at that annual solemnity, there enters the temple, with fear and trembling, a penitent Israelite. Like the publican that went up to the temple to pray, he is burdened with a sense of enormous guilt. He durst not lift up so much as his eyes to heaven, but smites upon his breast. He would fain entreat for mercy, but dreads lest, by so doing, he should aggravate his guilt. Now, at the moment when the high priest went within the veil, how powerfully might this dejected and desponding penitent have been urged and encouraged to lift up his own voice for mercy! "It is true you are a sinner" (a pious friend might have said to him)—"you cannot well *overrate* the enormity of your guilt, but then do not *underrate* the mercy of God through an atonement. Has He not promised that, on the ground of sacrifice, He will forgive the broken and contrite spirit? Do not all the appointments of the economy, and all the services of the temple, centre in the *sacrifices?* Do not all the daily and diversified sacrifices of the whole year centre, and find *their* completion, in the sacrifice just offered by the head and high priest of our nation? And does not *his* sacrifice find *its* high application and end in the *blood-sprinkling* on the mercy-seat? And is not the high priest, *at this moment*, within the veil presenting it to God? Now, then, *now*, while he is there pleading in our behalf—now, while God is in the act of accepting the offering—now, ask for remission, cry for mercy, and, as far as the east is from the west, so far will he remove our transgressions from us." What an encouragement was this to pray!

The application of all this is obvious. "We have a great high priest, who is passed into the heavens, Jesus, the Son of God." "We have an advocate with the Father, Jesus Christ the righteous." Now, suppose the intercession of Christ were at present unknown to you—unknown to the world. You have, let it be supposed, long since emerged from the darkness of sin into the light of a large amount of Christian truth; but, though standing in that light, you have sinned. You have not *purposed* to sin—that would be inconsistent with the very idea of the Christian character; but your purposes *not* to sin have not always been strong enough to restrain the evil tendencies of your nature. How often have you left the throne of grace radiant with hope, and confident of security! How often have you had to return to it again to confess that your hope was premature, and your confidence misplaced? Could all your broken *vows* take shape and become visible, what altars would be seen overturned, what temples in ruins! Could the *sins* which have led to this unhappy result take form and be seen, what dark and demon shapes would come into view—foul enough to amaze you that they could ever have been the means of your guilty infatuation! Could your own *thoughts* respecting your condition—your passing reflections and fears respecting your own *character*—take shape and be seen, what drooping and disheartened forms would appear, and how haggard and ominous the looks they would be seen to cast towards the future! And could form be given to your apprehensions of God—could they be painted to the eye as guilt makes them present to your mind—what dark clouds would be seen round about His throne, and what aspects of terror looking forth from those clouds! All confidence in *yourself* you have lost, while you feel as if confidence in God would be presumption. At the same time, you know that His mercy you must have or perish—that if a single ray of hope remain, it must come direct from the throne of God.

From what quarter, then, shall we draw the encouragement which shall induce you, not merely to approach the mercy-seat, but to approach it in the assured confidence of Divine acceptance? What is the condition on which you would consent to go, to-day, or to-morrow, at any given hour, and fall down before God in prayer, in the full expectation of mercy? Would you feel emboldened to do this, could you be assured that at the moment when you were falling before God you should be accompanied by the earnest intercessions of every Christian friend whose name you know and revere? You believe that "the effectual, fervent prayer of a righteous man availeth much"—that the intercession of Abraham suspended, for a time, the descending fire which destroyed Sodom—that the prayer of Moses held back the arm of God from destroying Israel—that the prayer of Elijah opened and shut the windows of heaven. Now, would you deem it a sufficient encouragement to go to God in the way we have described could we guarantee that, in the same hour, every righteous man in all our various Christian denominations should enter into his closet, and supplicate God in your behalf? Or, beyond this, could we assemble together, in your behalf, a solemn convocation of all the Christian Churches upon earth—could we bring all flesh before God—could we enlist for you all the power of prayer which exists at present upon earth—and, carrying the supposition out to the utmost, could we even ensure to you the mightier supplications of the Church above—of all its thrones and dominions, principalities and powers—were all the created universe to obtain a special audience of God, and to surround His throne together, for the sole object of entreating Him in your behalf—could you doubt of your success? Could you refuse to pray, if you knew that your prayers would thus be seconded and urged by the combined importunity of all the holy creation in prayer?

But what if in that solemn hour, when the violent were taking heaven for you by force—if at the very crisis when their prayers had risen to strong crying and tears—what if then the Church should, for the first time, hear the announcement, "If any man sin, we *have* an advocate with the Father, Jesus Christ the righteous"—what if then you could behold the Great Advocate himself come forth and stand at the golden altar—and what if you should hear Him announce, "*I* will pray the Father for you"—Oh, what a day of hope would forthwith dawn upon your soul—your fears would be forgotten, your unbelief exchanged for exultation—you would feel that having HIM for an advocate, you could dispense with all inferior aid—that even your own feeble supplications became invested, in His hands, with the force of Omnipotence.

But you need no *vision* to reveal and certify this glorious truth. You believe that Jesus Christ the righteous IS our advocate with the Father—that He "ever liveth to make intercession for us"—in other words, you believe—for this is the meaning, the *heart* of the doctrine—that all that Christ *is*, all He has *done*, all the relations He sustains to God, and all His resources for man—the *whole* is, at this moment, freely and fully available for you. Now, you cannot thoughtfully pass in review all that belongs to this glorious fact, without feeling that every part of it shames you out of your guilty fears, and impels you to go boldly to the throne of grace.

1. Think, it is *Jesus Christ* who is your advocate—JESUS CHRIST. The very name is identical with compassion, mercy, love. JESUS CHRIST—the very sound is music, and calls up a host of the tenderest associations. Does it not remind you that, when on earth, He had ears only for one sound, and that was the voice of penitence confessing sin; eyes only for one sight—the spectacle of human want and woe? He remembered only that we were perishing, and felt only that He could save. Does it not remind you of lessons steeped in love, of remonstrances and invitations mingled with tears? Does it not recall the scenes at the gate of Nain, and the grave of Lazarus; in the family at Bethany, and in the "upper room"? Does it not bring back Gethsemane, and "the place called Calvary," and the sepulchre, and the scene in which "he shewed them his hands and his feet"? Blessed Saviour! why did sorrow come to Thee to have its tears wiped away? Why did guilt fall at Thy feet with an uplifted eye of hope? Why did unsheltered weakness run, as by instinct, to take sanctuary in Thy presence? and penitence lay bare its wounds to catch the balm that fell from Thy lips? Why? "Ye know the grace of our Lord Jesus Christ." And ye know that all that grace is now at the altar of intercession, ready to interpose for you.

2. But if His being Christ the compassionate implies His *willingness* to intercede, His being "Jesus Christ the righteous" denotes His *power*. It implies, not merely that, being righteous, He needs no intercession for himself—this is the least and lowest thing implied. It implies that He can plead for the unrighteous—plead for them with all the power of a righteous being; that His very intercession is righteous—that it possesses all the force of authority and law—of the very laws which we had armed against us; so that now, "if we confess our sins, God is faithful and just—not merely compassionate but just in forgiving us." Justice itself comes over, and stands at our side, and pleads for us. Sinai unites with Calvary. It implies that the intercession of Christ re-

poses on His *character*—looks back to the whole of His earthly history—takes in all the righteousness of His life—includes Bethlehem and Calvary, with all that lies between. It implies that, while upon earth, nothing He did was done for himself—that whatever He did was done solely for man—and that, as our Intercessor, the entire merit of the whole ascends as incense with the prayers of the suppliant.

3. Remember, too, that we have not only such an advocate *before* the throne, but that He who fills the throne is a *Father*—our *Father*—implying that we have an intercessor in the very heart of God—that his own fatherly heart pleads for us; that the intercession of Christ implies no original unwillingness on the part of God to forgive—but that, on the contrary, He so loved the world as to make this provision—make it as the only means of gratifying His love. He is our Father—reminding us that *He requires* intercession, in no other sense, and for no other reason, than that on which Christ renders it—that, in this respect, they might even exchange offices—that even in the act of intercession the language of Christ is strictly true: "He that hath seen me hath seen the Father also;" and the still more remarkable language: "Ask in my name; and I do not say that I will pray the Father for you, for the Father himself loveth you, because ye have loved me."

4. To this nothing can be added. Brethren, there is no reason *in God* why the guiltiest present should not be forgiven—there is no reason *in God* why the guiltiest man at this moment on the face of the earth should not find mercy. For the atonement—the *ground* of mercy—was made, not for sins of a certain kind merely, nor for a certain number of sins, but for SIN. It was a *moral* compensation for a moral evil—for sin as sin. And hence (says the apostle), "He is the propitiation for our sins, and not for ours only, but also for the sins of the whole world;" so that, if you were not only the guiltiest man on the face of the earth, but even if you could gather into your own individual person the guilt of every

other human being, there is still no reason in God why you should not be freely and fully forgiven, "For the blood of Jesus Christ his Son cleanseth from *all* sin." And then, while the atonement is for sin as sin, the intercession of Christ is for the sinner as suppliant. And if, as I have said, the meaning, the *heart,* of the doctrine be, that all the resources of Christ are at this moment freely available to you, then there is no reason in Christ—no reason in the universe—why you should not be "accepted in the Beloved."

Possibly, however, you may now be ready to shift your ground. Admitting that there is no reason in God why you should not obtain mercy, you may be ready to confess that your great reason for dismay is in yourself—that you have so often recovered and relapsed—sinned and sorrowed, only to sin again—and all this while standing within sight of the cross of Christ—that you begin to question your own susceptibility to the renewing influence of the Holy Spirit. The readiness of God to pardon you profess to admit, but your own readiness to repent and forsake sin you more than question. Possibly there may be ample ground why you should take this low view of your character. I would say nothing to lessen, but everything to deepen your humility. But do not deceive yourself. In putting away from you the consolation I offer—and in doing this under the idea that you are only condemning yourself—you are doing despite to the Spirit of grace. You are still questioning the *willingness* of God to renew you. His *power* to do it you surely would not question. You *cannot* doubt the *ability* of the infinite Spirit to "create you anew in Christ Jesus." To do this is as much a *Divine* work, in a sense, as to provide for your forgiveness. And can you doubt His *readiness* to give to you "a new heart and a right spirit"? This is the great promise of the dispensation under which you live. The agency and outpouring of the Spirit was the first great gift obtained by the intercession of Christ. "It is" (said He) "expedient for you that I go away." And when He went from the place of sacrifice, and stood in the presence of God for us—when He arrived there to find that the incense of His offering had preceded Him, and had filled the entire temple with its odours—He found also that the Spirit himself was waiting to descend to plead and strive *with men*, while He became *their* advocate *with the* Father. And still Christ is interceding, and the Spirit is acting. Not only, therefore, is there no reason in God why you should not obtain the renewal you need, as it is a part of the great work of human salvation, there is *every reason* in God why you should. The same infinite love, which led Him to provide for your redemption by the atonement, now leads Him to seek your renewal by the agency of the Holy Spirit. Disbelieve this, and you are committing the only sin which can make your recovery impossible; doubt this, and you are defrauding Christ of the joy which was set before Him—robbing Him of a pleasure greater than the songs of angels can impart. Absent yourself from the throne of grace, and you are staying away from the only place of meeting—of contact—between the soul and its Saviour. Go there, and cry for mercy; and your voice, ere it reaches the ear of God, shall fall in and blend with the voice of Him "whom the Father heareth always." And if there be truth in the text—if any veracity in the word of God—*your* prayer becomes His *desire*—your success becomes identified with His *honour;* so that in representing himself as your advocate, He is, in effect, pledging himself to your salvation.

And, now, why was this glorious truth placed on record? Precisely for the same reason the apostle assigns for recording the preceding truths—"that ye sin not." He knew that a sense of insecurity makes the soul sullen, and obedience impossible. He knew the force of the sentiment, "Then shall I run in the path of thy commandments when thou hast enlarged my heart"—that it is only as the soul is set free from the bondage of sin and fear that it bounds away in the path of duty, and soars where before it hardly crept.

For "love casteth out fear." Happy they who repair to the mercy-seat, only to leave there their sense of guilt, who go to the throne of grace, only to bring away with them a portion of its royalty—to become themselves living and sceptred powers, who rely on their Lord's intercession, only to "go and sin no more."

For another practical result of this is, that they themselves are prepared to intercede for others. Christian parents and friends, can those dear to you point to you, and say, We have intercessors—human advocates—with the Father? Whatever else you may have done for them, if you have not yet wrestled in prayer for them, you have yet to employ the mightiest agency of all at a throne of grace.

Prayer for the *world* is the sublimest office of the Church. And how cheering the thought, that of all the prayers which are thus offered—making one continued strain of supplication—not one ever *has* been, or *can* be lost. It is a prayer for the kingdom of Christ; and as such it is music in the ear of God, of which He loses not a single note. It is a prayer for the hastening of His own glory; and, as such, He places it among the perfumed supplications already offered by the saints of past generations—He places it among the last aspirations breathed from the deathbed of David the son of Jesse, and of every ancient worthy—among the mighty prayers which ascended from the fires of the early martyrs—among the loud cries of those whose souls are heard from under the altar—among the earnest entreaties of the wide creation sighing to be delivered from the bondage of corruption into the glorious liberty of the children of God. It is a prayer for the salvation of a world which He loves; and, with delight, He beholds it flow into that channel into which a stream of prayer has been for ages flowing and accumulating without a moment's pause—and which shall finally overflow, and pour forth a healing flood of heavenly grace over the whole earth. "Ye, then, that make mention of the Lord, keep not silence."

Pray for the world. That is your office. You are made priests unto God. In this way our "Advocate with the Father" would plead with *our* lips as well as with His own—clothing us in effect with priestly vestments—placing us by His side at the altar—putting into our hands a censer filled with incense like His own—and thus multiplying the voice and power of His own intercession. "The effectual fervent prayer of a righteous man availeth much"—how much the day of judgment alone will disclose. We are not yet alive to the efficacy of prayer—the Church of Christ at large is not. It is an invisible cord by which we can draw men towards heaven—it links our weakness to the power of God—it invests us with indefinite power over the destiny and happiness of the race—its history is the history of wonders. But the *full* efficacy of prayer is as yet unknown, for it has never yet been tried—we allow it to remain a mystery. Like some of the elements of nature, it contains a power which, if put forth to the utmost, would infallibly change the face of the earth. And the day is hastening on when its efficacy shall be tried on a scale before unknown, for "all flesh shall come to pray before the Lord," and Christ shall lead their devotions, and shall give to them the infinite weight of His own intercession. And, then, when the last sin is pardoned, and the last soul saved—when nothing shall remain but for "the righteous to go away into everlasting life," it shall be seen that, like this epistle, the whole Christian economy is but God's epistle inscribed to us "that we sin not"—that for the utter extinction of our sin and guilt we are indebted to Him who is our advocate with the Father;—and that prayer, in His name, is the mightiest instrument for the salvation of the world.

SERMON VII.

THE EPISTLE TO THE CHURCH IN SMYRNA.

REV. ii. 8-11.—"And unto the angel of the church in Smyrna write: These things saith the first and the last, which was dead and is alive; I know thy works, and tribulation, and poverty, (but thou art rich,) and I know the blasphemy of them which say they are Jews, and are not, but are the synagogue of Satan. Fear none of those things which thou shalt suffer: behold, the devil shall cast some of you into prison, that ye may be tried; and ye shall have tribulation ten days: be thou faithful unto death, and I will give thee a crown of life. He that hath an ear, let him hear what the Spirit saith unto the churches: He that overcometh shall not be hurt of the second death."

HERE, then, is a letter from Christ—one of seven—addressed to the seven Asiatic Churches. If you look at them, you will find that the structure of each is alike. Opening with an inscription to the particular Church for which it is intended, and of the Divine authority from whom it is sent, each of them is found to contain a commendation of whatever in that Church was praiseworthy, a rebuke for whatever was wrong, followed with counsels and appeals to arouse the slumbering, to encourage perseverance, and animate hope; and each concludes with a call to universal attention, and a promise to the triumphant Christian of distinguished honours in the world above.

But, beyond this similarity of structure, these epistles are all characterized by the same general principles; and the call on every man to "hear what the Spirit saith unto the churches," demonstrates that these principles were intended for universal application to the Churches of Christ in all after times. I have selected the text as the basis of a few remarks on some of these great general principles.

I.

And, first, our Lord would teach us that *His Churches are objects of His supreme regard.* More than half a century had now elapsed since He had ascended up far above all heavens; and during that period, whether He made himself visible to His martyr Stephen—or called to the persecuting Saul of Tarsus—or graciously deigned any other manifestation—He shewed on each occasion that the interests of His Church were always present to His mind. And now, that He once more comes forth to shut up the vision, and complete the canon of Scripture, what is His burden still but the welfare of His Church? Behold Him! Every part of His august appearance is deeply significant. His robe of priestly and regal dignity—His head of blinding whiteness, and eyes of piercing flame—His voice as the sound of many waters—His right hand holding seven stars—and the serene splendour of His countenance, like the sun shining in his strength—all denoting the greatness of the occasion. Listen to Him! He once more breaks the silence of eternity—calls the universe to attend. "He that hath ears to hear, let him hear what the Spirit saith unto the churches." And what do we hear? The destruction of Jerusalem was at that time impending—do we hear a reference to its doom? All the governments of the world were at that time in a crisis—do His disclosures relate to *their* destinies? No; topics like these, though all-engrossing to the world, are passed over by Him as comparatively unimportant, and every syllable He utters relates entirely to the welfare of the Church which He hath purchased with His own blood.

The affairs of the *world,* indeed, are under His superintendence, but always with an especial view to the prosperity of His Church. While He extends His sceptre, and despatches His messengers to every part of the earth, He represents *himself* as walking in the midst of the Churches, and as holding their stars in his right hand. The Church is the theatre of His grace in which He is making experiments of mercy on human hearts. It is the sacred school in which He is educating and training some who were heirs of wrath to take part in the business and pleasures of heaven. It is His temple—each living Church is His very Shekinah—the sign and embodiment of His presence. Had you entered the Jewish temple during the period of the theocracy, would you have been awed by the reflection that THERE, within that solemn veil, was the symbol of the present God? And do you suppose He is present here less really, personally, certainly than He was there? I am more certain of His presence here than I should have been there. That was but the sign; here is the thing signified. Every thing in His Church is sprinkled with His blood, and inscribed with His name. He has formed it for himself. His eyes and His heart are there continually.

II.

A second truth implied in the text is—that *Christ possesses the most intimate acquaintance with the state of His Churches, and of every individual member.* Each of these epistles begins with the declaration, "I know thy work,"—and, to prove this, the Saviour lays before each a sketch of its history and state.

He knows the *number* of those who are in the habit of attendance on the ministry of His Gospel in any given place—and in His census there are no mistakes. He distinguishes between those who worship God in the spirit, and those who only go through the attitudes and signs of devotion; for His statistics are all spiritual. When he sees His professed worshippers at His footstool, His eyes are as a flame of fire making inquisition for hearts—going from bosom to bosom—and penetrating through every veil to see if they throb heavenwards. He follows them from the sanctuary to see if their devotion will live till it reach the closet—and into the world to see if their piety be more than a name. Many of you are known as His professed people—your names are enrolled in His earthly Church. He also has a book in which your names are inscribed. But *there* are inserted, in addition to your names, all the particulars of your moral history—the religious advantages you have enjoyed—all which you might have enjoyed, but have lost through neglect—all the impressions you have felt—the resolutions you have formed—and the discipline by which you have been exercised. From that volume He could read forth at this moment a minute account of your religious character, specifying the particular sins in which you may have indulged—the causes which have checked the growth of your religious life—the manner in which you may have restrained prayer before God—all the particulars of your religious habits. "Behold" (saith he) "I stand at the door and knock,"—and He knows what guests are already within—what sins are entertained and regaled in the chambers of your heart, while He is kept standing without and refused admission. Or, if you have opened and received Him, He construes every thought and movement of your heart into a sign of welcome, or a symptom of estrangement.

And oh, were He now to open that book of remembrance at the page which contains your name or mine, what may we suppose would be the disclosures He would make? Would not the very first sentence, "I know thy works," instantly remind us of resolutions broken, of privileges abused, and of duties neglected? Would there not flash upon our minds the recollection of many a struggle in which conscience was vanquished by inclination—the love of ease had overcome a sense of duty—the influence of custom had triumphed over a dawning conviction of obligation and right? Would not the first item He might name in the catalogue of our doings, be of a nature to cover us with confusion—to prepare us to hear the account closed with a sentence of condemnation? Brethren, the day is approaching when that account will be proclaimed in the hearing of the universe; and the first and the least effect which the prospect of that day should produce is, to lead us to institute great searchings of heart.

III.

A third truth derivable from the text is, that *the Saviour despises not the least indications of piety, but would have those who are the subjects of such inclinations to cherish the most encouraging views of His character.* We infer this from his appearance to John—demonstrating that He had not dissolved His relationship to His people—had not divested Him of His tender concern for their welfare. We infer it from His making this appearance in *human nature*—He was "like unto a Son of man," and was clothed partly in priestly attire. Reminding us that, in heaven, the golden censer is never out of His hand—the altar of incense never deserted—His priestly vestments never laid aside—that He ever liveth to make intercession there.

We infer His deep sympathy too from the view which He gives of His character to the particular Church addressed in the text. It is observable that as each Church had a character peculiar to itself, so He turned towards each that particular aspect of His own character which was most important for it to keep in view. For example, the Church of Pergamos was overrun with deadly errors; and therefore to that Church He writes as "He that hath the sharp sword with two edges"—that weapon of celestial temper which is quick and powerful to exterminate error from the soul, and heresy from the Church. But the Church at Smyrna was in a condition to require encouragement; and therefore He turns on *it* a benignant aspect—reminding it that He is "the First and the Last, who was dead and is alive again." As if He had said, Having resumed the life which for your redemption I had laid down, I have now no other employment but to bring the happiness of my people to perfection. All the difficult part of the work is over. Had there been doubts concerning my love for man—objections to my power to save, they should have been made prior to my incarnation and death. The time for making them is now gone by. Then was indeed the travail and pang of infinite love—but it is past. I am to be scourged no more—buffeted no more—in agony no more. I die no more—death hath no more dominion over me. All that is penal is exhausted—the cup of suffering is drained—the ignominy is ended, never, never to be repeated. It is finished. All that was toilsome I have done—all that was painful I have borne—nothing now remains but what is pleasant, Godlike, glorious. "The head that once was crowned with thorns is crowned with glory now." I am now on my throne, with all things at my disposal. Unless you could suppose, therefore, that I could abandon my design—forget the very purpose for which I endured the cross—sacrifice the intention which has always been nearest my heart—you *must* believe that I, who was dead and am alive again, live for those for whom I died. Christians, your Lord hath no other employment for His infinite power but in saving His people—no other occupation for His boundless resources of wisdom and grace but in blessing and making them happy. And never will He rest—never will He count His work accomplished, or His own happiness complete, till He has placed them by His side, and crowned them with His glory. And that He despises not the least indications of piety is evident also in this, that while He has to complain of most of the Churches, "I have a few things against thee," He graciously stoops to enumerate and point out every particular in which they approved themselves faithful and sincere. Not more fondly does a parent search in the features of his infant child for the least trace of resemblance to himself—not more minutely do men search whole districts of land, examine particle by particle, in quest of gems or gold, than the Saviour investigates whole Churches in quest of the treasures of piety—the features of a renewed mind. And lest there should be but one such partaker of piety in a whole Church, He addresses His promise individually "to *him* that overcometh." As if He should say, Though my Church had become so pervaded with worldliness, and overrun with error, that only one member continued faithful and true, he should not escape my notice. I would lead him forth from the crowd around him—honour him in the presence of my Father—crown him before the universe. Some of these Churches had almost outlived their piety; what remained of it He described as ready to die. Instead, however, of extinguishing the smoking flax, He sought to kindle it afresh, by awakening within them emulation and hope; by shewing them that although their Christian character was reduced to a mere wreck, there were still materials out of which might be built up a temple of holiness—a habitation of God through the Spirit.

IV.

But then, fourthly, in order that we may not abuse this goodness, by resting satisfied with slender godliness, our Lord intimates that *the life of the Christian is a state of warfare, and, as such, requiring constant activity and effort.* He here addresses His people as warriors—speaks of the persevering Christian as of one that overcometh—and of heaven itself as a world of conquerors.

At that time, it is true, the faithful were exposed not only to foes within, but also to fightings without. Many of them could boast that their persons were covered with the scars of the Christian conflict. They led the van of the army of the cross. They stormed the very strongholds of sin. They proclaimed the name of their sovereign Lord where Satan's seat was. Would you know the result of their warfare? Their progress from place to place was marked, not indeed with blood, or if so, with no blood but their own—but with the fall of idol temples, the plantation of Christian churches, the trophies of ransomed human souls, and with the song of the Christian warrior exulting, "Now thanks be unto God, who always causeth us to triumph in every place!"

Do you admire their heroic devotion—their self-sacrificing

spirit? It is meant that you should more than admire—that you should imbibe and copy it. You may not indeed be called to put it into actual practice to anything like the extent to which they did. But the spirit of their piety you must have, for the Christian life is a conflict still. The same principle of loyalty and love to Christ you must posess; and from that same principle must you resolutely pass by, without entering, all the avenues of sinful pleasure, and close your eyes on the dazzling but empty illusions by which the children of this world are enchanted; you must resist temptation, rise superior to selfish indulgence, disregard the derision which men may cast against piety, and challenge and put to flight whatever would come between you and the gate of heaven. "If any man love his life more than me" (said Christ) "he is not worthy of me." The question whether you do or not may never in this world be put to the *test;* but the importance of possessing the *principle* is precisely the same. If you do not possess that attachment to Him which would enable you to shew, if called to the test, that you love Him more than life itself, you are not worthy of Him. Destitute of this principle, it will not be necessary to put your sincerity to a very severe trial; any little temptation—every little obstacle—will be sufficient to move you away from Him. The world need not frown and threaten you with persecution—her pleasures will allure—her snares will entangle and ruin you. But possessed by the love of Christ—feeling your obligations to Him—looking forwards to a crown and a kingdom with Him—none of these things will move you—life itself will be held in submission to His pleasure; and, like a Christian soldier, you will be animated, through every change and season of life, with the desire that you may fight the good fight of faith, and be crowned with the approbation of your Lord and Saviour.

V.

And then, fifthly, *to secure the persevering fidelity of His people, the Saviour promises them a heavenly reward.* A promise to this effect is here made to each of His Churches, and to each is promised a different reward. By which He would probably remind us, both of His vast and various resources in being able to give to every one a different blessing, and also that He will dispense His gifts indiscriminately, each being appropriate to the character that receives it.

The gift which He here holds up before the eyes of the Church at Smyrna is a crown of life: a crown—the emblem of royalty—the summit of human ambition. To obtain it what deeds of daring have men achieved—what rivers of blood have they shed—what enormous guilt have they incurred! "Now they do it to obtain a corruptible crown, our aim is at an incorruptible." And do the annals of the Church record no deeds of heroism achieved for that living crown? Who does not instantly think of Paul? Who does not hear him, in imagination, as he stands tranquilly gazing for a moment on the axe and the block, then raising his eyes to his promised crown, and exclaiming with delight, "I am ready—ready to be offered—and the time of my departure is at hand."

But Paul was only one of a noble army of martyrs. Fired by the same prospects of glory, the weak became irresistibly strong—the timid dared to do and to die for Christ. These principles retain their efficacy still, and you profess to be influenced by them. And still does your Lord continue to unveil the prize which He has promised to holy perseverance—bringing out the crowns, the regalia of heaven, and suspending them from His throne, He reminds you that they are placed there to be won. Oh, reflect that the prize for which, as Christians, you are candidates, is a crown—a crown of life. When tempted to relax in your Christian course, it will nerve you afresh to remember that you are on your way to the enjoyment of eternal life—of life with God—of the life of God himself. All other things, at best, are mere adjuncts—accessories—to blessedness; this life at which you are aiming is blessedness itself. It is more than a bare perpetuity of existence; it is life enriched with the highest possible excellence—life purified, exalted, applied to the loftiest purposes, carried out to its utmost extent of enjoyment—the very *crown of life.* And should the contest for such a prize be feebly carried on? Christians! know you not that you are surrounded by a great cloud of witnesses? Invisible spirits behold you: at the moment of your conversion there was joy among them in the presence of God; and still they mark every step you take, and tune their harps afresh every time you triumph over sin, and throw wider open the gates of heaven for your reception every time you put forth a successful effort after holiness. But more than all, God your Saviour beholds you—*He* is a witness of your course, He commands you to advance, He stretches forth His hand to your aid; and while He holds up to view in the radiance of His throne the prize of your high calling, His voice from heaven proclaims, Be thou faithful unto death, and I will give thee a *crown of life.*

VI.

And then, sixthly, *the text suggests certain methods by which the individual Christian, or particular Churches, are to be excited to achieve this warfare, and to win this crown.* It calls on the members of every Church to which it comes to institute a solemn examination of its spiritual history and state. " He that hath ears to hear let him hear what the Spirit saith unto the churches"—what the Spirit saith to *this* Church. "Blow ye the trumpet, sanctify a fast, call a solemn assembly." As if the trumpets of Sinai had convoked us together here—as if we belonged to certain Churches to which Christ had but this day despatched an epistle—let us suffer the word of exhortation, and lay ourselves open to its searching influence. As if He himself had come down to conduct the solemn investigation, let us humbly ask Him to ascênd the seat of judgment, and say, " Search us, O God, and see what evil there is in us, and lead us in the way everlasting."

As private Christians, then, are you looking upon character, holy character, as of the highest order of excellence—"labouring to attain it"—daily renewing your dedication to God? As heads of families, is the daily sacrifice presented on the domestic altar, and are you walking before your households in the fear of the Lord? As members of civil society, does your conduct recommend your religion—is your life exhaling the incense of Christian consistency and excellence? As members of the Church of Christ, are you sufficiently alive to the dignity and duties of the relation? Are you tender of each other's reputation, bearing each other's burthens, praying for each other's welfare, sympathetically united as members of the same body? Is a spirit of social prayer among you? Is the Great Spirit of the Church—the Holy Spirit of God—invoked, cried out for, as the only power which can give the ministry here success?

Were I addressing some Churches, I might still further ask, Has good been done here—have men's souls been saved—are children collected, taught, and trained for heaven? Are visits of mercy made—has the neighbourhood been benefited—is the influence of your Christian activity made to be felt around—are other Churches glorifying God in you? I know that, in your case, these questions can be answered in the affirmative. All the more important is it that your prevailing spirit should be, "Not unto us, O God, not unto us, but unto thy name be all the glory."

A word to those of you who merely attend on the ministry of the Gospel here. Like Israel of old, you come as the people come, and sit as the people sit. What is the result? Every time you assemble, the Bible—God's great epistle addressed to you—is opened in your midst. Have you ever considered its hallowed character, and its direct relation to you? In every age it may be said to have been sprinkled with blood; a drop has fallen even on the text—for it speaks of suffering, imprisonment, and martyrdom for the Word of God. It has been baptized with fire. Its central subject is the cross. Its original propagators and possessors endured death oft in preserving it. It has been transmitted to us through ages of persecution and sorrow—committed to us by a hand stretched out of the midst of the fire. It has been sent to us from the dungeon, bequeathed to us from the rack. It is the precious legacy of a host of martyred saints. Do you, I ask, sufficiently prize it? Do you receive and press it to your heart as the true sayings of God? They all expect it from you. They will demand it at your hands when you meet them at the bar of God. Hearers of the Gospel! are you aware of your position? The Gospel is the power of God unto salvation to every one that believeth. Every time you hear it, you stand as in the focus of all the threatenings, promises, invitations, commands, and doctrines of the Bible—they all gather around you—settle upon you. Have you not felt them?—trembled, believed, surrendered yourselves up to their influence?

As often as you come here, the Spirit of God is here—here to enlighten dark minds, and to renew depraved hearts. Every time you have come, you have come within the scope, passed within the verge of His influence; you have been surrounded by it as by an all-encompassing element. Have you not heard at times His still small voice—felt His startling touch—invoked His regenerating breath to breathe upon you? Have you ever come with a conscious desire to be made a new creature in Christ Jesus?

How many, brethren, how many of the charges and commendations contained in these seven epistles are applicable to this assembly? Were the Divine Redeemer to dictate an epistle to *this* Church, say, what would be its prevailing tone? Granted that it would not be the tone of stern and withering rebuke, but of sympathy and approval, would its commendation be unmixed?

But if the text thus summons you to an examination of

the past and the present, it charges you indirectly to act on a wise and comprehensive plan for the future. In engaging that if you are faithful unto death He will give you a crown of life, what is the Saviour doing, but leading you to a mount of vision which commands a view of eternity? and what is He but saying to you there, Let the sweep and compass of your views take in that eternity? View existence as a whole. Let a grand and comprehensive purpose connect to-day with a period ten thousand ages hence. My young friends, resolve to wear a crown in heaven. "I" (said one in early life, and the resolution was a splendid instance of moral sublimity), "I will do whatever I think to be most for God's glory and my own good, *on the whole,* without any consideration of time, whether now, or ever so many myriads of ages hence." What is this but simply echoing back the language of Christ in the text? It is time doing homage to eternity —faith taking the man to an immeasurable distance from the earth, and bidding him look down, and look back upon this world, shrunk in its dimensions, and dwindled to a point. It is the soul enjoying a foretaste of future freedom—ascending the throne—asserting its royalty, and putting on its promised crown before the time. Go thou; and, in the strength of God, do likewise.

Finally, our Lord reminds us here, in effect, that the Spirit is present in the Church expressly to reprove, assist, and animate its members. By commanding us to hear what the Spirit saith—though He himself is the speaker, He would remind us that this is emphatically the dispensation of the Spirit—that everything in the Church—every voice—even His own voice—is in a sense subordinated to the Spirit, and can be heard with effect only as the Spirit repeats it and conveys it into the soul. And is it true that a regard to the voice of the Spirit would have saved those seven Churches from decay and death? and is it true that this Divine Spirit is in the Church still?—that *we* can obtain His unmeasured influence?

Oh, were there some one spot on this wide earth where the presence of Christ was visible—the earth's holiest of all—where, whoever entered heard His voice, saw coruscations of His glory; slept only to have visions of the Son of man as seen by John; and awoke only to feel that all around was instinct with His Divine presence;—who would not make a pilgrimage thither, though it should be as far as Patmos, where John was? Brethren, that pilgrimage would end only in disappointment, if the sacred precincts were entered with an *unprepared* heart; and with a prepared heart the pilgrimage is unnecessary. That presence is nigh to us—surrounds us—is here. Without the heart to desire it, and the eye to perceive it, that presence might indeed as well be far off, at the outskirts of the universe. The preoccupied mind might sleep at the very gate of heaven and no celestial dreams would visit it. The worldly mind might find itself even in the holiest of all—but the skirts of the Divine glory would sweep by it unnoticed. A mind keen after earthly objects—engrossed by the interests of time, might live here threescore years and ten—with the powers of the world to come all the time surrounding it, soliciting it, pressing in upon it—and yet never once recognize a single indication of the Divine presence. And he who finds nothing of heaven on earth would find nothing but earth even in heaven. It is the pure in heart that sees God—that beholds Him even here—the impure could not see Him there. Let there be a congregation of such hearts—let there be here an assembly of hearts humbled before Him—craving His aid—yearning for His spirit—and visions, precious as those which John saw, would stand disclosed to us. No sight of angels round about the throne might flash on our view; but "I say unto you, there would be joy among the angels in the presence of God." The gates of the celestial city might not brighten to our eye, nor the music of its harps fall on our ear:—but the reality would be here without the imagery; the Spirit without the rushing mighty wind; Pentecost, in its converting and transforming results; Patmos, in its manifestation of a present Saviour; Truth, in the calmness of its power; Love, in its purifying flame; the kingdom of heaven in the soul. He that hath an ear to hear, let him hear what the Spirit saith unto the Churches. Let the Churches hear and suitably respond to the Divine Spirit, and a new apocalypse—an era of glorious prosperity—should be the result.

SERMON VIII.

VITAL CHRISTIANITY BOTH EXCLUSIVE AND COMPREHENSIVE.

1 COR. xvi. 22.—"If any man love not our Lord Jesus Christ, let him be anathema, maran-atha."

THE apostle, you remember, had written this epistle by another hand. It ends at the 20th verse. But no sooner has his amanuensis laid down the pen, than he himself takes it up. And the text is the substance of his weighty postscript. "The salutation of me Paul with mine own hand. If any man love not our Lord Jesus Christ, let him be anathema, maran-atha—reserved to the coming judgment of the Lord." Here is Christianity in its *vital substance*, its *stern exclusiveness*, and its *loving comprehensiveness*. To this threefold aspect of Christianity let me now invite your devout attention, as bringing us into contact with some of the questions of the day.

I.

Here is, first, Christianity—personal, subjective Christianity—in its vital substance, *love to Christ*. What is implied in the fact that the essence of Christianity consists in *love to Christ?* Evidently, in the estimate of the apostle, Christ could not have been a mere myth, as some would have us believe—a bare impersonal idea—the poetic creation of man's hopes. Strictly speaking, you cannot love an *idea;* you may *conceive* it, *believe* it, *admire* it, *act on* it, but love must have a personal object. Loosely and popularly, indeed, we speak of loving a *place*, a *thing*, and even an *occurrence*. We may be *gratified* by it, have *pleasant associations* with it; but, correctly speaking, we can be said to love intelligently only objects having affections—beings capable of returning our love.

"But what matters it" (it is said), "will not the bare *idea* of such a being as Christ produce the same effects as the reality? Is it not the idea only that exists for us?" Ay, but the idea of a *person,* not the idea of an idea. The thin impalpable notion of an abstraction has done nothing for the world; the conviction of a *loving, present, historical, ever-living* Saviour has done everything. Now, that the character of Christ *is* a personal reality, might be argued from its very *sublimity* and *perfection.* A thing may be so wonderful as to surpass invention, and therefore be independent of all proof, or rather constitute its own proof. Such an object we believe the character of Christ to be—the great moral miracle of the Bible. Alone it forms a demonstration of the truth of the record which enshrines it. Infidelity itself, in the person of Rousseau, has bowed down and adored it. Its very perfection guarantees its reality. If we deny the *reality,* we create, if possible, a greater wonder in ascribing the invention *to such men as conceived it.* True, a man may conceive of excellence which he does not practise, and imagine greatness far above his attainment. But that men *like the evangelists* could have originated the idea of the character of Christ, is "as contrary to the *ordinary processes* of the mind as if it exceeded our *constitutional capacity.*" The *moral* wonder in the one case would be as improbable as the *natural miracle* in the other. They could have drawn the Divine portrait only from knowing and observing the living original.

Besides, such an idea was a new thing in the earth. Why, if it is a mere creation of the intellect, why have not other religions imagined the same? The canvas has been spread in every age. They have drawn heroes, philosophers, gods in profusion—no limit was imposed on their imagination. But where, among them all, is an ideal character approaching to that of Christ? And why not, but because they had never beheld such a living reality! And why have the evangelists pourtrayed Him, but because, instead of modelling His life according to their ideas, their own ideas were modelled by His life? Why, but because the representation did not originate in any previous idea of perfection, but because this idea itself was originated by the observation of His life?

And for the same reason that the idea of the character of Christ had never before entered the human mind, the apostles themselves could not, at first, take it in. He had to unveil himself slowly, as they could bear it. They had to look at Him again and again. It was long before they could embrace in one view the lofty spiritual image which the whole of His life held out. Their minds had to grow up to it. And the very process made them new creatures. Nor do they, after all, attempt a formal sketch, or a set eulogy of His character. They simply and incidentally relate what He said, and what He did, and leave the account to speak for itself.

Paul assuredly did not regard Christ as a mere idea. He saw Him in a light brighter than that of the mid-day sun. The sight smote him to the ground. From that moment he never *ceased* to see Him. In a sense, he saw nothing else. Nor can *he*, by any extravagance of scepticism, be supposed to have *invented* the idea of Christ for himself. Up to the moment of his conversion, he was exceedingly mad against it. The moment after, he was prostrate at the feet of Christ. The very same instant in which he saw Christ, and conceived aright of Him, revolutionized his whole nature. And thus it has been ever since. The character of Christ stands up alone in the world's history. It is a fact the most pure, precious, transforming, ennobling, known to our race. The bare presentation of it is an era in the history of the mind which receives it. It lifts man's whole nature. As it has been said, "One might well consent to be branded, broken on the wheel, merely for the knowledge of such a character as Christ's."

And like everything perfect—like God himself, of which it is the image—it has this characteristic, that the higher our own moral attainments, the loftier our appreciation of it. Like the blue arch above, which seems higher seen from the mountain-top than it did in the valley, just because we have ascended into a purer atmosphere, the character of Christ rises as we rise—lifts itself up in unattainable purity and dignity, and always towers increasingly above us.

2. Next, if Christianity consist in love to Christ, He could not have been a mere teacher of doctrine, however sublime, but must himself have *been* or *done* that which is calculated to excite affection. This is an important distinction. No man is loved—no man *can* be loved as a mere teacher—as the *mere* bringer or channel of truth to other men, any more than the mere paper of a book. The *truth* he brings may be heavenly, but *he*, the channel, may be earthly, sensual, devilish. The two things are totally distinct. The utmost which he can excite or expect as a mere teacher is a feeling of gratitude. If he is to be loved, in addition, it must be on account of his *manner* of teaching; or because his own character is in harmony with his teaching; or because his teaching, sublime as it is, is only an exposition of his own *being* and *doing*. If he is to be loved, that is, he himself—independently of the subjects which he teaches—he himself, in his *personal being* and *doing*, must be an object of affection.

Tell me not, then, merely that the doctrine of Christ was more spiritual than any which had before been propounded and that He even sealed its truth with His blood. I admit its spirituality, admire its sublimity, deem Him my benefactor. But, if this be all, He is only one among many. He avowedly left the more spiritual truths to be taught by others. For these I am indebted to His followers. And they, too, *died* for their testimony. Nor was their death *less* demonstrative of *sincerity* than His ; while it was more *exemplary:* more exemplary either in the tranquillity which philosophy demands, or else in the exulting joy of conscious triumph. If these, then, were His only claims, He could only share my regard with others. If I am to love Him, He must *be* and *do* something distinct from them all.

Accordingly, the fact that this distinction belongs to Him is the burden of the New Testament. From the time when John pointed to Him—not as a mere teacher—but as "the Lamb of God which taketh away the sin of the world," to the time when Paul wrote of Him as having expiated our sins—His *being* and *doing,* His *person* and *work,* are the one theme of the New Testament.

Even our Lord's own oral teaching had this significant peculiarity, that it pointed away from itself (if I may so say) to what He *was* and what He *did.* What portion of it was not either a vindication of acts which He had already performed, or intimations of purposes He was about to accomplish? What was His Sermon on the Mount, and, indeed, the burden of all His parables, but a foreshadowing of the kingdom He was about to set up—of its impediments and its growth, its spirituality and the character of its accepted subjects? All that was expository, hortatory, and of the nature of promise in His teaching—what was it but an illustration of the blessings He had come to procure, or an invitation to partake of them.

The object of His mission, say some, was to teach the doctrine of a resurrection. Nay, He *proved* it—proved it, not by words but by deeds—by His own resurrection and ascension. The object of His mission, say others, was to teach the doctrine of the love of God. Nay, He presented himself as the *proof* of it. He himself stood forth as the great gift of God—the embodiment of His love. He was pre-eminently the subject of His own teaching. He came to *be* the manifestation of God rather than to speak it—to speak it by being it. "He that hath seen me" (said he) "hath seen the Father also." "Never man spake like this man" in this respect—that He was the text of His own preaching. His words were only a running commentary on himself and His deeds.

Now, on the assumption that Christ was "God manifest in the flesh," all this is explicable enough. It is only in strict analogy with His procedure as God manifest in creation. The method in each case is the same. He speaks by actions. His words are deeds. He teaches by objects and events. "The heavens declare the glory of God." In other words, the language of creation is, "He that hath seen *me*, hath seen *so much* of the power of God and the wisdom of God." He does not orally teach us the laws and the science of nature. He supplies the facts from which we ourselves derive the science. "He speaks and it is done;" and it is from the things *done* that we come to know and adore the Doer. Similarly, but in a far loftier sense, "to them that are saved, *Christ* is the wisdom of God and the power of God." He *himself* is this. His influence streams from His person. His teaching derives its power and meaning from His character. He suggests ideas by realizing them; exhibits spirit, by being himself the living incarnation of it. His actual doing supplies the facts whence the apostles derived their doctrines; forms the quarry whence we hew the stones which form the temple of sacred science. Both His teaching and doing were but an exposition, or (if I may employ the word) an *externalization* of himself.

And was not this what man wanted? The necessities of the world were beyond the reach of mere teaching. Was information all that man wanted? Was his sin only synonymous with ignorance? The groans of the world told a different tale. Others had theorized and taught. Ages of *talk* had passed. But man's condition called for one who could *perform* what others had only promised; who could embody and make actual that which others had only imagined as possible, or admired as desirable; one who would not think to *save* by *teaching*, but would *teach* by *saving*. It was a condition of guilt, depravity, death. It required not a *theory of life*, but life, for that alone produces life; not a *system*, but *deliverance*. A *Deliverer—a personal Redeemer—a* being who, taking a survey of man's spiritual wants, can meet them all—can take humanity into his embrace, and invite it to cast itself on his beating heart for repose—One whose words are deeds—the deeds of a being mighty to save.

3. If Christianity—if the very essence of religion—consists in love to Christ, He could not have been *a mere man;* and, *as Divine,* cannot be regarded as having saved us by some cheap and easy method of deliverance. His being and doing must be of a kind corresponding with the love which He challenges. That I should be required to love God supremely, I can well understand. That such love should be the first and great command—the principle of *all* law, the essence of all obedience—to this my entire nature responds. But who is this that, according to the apostle, challenges the love which I owe to God alone? What must *He* be that I can only love God truly through Him? If Christianity itself be the highest form of religion, and if the essence of this highest form be love to Christ, what must He *be,* and what have *done,* that loving Him should be identical with the loving of God?

Brethren, to this "great mystery of godliness," there is but one solution—"God was manifest in the flesh." "He who thought it not robbery to be equal with God, took on him our nature, and assumed our liabilities. Ye know the grace of our Lord Jesus Christ; how though he was rich, for our sakes he became poor, that we through his poverty might be made rich." Our condition required that He should die; and, with all the fulness of the Godhead bodily, He advanced to the place of sacrifice. Our redemption demanded that the holy and outraged law should receive no less a compensation than His obedience unto death; and He humbled, and humbled, and humbled himself, till He had become obedient unto death, even the death of the cross. Beyond this, He *could not* go, even *He* could not go. Yes, when *He* could say no more He made the *Cross* begin to speak. When His *lips* had uttered *their* testimony, He opened His *heart* and spake in *blood.* When His *life* had ended its proclamation of mercy, He summoned up and exceeded all in the utterance of His *death.* Hide from me, if you will, every other object —throw a veil, if you will, over every other act which even *He* performed—silence, if you will, every other utterance of *His* love, but let me see His *cross*—let me never cease to hear the assurance constantly issuing thence; for it tells me at once that He is infinite love, and my tender, compassionate, all-sufficient Saviour.

Ah! little do they consider either the nature of man, or the doctrine of Scripture, who tell us that it matters not—provided eternal life is bestowed—how it is procured, or by whom. Brethren, we have not so learned Christ. The stupendous nature of His sacrificial obedience is a more affecting display of love than even the blessings of salvation resulting from it. Granted the Divine dignity of Christ—that pardon and eternal life should result from His mediation appears to be only a natural consequence. The cause is felt to be adequate to the effect. The effect is but worthy of the cause. No argument is employed to enforce it; no effort necessary to believe it. How *could* so stupendous an arrangement result in consequences less glorious! The wonder turns on that arrangement itself. That God should have *so* loved the world! That we should be not merely "*redeemed,*" but "redeemed with the *precious blood of Christ!*" That He should have so loved us as to *give himself* for us—"as to bear our sins in his own body on the tree!" To convince us of this fact, God himself has to testify—solemnly to affirm —to reiterate the testimony. Much as the gift of eternal life may excite our gratitude, that that gift should have been provided by such a method—at such a cost—is incomparably more astonishing! It is the last point on which unbelief makes a stand, and, in making that stand, unconsciously renders the highest homage to the magnitude of the love which thus confounds it. Such unbelief is the involuntary tribute of human selfishness on finding itself standing in the presence of a love too vast for its conception. The fact of that love believed, all is believed; and he who believes it is himself absorbed by it.

And, thus the reasons we have for loving Christ at all, determine also the nature and the *supremacy* of that love It is love rising to religion. *Some* characteristic Christianity *must* have. Even if it were a *false* system—one among many—it must have something unique, in order to make it *one* among many. How much more, then, must it have a distinctive character as the *true* religion? Every *other* system called for trust, gratitude, worship—even though it presented a *false* manifestation of God. Here is a *true* manifestation—the true God himself—the true God and eternal life manifest in the flesh. Surely, less than *love, confidence, adoration,* cannot be justly accorded to HIM. Here is more than a voice commanding, "thou shalt love the Lord thy God with all thy heart;" here is One *exciting* that love—doing *that before our eyes,* which constrains it. Here is a love for us so great, that even after obtaining Divine help to comprehend it, we have yet to confess that it passeth knowledge. And can the love which it *begets* be less than supreme?

But if *less* would argue ignorance or impiety, so *more* would be unnecessary, even if possible. Love is the fulfilling of the law, and of the gospel too. Gratitude, confidence, homage—all piety—resolves itself into this; and this branches out into all piety. Look through the New Testament, and you will find that love to Christ is made the motive to all obedience, the pervading element of all piety. "Lovest thou me?" is our Lord's inquiry to *every* candidate for a place in His service. "For me to live is Christ," is the oath-like response of every one of His true followers. And in thus saying and feeling, he is conscious, not merely of *pleasing* God, but of *loving* Him. In thus carrying his affections to Christ—yielding up his heart to Christ—he is loving all that he knows of *God*—all that God himself can enable him to know. So that love to Christ is *religion*—the *heart* and *core* of Christianity.

II.

Here, then, is a test for everything pretending to the Christian name; or, secondly, here is Christianity in its *exclusiveness.* "If any man love *not* our Lord Jesus Christ, let him be anathema, maran-atha."

The Christendom of to-day includes parties standing in almost every possible variety of relation to Christ, and yet all of them equally assuming the Christian name. Now, obviously, this must be wrong. There must be delusion somewhere. To say the least, some of these parties must be standing nearer to Christ—the centre of the great Christian circle—than others. Indeed, if Christianity be a system—if it have any centre at all—some of these parties must be standing not within the circle but without—must belong to some other system, even while usurping the Christian name. But how are we to determine the parties and their position? The text supplies us with a test.

Can we, for example, doubt for a moment what the apostolic estimate would have been of those who dissipate the whole history of Christ into thin air—who sublimate even His person into an idea—who reduce His character to an abstraction? Love Christ! Why, according to them, there is no Christ to love—no object for the hungry heart to embrace! For an *ideal* Christ, what more proper than a mere ideal love! Religion with them is an affair of the intellect only. They have achieved the supposed impossibility of imagining a circle which has no centre—a salvation without a Saviour! Love Christ! Why, *they* have *made Him,* and not *He them.* According to them, the Church has made Christ, and not Christ the Church! He is an ideal creation of the human mind! If anything therefore is to be loved, it is man himself, the creator of the idea. And accordingly, it will be found universally to hold true, that, in proportion as man thinks little of Christ, he idolizes himself. Something he must love; and it may be laid down as a maxim that, in the same proportion as Christ is degraded, man himself takes His place. "You told me I was a god" (said one of the lights of this pantheistic school, reproaching his brother philosophers when he lately found himself on the bed of death)—"you told me I was a god, but I find myself a suffering, dying man, and I want a God—a personal God—who can love *me*, and whom I can love." This is the great want which Christianity supplies. But the idealist robs us of the glorious reality. "Beloved, believe not every spirit, but try the spirits whether they be of God; because many false prophets are gone out into the world. . . . Every spirit that confesseth not that Jesus Christ is come in the flesh, is not of God; and *this* is that spirit of antichrist."

2. Let us apply this test to another party; to those who regard our Saviour as a mere man, and His office as confined to mere teaching. Can we, for a moment, doubt what the apostle's estimate of such would be? Why, their chief occupation is to tame down, and reduce to insignificance, all that he has said concerning Christ. According to *him*, the highest titles belong to Christ. *He* prayed for the help of the Spirit to enable him to know Christ, and to conceive aright of His love; this, in their eyes, *must* be sheer extravagance; for the love of a creature cannot transcend a creature's conception. "He" (said our Lord himself, when speaking of the Holy Spirit), "*He* shall glorify me."—Do *they* do anything of the kind? According to *Paul*, Christ is our Redeemer from the guilt of sin—our propitiatory Saviour—*they*, on the contrary, inquire (I use the language of one of them), "Why do we call Jesus Christ our *Saviour?* Our teacher He certainly was. But does not *Saviour* imply something more?" Unquestionably it does, we reply, and therefore the sacred writers employ it—a fact which the inquirer appears to have forgotten. For the *apostle*, Christ

was still living—living *for* him—present *with* him—his loving, all-sufficient Saviour. Not so for *them.* In their view, our relation to Him is *past* and not present. In effect, He is a dead Saviour, one of the departed. He is literally dead and gone. He is not an object of present adoration and joy.

To my own mind, this is one of the most repulsive aspects of the system. I believe it to have been one of the great designs of Christianity to present man with an object of worship such as he can at once love and apprehend—to meet that craving of the human heart, which every *false* religion sought in vain to supply—by giving to us a human manifestation of the invisible God. In the person of Christ, I behold Him, and adore. But here is a system which ignores Him for all present purposes. He is still virtually dead. He is simply a departed spirit. "They have taken away my Lord, and I know not where they have laid him." I look into the Scriptures, and I find the apostles labouring to exalt Christ; inflamed themselves, and inflaming others, with the love of Him. I listen to *them,* and the whole scene is changed—I must not bow the knee to Christ, nor call upon His name. While I live, I must watch against the danger of thinking too highly of Him; and when I die, whatever my parting prayer may be, it must not be, "Lord Jesus, receive my spirit." The language of the Gospel is, "If any man love not our Lord Jesus Christ, let him be anathema;" *their* language is, "if any man attach any *special efficacy to His death,* let him be deemed a weak enthusiast; if any man *worship* Him, let him be denounced as an idolater; if any man in this sense *loves* Christ, let him be anathema."

And here, let me not be met by the inconsiderate objection, that my views tend to unchristianize many excellent men. You would not call a Deist a Christian; he himself would reject the name; and yet he may be, in many respects, an excellent man. The truth is, I would withhold the Christian name from no man, whatever his denominational appellation may be, who truly loves Christ, and confides in Him as his Saviour. And would you give it to him if he did not? But that with which I have to do is—not with individuals—but with systems and parties. Take the party which, *as a party,* is a mere abstraction, and, it may be, unchristian—the peculiar views, that is, which form the bond of union among its members may be undeserving the Christian name. But take an individual member of the party, and he may be better than his party-views;—he may be a good man in spite of his views;—his character may be made up of other elements than those which constitute the peculiarities of his party—and if Christ be his Saviour, he is a Christian. But, I repeat, that with which I have to do is the party or system. Nor would I care to know what is its creed—its doctrinal views—except as it enables me to judge of its religious *tendency.* But shew me a system whose pervading tone is essentially different from that of the apostolic epistles;—whose direct tendency is to reduce my sense of guilt, and my estimate of Christ as a Saviour—to bring down to the lowest point my sense of obligation to Christ; and, unless I deny "the Lord that bought me," I must regard it as wanting the very life-blood of Christianity.

3. But the test supplied by the text is of still wider application. Here is a man who, in his inquiries respecting Christ, professes the utmost freedom from bias—perfect indifferentism. Of course, he would like to read an account of Christ written by one equally indifferent. But this could not fail to be an unchristian account; and, therefore, prejudiced, biassed, *untrue.* For no one who acknowledges Christ can be *indifferent* to Him; but finds himself standing in relations to Him, calling for the profoundest veneration and love. Indifference here is impossible. It is to require that a man should neither be a Christian, nor yet *not* a Christian, at the same time. It is to assume that Christ is *one* thing, in a professed endeavour to ascertain whether He is not *something else.* Grant Him to be only a human being;

and, however excellent he may be, I can judge of Him impartially; that is, I assume that there are faults and imperfections in His character, and on these I can pass judgment. But grant Him to be Divine, and I must *believe* in Him. I am not His *judge*, but His *servant and creature.* He claims the devotion of my whole nature. He himself is identical with holiness, love, perfection; and I cannot but aim to be identified with Him. And to bring indifference to the inquiry is actually to prejudge Him, virtually to deny Him, and to contradict the most sacred laws of our own being. Indifferent! What—indifferent whether I have a Saviour or not?—indifferent whether I am confiding my soul to a mere creature, or to One able to save unto the uttermost?—indifferent who or what is to be the object of my trust and worship? Why, it would be treason alike to Him and to my own soul.

4. Nearly allied to this indifference, in reality, though not in form, is that cold apathy which belongs to what may be called fashionable religion. The *nil admirari* of the world is carried by many into religion. An orthodox creed suffices; any emotional interest in it they leave to enthusiasts. Not to call Christ *Lord, Lord,* they would deem wrong; but to do the things which He says, or, at least, to be thought to *feel* any concern on the subject, *that* they would repudiate as an insult. Manliness, with them, consists in repressing the finest part of their nature, the best protection against everything low and polluting—in feeling enthusiasm for nothing—in adoring nothing—in becoming a moral petrifaction. From youth up, all emotion in religion has been repressed; till now, though standing even in the presence of Christ, they are "past feeling."

5. Others there are, who are consumed with zeal about almost anything and everything in religion, except about Christ. Like the Judaizing Christians of old, contending for circumcision; or like those of a later period, contending for the worship of the Virgin, they contend for a Christianity

without a Christ; a Christianity, of which the centre is a priesthood, or a Church, or a sacrament. In opposition to all such idolatry, the apostle holds forth the doctrine of the *person of Christ;* not His Church, not His teachings, not even the virtues which He recommends, but *himself*—the only object which can banish will-worship on the one hand, or impart life and power to Godliness on the other.

And the reason of all this is obvious—is implied in the text—namely, that personal Christianity is rather a state of heart than of the intellect—consists rather in the *love* than in the *knowledge* of Christ—in right *feelings* towards Him than in right *opinions* respecting Him. Doubtless, my *opinions* are likely to influence my *feelings*, and hence the importance of correct opinions. If I am self-consistent, my belief cannot but react upon my heart—a fact which proclaims the folly of those who decry all creeds, for they have one of their own—every man has—who fancy themselves wonderfully large-minded in dispensing with all doctrinal views—unconscious that they are simply disclosing a certain *animus* against Christian truth, and a discreditable ignorance of human nature. But, then, while we would strenuously contend for the great system of Christian truth, we contend for it, not as an *end*, but as a *means to an end;* and *that* end, a right state of *heart* towards *Christ;* and we contend for it, with the distinct confession, that it is possible to hold right *views* of Christ, not only without the right *feelings*, but possible even to make the *views* a substitute for the *feelings*. Now, if any man merits an anathema who loves not Christ, because he views not Christ as he ought, of how much sorer punishment is he worthy, who, professing to behold in Christ an Almighty Saviour, is yet conscious of no glorying in His cross, no love to His person? For such the inspired apostle reserves his most fearful denunciation.

We are aware, indeed, of some mawkish sentimentalists, who would repeal even this anathema. To them, all discrimination of character or sentiment is narrow-mindedness—

all discipline, severity—all punishment, cruelty. And this indifference of theirs to the immutable distinctions of right and wrong, they call charity, liberality. Touch their selfishness—wrong their own little interests of an atom—and all the resentment of which their nature is capable, flames up in indignation. But if it is only one of the pillars of the Divine throne that is shaken—only the character of God manifest in the flesh that is sported with—*that* receives their utmost indulgence, and their resentment is reserved only for those who denounce it. Besides, their conception of the character of Christ is, that He is all and only amiable. They forget that He could thunder and lighten as well as weep. They are deaf to the woes He denounced; blind to the judgment-scene which He painted. They forget that, in effect, He himself gave utterance to the text, when He said, "Whosoever shall be ashamed of me, of him will I be ashamed in that day." Had *they* lived in the first ages of Christianity, they would have joined with the heathen of the day in denouncing the Gospel for its stern exclusiveness—for its refusal to symbolize with idolatry—for its not being satisfied at the admission of Christ to a seat on Olympus, or a place in the Pantheon, as *one* of the gods.

Brethren, there is a point at which charity itself must stop. There are those whom patience itself must give up. And surely, if that point, and those parties, are anywhere to be found, they are specified in the text—they who love not our Lord Jesus Christ—who are insensible even to *His* claims.

Had the text been an unfinished sentence—had it been, "If any man love not—love not at all—love nothing"—how would you have filled up the sentence? If any man love nothing, he must be a monster. Let society guard against him—"cast him out." And is Christ to be the only being from whom men may withhold their affections with impunity? The anathema in the text is not directed against men who have no affections; but against those who, having affections, are so much in love with self, as to have morally disqualified themselves for all sympathy with essential excellence; so enamoured of the low, the mean, the sensuous, or the speculative, that Divine Perfection itself may approach them, without awakening in them any consciousness of its presence, or only to render them conscious of uneasiness and hostility. To denounce such, is not to utter the anathema of *haste and rashness.* For they are resisting God's last appeal to their hearts. Who has not been thrilled at reading the touching language of the lord of the vineyard, when, after the husbandmen had beaten and wounded every messenger he had sent, he said, in his perplexity, "What *shall* I do? I will send my beloved son; it may be they *will* reverence him when they see him." It was his last resource; and you know the result, and have, doubtless, often sympathized with the doom which finally overtook them. The denunciation in the text is but that doom applied to a far more revolting form of guilt. It is not the anathema of *bigotry.* To commend the lovers of Christ, is virtually to denounce them who love Him not. It is not the anathema of *anger.* It may be uttered with tears. It is so consonant with truth and holiness—with all the best feelings of man's nature, and all the laws of God's government—that when they who love not our Lord Jesus Christ shall at last behold what they have neglected—they will pronounce the anathema on themselves. They will see that if any man love not the Incarnation of all excellence, he avows himself an alien from all goodness—feel that any external sentence does but interpret the doom which He himself has already pronounced—and for ever will feel that the severest infliction which can come on him from without is, to be pointed at as a man who loved not our Lord Jesus Christ.

III.

But in thus pronouncing a sentence of exclusion against all who love not Christ, the apostle was, in effect, saying—"Grace be with all them that *do* love our Lord Jesus Christ in sincerity." So that here is, thirdly, Christianity in its *comprehensiveness.*

In giving to his letter this affecting close, the apostle aimed probably to remind the Corinthians that the essence of Christianity is *love to Christ;* intended to turn away their minds from the disputes and discussions which had rent the Church into factions, to *Him* who could unite them all into one loving community—designed to remind them that in such disputes, even though one party might be right and the other wrong, both might be wrong—heretical—as to Christianity itself, by leading men away from Christ to questions tempting to the intellect, but of no avail whatever in relation to eternal life. It is as if he had said, "Love Christ, and you form a Church;" love anything else, and you form a faction. You cannot *argue* yourselves into Christian fellowship; but love Christ, and you will find yourselves already in fellowship. Quarrel about other things, even Christian things—and you will cease to love Him; love *Him*, and you will cease to quarrel about anything. If any man love Christ, however little he may know of the *body* of Christianity, he has at least the very centre and soul of it. If his heart be right with Christ, he will judge kindly of those who give evidence that their hearts are in the same state, even though many of their Christian opinions may differ. If he have felt the attraction of the Cross, he will open his arms and embrace all who have been drawn within the same circle. If he love *not* our Lord Jesus Christ, his creed has no centre, his heart no sufficient object, he has no guarantee of hope either for himself or others. But if he do love Christ, everything else will follow; he will love his people, love everything he enjoins, love all that Christ loves—he will be Christ-like.

Sublime conception! the organization of a new community, distinguishable from all the forms of civil society by the redeemed character of its members, and the spiritual design of its government! Eventful period! when Christ came to realize the sublime idea; to be himself the heart of the Church ; the centre around which it should collect and form, and, in His own person,—humanity inhabited by Deity—presenting at once the image and the nucleus of the unearthly society. And mighty the force which He has ever since exerted—giving a new date to time, and a new aspect to life—increasing the interest of man in man—creating specimens of heavenly excellence—giving to the spiritual ascendancy over the material—establishing a brotherhood of souls—and doing all this by a new power—the power of *love* —His own *person* being the *centre,* His own *heart* the *source* of the whole! And, oh, happy the time when that love shall unite all His true followers into one heart and one soul! when all shall be recognized as real Christians who *do* love Him, and they only shall be disowned who love him not! And wise and happy the people who, forestalling that time, and preparing for it, make love for the person and work of Christ their only condition of union with His Church! "Grace be with all them that love our Lord Jesus Christ in sincerity."

Christians, we love Him because He first loved us. To His love we owe everything. But for His love, we soon should have had nothing in the universe to love, but have been eternally hateful even to ourselves. But now we love *Him* —this is our title—our high distinction. Whatever others may love, we are able to love *Him*—have risen to the height of identifying ourselves with Him. One manifestation the world has had of perfect excellence, and we find ourselves capable of sympathizing with *that*—God has given us power to do it. What manner of persons ought we to be! visible transformations into His image—centres of attraction to Him, repellent of everything unlike Him—in affinity with all that loves Him—epistles of Christ addressed to the world—inviting the world to look at the embodiment of Christianity —to behold in us Christ living and walking the earth again! What manner of persons ought we to be; rejoicing in Him; yearning for the progress of His cause; not waiting for great occasions to serve Him; seizing the least; giving thanks at every sign of success; pouring out our hearts in prayer, that these walls may resound with the love of Christ; and the Church assembling here, with their beloved pastor, be knit together by love to Him; and that many a worldly heart may here be melted and moulded and fitted for the celebration of His love in heaven.

Some such hearts may be here to-day—hearts sensitive, it may be, to every kind of appeal but the highest; ready to love every object but Christ; flattering themselves that they are lovers of truth—admirers of the beauty of virtue—susceptible of the deepest gratitude—but yet insensible to the claims of the highest excellence, and of the only love which passeth knowledge. Need I remind you that you *must love;* that you are created under a necessity of loving; and that your love must have, in order that you may be happy, an *infinite object?* Anything less would be infinitely too little. You may be slow in making the discovery—though even now you are not without premonitions of it—but the time will come when you will be alive to nothing else. It must not be a *gross material object*—that would reduce to its own littleness a nature capable of perpetual enlargement. He must be *spiritual*—connatural with yourself—*and such a being is Christ.* He must not be even *tainted with sin,* otherwise your love would be often clouded with suspicion—your happiness marred with apprehension. He must rise above you in unclouded purity—elevating your own conceptions of excellence, and inspiring you with a sleepless desire to rise *to* it. And *such a being is Christ.* He must not be *finite, limited, dependent,* in His resources; otherwise the time would come when you would have comprehended *Him,* and have exhausted His *resources;* when you would find that you still had faculties unused, capacities unfilled, affections to spare. The highest use you could make of such a being, however excellent, would be to make Him the point from which to soar away in quest of an object which is infinite;

and *such an infinite object is Christ.* But you may fear that with His greatness comes another danger—the danger of His lofty self-isolation. Is He capable of disinterested love—capable of loving *me?* Capable of disinterested love! the world would have known nothing certain respecting such love but for Him. He has made the idea familiar to us. He is the embodiment of it for all time, and for all eternity. "Ye know the grace of our Lord Jesus Christ." His greatness is the greatness of self-sacrificing love. Yes; this is the very soul of the Gospel, and the secret of its power: God giving himself *to* man, by first giving himself *for* him. "He loved us, and gave himself *for* us;" and is now offering himself *to* us. He waits not for you to solicit Him; He is soliciting you. Infinite love is pressing itself on your acceptance. Receive Him; and of you it shall then be said, "Whom having not seen ye love; in whom, though now ye see him not, yet believing, ye rejoice with a joy unspeakable and full of glory." Amen!

SERMON IX.

THE ORACLES OF GOD.

ROM. iii. 1-2—"What advantage then hath the Jew? or what profit is there of circumcision? Much, every way: chiefly, because that *unto them were committed the oracles of God.*"

WHO by searching can find out God? who can find out the Almighty unto perfection? And yet who, deserving the name of a rational being, has not attempted it? The character of God, and the nature of our relations to Him, are subjects, before which every other sinks into insignificance. In the absence of Divine revelation concerning them, the anxious inquirer has been heard exclaiming, "Who shall go up for us to heaven, and bring it unto us? or who shall go over the sea for us, and bring it unto us?" And as the height and the depth have replied, "It is not in us," he has sunk in despondency, exclaiming, "O that I knew where I could find Him!" In the absence of light he has gazed intently on the darkness, till, in the language of Eliphaz, a something passed before his face and the hair of his flesh stood up. Unable to raise the vexatious veil, which obscured without quite concealing the objects of his search, he has laboured to interpret the shadowy forms and movements behind. Despairing of help from the living, he has inquired of the dead. No whisper of nature has passed him unheeded—no object unquestioned, unracked. Every element without, every faculty within him, has been invoked, solicited, and exhausted, in the hope of compelling it to disclose something.

In compassion to this exigence, and as a part of a great purpose of mercy, the Almighty has condescended to speak to man at sundry times and in divers manners. One of these methods was by oracle; that is to say, besides imparting His mind to man *spontaneously*, He graciously allowed himself, under certain conditions of place, and person, and manner—conditions of His own appointment—to be questioned, or inquired of, and His reply was called an utterance, a response, or an oracle. But then, as all the communications of God to man, however made, are on topics of solemn import, they may all be regarded as replies to human inquiries, although these inquiries may never have been put to God formally, and in so many words; and hence the other parts of the Bible, as well as those which contain His direct responses, came to be denominated *oracles* also. For instance, the law of ten commands; each of these is, in effect, a reply to a solemn enquiry. In all ages, the idolatrous tendencies of the human heart have been asking—and a large majority of mankind still continue to repeat the question, "May we not have a plurality of gods?" And the first command comes, like an oracle from amidst the thunders and lightnings of Sinai, saying, "Thou shalt have none other gods before me." Then if we may not—continues the same persisting perverseness—if our worship is to be confined to the one living and true God, may we not, at least, indulge our senses with symbolical representations of Him? "To what will ye liken me? saith the Lord; or whereunto shall I be compared? Thou shalt *not* make unto thyself any graven image." Anger, and hatred, and revenge—intent on blood—have each been ever glaring defiance at the heavens, and saying, "May I not avenge myself?" But what saith the answer of God? "Thou shalt do no murder." And hence all the commands of the moral law are denominated *oracles;* for, saith Stephen, when speaking of Moses, "This is he, who, in Mount Sinai, received the lively oracles to give unto us."

On the same principle, the *whole* of the Old Testament Scriptures are in the New repeatedly called *oracles.* For what part of them does not apply to some important and importunate enquiry of the human mind? Has man, for instance, anxiously pressed the question in every age, "What was the origin of the world? and what the early history of the nations of antiquity?" The fictions of early poetry, the theories of ancient philosophy, the endless mythologies of idolatry—all prove that he has. Accordingly, the historical books of the Bible may be regarded as God's oracular and sufficient reply. What are all its *threatenings,* but the oracles of His holiness, responding to the questionings of human fear concerning the punishment of sin, and a judgment to come? What are all its *promises,* but the oracles of mercy, replying to the hopes of man concerning pardon and endless life? And what its *prophecies,* but the answers of the omniscient oracle to our eager inquiries concerning the eventful future? Hence, the entire Bible is described as oracular; for, in answer to the supposed objection of the Jew in the text, "What advantage then hath the Jew, or what profit is there in circumcision?" the apostle replies, "Much every way; chiefly, because that unto them were committed the oracles, or Scriptures of God."

Brethren, we profess to believe that these ancient oracles, and others subsequently added to them, are in our possession—that the Scriptures of the Old and New Testament form a collection of adjudged cases—of laws never to be repealed—of infallible judgments never to be reversed or disturbed—of answers to the most momentous inquiries man can ever propose, answers never to be recalled—all the information which heaven deems necessary for earth—so sufficient, that no serious doubt can ever be started, no important question ever arise on any moral subject, which it has not anticipated, and to which it does not reply. How important, then, first, that we should have an enlightened conviction of their Divine origin; and, secondly, that we should appreciate the important subjects of which they treat; and, thirdly, be aware of the responsibility which their possession entails on us.

I.

First, *it is important that we should acquire an enlightened conviction of the truth and divinity of these oracles.* Let it be supposed that we had now assembled to hear these oracles for the first time—that we had come from the ends of the earth to consult them—that for years we had been labouring under a distracting consciousness of guilt for which nothing had brought us relief—and that now we had come together to hear what professed to be the true sayings of God on the subject. Should we not feel that we had reached a crisis in our history—that disappointment now would leave us to despair—that delusion would involve us in destruction? Our only wise course, in such circumstances, would be to call first for satisfactory evidence that we were not about to listen to the voice of a deceiver. The very fact that the Scriptures are called the oracles *of God,* implies that there have been other oracles, real or pretended, *not* of God. And it was to have been expected that whatever method God might adopt for disclosing His mind to us, men, either disliking His disclosures, or not being able easily to obtain them, would attempt to do the same by their enchantments—to institute oracles of their own. Accordingly, the heathen world abounded with pretended oracles, to which numbers flocked from all directions, in order to obtain instruction in their difficulty, and direction in their perplexity. But all these were only parts of a great system of imposture; and hence the importance of our being convinced, before we yield our confidence—before we lend even our ear to the voice of the Christian oracle, that we are listening to the voice of God. To assure us that it is the voice of truth only would not suffice—a thoughtful heathen might sometimes have stumbled on a truth; but by what mark was he to know it—how was he to distinguish it from error?—truth and error would both come to him in the same unsatisfactory form, the form of guess or conjecture. Not only must we be assured, therefore, that the oracle we are required to believe is true—but that it is the right truth—that it is God's own reply to our inquiry. It must come directly from God—sealed and authenticated by Him as His Divine response.

Now that we should not be requiring too much in asking this, is evident from the fact that God himself has graciously provided for it. In the 45th chapter of Isaiah, He challenges a comparison between *His* revelations and the oracles of the heathen—dares an examination into His claims in the full confidence of their Divine superiority. "*I* have not spoken in secret, saith He, in a dark place of the earth; I said not unto the seed of Jacob, Seek ye me in vain; I the Lord speak righteousness, I declare things that are right." Would you look on *publicity* as one mark to be expected in a communication from heaven? The heathen oracles gave their responses from gloomy woods, and caverns, and dark recesses. The oracle at Delphi—the most renowned of them all—gave its pretended answers from a chasm or deep cleft in the earth. "But I," saith God, "have not spoken in secret, in a dark place of the earth—my law was given from the top of Sinai, in the face of an assembled nation—my prophets are public men—my Gospel challenges the inspection of the world—deprecates nothing so much as the neglect of the evidence on which it rests."

Would you expect that the subjects of a Divine revelation would be distinguished by the *vital importance of their character?* The heathen oracles responded alike to the questions of the trifler and of the anxious—of the curious and of the devout. But, saith God, I have never said, "Seek ye me in vain, or to no purpose, or on vain subjects." One of the principal faults which men are disposed to find with the Bible is, that it confines its disclosures to important subjects—that it will not gratify their curiosity and wonder—that it will not furnish them with an excuse for neglecting the great, by dealing in the little—that all the light which it supplies falls exclusively on the path to heaven. No, saith God, I trifle with no man—Mine is an oracle for the solemn and sublime—for the soul and eternity.

Would you expect that a Divine response would be clear and determinate? The heathen oracles were doubtful and ambiguous—notorious for returning uncertain answers—answers by the misinterpretation of which many of their votaries were ruined. Thus Crœsus, who was conquered by the very Cyrus predicted in the 45th of Isaiah, on consulting the Delphian oracle before he marched against Cyrus, received this answer, "If you march across the river Halys, you shall overthrow a great nation." He imagined that the nation he was to overthrow was that of Cyrus, but it proved to be his own. But, saith God, in relation to such ambiguity, "I, Jehovah, speak righteousness—I give direct answers." The truths which He has disclosed are of a nature, that had He chosen to conceal them, He had only to remain silent—never could men have discovered them by their own endeavours. If He speak, therefore, it can only be to instruct and enlighten; and, in order to this, His communication must be clear and explicit. And this is its character; "the entrance of His word giveth light, it giveth understanding to the simple." Ignorance itself is made wise by it—wise unto salvation. Even the wilfully blind cannot shut out all its light. Close their eyes as they may, some rays will beam across their path. Close their ears as they may, some warning sounds from the oracle will reach them at times—sounds of which they would be glad to plead the ambiguity, if they could, as an excuse for neglecting them; but, no, they cannot misunderstand their meaning.

Would you expect that all the predictions of a Divine oracle would be verified by the event? That those of the heathen were only occasionally verified, and then only by accident as far as they were concerned, you need not be told. But, saith God, in allusion to this deception, "I speak things that are right—that are faithful and true." And hence, while He challenges the heathen to adduce a single prediction of theirs which was justified by the event, He often appeals to the Israelites that not one thing had failed them of all that He had foretold. But with how much greater force might He repeat the appeal to us of the present day! Go, search His predictions of Babylon and Egypt, of Jerusalem and Tyre—you have only to turn the future tense of the sacred oracle into the past, and the prediction of what *should* befall them becomes an accurate and minute history of what *has* actually transpired.

Are we now, then, prepared to ascend and consult the oracle for ourselves? or do we ask for greater evidence of its divinity yet? Should it signify nothing, that the oracles of God, after displacing all their ancient competitors are enshrined and enthroned on a mountain of evidence which still continues to enlarge its base, and to lift higher its summit? Let us mark the spoils which lie around the foot of the mount—the spoils which Truth has won from error—the religion of the Bible, from the imposture of idolatry and paganism. There lie the broken tripod—the mutilated altar—fragments of oracular shrines—of the idol blackened with the incense of the priest—and of the pavement of the portico worn with the foot of the philosopher.

Can we help remarking, as we ascend the mountain of the Lord's house, that our way lies through the sepulchres of the dead? They are the tombs of prophets, apostles, and saints, who sealed the truth of the oracles they delivered with their blood. Do we find the approach to the temple thronged with a multitude of worshippers, and do we admire the contrast they present to the profligate and the wretched of mankind? Such were some of these—but they have consulted the holy oracle—they have felt, believed, and acted on its response; and the consequence is, that the savage is civilized—the vicious is reclaimed—the miserable, happy. Are we struck on entering the temple with the pictured representations on its walls of the blind receiving their sight, the dying restored, the dead brought to life again? Are we met, in one part, with the sight of an angel lighting up the earth with his presence; and in another with the spectacle of a darkened sun, a quaking globe, a collapsing universe? They represent the miracles which have been wrought to attest the truth of the oracle. Do we mark how thoughtlessness, as it bends its ear to the oracle, becomes reflective—how hardened obstinacy smites upon its breast, and falls prostrate—how the brow of perplexity is smoothed—and the countenance of care lighted up with the smile of satisfaction? The oracle has spoken to each a word in season. And, besides all this, do we mark, as it speaks, how everything seems to echo its voice? All things seem in harmony with it. How amazing this property, that its voice should cause objects, otherwise silent, to become vocal! It speaks to the individual man, and something within him speaks in return—a still small voice within him replies; it is the oracle of the breast. And whether the Divine oracle commands, or prohibits, or instructs, that oracle within him repeats and confirms the sentence. While, at the same time, every object in nature, and every event in providence, becomes oracular also, and corroborates its truth.

And now, having reached the place of the oracle—having come to the oracles themselves—let us remember, that in the very fact of their preservation, through so many ages of time, and amidst a world of hostile depravity labouring for their destruction, we behold a crowning proof of their divinity. For could we but see a volume bearing marks of all that these holy oracles have passed through, what should we behold but an ancient volume, exhibiting signs of having been at one time trampled on by rage, at another moth-eaten by neglect; now interpolated by error, then erased by pride; here, scorched by the fires of bigotry; there, stained with the venom of infidelity; in every page, sprinkled with the blood of its martyred defenders; and yet, so substantially entire in every part as to shew that it has always been in the keeping of Omnipotence—in the hollow of His hand.

II.

Having come to the holy oracles, then, with an enlightened conviction of their Divine authority, let us, 2dly, *reverently consult them,* and appreciate the important subjects on which they speak. We have said that they contain replies to every essential inquiry. But though all these subjects of inquiry were equally important—which they are not—it would still be true that, in the order of time, some would claim our consideration earlier than others, and that these are "the first principles of the oracles of God." Now, what are these?

1. If we had hitherto been destitute of all the knowledge which Revelation supplies—if we had now assembled to consult the living oracle, but were required to limit our inquiries to two or three subjects—what should they be? Could we possibly hesitate? Has not the Bible itself suggested and repeated the first inquiry in every possible form? "What must I do to be saved? How, then, can man be just with God? How can God be just and yet a Saviour?" Vary or disguise it as he may, this is the cry of universal man. What else was meant by erecting an altar to the unknown God? It discovered an anxiety lest, in the wide realms of invisible and immortal natures, there should be even one superior being left unappeased and unpropitiated—a desire to secure the favour of every invisible power in the universe. What else was meant, too, by the anxious language of the awakened sinner, as described by the prophet Micah:—"Wherewith shall I come before the Lord, and bow myself before the high God? Shall I come before him with burnt-offerings, with calves of a year old? Will the Lord be pleased with thousands of rams, or with ten thousands of rivers of oil? Shall I give my first-born for my transgression? the fruit of my body for the sin of my soul?" This was only saying, in effect, that no anguish could be deemed too great—no sacrifice too costly—if it did but propitiate the favour of God in his behalf. But how shall

he do this? By pleading that he is not so guilty as many? Go to him and say, "Why this excessive sorrow?—you have committed no enormous crime: others are as bad, and even worse than you." Say this to him, and he will reply, and reply truly—Is the conduct of others the standard by which I am to be judged?—if not, the fact that others are possibly worse than me is no solace to me. And even to think of pleading it in palliation would only aggravate the guilt which it seeks to excuse. How shall he obtain the peace he seeks? By the assurance that God will accept his repentance? "How do you know that?" he will reply. Does repentance save the criminal from the sentence of human law? Does repentance deliver him from the frown of Providence even in this life? If so, how is it that the penniless and broken-hearted profligate does not recover his health and his property again, but perishes in tears, and want, and wretchedness? Who, then, shall comfort him? The world with its delights? As well might you offer them to the suffering or the dying—he sees their emptiness—resents their intrusion as impertinent folly. Do you remind him that God is benevolent? "*That* is the very thought," he will reply, "which gives me the keenest sense of my guilt—that He should have been the best of Fathers, and I one of the most ungrateful of His children—that He should have been ever blessing me, and I as constantly abusing His goodness." Whither shall he repair?—to the temple of nature? Throughout her ample dome no accent is heard to give hope of pardon to the guilty. To the mosque of Mohammed? No oracle is there; or one which speaks only of defiling, sensual indulgences. To the altar of Judaism? "The blood of bulls and of goats cannot take away sin." One only resource is left, and if that fail, darkness profound and despair eternal will settle around him—it is the oracle of the cross. And how does that minister relief?—by extenuating his guilt? On the contrary, it tells him that his guilt exceeds his worst apprehensions—that were his alarm a thousandfold greater than it is, it would not, could not be exaggerated. How, then, does it minister relief?—by repealing the law of God?—by overruling the requirements of His justice? This the penitent sinner himself would deprecate. Salvation, on such terms, would be no salvation to him. He could not confide in a being who could thus trifle with His own laws. Besides, his own conscience would continue to demand reparation for the dishonoured law, even if the law itself did not. His own conscience insists on an atonement. He would not be saved but by a just and a holy God. Hear, then, the response of the heavenly oracle—"I am a just God and yet a Saviour." Does the penitent ask how justice and mercy can thus be reconciled? "Behold," saith the oracle, "behold the Lamb of God, which taketh away the sin of the world." Is he concerned lest that atonement should not be satisfactory to God? He is assured that it was God himself who provided it. Does he fear lest that sacrifice should avail only for some sins? The blood of Jesus Christ, he is assured, cleanseth from all sins. Can he yet fear that he shall perish? He is assured that God so loved the world as to make this vast provision that he might not perish but have everlasting life. Nothing now, then, is wanting to his forgiveness, but his cordial belief of these wondrous truths. "In Christ Jesus the Lord," he can now say, "have I righteousness and strength—the wrath to come is not for me—for who is he that condemneth?—there is no condemnation to them that are in Christ Jesus."

2. But now another inquiry arises. The Gospel has assured him of pardon for the past; can it secure him holiness for the future? It has saved him from the guilt of sin; but unless it delivers him from its practice and its power, his deliverance will be incomplete. Saved him from hell it has; but unless it renews his nature, and prepares him for heaven, impenetrable darkness will still hang over his eternal future—for the breath of a polluted heart would wither the bloom of Paradise itself. But how can this change be effected?—

by the outward reformation of his conduct merely? That *may* take place, and yet the heart be unchanged. By baptism? Facts demonstrate that that only *denotes* a change, or signifies what it *should* be, but does not effect it. By the impartation of knowledge? The history of the world has proved—and its present state confirms the humbling truth—that arts, learning, science, all the machinery of civilization, so far from being necessarily connected with moral improvement, may only serve to make men mightier in depravity—giants in evil. By judgments? Do the unquenchable flames renew the heart? By enacting laws merely?—instructing him how he ought to think and act? Law, at best, can only convict of sin. By forcing his will?—doing violence to his moral nature? That would make obedience impossible; for forced obedience is only the compelled and passive movement of a machine. How, then, is the seemingly impossible but yet indispensable change to be effected? Let him take the question to the Holy Oracle, and listen to the reply—"A new heart will I give you, and a new spirit will I put within you; and I will put my spirit within you, and cause you to walk in my statutes, and ye shall keep my judgments, and do them." Here all his difficulties vanish. The spirit of life in Jesus Christ having quickened him from a death of sin, engages all his powers, and carries along his whole nature in an earnest pursuit after holiness. Finding the powers of his mind possessed and polluted by the spirit of evil, it expels the unholy usurper, and gives back his soul to the hallowing influence of God. Finding him feeble and helpless in moral purpose, it takes him to the cross, and there brings daily to bear on him the full force of love and gratitude and faith—of motives strong enough to move all heaven. And as it shews him how the heart that bled there beats for him—and how the hand that was nailed there is the hand that caught him in his fall—that shut for him the gate of hell, and opened for him the gate of heaven—and as it unfolds to his view the visions of that immortality, and calls him to live under the influence of that other world—what can become of this? It is crucified to him, and he to it. And thus the same oracle which tells him of pardon, tells him that that is only the first of its blessings—that in coming to him first, it comes only as the leader of a train which reaches from earth to heaven—from the cross to the right hand of the throne of God.

3. And then comes a third inquiry connected with these disclosures of pardon and holiness; to what will they lead? —or what is the state in which they will terminate? Who that has felt the natural longing after immortality—who that has felt this longing in connexion with a sense of the uncertainity of life, and of the insufficiency of all created nature to fill his capacity for enjoyment—who that has felt these when he supposed himself to be standing on the extreme verge of life, and was casting an anxious gaze on the untried world beyond—who has not then felt a throng of questions rise to his lips which none but a heavenly oracle could resolve? A Socrates and a Plato, a Cicero and a Seneca, often felt this to a degree which, while it made life a burthen, made death at the same time an object of appalling dread. They saw the human race walking in gloomy procession to the grave; and as they saw them pass into the land of shadows, they sought with strained and untiring gaze to watch their steps and learn their fate. But all in vain; if at one time they spoke as from the skies, at another they uttered the language of the sepulchre, according as hope or fear was the oracle of the moment. But there, where every other religion vanishes like an extinguished taper and leaves us in darkness, the gospel holds up a torch which not only discloses a world beyond, but the separate states of the righteous and the wicked. Is the important question asked, "If a man die, shall he live again?"—how distinct and solemn is the reply of the oracle, "Verily, verily, I say unto you, *all* that are in their graves shall come forth, they that have done good unto the resur-

rection of life, and they that have done evil unto the resurrection of damnation.

Indeed, on no subject is the heavenly oracle more copious and explicit than on this; often prefacing its responses with solemn asseverations—and repeating them again and again; while one of its latest communications was in these words, "Write, Blessed are the dead that die in the Lord." I heard an oracle from heaven, saying this, saith John; and immediately the Eternal Spirit taking up the strain, added, "They rest from their labours, and their works do follow them." It tells us, that for the righteous to be absent from the body is to be present with the Lord. It assures us that in that day of final awakening, their life will not only be restored but ennobled, exalted to the highest state of security and glory it can sustain—that from the ruinous heap of every grave a living structure shall arise, built up into an imperishable monument of Him who is the resurrection and the life—that in the stead of dishonour, it shall be raised in glory—that in the place of weakness it shall be clothed with the vigour of immortal youth—that the original grossness of its materiality shall be purged away—that in the place of a natural body, it shall be refined and etherealized into a spiritual body—into a robe of light rivalling the purer essence of the soul itself—while each of its senses shall form an inlet to floods of enjoyment, and all its powers be instinct and emulous with zeal for the Divine glory.

Would we ask any question of the holy oracle concerning the scenes of the final day? It tells us that the saved and the lost will then meet together for the last time before the throne of the judge—it tells us that sin will have reached maturity in the wicked and have prepared them for hell—that holiness will have attained maturity in the righteous and have prepared them for heaven—and when the purity and beauty, the joy and glory on the right hand, shall be seen in immediate contrast with the fearful array on the left, all will acknowledge that the salvation of His people, as there displayed, is a worthy result of all His stupendous plans, and abundantly exceeds all the lofty things which He had spoken concerning them. Then will He, whose voice had often been heard, be visible to the eye as well as audible to the ear—then will He challenge the universe to say if one of all His oracles has failed—then will He speak once more, and every word He utters will be laden with fate. Concerning the great system of Providence, He will say, "It is finished;" of Time, He will say, "Let it end;" and of Eternity, "Let it begin." To the righteous, He will say "Come;" and to the wicked, "Depart;" and as the universe takes up and reverberates the oracle, "these shall go into everlasting punishment, but the righteous into life eternal."

III.

Then need I repeat, thirdly, that *the possession of the oracles of God involves us in deep responsibility?* The very phraseology of the text implies this; for it speaks of them as a sacred trust of pre-eminent importance. "Do you ask me," says the apostle to the objecting Israelite, "what advantage your nation possesses over the idolatrous Gentile, if you are yet to be placed on the same footing as sinners before God? Much every way. For do not suppose that your religious privileges are to be thought unimportant because you neglected to improve them. Enumerate those privileges. There was the supernatural origin of your nation—there was your miraculous march through the wilderness—there was the perpetual Providence which sustained your national existence—your theocratic government, or Divine administration of your public affairs—your temple-service—the mass of living light within the veil—the types, as perpetual remembrancers of great truths, and as foreshadowing good things to come—and the oracles of God. But—as if he had said—I will name but one of these; for that comprehends and forms the charter of all the rest—the oracles of God."

And if they formed the richest blessing of that dispensation, are they to be valued less now that "God, in these last days, hath spoken to us by His Son?" "Yea, doubtless," saith Paul, "I count all things but loss—my Hebrew descent, my denominational distinction as a Pharisee, my zeal for the law, my ceremonial righteousness—things which lately constituted my pride and boast—here I trample them all under foot, and count them but loss, for the excellency of the knowledge of Christ Jesus my Lord."

Can you, my friends, sympathize with the apostle in this new preference? Bring out your wealth, and place it by itself—your reputation, and place it by itself—your worldly pleasures, and set them apart—and the oracles of God, as a fourth object of value—and now make your selection. Take away with you but one of these four objects; and say, which shall it be? Are you perplexed in your choice? Consult the oracle, and hear the reply: "Thus saith the Lord, Let not the wise man glory in his wisdom; neither let the mighty man glory in his might; let not the rich man glory in his riches: But let him that glorieth glory in this, that he understandeth and knoweth me; that I am the Lord, who exercise loving-kindness, judgment, and righteousness in the earth; for in these things I delight, saith the Lord." Yes, and the possession of that knowledge entails on you greater responsibility than would rest on you by your possessing all the riches of the rich, all the power of the mighty, and all the wisdom of the wise. So that, hereafter, should you ask, "What means of salvation did I possess? What peculiar advantages for eternity did I enjoy?" the emphatic reply will be, "Much in every way: but chiefly that unto you were committed the oracles of God."

By the mercies of God, then, will you not now reverently consult them? It is for your life. Refuse not on the ground that the answer of the oracle may inspire you with gloom. True, its answers will be solemn; but then they relate to solemn and momentous things. It will tell you that death is a curse; and that, in consequence of sin, you are exposed to it. But then death is a curse, whether the Gospel tells you of it or not; and you are exposed to that curse, whether the Gospel warns you of it or not. You are not in danger of destruction because the Gospel says so; but the Gospel says so because you are exposed to destruction. And your not attending to the Gospel does not alter the case—your being deaf to the warning does not lessen the danger. If you were never more to hear a word on the subject, it would still be true every day and hour and moment of your life, that you are exposed to eternal death. The Gospel alludes to the painful subject only with a view of telling you of the way of life. The inscription over the sacred oracle is this, "Hear, and your soul shall live." "The words that I speak unto you, they are spirit, and they are life." Will you not, then, I ask again, hasten and reverently consult it? At this moment it is speaking—and will you not hear it? It has something to say to each of you. Only let the subject be suitable, and it will answer the inquiries of every one present—of the young and the old, of the rich and the poor:—will you not go and inquire of it? Centuries ago, it told the Israelites how they would be circumstanced at this day. You have often longed to look into the future—wondered *where* you would be, and *how* you would be occupied at some distant time. Have you no anxiety—at least, have you no curiosity to know how you will be circumstanced centuries hence? The oracle can tell you. Only go to it, and honestly explain your character—that you never pray—that you are living in the practice of secret sin—and that, though you possess the opportunities of religion, you are not improving them; or else that, through the grace of God, you are the reverse of all this; only consult it honestly, and it will tell you whether centuries hence, whether a few years hence, you will be happy or miserable—what world you will be in, whether in heaven or hell. And will you not consult it? Do you ask *when?* The oracle itself replies, "*To-day,* if ye will hear my voice—*to-day.*"

Or, if you are in the habit of listening to it, what is the result? Others have been pierced and prostrated by its power; for the Word of God is quick and powerful, sharper than any two-edged sword, cutting deep into the conscience, and wounding the very soul. How is it that you have never quailed under its soul-subduing edge?

Or if you did once quail, what has enabled you to regain your self-possession? If you once trembled at the thunders of Sinai, what enables you now to walk among the most forked of its lightnings undisturbed? By what mysterious charm can you now stand unmoved, where you once exceedingly feared and quaked? At one time the voice of heaven could not speak, but a voice from within you answered; you carried about an oracle in your breast. When did you last hear its faint and dying tones? My fellow-sinner, if, in turning up the ruins of some ancient temple, you would hang with interest over the relics of the tripod, or the shrine of its long-forgotten oracle, believe me, you yourself present to the eyes of the righteous in heaven and on earth an object of intenser interest still. Pointing to your breast, they can say, "Behold the ruins of a deserted temple; here, once an oracle spake, and gave its responses as from heaven. Every word it uttered was received as the voice of God. But now long since that voice has ceased; that oracle has sunk into silence. Nothing is ever heard now, but sounds resembling the hollow and ominous echoes of the sepulchre—ominous of the eventual resurrection of the murdered dead. Yes, that violated conscience will again speak, speak in the hoarse and aggravated accents of retribution; and this will be the burden of its response to your every excuse, "much was your advantage every way—chiefly that unto you were committed the oracles of God." And the gloomy caverns of perdition, taking up the fearful burden, will tell it to all the myriads of the lost, that unto you were committed the oracles of God.

My fellow-sinner, do you wonder at the urgency of our

representations? It is because those written oracles are still addressing you, though the voice in your breast has long been silent. It is because that organ of God within you seems to be gone, that we need to call on you all the louder. It is because no human urgency can truly represent the earnestness of God—though all the voices of earth, and of ocean, and of air—of every note and every power—were all collected and condensed into one emphatic utterance of concern—on this account it is that we now so earnestly entreat you in Christ's stead, "Be ye reconciled to God."

But if you have been subdued by the voice of mercy—if there be no sounds so melting and welcome to you as those which come from the oracles of God, are you repeating them to others—republishing the truths they utter to others—anxious that your children and connexions should hear the sweet and solemn sounds—assisting to propagate them till their line shall have gone out through all the earth, and their words unto the ends of the world? Are you practically acknowledging the sufficiency of the holy oracles? When an ancient Jewish believer went up to the temple to consult the oracle, the response which he received was held decisive. Is each verse of Scripture enshrined—each sentence so enthroned in the temple of your heart, that you no sooner hear it speak than you hold it as final and decisive? Do you pay it the same homage in your public capacity as members of the church? All the plausible errors—the crude notions—the popular and spreading heresies of the day, originate in the practical denial of the sufficiency of the Scriptures—in the substitution of some human oracle in their stead. Of a certain Old Testament character we read, that "his counsel was as if a man had inquired of the oracle of God." The noisy responses of these fallible oracles drown the voice, and disparage the authority, of the Divine oracle. Let *your* appeal be to the law and to the testimony.

Do you love the place of the oracle? The Psalmist regarded the whole sanctuary as an oracle—"hear my voice," said he, "when I cry unto thee—when I lift up my hands towards thy holy oracle." To his sanctified imagination the entire temple was vocal with the responses of heaven. He had already received answers to the great questions which related to his pardon and acceptance with God. On these subjects he was himself prepared to answer the inquiries of others. But he knew that he needed to be reminded of old truths, and to be instructed in new duties. He knew that God has a will concerning our every day, and hour, and moment; and he came to ascertain that will for the present day and the passing moment. Christians, you have found acceptance with God—do you now come to the place of the oracle, saying, like the Psalmist, "I will hear what God the Lord will speak?" The age in which you live has its duties—have you ascertained them? The present day—this passing hour—has its duties—do you know them? The oracle is now saying, "Whatsoever thy hand findeth to do, do it with thy might:"—and you now find this to do—to lay an offering on the altar of God. The occasion which has brought us together renders this the duty of the moment. A regard for Christian character, and for the character of the house of God, renders this the duty of the moment. And if, when you shall have passed from the sound of the oracles of God on earth—when the last day of time, the last hour of the Christian dispensation shall have arrived—if, when only one oracle more shall remain to be given—if you would then hear that "well done, good and faithful servant," addressed to you—and hear it without shame and self-reproach—it can only be by now humbly, and in the strength of God, discharging the duty belonging to each successive hour in the vivid anticipation of that final hour.

"Now unto Him that is able to keep you from falling, and to present you faultless before the presence of His glory with exceeding joy; to the only wise God our Saviour, be glory and majesty, dominion and power, both now and ever, Amen."

SERMON X.

THE WORDS OF LIFE SPOKEN IN GOD'S TEMPLE.

ACTS v. 20.—"Go, stand and speak in the temple to the people, all the words of this life."

EVERY circumstance connected with the utterance of these words deserves attention. *Think of the time of the occurrence.* It was when the Christian Church was yet in the opening dawn of its freshness and glory. Its Divine Founder and Head had just ascended to the throne of heaven. Its Divine Endowment, the Holy Spirit of God, had just been poured out with a copiousness and a power which enriched and filled it with miraculous influence. Its teachers were prophets and apostles—men whose words were revelations, and their acts miracles. Its numbers were increased, not by units, nor by tens merely, but by hundreds and thousands in a day. Numerous as its members were, and diversified as had been their previous character and circumstances, they were now all of one heart and one mind. In the midst of persecution and danger, they knew nothing of fear; in the employment of their property, they thought of nothing but the support of their poorer brethren, and of the general good. One theme employed their tongues—salvation by the cross of Christ. One object animated and engrossed their souls—to promote the glory of that cross in the salvation of their fellow-men. One heart sent its pulsations through their whole body, diffusing life, and warmth, and spiritual vigour through every part.

Equally noticeable is *the immediate occasion of these words.* Bright as the morning of the Christian Church had arisen, and early as it yet was, a cloud had already appeared in the horizon; though it hung there only for a moment. The sin of Ananias and Sapphira—compounded of ostentation and fraud, of covetousness and impiety—had lately startled the tranquillity of the Church, and had shewn that into this new, this spiritual Eden, the ancient serpent was essaying to enter. The apparent severity of the judgment which alighted on this guilty pair was doubtless real mercy to numbers. The dead bodies of the culprits seemed to lie in the very doorway of the church, and kept back many from entering, who would otherwise have intruded from sinful motives, and by their temper and conduct have blighted the Church in the very infancy of its being. "And great fear came upon all the church, and upon as many as heard these things." *Within* the Church, all was purity, vigour, life. *Without*, all was attention and high-wrought expectation. Other wonders followed; the neighbourhood of the Church became a Bethesda, to which the sick and the dying repaired for restoration; the circle of apostolic influence was thus enlarged; "and believers were the more added unto the Lord, multitudes both of men and women."

The result, as far as their enemies were concerned, was such as might have been expected; for persecution is one of the most ancient and highly-valued ordinances of bigotry and power. "Then the high priest rose up, and all they that were with him (which is the sect of the Sadducees), and were filled with indignation; and laid their hands on the apostles, and put them into the common prison." Vain and infatuated attempt! Did they think to imprison celestial light?—to inter, as in a sepulchre, immortal life? "The angel of the Lord by night opened the prison doors, and brought them forth."

The nature of the being who uttered the text is also remarkable—it was "an angel of the Lord"—a being of an order of which we know comparatively little; but that little is of a nature to excite our curiosity and astonishment, especially as it discloses the fact that they are in some way mysteriously related to us. Here, one of them is found appropriately engaged in liberating the newly-appointed messengers of mercy from their confinement—an agent from the upper province of the kingdom of heaven, ministering to the advancement of the kingdom of heaven, as newly set up in this lower province on earth. Force has been employed to coerce the apostles; but here is an agency employed to which walls are no impediment—to which fetters and bolts can offer no resistance. The parties who have employed this force are *Sadducees*—"who say there is neither angel nor spirit;" but here, in just retribution, an angel is employed to frustrate their designs. Bringing with him the laws of his own nature, and of his own region, by a mode of action unknown to our material sphere, he made himself present in the prison, opened the doors for the exit of the apostles, and yet left them shut. This we call supernatural; to him, doubtless, it was natural—perhaps the only mode of action he had ever known. "The angel of the Lord opened the prison doors, and brought them forth, and said, Go, stand and speak unto the people, in the temple, all the words *of this life.*"

Mark the instructive *indefiniteness of their subject*, as described in the phrase, "*this life.*" This indefiniteness is a characteristic of Scripture sublimity. Such, for example, is the language of the apostle Paul, when he declares, "I know in whom I have believed"—though he does not specify *in whom;* "and I am persuaded that he is able to keep that which I have committed to him"—though he does not specify *what;* "that he is able to keep it against *that* day"—but he does not name *what day.* This is the indefiniteness of a mind so absorbed with the grand outlines of its theme, as to forget the details and particulars—of a mind so full, so overflowing with its favourite subject, so constantly dwelling on it, as to take it for granted that every one addressed is full of it likewise—that words are almost unnecessary—that mere hints are sufficient. So, here, the celestial messenger designates the Gospel by the grand generality of "*the words of this life*," or, "of *this same life*." By the phrase "*this life*," indeed, we commonly understand *the present life;* but the apostles had no controversy with the Jews about the passing affairs of this world—about the few days they were to live on earth. They were in no danger of mistaking the angel as to the nature of the life he meant. They well knew that it was this life and immortality which had been recently brought to light; this life which they had been divinely commissioned to offer to a death-stricken world—this life which they were always thinking and conversing about—this life for the preaching of which they had been cast into prison. When the angel spoke of *this life,* they well knew that he meant this peculiar life—this life, compared with which every other kind of life is only death—a life incomparably transcending every other kind of life.

And mark also where these words of life were to be proclaimed—*in the temple.* There, amidst an array of symbols, and types, and enigmatic signs, the apostles were to announce the living truth which explained and gave Divine significance to the whole. There, where the piety of the old economy had sunk into a dead formalism, and had found a grave—there the spirit of the new economy was to spring into life; and thence its life-words were to wing their way in all directions: thus fulfilling the prophecy, "Out of Zion shall go forth the law."

In these words, then, we may regard ourselves as supplied with an angel's estimate of the peculiar character and excellence of the Gospel—it is *a system of life.* Doubtless, as contemplated from different points of view, it presents different aspects; and, as regarded by different orders of beings, it exhibits various excellencies. But to the eye of that order of beings from whose ranks this angel had descended, its grand attraction appears to be that it is a life-giving system. Elsewhere, it is called "the word of *this salvation*"—of salvation, that is, *from death.* But the phrase in our text includes this idea of deliverance, and the glorious life-giving effect which follows, in addition. And it is to this aspect of Christianity, *as a principle and means of Divine life,* that I would now direct your devout attention. May the Spirit of Life himself be present in His renewing power!

I.

Now, let us inquire, first, *whence the necessity for this life?* for its introduction implies that something was previously wanting or lost which this was meant to supply; that it comes in the stead of some kind of death. And the scriptural explanation of the fact is, that there is a profound sense in which men are dead while they live; that the introduction of sin has occasioned the loss of a whole order of life from our nature. This is a kind of death which men generally do not consider. The only death they think of is that of the departure of natural life from the body. They look abroad on the world, and see everything clothed with animation, and stirred with excitement; and they cannot conceive that death, in any sense except the animal life to which I have referred, can belong to such a state. And yet a little reflection might shew them that man can die in more senses than one. The criminal who has forfeited his life to the laws of his country, is *dead legally*—incapable of any civil transaction. Question him; and you may find still further that his heart is hardened, and his conscience seared—he is lost to virtue, *morally dead.* Wait awhile; and you may hear that his mind is gone—he is *intellectually dead.* It may be years after that before his *animal* life departs. And even when that is gone, and he has become insensible, another system of life remains—that which depends on the involuntary action of the heart and the lungs—and it may be hours and even days before this last form of life becomes extinct. Now, observe, each of these kinds of life has laws of its own; and it is on the violation or cessation of these laws that its death ensues. His lowest, or mere vegetative life, is related to the air, and sustained by it. His animal life involves relations to exercise and nourishment. His intellectual life sustains relations to the various objects around him, as objects of knowledge. His social or moral life stands related to the existence and wellbeing of society. His legal life denotes his relation to the juridical and political government under which he lives. But, now, is he capable of no other, no higher form of life? Hitherto, we have spoken only of his living relations to the created, the visible, and the passing; there is the Infinite Creator, the region of the invisible, and the duration which is eternal—has he no living relation to these? For if he have—and if the importance of each kind of life is to be estimated by the nature of the objects to which it relates—his life, derived from union to the invisible and the Divine, must be incomparably his noblest and his highest life.

Need I remind you that for this life chiefly man was made and meant; a life whose highest law was that of love to God—whose motives were to be drawn from the slightest intimations of *His* will—whose supports were to come direct from intercourse with Him—whose model was no less than that of His own ineffable life—and whose ultimate home was to be in the light of His own immediate presence? Need I remind you that man has lost this life?—that by voluntary disobedience against God, he incurred the penalty of the law which had said, "the soul that sinneth it shall die"? and does not this account for that feeling of which you are often conscious—of a dignity departed—of a happiness blighted—of moral conflicts ending in defeat—and a lingering, but too faint admiration of spiritual excellence and worth? Does it not account for the consciousness you feel at times, that your conscience is dethroned, that your heart is depraved, and your nature tainted in its springs and principles? Yes, the explanation is—God's own explanation is—that you were made for a life which you are not living; that your highest order of life has been sinned away, and lost out of your nature.

Need I remind you, further, of the state of things superinduced by this absence of spiritual life, prior to the advent of Christ? True, the patriarchal and the Jewish dispensations of religion, which God had graciously set up, had partially kept the natural tendencies of sin in check. But notwithstanding this palliation, could you have taken an intelligent survey of the dark scene—could you, like some ancient prophet, have ascended the mount of vision—what would you have beheld man doing in relation to God? What mean those altars ever streaming blood—those keen self-upbraidings, those cruel self-inflictions, that offer to sacrifice even the fruit of the body for the sin of the soul? Do they not all proclaim a deep-seated sense of personal sinfulness? remorse which calls for atonement? self-dissatisfaction which can be allayed by nothing less than a new nature? Yet no worship ascends to God; His footstool is deserted; idols without number usurp His place, and intercept the homage which should ascend to His throne. Could you, further, have looked beneath the surface of society, what would you have beheld? "Their fleshly mind was darkened," saith the apostle. Their very mind had sunk into matter—had become its slave. Their flesh should have become spiritual; but their spirit instead had become fleshly. True, Greece was still possessed of intellectual life. Rome was nerved with martial and political power. But death was sapping the peculiar life of each. The earth which had proved the grave of *piety,* seemed destined to be the grave of every other kind of life. Had that other, that spiritual life, survived, it would have drawn up into its own ennobling region every lower form of life. But *that* entombed, everything else descended after it. Power, wealth, painting, poetry, music, statuary, science—all were pressed into the service of sin; made to become the ministers of the passions; and to serve at the shrines of vice—the shrines of a living death. And the race, what had become of them? Generation after generation had passed away—whither had they gone? Philosophy had watched them with dismay walking in gloomy procession to the grave, and as it saw them disappear in the land of shadows, had gazed, and strained, and tried to pierce the darkness, and learn their fate; but all in vain. "Death had passed upon all men, for that all had sinned."

Conceive, now, what an aspect of death the world must have presented to a being like the angelic agent in our text —all purity of life. Conceive him to have known the earth from the time of man's creation—to have watched its history up to the moment of which we are speaking—to have been *absorbed*—as the earth turned round its cities and nations to the light of day—*absorbed* in the spectacle of vast crowded tracts of spiritual beings—immortal essences—wasted, ruined, murdered, lost; a captive world, chained to the wheels of the great spoiler, and moving along to perdition. Conceive *him*—a being incapable of death, at the furthest remove from death, and aware that man was made for life also; conceive him to have been watching and marking, age after age, how, as God replenished the earth with human life, death had thrown a pall over each generation—had never allowed the grave to be closed—had conveyed them all away to his subterraneous caverns; conceive this, and then say, what image there is gloomy and appalling enough to set forth his view of the world's death-like condition! I know but of one; and that the Bible itself supplies, when it speaks of humanity as a corpse, lying shrouded, and with the face-cloth covering its features. "And in this mountain the Lord will remove the face of the covering cast over all people; and the veil spread over all nations; he will swallow up death in victory."

II.

This brings us to speak, secondly, of *the life which the gospel reveals, as the remedy for this state of death.* That state exhibits a threefold aspect. 1. It is *a penalty affecting our condition.* Man has placed himself, by sin, in hostility to the government of God. Banishment from the favour and presence of God is the penalty incurred. It is in perfect accordance with right, that the law should take its course, in order that holiness might be protected, sin discouraged, and the Divine determination to maintain the order of His government might be emphatically proclaimed. How, then, can He reverse the sentence, without impeaching its rectitude, and appearing to judge Himself? Come, and we will shew you a sight which has already moved all heaven, and which is destined to move all earth. We lead you to it through a long array of types and emblems, and impressive rites; these are only the august preparations for the event. Behold that cross; and know that in the person of Him who there expires, you see God manifest in the flesh. It was our only means of escape from destruction; and He voluntarily submitted to it. By stooping from His glory—assuming our nature—and suffering before the eyes of the universe all that humanity sustained by Divinity could endure, He has answered the very ends which our punishment would have secured—and more. He has more than satisfied the demands of the law; by His obedience unto death, the law is *magnified,* honoured, enthroned for eternity. God himself, as the giver of the law, can now remit its penalty without relaxing its obligations. He can say to the penitent sinner, you are free—for Christ's sake, you are free—go, and sin no more. And thus He can be just while justifying the ungodly.

2. But the deathlike state of sinful man is not merely a penalty affecting his condition, it is *a disease affecting his nature;* and the gospel remedies and replaces it with a principle of indwelling life. "I am come," said Christ, "that they may have life." "Whosoever drinketh of the water that I shall give him shall never thirst; but the water that I shall give him shall be in him a well of water springing up into everlasting life. This spake He of the Spirit which they that believe on Him should receive." By the agency of His Holy Spirit, He brings them into the presence, and

places them under the power, of His cross. "Not by might, nor by power, but by my Spirit, saith the Lord"—by my Spirit taking of the things of Christ—taking of His *voluntary obedience,* and shewing that He, though in the form of God, made himself of no reputation—assumed a dependent life expressly that He might be able to obey the very law which man had ruined himself by resisting;—taking of His *love,* and shewing how He wept, how freely He poured out *His* blood in order that the law might not take ours, might be satisfied without, might surrender us up to the pardoning mercy of God;—taking of His *mediatorial glory,* and shewing us that He is now seated upon a throne—seated there to receive our submission, to welcome our return, to place us once more in harmony with the throne of God, and to assure us of His favour. In this way, the heart is relieved of its burden, and is inspired with hope. The sensibility of the conscience is quickened, and its fears allayed. The pangs of penitence are followed by a peace which sets the mind at liberty for a career of active duty. "The hour is coming," said Christ, "and *now* is, when the dead shall hear the voice of the Son of God; and they that hear shall live." And in this way, starting from the slumbers of sin, they awake to newness of life—a resurrection to holiness. Dissevering themselves from their former bonds, they ask to be trained for every duty His service may require. In this way the Spirit of God becomes the very soul of their soul—lifting it out of its materiality, and restoring it again to its lost dominion—makes it *spirit.* Henceforth, they not only live themselves, they throw a life into all their religious activities. In the enjoyment of this new-found existence—this life from the dead—they pant after God—can be satisfied with nothing less than felt communion with Him. One of the distinctive characteristics of physical life is its power of assimilating materials to its own substance and support; and, like that, the regenerated are endowed with the power of converting the various events of time into the mysterious means of their spiritual nourishment, and even of turning obstacles into their own form and character. Conscious that they are once more breathing the only atmosphere in which the soul can truly live—in the complacent favour of God—they feel within themselves an earnest of immortality—feel that the new principle of which they have been made the subjects has nothing to fear from death—that it is made for eternity—that it is destined to spring from the bed of death to immortality. Henceforth they live; yet not they, but Christ liveth in them.

3. The death-like state of sinful man is not merely a penalty affecting his condition, and a disease affecting his nature, it is also *a fearful gloom involving his destiny.* It abandons man to mere conjecture respecting the whole futurity of his being—both as to whether he will continue in being or not; and, if so, what the character of that existence will be. All heathen philosophy halted at the grave. Jewish revelation, indeed, conducted its disciples a little beyond—into Sheol, Hades, the unknown state; but the light which it held over the sepulchre flickered. It remained for Christ to bring life and immortality to light. He may be said to have embodied the truth—to have fashioned and personified it in His own glorious body. Not only did He repeatedly raise the dead, He arose himself. Having rolled away the stone from the sepulchre of human hope, He invites us to look in; and, lo! angels in white sitting, to reassure our hope, and to point us to the skies. Having descended into the dreary domains of death, and finished His work, on the morning of the appointed day, He came forth as He had said—stood at the mouth of the sepulchre radiant with immortality, and called on the world to behold and to share in His triumph. "I am," said He, "the resurrection and the life"—the great principle of life; I *could* end the reign of death at once; I have only to speak, and all the dead would recognize My voice and start into life. "Marvel not at this; the hour is coming in which all that are in the

graves shall hear the voice of the Son of Man, and shall come forth." So certain is this, that He sometimes speaks of death in terms of disparagement, as if it were not. "Whosoever believeth in me shall never die." "If a man keep my sayings, he shall never taste of death." His eye is fixed on the scenes beyond—on the vision of dissolving elements—the rising dead—the great white throne—the opened books—the assembled universe—the completion of all His plans of mercy. Do you ask what then awaits His people? Do you feel a capacity for ever-advancing excellence—a longing for ever-increasing happiness? He declares that heaven is eternally set apart for both. There nothing that defileth can enter. There excellence will know no pause in its ascent from throne to throne—happiness no interruption to its ever-widening, deepening stream. Because He lives, His people shall live also.

Now, in this manner, Christ hath brought both the *means* of spiritual life, and the *immortality* of that life to light—brought them from an unknown distance, and placed them before us—brought heaven with all its glories into our horizon—brought the very throne of judgment so near to us, that, whenever we will, we can place ourselves before it—surrounded us with the solemn pomp and the spiritual inhabitants of the unseen world; so surrounded us that they look down on us, press in on us, that, do what we will, we feel that we are moving under the powers of the world to come. So perfectly is the Gospel—in its threefold aspect of pardon, purity, and immortal life—adapted to the death-like condition of sinful man, that no one present can reject it without wronging his own soul. Yes; his *soul.* His health may not suffer in consequence—his worldly prosperity may not decline—but his soul, the noblest part of his nature, is wronged. This whole system of Gospel-truth was meant for his soul's life—they were designed for each other; so that as long as he stands aloof from it, he is wronging his own soul. Here is the rich inheritance—his soul is the only part of him capable of enjoying it—and he is wronging the immortal heir of the immortal inheritance. And dying thus, the wrong will be irretrievable, eternal. He will ever carry about with him a wronged soul; for he will ever carry about in his soul some faculties unused—capacitles unfilled—powers undeveloped; for of the only thing which could have developed and filled them, he wronged it. The full extent of the wrong he will never know. Though his sense of the wrong will be perpetually increasing, ten thousand ages will have only partially revealed to him its untold extent. But then, in proportion to that loss, if he neglect it, is his gain if he accept and embrace it—*he finds life.* Not merely existence, but all that can enrich, expand, and make existence infinitely desirable — motives for all its actions, and objects for its noblest affections. Not merely deliverance from *death,* but its very opposite—the favour of the Lord; finds himself standing in the light of that favour, sharing it with the cherubim—sharing it with Christ himself. Finds a world in which to enjoy it; this world is too confined for it—it asks the scope of infinity for its expansion. And after the lapse of ten thousand ages he will feel as if he were only just commencing its enjoyment. It is the very *crown* of life.

Oh, with what subduing power must these living truths have fallen on the heart of those penitents who first heard them proclaimed! Had it ever been their lot to gaze on the spectacle of an ordinary crucifixion, the sight must have left an image on their minds never to be effaced. Was it possible for them, then, to behold Jesus Christ evidently set forth crucified before their eyes—to know the dignity of the sufferer as God manifest in the flesh—to know that He hates the sin as deeply as He loves the sinner—to look into the heart of this great mystery of godliness and find it to be love, without experiencing a change? If every word they hear spoken, even by a fellow man, leaves some impression on their mind—can they hear that they are *saved,* and believe that the voice which assures them of salvation is the voice of God, without feeling it thrill through every faculty of their soul? If every object and event they may witness produces *some* effect on their character, is it possible that the event which is to affect their whole being for ever—which for them shuts for ever the gates of hell, and throws open and fills with visions of glory the ample spaces of eternity—should produce only a transient and slender impression? Must they not, by necessity of nature, love Him, without whom they would soon have had nothing in the universe to love, but have been eternally hateful, even to themselves? They wait not for a reply; they need not a command. They are under the mastery of a principle which is its own law—a principle of boundless gratitude and love.

And you know the happy result. The new Church became one region of life—of Divine vitality throughout. Believers themselves seemed reconverted. If sinners became saints, saints themselves became as angels; thus fulfilling the prophecy which had said, "The weak shall be as David, and David as an angel of the Lord." Every Christian beheld in every other the face of a brother. One interest prevailed, one subject of emulation swallowed up every other—who should approach nearest to the likeness of Christ—which should do most for the enlargement of His reign. Even death for them was divested of all its terror. The rack, the axe, the cross—none of these things moved *them*. What had *they* to do with death? If persecution *would* have their body, the soul surrendered it, left it behind, dropped it in the grave, and passed right on to immortality. What to them was the loss of this world, they lived within sight of heaven. "Absent from the body, present with the Lord"—this was the primary article of their martyr-creed. They felt that their noblest life was "hid with Christ in God"—was seated high up, beyond the reach of harm, in the very fountain and summit of creation. At thought of this the instruments of torture became consecrated in their eyes—glowed with a glory reflected from His throne—the very flames were chariots of fire to convey them in triumph to their appointed seats. In a word, they thus judged, that "if one died for all, then were all dead, and that he died for all, that they which live should not henceforth live unto themselves, but unto him which died for them, and rose again." Religion with them was *a life.*

III.

Let me glance, thirdly, at *some of the attributes of this life,* and we shall see the pernicious errors entertained respecting it. If the view we have taken of *this life* which the apostles were to preach be correct, it needed no prophet to foresee and foretell that it would not be long before attempts would be made to modify and corrupt it. Such had been the history of every religion; so that even every false religion had soon lost the modicum of truth which it at first contained; and as for the true religion itself, that had become so stagnant and corrupt, that it bred nothing but Pharisees and Sadducees, and swarms of sanctimonious hypocrites. But if such had been the fate of Judaism, still more likely was it that Christianity should encounter the hostility of human ignorance, selfishness, and pride; for against every form of these it proclaims open war.

1. Like the principle of natural life, *this new evangelical life is first a divinely-derived and invisible power.* But will the world be satisfied with a thing so secret, subtle, intangible as this? They who experience it, indeed, will be satisfied with its silent indwelling power. But in proportion as the world tampers with it, it will be transformed into a worldly thing—a material, gaudy, temporal thing. If this cross can be gilded over—these thorns can be hid in jewels—this broken reed become a sceptre—they may be retained; but if not, persecution will do its utmost to chase the Gospel from the earth. You know the result. It was only the history of Judaism over again; rather, it was that

history repeated, and abundantly surpassed. The Jews were only *looking* for a temporal kingdom when Messiah came; the Christians, falsely so called, actually founded one. Yes, that which the Jews had only indulged in as a vision, and which our Lord had denounced as entirely subversive of His claims, His professed followers actually laboured at and realized. There it arose, ranged in hierarchical order, gradation above gradation, a towering structure of political grandeur, a living pyramid, whose summit was crowned with the throne of one invested with universal supremacy, and at whose base was stretched out, in glorious perspective, the kneeling and admiring homage of the world.

Now, here was *temporal* dominion—*political* life; but, oh, how different from *that Divine life* which the apostles had proclaimed! so different that that life was displaced and destroyed by it. True, the living power which the Gospel sets up is not inimical to human governments; it pre-supposes them—tends to invigorate them—arms their sanctions with additional power. But all this it does indirectly; and only as the effect of what it does primarily and directly to the individual man. True, this living and transforming power is itself a kingdom; but "my kingdom," said its Heavenly Founder, "is not of this world." It came down complete from heaven, and conducts thither again. It does not contemplate man specifically in his national, secular, or artificial relations, but in his moral and spiritual capacity. Primarily, it does not deal with men collectively; it individualizes; lays its arresting hand on the individual conscience; leads the man apart; causes him to feel that heavenly, like earthly, life is a personal affair. It proposes to form him into a subject, and to secure his allegiance by laws and influences unknown to the resources of worldly powers, and mysterious as the operation of the wind—an agency derived direct from heaven. True, it is a kingdom; but "the kingdom of God cometh not with observation." Its basis was laid in an ignominious cross; and all its subjects enter it in tears—the tears of "repentance *unto life.*" Unlike the dominions of the kings of the earth, it knows nothing of territorial divisions and geographical bounds. "That which is born of the Spirit is *spirit,*" and belongs to His domains. So much of the man as is sanctified belongs to this state, and no more; and only so much of society as is reclaimed to holiness comes within its spiritual scope and verge. The lengths and breadths of Immanuel's land are not capable of being mapped; it is a region too ethereal to be subjected to the lines of latitude and longitude; it is commensurate with actual faith and actual holiness, *and knows no limit but where these terminate.* "Whereunto," said Christ, "shall I liken the kingdom of God, and with what comparison shall I compare it?" None of the governments of this world supplied Him with an analogy. He who is the wisdom of God seemed embarrassed as He looked around the world of civil society for a similitude, and saw that it contained none. The illustration which He sought for He found in the principle of vegetable life—in the silent and unobtrusive growth of the mustard seed to a tree. So the seed of spiritual life deposited in the heart germinates, and brings forth the fruits of righteousness, and is destined to fill the world with its fragrance and its fruits.

2. Again; like the principle of physical life, this divinely-derived and invisible power *is internal and pervading.* Then it is not a *ritual.* Life operates from within, outwards. And "the kingdom of God is *within you,*" saith Christ. When He came upon earth, He found it made up of mere outward acts and ceremonial observances. And there, in that temple which had become the tomb of piety—where every object had become an idol, and every exercise an act of hypocrisy—*there* His apostles were commanded to go, and to proclaim "the words of this life." They were to pass from the elaborate and pompous ritual of Judaism to the severe simplicity of spiritual worship. They were to leave the rites, to find themselves standing in the presence of

God. They were to emerge from the cloud of incense, to find themselves alone with the Great Spirit of the new dispensation. Henceforth they were to serve at an altar on which nothing was to be laid but "spiritual sacrifices." And, as if to make it impossible for His followers ever to substitute ceremonial worship for spiritual, He swept away every vestige of the ancient rites, and the only symbolic services He introduced instead were two of the simplest kind—while any additions to them were forbidden at the awful peril of His displeasure. And yet who does not know that out of these two there came to be constructed a whole system of ceremonial observances, and that others were added to them from time to time, till the preaching of the words of this life came to be silenced—the book containing the words came to be lost—and religion, instead of being a life, came to be a prolonged ceremony? What is it even now that passes generally for the Christian life? What but an elaborate accumulation of penances and mortifications, of splendid sights and melodious sounds, of fasts and festivals, a constantly recurring round of outward observances? As if aware that they have no more of religion than the lifeless form—the body from which the spirit has fled—men have endeavoured to conceal its death-like features by overlaying it with a profusion of costly decorations. Even among those who profess to have adopted a purer form, is there not a constant effort made to substitute something outward for this inward life? One relies chiefly on his belonging to a certain Christian community—another on his descent from a pious ancestry—a third on his unfailing attendance at the house of God—a fourth on his occasional activity and liberality in the outward service of God—a fifth supposes himself to have been actually regenerated in baptism; and a sixth, that in eating the sacramental bread he is literally eating the flesh of Christ—incorporating the Saviour's body with his own body—as if that could save his soul. Alas, the perverse ingenuity, the indomitable perseverance of men, to substitute anything, everything, in the stead of an inward spiritual life. Oh, it is so much more easy to endure even bodily torture than to bend the will; there is so much in the idea of personal merit to sustain the endurance of physical suffering; and so much food for complacency afterwards in the review, that it would be only necessary for the Gospel to proclaim its acceptance of outward rites, penances, tortures, in the stead of spiritual religion, in order to enrol among its followers multitudes who now stand aloof from it in aversion and despair.

But no, religion is an inward life. It is the restoration of a lost life, or it is nothing. Having wandered from God, we are accounted dead, in the highest sense, till we are again restored to Him — destitute of that highest order of life which originally pervaded our faculties, and was diffused through our nature. And the great object of Christ was to remove every impediment to the recovery of this lost life, and to aid us in its exercise. "This is the record, that God hath given to us eternal life, and this life is in his Son." "He that hath the Son hath life"—and He only hath life. And in order to this, "Verily I say unto you, ye must be born again." If you would "worship God in the spirit," you must be "born of the Spirit." "The Father seeketh such to worship him"—He looks around for them. When you come into His courts, He looks for an assembly of human hearts — of naked human hearts — and when He beholds them engaged, delighted, absorbed in His worship, He contemplates an object far more acceptable than the flaming sacrifice of the whole material world. Brethren, if the Spirit has put forth *His* power to renew you, so *your* spirit is to put forth a corresponding power in earnest endeavours after holiness, and to be ever aiming at an expansion and increase of that life till mortality itself shall be swallowed up of life.

3. Again; like physical life, this spiritual and pervading principle *is active and practical.* Then it is not *a creed*

merely. True, it begins in faith, and is maintained by it. "He that *believeth* hath the witness in himself." "And the life which I live," said the apostle, "I live by the *faith* of the Son of God." But the prevailing error lies in making the reception of a certain form of truth an end, instead of regarding it as a means to an end. *Not* to subscribe to certain truths would be thought highly blameworthy; but to do anything more than subscribe to them is very generally deemed quite unnecessary. Not to hold the doctrine of justification by faith alone, would be denounced as heterodox; but to be actually looking to *Him* who is the object of that justifying faith, trusting in Him, loving Him, rejoicing in Him—this would be deemed by the same parties fanatical, so that the adoption of the right views respecting justification actually becomes an impediment to their looking to *Him* through whom alone the justification comes. Not to admit the claims which Christ has upon them, they would deem impious; practically to yield themselves up to those claims is a thing they leave to enthusiasts—as if the admission of a debt were a full discharge from the payment of it. Not to hold an orthodox creed would, in their eyes, be unchristian; to think of acting out that creed they would account irrational. And how is all this soul-destroying inconsistency to be explained, except by their willing ignorance of the fact that religion *is an active and a practical life?* The faith from which it springs is not inactive and unproductive; it works and works by love, and shews its existence by its works. It can neither live without food, nor be satisfied with merely looking at food; it hungers and thirsts after righteousness—cannot breathe the impure and polluted atmosphere of sin—carries up the soul into a purer region, where it can draw congenial breath. It yields the fruits of the Spirit, brings forth the fruits of righteousness which are by Jesus Christ unto the praise and glory of God.

4. And, then, like physical life, this Divine, internal, active

principle is *continuous*. Then it is not merely a single act, an occasional impulse, an abrupt gush of feeling, a passing resolution. It is a growth from a heaven-implanted seed—a growth in which there is, "first, the blade, then the ear; and after that, the full corn in the ear." In opposition to this, how generally do men regard salvation as a mere outward deliverance, and as, therefore, consisting of a single act. They profess to be infinitely indebted to Christ; for they suppose Him to have done everything for them in such a sense, that now they have only to give their consent in order to be taken to heaven—forgetting that before He can be said to have done anything for them personally, He must actually commence a renewing, life-giving process within them. They estimate their deliverance from hell as from a place of outward torment merely—forgetting that sin has created a hell within them, that an angry and polluted conscience is a worm which dieth not, and that unsubdued propensities to sin are fires which, if now left unquenched, will continue to burn on for ever. And, in the same way, they are accustomed to anticipate heaven as a mere spectacle of splendour, an elysium in which they are to find happiness prepared and awaiting their arrival, whatever the state in which they may reach it. They entirely lose sight of the fact, that their present character is creating their future destiny; that their principles and actions, preceding their own departure, have already arrived in eternity, and are there preparing for them a place of reception.

Oh, what would that kingdom, of which Christ is the author and glory, have become, had it been left to be moulded by the hands of man! It would have been made to consist of mere occasional acts and outward observances, and those of the most trivial description; whereas it is composed "of righteousness, and peace, and joy in the Holy Ghost!" Never, never let us forget that the happiness of heaven will result chiefly from its holiness; that, so far, heaven commences with the believer here on earth;

that, when he leaves the world, he takes the elements of heavenly happiness with him ; that the ultimate glorification of the saints will be only the last step of a previous course, the culminating point of a process which transformed them while they were here below ; so that it is only by entering on the way of life now, that we can enter on eternal life hereafter.

IV.

Now, fourthly, it is the duty and office of the ministers of the Gospel to proclaim "the words of this life." This they are *commanded to do* by more than angelic authority—by the Lord of Angels himself. As to the *manner* in which they are to do it—"Say to them, saith God, As I live, saith the Lord God, I have no pleasure in the death of the wicked, but that the wicked turn from his way and live. Turn ye, turn ye, for why will ye die?" Earnestly, as if speaking on oath—solemnly, as if entrusted with the oath of God, they are to set before the people life and death. Neglecting to do this, they are *threatened* that the blood of lost souls shall be required at their hands. In the *discharge* of their duty, they are assured of Divine assistance. If the aid of Heaven were withheld from every other being, it should yet be accorded to *them;* for the world is continued only to await the result, and to reap the fruit of their labours. They are *urged and animated* to fidelity and perseverance by the prospect of high reward; for they are given to understand that "he who converteth a sinner from the error of his ways, saves a soul from death, and hides a multitude of sins;" and that "they who turn many to righteousness shall shine forth as the stars for ever and ever." They are assured of the Divine complacency in their labours, even though they fail of success. For "we are a sweet savour of Christ, in them that are saved, and in them that perish; to the one we are the savour of death unto death; to the other the savour of life unto life." To *Him* our ministry is as acceptable as the perpetual ascent of sacrificial incense.

Now, it is to the exercise of this ministry that this house of God has been set apart;—to "the words of this life" these walls resound. True, no splendid temple-service here meets the eye, as it met that of the apostles, testifying and illustrating the truths they proclaimed. But what though no altar of sacrifice here streams with blood? "We have an altar," says the apostle—an altar invisible to sense, and on that altar there is a victim—"the Lamb of God that taketh away the sin of the world." "*God* hath set him forth as a propitiation for sin through faith in his blood." What though no *ark* of the covenant appears here? The *covenant* itself we have. What means this sacred volume? "All that the ark did once contain could no such grace afford." "This is the *new* covenant," saith Christ — "the new covenant in my blood"—the covenant of life; every page of it proclaims, "Hear, and your soul shall live." We know of no mysterious veil to conceal the mercy-seat; we have access into the holiest of all. The only veil we know of is that which separates earth from heaven; and as to our High Priest, He has passed within that veil. He is gone into heaven itself, now to appear in the presence of God for us. Everything valuable in the former economy here finds accomplishment, stability, and perfection. Religion, disencumbered of its body, comes to us as *spirit and life.* He whom we preach is "the way, the truth, and *the life!*" And God forbid that these walls should ever echo to any other theme than that of eternal life through the mediation of Christ.

In this way the ancient temple itself may be regarded as still standing, and its solemn services as still proceeding. Here, in the preaching of the Gospel, its fires still burn—its victims bleed—its day of atonement still returns. Here its prophets repeat their sacred strains, testifying of the sufferings of Christ, and the glory that should follow; and its priests typify "the offering of the body of Christ once for all." And here, too, exalted beings, of the order brought before us in the text, come, as to a point of friendly communication established between earth and heaven—come to rejoice over the returning and repenting sinner. As a house of God, all the influences of the past come and gather around it, and settle down upon it; while, for the future, heaven is awake with expectation—a page is newly opened for it in the Book of the Divine remembrance—from this day its history begins for eternity; for it is a part of that vast combination of means by which God is reducing and restoring all things unto Himself.

V.

Let me remind you, once more, that there ought to be a correspondence between what the Gospel is in itself and the manner in which we attend to the preaching of it. Does it consist of the words of life? Oh, if you duly apprehended it in this light, with what seriousness, what searchings of heart, what deep workings of spirit would you attend to it? If you apprehended it in this light, with what point and pungency would its appeals come home to your consciences; with what commanding power would its precepts bind themselves down upon your hearts; with what a melting influence would its doctrines and gracious promises penetrate your souls; with what lifegiving effect would you listen to it! Ask yourselves, then, whether you have ever attended on the Gospel as containing the words of life? Ask yourselves, Have I got *life* by it? Did it ever enter into *my* heart as the means of life? Did I ever so much as *design*, *expect*, or *wish*, that it should?

And if you have not, how much to be deplored is your case! Week after week, and year after year, the words of life have been breathed forth in your hearing—and others have been quickened by them—but as for you, if you utter the language of truth, you may say, my heart is still dead towards God—no words that I have heard have awakened my heart—have purified, melted, taken possession of my heart. Dead I was in trespasses in sins, and dead I remain, notwithstanding all the words of life which I have heard.

But why, why will you remain dead? "The words that I speak unto you," saith Christ, "they are spirit and they are life." You have never heard the Gospel preached but He was passing by to do you good; why did you not call upon Him to give life? No, never have you heard His Gospel preached but He was standing at the door of your heart and knocking; why did you not open to admit Him that you might have life? You are listening to His Gospel now, and He is waiting to make it the power of God for your salvation; why will you not breathe forth the prayer, "O make these words beget life in me—let them transmit life into the very centre of my being, and make my soul live?"

Could I have come to you this morning with the proofs that an angel had bid me to say all this—that the bright and happy being who directed the apostles to preach in the temple had directed me to address you as I have done—would not a very solemn interest have invested the occasion? Brethren, the Lord of Life himself directs it, and is present to witness the result. What, more can I say to affect and to impress? Shall I remind you that you are passing through the very valley of the shadow of death? Ought not the very *name* of *life* to be pleasant and welcome to you? Oh then admit, draw in, as vital breath, the words of this life; words so lifegiving, that even the Being in this text—a Being who is emphatically "a living creature"—a creature all life, the inhabitant of a region all life—yet calls them "words of life." Here is a life which death cannot touch—a life which shall finally prove victorious over every form of death—a life which rises and rises till it emerges into a sphere where no death can come—where its shadow never falls—a sphere full of vitality and eternal life. "Come from the four winds, O breath, and breathe upon these slain, that they may live."

Finally, what manner of persons ought *we* to be who profess to be partakers of this life? In reply to this question, I might ask another—

1. What manner of persons were its first recipients; and yet what had the Saviour done for them which He has not done for us? They did not hope for more than eternal life; we do not hope for less. Yet so mightily did this hope animate them, that their piety was all flame—a flame in which they were ready to offer up everything earthly, even life itself, as a sacrifice.

2. I might remind you further of what its early recipients actually *endured* in order to transmit to you "the words of this life." In almost every age the Gospel has been sprinkled with blood—baptized with fire. Its original propagators endured imprisonments and deaths oft in preserving it. It has come down to us through ages of persecution and sorrow. It has been committed to our keeping by a hand stretched out of the midst of the fires. It has been sent to us from the dungeon—bequeathed to us from the rack. It is the precious legacy of a host of martyred saints. And shall *we* not shew the living power of that for which they died?

3. But let me especially remind each Christian present, that he has been called forth from more than an earthly prison—liberated by more than angelic interference—experienced a rescue to which the universe can never know a parallel. "What, know ye not that ye are the temple of the Holy Ghost which is in you—which ye have of God—and ye are not your own—for ye are bought with a price—therefore glorify God in your bodies and spirits which are his." Glorify him—the apostles were set at liberty to proclaim His Gospel. The salvation of that Gospel was meant to set every part of your nature at liberty to glorify Him. And, oh, as if your redemption had just been accomplished by the Son of God, and as if you had been actually recalled from the dark prisonhouse of perdition, we beseech you—by His baptism, fasting, and temptation—by His agony and

bloody sweat—by His cross and passion—by His precious death and burial—by His glorious resurrection and ascension—by the bitter pains of eternal death from which He has redeemed you—by "the words of *this life*," to which He hath raised you—by the radiance of that throne to which He is leading you—and that crown of life which there awaits you—we beseech you, brethren, that ye now present yourselves to God a *living* sacrifice.

4. And, then, is it nothing to know that the cause you are called on to serve is one destined to absorb every other, and to achieve universal triumph? As certainly as the prison opened its bolts and bars for the apostles to walk forth, every obstacle to the progress of His Gospel shall fall prostrate and do it homage. As surely as an angel ministered to their escape, so surely shall the highest agencies in the universe unite in His service. Alas, that the agency of His people should be so grudgingly given. Time was, when the *followers* of Christ were liable to the prison and the stake—but then "the *Word of God* was not bound"—the living Spirit of the Gospel was unimprisoned and at large. Now, on the other hand, His followers are at large, but *the Life of Christianity*—is not that imprisoned? And who are its jailers? Who or what but the selfishness and the worldliness of its professed friends? But even this is destined to yield. Happy they who shall witness the change. But happier still are they who contribute to hasten its arrival;—who uninfluenced by the spiritless example of others—and without waiting to be dragooned into duty—simply ask themselves, "How much owest thou unto thy Lord?" and live to express their sense of the magnitude of the obligation.

SERMON XI.

THE CHRISTIAN MINISTRY.

2 Tim. iii. 16, 17.—"All scripture is given by inspiration of God, and is profitable for doctrine, for reproof, for correction, for instruction in righteousness; that the man of God may be perfect, throughly furnished unto all good works."

If the ultimate design of Christ, in the institution of a Church, be the conversion of the world—and if the preaching of the Gospel be the chief instrument by which the Church is to answer that end—how important to determine the characteristics of the most efficient ministry, and the way in which the Church may obtain it.

Now, it would be extremely easy to describe such a ministry; for it would be only necessary to enumerate the attributes of ministerial perfection, and then to suppose them all combined in real forms of living and personal activity. And we have no doubt that many a Christian congregation has listened to such a description of ministerial excellence till they have been conscious of feelings, which, if translated into language, would have said, "Oh, for such a ministry!—would that such were the qualifications of *our* minister—how different a people should we then be!" And this latter part of the ejaculation, if explained, would *often* have proved to mean, "We should prosper then without any trouble on our part—our minister would do, and would be, everything for us—we should enjoy the distinction arising from *his* excellence, without having to cultivate corresponding qualities for ourselves." Now, to shew that this *is* the correct interpretation of many such a wish, we think it only necessary to suggest, that could the persons entertaining it have seen at the moment, as by a flash of light, that every approach to official perfection on the part of the minister would involve the necessity of a corresponding advance in practical piety on their part—that if *he* became all that they could desire, it implied a readiness and an obligation on their part to become all that *he* could desire—not merely liberal, but self-denying; not merely active, but laborious; not merely professing, but possessing and exemplifying the distinguished piety and devotedness of apostolic times—could they have seen that all this would have been indispensable on *their* part, we can easily conceive, without any painful effort of the imagination, how the ardour of their desire for an efficient ministry would have died away into a very languid sigh—and that, if such were the hard condition on which alone they could obtain it, they would readily signify their willingness to languish on together, people and priest alike inefficient. We propose, then, not so much to enumerate the characteristics of an efficient ministry, as to shew why such characteristics are necessary; and that on the Church it devolves, under God, to cultivate and maintain such a ministry.

I.

To say that *piety* is necessary for the Christian minister is saying but little—it is indispensable even for the private Christian. *Every* believer is a living temple, and what is a temple without piety? Gratitude must bring its oblations—love must kindle and feed its altar fires—and penitence come with its sacrifice—and faith present it—and holiness guard and consecrate the whole for God. But there is a sense in which not only the *individual* Christian, but each particular church, is a living temple—and the office of the minister is to conduct its worship. If piety was essential for him as a private Christian, from the moment he comes forward to conduct the services of this whole collective temple, *eminent* piety is indispensable. He is emphatically "a man of God"—

virtually commissioned, like an ancient prophet, to transact with the people the affairs of heaven; can he form too high an estimate of the duties of his office? He is an ambassador for Christ to the guilty and the perishing; how necessary that he should be baptized in the very spirit of compassion and love. He knows the fearful consequences of the state into which they have sunk; and, as if he foresaw the end of their course—heard already their doom pronounced—beheld the pit opening to receive them—and heard, by anticipation, their hopeless cries for deliverance, he is to evince the deepest tenderness and the most earnest solicitude "to pluck the firebrands from the flames," and to quench them in the blood of the cross. He is to feed the Church of God which He hath purchased with His own blood; how important that he should relish and feast on the manna which he distributes to others—that he should be able to say with a spiritual gust which marks his own intense enjoyment, "His flesh is meat indeed! His blood is drink indeed!" What a depth of solemnity may we suppose to have rested on the mind of the high priest on the morning of the great day of atonement—how weighty the interests pressing upon him—how holy and awful the act of entering within the veil to officiate there in the immediate presence of God! As the official intercessor for His Church upon earth, the Christian minister has, in effect, to do this weekly—daily; how important that he should be able to say, "Truly our fellowship is with the Father, and with his Son Jesus Christ!" His sacred duties are of regular and constant recurrence—what but eminent piety can save him from sinking into formality—from discharging them with that cold, professional indifference which is the certain death of all usefulness—can impart that spiritual freshness of fervour essential to his own enjoyment, and to excite and secure the sympathy of others? While the private Christian is expected to be an example to the world, *he* is to be "an example to his flock"—a model among models. His central station and official character invest him with influences which must render his every movement an object of interest to superior beings, for they deeply implicate the everlasting welfare of all around him; how important that the whole of that influence should be eminently holy; and how can that be but by issuing from a character eminently pious?

2. But essential as distinguished piety is, it is not all-sufficient—otherwise, every good man would be eligible to the ministry. We remark, next, that an efficient ministry must be a *learned* ministry—or, if you please, an *educated* ministry. We are aware, indeed, that against this position there are numerous prejudices—prejudices, however, which have nothing respectable in them except their antiquity; but, long-cherished as they have been, we trust that their days are nearly numbered. Meanwhile, it would be easy to shew that most of these prejudices originate in ignorance; and thus furnish in themselves the most apposite proof of the value of education, since a very little instruction is commonly found sufficient to put them all to flight.

"God," says an objector to an educated ministry—"God has greatly blessed the preaching of many uneducated ministers." We gratefully admit it. He did not bless them, however, on *account* of their ignorance, but *in spite* of it. It was not their ignorance He blessed, but certain other qualities which are common alike to the educated and the uneducated minister if they are men of God—zealous devotedness, and believing prayer for the influence of the Holy Spirit. Besides which, we would suggest to the objector whether the class referred to did not consist of men who had never enjoyed the opportunity of obtaining an education? For we would remind him that it seems to be a rule of the Divine conduct to require from His people the very best instrumentality they can furnish—as He required the best animal of the flock for sacrifice—and therefore to accept the service of the ignorant, and to bless the zeal of the obscurest, as long as it is the best. But from the moment they possess the means of improving it, that improvement He requires; nor are they then warranted to expect His blessing till that improvement has been effected.

"But," continues the objector, "the efficacy of the ministry depends on the influence of the Spirit, and that influence is not limited by the quality of the means." The former part of this proposition we not only admit but contend for. The latter part may contain an error; and, in the sense in which you employ it, we suspect that it does. If you only intend that the operations of the Holy Spirit are *originally* independent of all human instrumentality, we freely admit it. But if you mean to say that they are still as unconnected with that instrumentality as ever—that His plan of operation does not include that instrumentality—that He has no preference for one kind of instrumentality above another—that He has not been pleased to bring himself under the gracious obligation of a promise to connect His blessing with the use of certain means—and your language goes to imply all this—then we demur to it, and deny it. You mean to say that He *can* give success to the most ignorant ministry. Yes; but you surely will not add that therefore He *will*—that He will make His *power* the rule of His conduct. He *could* teach His servants the knowledge of the alphabet; but you would not have had your minister wait till that knowledge was supernaturally imparted to Him; nor, we presume, do you deem that knowledge a very superfluous attainment. He *can* make the naked rock or the sea-shore sand spontaneously yield corn; but, we presume, you look for it rather in the adjoining field; nor do you expect to find it even there without cultivation. You do not make what He *can* do the rule of what He *will* do in any other department of the Divine conduct—why do you look for it here? Because He has condescended to bless the humble and pious ministry of the uneducated when learning could not be had, you surely will not try to take advantage of His goodness, and to put Him off with ignorance when knowledge *can* be obtained. Because

He graciously accepted the torn and the lame of your flock when it contained nothing better, you surely will not try to make Him serve with the same now that it contains the young and the healthy. Above all, you surely do not do this under the pretence of honouring God. You do not expect that He will distinguish you in the last day as having pre-eminently proved your concern for the progress of His Gospel, by having been pre-eminently unconcerned about the qualifications of the instruments you employed.

Do not practise on yourself another deception—that God has put greater honour on the pious instrumentality of the uneducated than on the equally pious instrumentality of the educated. To say nothing of Moses—"God's first pen," as Lord Bacon calls him—learned in all the wisdom of the Egyptians—think of the success which attended the ministry of the apostles; and they, you will remember, were made learned by miracle—nor was their ministry allowed to begin till their illiteracy had been thus miraculously surmounted; while the most useful among them—he who laboured more than they all, and who filled the Roman empire with the sound of salvation, was he who had been brought up at the feet of Gamaliel—the scholar and philosopher Paul. With what signal effect the weapon of sanctified learning may be wielded, the history of the Reformation attests. "If we lose the learned languages by neglect," said Luther, "we shall lose the Gospel." "An unlearned theology," said Melancthon, "is an Iliad of evils;" a sentiment often reiterated by Calvin also. Among the greatest men of modern days are our Christian missionaries; and among these, perhaps, the most useful are the most learned—the translators of the Bible into other tongues—men who thus partake of the dignity of prophets and apostles—the benefactors of nations—whose memory will be illuminated for ever with the radiance which they are means of shedding over myriads of benighted minds.

And, after all, remember that the most uneducated minister of the present day is largely indebted to the learned labours of his predecessors. However slender his mental resources may be, he obtains them only by availing himself of the toils of others. If he can only just read his Bible, and some favourite religious author, he is enjoying the results of learning—of prodigious labour and abundant learning. Think what has been necessary in order to put that translation of the Bible into his hands—what studying of languages, collating of manuscripts, recension of copies—what years of persevering application! So that he is living on the learning and labour of others! Surely, it is not for him to decry education—for the drone to depreciate the process by which the truth, sweeter than honey or the honey-comb, has been hived and made ready for his use.

But still the objector may urge, "the text intimates that a knowledge of the Bible alone is sufficient to furnish the man of God for his office." We say the same—but then comes the question, What is to be the amount of that Scriptural knowledge, and how is it to be acquired? You say, "the Bible, and nothing but the Bible;" and so say we—but with this important addition, "the Bible, *the whole Bible*, and then nothing but the Bible;" whereas we fear that you are disposed to be content with much less than the Bible—with a very small portion of it—that is to say, with two or three of its leading truths. And to this remark it would be out of place for you here to reply, that the knowledge of these leading truths is all that is necessary to salvation—for then, to be consistent, you should discard all the Old Testament and indeed the greater part of the New; because many have been saved without them. It is not for us to say how little sanctified knowledge may be sufficient for salvation—and yet you seem disposed to make the dangerous experiment. But while God, on the one hand, is graciously pleased, in certain circumstances, to render the minimum of that knowledge sufficient, His people, on the other, should be ever aiming to reach the maximum—to acquire the utmost amount of Scriptural knowledge. Now all the education we advocate for "the man of God" is such, and such only, as can be made subservient to his office as an expositor of the Bible, either by strengthening and preparing his mind as the instrument to be employed on it, or by furnishing him with the means of developing and illustrating its truths. In a word, we are anxious to put all the honour on the Bible we can—to extract from it, if possible, all that it contains—to make the most of it as God's instrument for the salvation of the world.

For instance, Timothy "knew the Scriptures"—he knew the Old Testament, most likely, in what we now term the original language; and he knew as much of the New Testament as was then written, in *its* original language—that probably was his mother tongue. So that in claiming for "the man of God" now a knowledge of these ancient languages, we are only aiming to place him, in relation to the Bible, as nearly as possible, on a footing with the youthful Timothy. Besides, there are beauties in every language not to be transferred, and idioms which cannot be translated into any other tongue—would it not be putting dishonour upon the Bible to allow its sacred beauties and idioms to lie neglected, simply to escape the trouble of acquiring the languages in which it is written? Is it anything more than an act of ordinary propriety for the professed expounder of that sacred volume to spare no labour in order to make himself acquainted with all that it contains? Then must he be able to read it in its original tongues.

But this is not all that is necessary. We believe that all knowledge is one—all truth one connected, entire, infinite idea—and though God has been pleased, in condescension to our limited capacity, to break down that great idea into parts, and to present us with such views of those parts as best suit our condition, yet we believe all those parts have points of connexion, and that he who, in a spirit of dependence on Divine teaching, most patiently studies them, is most likely to perceive that connexion and unity—that every such perception will constrain him to admire "the depth of the riches both of the wisdom and knowledge of God"—and will enable him to present the truth in a compacted, convincing, comprehensive, and impressive form to others. Hence, partly, we advocate a course of mathematical training as highly conducive to habits of patient, connected, mental application.

We believe that all nature is in analogy to religion—that the works of God in creation and providence are His own connected comment on His Word. What an important use has Butler made of this idea in his well known "Analogy!" And we believe that hereafter it will be seen that the universe was only a vast temple, with the cross standing in the centre, while every object and event was related and subordinated to it—that it never moved but all things fell into its train—never stood but they all bowed down before it—never spoke but they all echoed its voice—and that the sight, when beheld in the light of eternity, will fill all heaven with adoration. But we would have the preacher of the cross to see something of it now—and hence we would have him to be generally acquainted with natural and moral philosophy, in order that he might feel the eminence on which he stands, and be conscious, as he looks down and marks how all things do homage to Christianity, of adoration now.

The Bible insists on the doctrine of human depravity. The history of the ancient world is an unbroken record of facts illustrative of this doctrine. An acquaintance with that history gives a depth to the meaning of the apostle in that sketch of the monster-man contained in his first chapter to the Romans, which no one ignorant of ancient history can ever perceive—shews that so far from being able to ameliorate our moral condition, our invariable tendency is to become worse and worse—that the highest point of the world's civilization was the lowest point of its morality—that, so far from reason or philosophy leading men to God, the religion which it has constructed and decorated for them has uniformly proved their greatest curse—that the advent of Christ was as necessary to save the world from temporal as from eternal ruin. Hence, partly, shall all this remain unknown to the man of God? If not, we claim for the man of God a knowledge of ancient history.

The Bible abounds with prophecies relative to the ancient monarchies and to the Church of God. These prophecies were recorded of course, that when they came to pass we might believe. Many of them have come to pass; and the question is, shall their fulfilment be known? Shall this part of the temple of truth be shut up and useless, or shall it be opened, admired, and worshipped in? Here is an important branch of evidence for the truth of Divine revelation—shall it lie waste and useless? shall God have spoken in vain? or shall His voice be heard? But if "the man of God" *is* to hear it, he must know something of ancient and modern history, that, by comparing the prophecy with the history, he may perceive its completion. Hence, again, the importance of secular history.

The Church of God has a history of its own. That part of it recorded in the Bible is written for our instruction. But its history did not end with what is there written; it is replete with interest and instruction down to the present moment. Shall the past errors of the Church afford no warning?—shall its sins and apostasies excite no penitence?—its Divine preservation amidst persecution no gratitude?—its gradual corruption no illustration of the New Testament prophecies concerning the man of sin? Shall its reformation excite no sense of obligation?—nor the Divine interpositions for its deliverance, its purification, and enlargement, no trust and zeal for the future? But all this supposes a knowledge of *ecclesiastical* history.

Owing to the influence of vicious causes some men are led to question the claims of the Bible. God has graciously supplied a variety of evidence expressly adapted for the conviction of such men, as well as for the confirmation of our own faith—evidence arising from prophetic, miraculous, moral, and historical sources. But this very evidence may be so exhibited, and often has been, as to excite their ridicule and confirm their unbelief. Is it not important that those who profess to exhibit and enforce it should themselves see its connexion, feel its convincing reasonableness, and be acquainted with the most useful modes of its application? Hence, we claim for "the man of God," who is placed, among other things, for the *defence* of the Gospel, an acquaintance with the philosophy of evidence.

Enough has been said, we trust, to shew that a ministry, to be efficient, must be educated—and that our great reason for advocating a liberal education is with a view to the increase of that ministerial efficiency. And, after all, what is it but saying that ignorance is imperfection; and that, in the case of the "man of God," we are anxious to lessen that imperfection as much as possible? What is it but saying that as sin is the parent of voluntary ignorance, and as the Gospel is the great remedy for sin, we believe that it was meant to remedy ignorance as well as every other effect of sin; and that we are anxious that the "man of God" should be an instance of its remedial influence in this as in every other respect. What is it but saying that, if there is something of God in every object and event around us, the "man of God" should be put in the way of finding and pointing it out to others? What is it but saying that if he speak for God, he should speak according to the rules of language—that if he reason for God, he should not do it irrationally, but according to the rules of reason—that if he believe all history to be an illustration of the Bible, he should possess an acquaintance with the past—that if he profess to be an interpreter of the Bible, he should spare no pains necessary to render himself a correct expositor—an able minister of the New Testament? What is it but saying that the "man of God" should be made as acceptable an offering to the Head of the Church, and as efficient an instrument for the conversion of the world, as his own personal endeavours, and the endeavours of the Church, combined with the earnest prayers of both for the impartation of the Spirit, can possibly render him?

3. But again, in order that a ministry be efficient, not only must it be pious and educated, it must be modified by a knowledge of present times, and adapted to the existing state of the Church and of the world. Though Moses, as the leader of Israel to Canaan, had always to follow the movements of the supernatural pillar, during no two days of the whole forty years of his ministrations were his duties perfectly identical. Though Paul went through the world with nothing but the cross of Christ, his mode of introducing and exhibiting that symbol of salvation differed with every new occasion. Had he cared nothing about success, he would not have shewn this versatility, and studied this adaptation; but so deeply was he convinced of the universal adaptation of the cross, and so supremely anxious to draw men into it, that he held it up in every variety of light, and became all things to all men in order that he might win some. And though in every succeeding age the chief duty of the Christian minister has been to unveil the same cross, yet as each age has materially differed from all its predecessors, his duty has been to vary and adapt his ministry accordingly.

Yes, the Saviour may be regarded as saying to His people, but especially to His ministers, in every age, "Can ye not discern the signs of the times?" Each period is preceded and attended with its own peculiar signs—and it is a part of your duty to mark them, that to the inquiry of the Church, "Watchman, what of the night?" you may be able to return the correct and seasonable reply. The office of the ministry, however, will be generally found to include three classes—men *behind* their day—men *before* their day—and men *of* their day. Those *behind* their day are always preaching to a former age; are conscious of alarm at every onward movement; and feel as little sympathy with their times as their times feel with them. Those who are *before* their day, are generally but few in number; nor is it perhaps desirable that they should be numerous, though the office they fill is something like that of the ancient prophet—pointing to the future, and preparing the Church for its arrival. Standing on a loftier eminence than their contemporaries, their eye sweeps an ampler horizon; and though the distant speck, no larger than a man's hand, enables them to speak of subjects which sound strange to the multitude, their voice never ceases to echo in the Church, correcting its views, animating its activity, and enlarging its expectations. The men *of* their day are those who, marking its peculiarities, and falling in with its movements, contribute something towards its progress to a better state of things. A considerable number of such the Church contains at present. They know, for instance, that it is partly their duty to assist in enlightening and directing public opinion; and, marking the mighty influence of the press for this end, they contribute what they can to the moral and religious literature of the day. They are placed for the defence of the Gospel—and aware that Popery, on the one hand, is no longer, in its outward policy and tactics, the Popery of the sixteenth century—and that Infidelity, on the other, is no longer the infidelity of Spinosa and the Pantheists, of Bayle and Academic doubts, of Hume, and Gibbon, and Voltaire, but a practical infidelity, with utilitarian science for its god, and the deification of man for its end, they aim to select their weapons from the armoury of the Gospel accordingly. They are to shew themselves philanthropists; if many around them, from sincere but mistaken notions, are seeking to benefit the world by human expedients alone, they must not be content with merely decrying such expedients, but must seek to surpass them by the strenuous application of God's remedy. If other sections of the Church than that to which they belong are abroad in the field of conflict, they should watch their movements, not to envy, but to emulate their activity, and to rejoice in their successes. If the world of Paganism is crying for instruction and spiritual help, and the Christian Church is disposed to minister to its relief, they should know something of the places to be occupied, and of the facilities for taking possession. And as the demand on the resources of the Church goes on increasing, they should be prepared to bring forth the strong reasons of the Gospel for entire self-consecration; taking care at the same time to blend their appeals for greater devotedness with appeals for greater devotion, for dependence on the Spirit, and louder cries for the impartation of His influence. And in thus saying that a ministry, to be effective, must be adapted to its age, what are we saying, after all, but that God is conducting the affairs of the universe on a plan—that in every age that plan advances—that His ministers are to mark that advance and to fall in with it—and that in proportion as they adjust their movements to His—link themselves on to His plans and keep pace with His progress, they move with the force of Omnipotence, simply by moving in a line and in harmony with it?

4. A fourth element of an effective ministry is a firm confidence in the sufficiency of the Gospel, and in its ultimate and universal triumph. Any doubt of its sufficiency as a remedy for the world's misery imparts feebleness to its ministry—creates indifference as to its diffusion—disposes the Church to seek for aid from that very world it is appointed instrumentally to save—fills the mind with alarm at every new test to which the discoveries of science may subject the Gospel lest it should fail to stand the ordeal, and thus invites the attacks of a world which it was intended to lead in glorious triumph. Yes, the Church of Christ has herself to thank for most of the assaults which infidelity has made on the grounds of her faith. That the world should voluntarily lay aside its hostility to holiness, do whatever the Church may, is not to be expected; but that hostility is divisible into two kinds—that which is

directed against Christianity, and that which is aimed at its professors. And what Christian would not rather that it should be levelled at *his* character than at that of the Gospel, or of his ever-blessed Lord? And who does not perceive, judging from the history of the Church, that Christians may generally choose which shall be the object of the world's attack—the Gospel, or its professors. Let them take the field—act on the aggressive—carry their arms into the enemies' country, and you hear scarcely a word against the truth of the Gospel—you give the world no leisure to indulge in speculative scepticism—it finds enough to do in stigmatizing your character as hypocrites, enthusiasts, and fanatics. But quit the field—shut yourselves up in self-indulgence within the walls of the Church, and the world will advance, as an earthly army in similar circumstances would do, and will sap and mine your *defences* as the only means of getting at and destroying you—your indolence, in that case, leaves it nothing else to do. But how does this guilty inactivity originate except in our want of sympathy with the design of the Gospel, and want of confidence in its sufficiency and success? As long as we consciously believe in its divinity and ultimate triumph, "we cannot but speak the things which we have seen and heard." "We believe, and therefore speak." Was not this enlightened confidence the secret of St Paul's activity and zeal? "I am not ashamed," said he, "of the Gospel of Christ—I am ready to preach the Gospel to you that are at Rome also—for it is the power of God unto salvation to every one that believeth." Had all the world been already at the feet of Christ, he could not have felt greater confidence in the Gospel than he felt while yet all the world was in hostility against it. And is not this holy confidence the secret of all the missionary enterprise of the present day? Oh! what an amazing volume is "the glorious Gospel of the blessed God!" How full of principles! How thickly sown with the seeds of things! How suggestive and fertile of good! Many a benevolent society of the present day has, on its first appearance, struck beholders as a perfect novelty—an original conception; and the first propounder has received the praise of all the Churches. But which of all these societies does not prove to be, in principle at least, as old as the Gospel, and does not plead accordingly the warrant of the Gospel?—nay, which of them all goes the length to which the Gospel requires it to go? And, knowing this, who does not feel assured that many an unthought-of agency for good yet lies slumbering in its hallowed page?—that many a verse, humble and familiar in appearance as the pebble which encloses a precious gem, conceals the type and principle of future societies, destined to scatter their blessings over the world? And what Christian does not feel assured that every such organization is as certain of fulfilling its course and answering its end, as if it came visibly accredited with the seal of Omnipotence? Yes, we ourselves are not carried through the regions of space by virtue of our union with the globe we inhabit more certainly than such instrumentality, simple as it may be in itself, and impotent as worked by man, is destined to succeed, by virtue of its sympathy and union with that Gospel which is moving steadily and majestically towards the lofty throne of God, and bearing the world along with it. Oh! what an amazing system is "the glorious Gospel of the blessed God!" An enlightened confidence in its Divine sufficiency will render the man of God independent of every other aid—thoroughly furnished for every emergency and every duty—while the firm persuasion of its ultimate and universal triumph will impart an ardour to his activity, and a moral dignity to his onward step, eminently conducive, through God, to the efficiency of his labours.

5. But the sufficiency of the Gospel depends, under God, on the free and full translation of its principles into active life on the part of the Christian Church. And hence, we add, next, that a ministry to be effective must be calculated to develope all the resources of the Church, and to bring

them into actual operation. A man of God is not the *servant* of his Church in the sense of having to perform *its* work. He has *his* work, and each several member has *his ;* but the work peculiarly his, as far as they are concerned, consists in exciting *their* diligence, directing their activity, and multiplying their agencies. The holder of the five talents was to increase them, not by labouring *without* them, but *with* them. And the man of God, when put in trust with the ministry of a particular church, is to look on each of its members as a talent, concerning which the Divine proprietor is saying, "Occupy till I come—employ every member—every moment and faculty of every member to the best advantage, that each may be the means of winning another, and that my Church of five hundred may be the means of gaining other five hundred more." With this solemn charge resting on his spirit, the man of God will feel that his first object is to make the most of that church with whose instrumentality his Lord has entrusted him. Its members may not be wealthy, educated, numerous, nor, in a worldly sense, influential. But they are such as God hath chosen and collected into a church to take part in His sublime purpose of saving the world. One thing is certain, therefore, that they are all to be employed. In this sense, there are to be no "private Christians" among them. Every Christian is a public man, taken up into the universal designs of the God of grace. In whatever sense they are private, then, like the ranks of an army, *all* are to take the field—the only concern of the man of God is to be, how to dispose of his forces so as to render them most effective in the cause of God. A ministry which begins and ends with itself—however pious, intelligent, and eloquent it may be—is, after all, the ministry of only one man ; and even that neutralized, counteracted, and rendered worse than useless in its effects on the world, by the slumbering and selfish inactivity of the hearers. But a ministry which sets and keeps in useful motion an entire church, however destitute it may be of other qualifications—becomes, in effect, the ministry of all its members, and thus proves an instrumentality of the widest influence and of the greatest efficacy. And never till the entire Church is thus stirred in all its depths, and all its resources put in actual requisition, will the full value of the Christian ministry be seen, for never till then will it answer the high object of its Divine appointment in the conversion of mankind.

6. But this supposes another requisite—unity of purpose, or entire devotedness to the objects of the ministry. The same exalted views of the duties of his office, which induce the man of God to covet and collect all the co-operation he can obtain, will induce him to give himself wholly to it. He who knows anything of the human mind, knows that its full energies are never put forth unless its object be single. He who knows anything of the design of the Christian ministry knows that it deserves the undivided attention and entire consecration of the whole man. And he who knows anything of the history of that ministry is aware that the men of God who effected the greatest good in their own age, and who are producing the greatest impression on posterity, were distinguished for the entireness with which they gave themselves up to their office. Not that they confined their activity to preaching. In addition to this, some of them, like the apostle, travelled, and wrote, and taught from house to house. Others of them, besides this, studied intensely—acquired the learned languages—translated and circulated the Holy Scriptures. But, however diversified their labours, they could each say, like the apostle, though in another sense, "One thing I do." One all-pervading passion—one all-controlling purpose—bound their various and versatile efforts together, causing the whole to result, like the intricate motions of a complicated machine, in one entire effect.

Christian brethren, this spirit of entire consecration is pre-eminently what we want. We have nearly everything else essential to success, in greater proportion than we have this. And yet this is, not among other things, but above all other things, in the order of means, indispensable. It can supply a thousand defects, while its place can be supplied by nothing. Talents which, without this spirit of entire devotedness, would have been comparatively wasted, or have ranked as insignificant, *by* it acquire a concentration and a power which arrest the attention, and move society. Feeble rays of knowledge which, without this, would have been useless to all but the possessor, *by* it are collected into a focus, and made to illuminate and to burn. Powers of persuasion and reasoning which, without it, would seldom move or convince, *by* it acquire an impassioned earnestness, which *will* be heard, and *must* be felt. Each appeal made for God is charged high with feeling and fervour—each sentence is an arrow with barbed and sharpened point—each attempt to reason for God, "logic set on fire." Opportunities of usefulness, which, without it, would have passed unseen and neglected, are, *by* it, anticipated, waited for, met, seized, improved, multiplied. Character, which, without it, would have lain unnoticed, *by* it acquires an air of originality and grandeur, and obtains a widespread ascendancy over other characters. There are men now occupied in the fields of ministerial and missionary labour, whose names, but for this, would never have been heard of beyond their own immediate circle, but whose praise is now in all the Churches, and will be to the end of time. Not a man of this kind ever lives without leaving on society permanent traces that he has been among them. So sublime is the design of the ministerial office, that to touch it—to approach it—is to catch the reflection of its grandeur; but steadily and devotedly to pursue it, is to be clothed in its greatness. And why? Partly for this reason—that the undivided and devoted man of God will be ever and anon impelled, by the very law of his devotedness, to advance a step beyond his contemporaries—to carry out into vigorous action some principle which they are content to retain slumbering in their creeds—to give himself up to the power of his principles. True, by so doing he may often attempt more than he can effect; but what then? He will effect more than most men attempt. Yes, we want enthusiasm—holy, sleepless, fearless, unquenchable enthusiasm!

7. But does not this most impressively remind us of the altar where alone this living fire is to be obtained? or, rather, of the source of all holy activity and power—the life-giving Spirit? And is not the man of God, whose devotedness to his work is such, that he cannot be satisfied with giving himself less than wholly to it, and who would fain see all the resources of the Christian Church pressed into the same service, and all its members co-operating with him to the utmost—is not he, for the very same reasons, likely to be the most earnest in his entreaties for the indispensable presence of the Spirit? Yes, whatever else may be essential in order to an efficient ministry, he will insist, first and last, on the influence of the Holy Spirit. Remembering that the present is emphatically the dispensation of the Spirit—that the bodily absence of Christ is supplied by the presence of the Spirit—that to convince men of sin is the office of the Spirit—that the ordinances of the Christian Church are the instruments of the Spirit—that that Church itself is the home of the Spirit—that the man of God is at once the mouth of that Church, and the organ of that Spirit in their united appeals to the world—remembering this, he feels as if he could not move without the Spirit; but remembering also that His influence is promised to prayer, he cannot do less than cry mightily for His aid. Thus earnestly sought, and appropriately honoured, the presence of the Spirit will be felt, nourishing and enlarging his piety into an element, not affecting a part of his character merely, but pervading the whole—consecrating his learning, and turning it into heavenly wisdom—keeping him on his watch-tower, looking out for the signs of the times and the means of improving them to the glory of God—inspiring him with

a growing confidence in the sufficiency of the Gospel to meet the wants of the Church and of the world—concentrating his powers to the one great object of his ministry—impelling him, under a sense of the magnitude of the work to be accomplished, to excite and engage the agencies of all around him—and yet deepening his conviction that, could all these agencies be put into full activity, the breath of the Spirit alone could crown that activity with success. As certainly as he believes this, he will pray—as certainly as he prays he will obtain the Holy Spirit—and as certainly as he obtains the Spirit, *his* will be an efficient ministry.

II.

But then comes the question, secondly, *how is such a ministry to be obtained?* For that it *can* be obtained, the fact of its existence here and there already, is proof sufficient. Now, though we shall only glance at the particulars, we think that glance will be enough to shew, that each of the requisites to an efficient ministry, which we have named, involves a corresponding obligation on the part of the Churches—an obligation which need only be conscientiously discharged in order to secure, under God, such a ministry. For instance, is eminent piety indispensable to a Scriptural ministry? But unless it could be shewn that the piety of the man of God is to exist independently of means, and uninfluenced by circumstances, it must follow that it will partake more or less of the character of those among whom he has moved. Christian parents, the next generation of ministers is already in embryo existence in the rising youth of your families—do you expect them to be pious in spite of your example, or, by the accompanying influence of heaven, in consequence of it? Christian Churches, the coming race of ministers is already existing in the youthful converts who are now joining your ranks. They do not come into our theological institutions and our pulpits direct from heaven—they come direct from your bosom. Will they not necessarily bring with them the marks of their Christian parentage, and the influence of your example? You expect them to be affected by the process they pass through in their way from you to the office of the ministry—by what spell are they to escape being influenced by the previous process they pass through in *your* hands? At present, then, they are in your training—train them in the way they should go, and the promise applies to the children of the Church as well as of the family, that when they are old they shall not depart from it. Let them see that whatever else you may value in them, it is their piety which chiefly endears them to your hearts—let them hear you confess your self-dissatisfaction, and importuning God for a loftier tone of piety in the Church at large—let them feel that to mingle with you is to move among examples of devotion, humility, and zeal—to be surrounded with an atmosphere of living piety—let this be your aim as Churches, and God will confer on you the honour of presenting to the next generation of Christians, a race of ministers whose only motto will be, "For us to live is Christ."

Have we shewn that education and intelligence are essential to the ministerial office? No argument can be necessary to convince you that it is for the Churches of Christ to supply these requisites. By selecting the more capable and intelligent, as well as pious among your youthful members to receive the necessary theological instruction—by liberally supporting the institutions which impart such instruction—by allowing those receiving it to enjoy the full advantages of such preparation, instead of hastily terminating their course of study, and hurrying them into the ministry unprepared—and by giving the preference, when called to choose a pastor, not to one of ignorant but of intelligent piety—by these means you cannot fail, under God, to secure an intelligent ministry. And by placing these means in your power, the Head of the Church is leaving you to say whether He shall be served by an illiterate or by an educated ministry.

Must a ministry, to be successful, be adapted to the peculiarities and wants of the times? Let the Churches encourage such a ministry, and they will obtain it. Here indeed, we admit, the influence of the pulpit and the pew is reciprocal. If the minister is silent concerning the signs of the times, and the movements which are visible on the face of society, it cannot be expected that the people should evince a desire for such information. On the other hand, if the people discover a reluctance to listen to anything which does not relate immediately to themselves—if the claims of the world at large are very slowly admitted and quickly dismissed by them—it cannot be expected that the minister will be eager or frequent in introducing them. Miserable, indeed, is the spectacle of a ministry or a Church which has outlived its day—which is living to itself instead of living to God for the good of the world—a relic of the past instead of a vital, useful, organic part of the present. But many a minister of this description is, I am persuaded, what he is solely owing to circumstances. Secluded in situation, straitened in pecuniary means, and depressed and corroded by domestic exigence, to him is denied the delight of ever ascending the mount of observation, and reporting on passing events. If freed from his trammels, and furnished with the means, he too would survey the moral horizon, and be conscious of sympathy with the entire scene.

But, with all deference, I would submit that of those ministers more advantageously situated, the number adequately acquainted with the present relative position of the Church and the world, and interested in it, is yet comparatively small; that the external affairs relating to the universal kingdom of Christ are introduced to the attention of the people too exclusively at stated times, on annual occasions, and in connexion with pecuniary collections, and too seldom as subjects forming a legitimate part of ordinary ministerial discourse, and to every part of which the heart of the Church should be supposed to be ever ready to vibrate and respond.

Let this department of their duty, then, be impressed on the *rising* ministry. Let them know that, besides their special relation to the respective Churches, they and their Churches sustain a universal relation—that the Gospel they preach embraces in its reach and sweep the universe and eternity—that the pulpit they occupy stands as the representative of the cross, in the centre of the universe—that there are lines of relationship connecting it with every object and event within that vast circumference—that they are placed in that central position to watch and report to their people the progress of events, to impress on them the dignity and responsibility of their character as the agents of "him for whom are all things, and by whom all things consist"—and thus to induce them, as their highest honour and happiness, to fall in with that vast procession, including all orders and all worlds, which even now is moving on to the one appointed spot, where all the diadems of the universe shall be cast at the feet of Him on whose head already are many crowns.

In the same way, let them be trained to an enlightened confidence in the Divine sufficiency of the Gospel they are called to preach. The foundation of this confidence, indeed, must be laid in their own personal experience of its converting and sanctifying power. Thus divinely prepared to "hope all things" great and good from the Gospel, let them be taken to that loftiest point of moral elevation attainable on earth—the cross of Christ—let them there see that God has only, *can* only have, one design concerning all around, a design of mercy—that He has only one instrument with which to fulfil that design, the Gospel of Christ—so that if any *other* science or agency is useful, it can only be by becoming related to that instrument, and subordinate to it. Inspired with such a conviction, they will not be ashamed of the Gospel, but will so preach it as to become mighty, through God, in asserting its transcendent claims, and hastening its ultimate triumphs.

If, again, a ministry, to be efficient, must be calculated to develop and draw out the resources of the Christian Church into benevolent activity, let there be a readiness on the part of the people to respond to that endeavour. If the minister, as the priest of the Christian temple, is to be a man of one object, it follows that the church of which he is the pastor is to be characterized by the same singleness of purpose. Where is the propriety of a minister devoted to *one* object, in a church devoted to *no* object, or distracted by the opposing claims of God and of the world? The obligations on the minister and the people are reciprocal. They can never consistently complain of his inactivity without meaning to say, "We ourselves are impatient to give more, pray more, labour more for God." They can never ask for a better leader, without implying their readiness to be better followers. He alone is not the Church; and it is by the Church that the world is to be instrumentally converted. His preaching alone is not to effect it; but his preaching, illustrated by their holy living, and followed up and enforced by their prayers and self-denying efforts. Let him feel that, as a leader, he has to direct rather than to stimulate—that, fast as he may advance, they are close at his heels—and they will not have to complain of the slowness of his movements. As a man of God, let *him* find that he has little to do in the way of "reproof and correction," and *they* will most likely find that he is not wanting in "doctrine and instruction in righteousness"—in any of the purposes of the Christian ministry.

And if the influence of the Spirit be, above all things, essential to ministerial success, remember that it is promised unconditionally to prayer. Not many months ago, a letter appeared in many of the religious periodicals, calling on the Churches, if I remember aright, to assemble at stated times for united prayer in behalf of our theological students and rising ministry. Meetings of this kind exist already in America; let us hope to see the practice obtain here. Let not the Churches pretend to deplore the comparative inefficiency of the Christian ministry, if they themselves never apply to the great Source of all efficiency in its behalf. If the weekly meeting for devotion be but scantily attended—and if, even then, the Christian ministry is forgotten, or but coldly glanced at, let them not wonder at its weakness. On the other hand, never can a minister hear the earnest entreaty of his people for an effusion of the Spirit on his work, without asking a double portion of the Spirit for them. Never could our theological students reflect that the Churches were wrestling in prayer on their behalf, without feeling as if they were already passing through the solemn service of their ordination—as if they were publicly kneeling before God, with the hand of the entire Church placed on their head—while all the members of the Church were imploring the Spirit, as with the voice of one man, to descend and anoint them to their office. And if they felt thus, simply from knowing that they were the objects of your deep and abiding solicitude at the throne of grace, what would they feel in *answer* to your prayer? They would receive the Spirit himself—feel that their sufficiency was entirely of God—and such would be the effect of their ministrations, that with the apostle they would be able exultingly to exclaim, "Now, thanks be unto God, who always causeth us to triumph in every place!"

Christian friends, I close with the remark with which I began—if the ultimate design of Christ in the institution of a Church be the conversion of the world—and if the preaching of the Gospel be the chief instrument by which the Church is to answer that end—how important to determine the characteristics of the most efficient ministry, and the way in which the Church may obtain it! This, I have very briefly, and, I am aware, very imperfectly, attempted to do. One thing I trust, however, is sufficiently apparent, that the influence of the ministry and of the Church is reciprocal—and that the object they are each to aim at is identical:—that influence, how important! that object, how unspeakably great! And who is sufficient for these things? Upon us the ends of the world are come; and rapidly do the scenes, the last scenes of the mighty drama thicken and hasten to a close. To us, as belonging to the Church of Christ, the sinful, helpless, and perishing world, "the whole creation, groaning and travailing in pain together until now," is looking in earnest expectation of approaching relief. On us the eyes of the universe are turned, expecting from us, at this momentous crisis, unwonted fidelity to Christ—entire consecration to His cause. But more and most of all—the Master—the Saviour—He who loved us and gave himself for us—expects it at our hands. Shall He be disappointed? Churches of Christ, do you in *your* capacity act as those whom He hath purchased with His own blood—we, in *our* capacity, as men of God, will aim to live for the perfecting of the saints for the *work* of the ministry, for the edifying of the body of Christ—and together we will see which, in the strength of God, can be most thoroughly furnished for His service, and press nearest to perfection in it—which can serve Him most efficiently on earth, and contribute most amply to His glory in heaven. Everything else is loss—this, this is infinite and eternal gain.

SERMON XII.

THE IMPORTANCE OF AN EDUCATED MINISTRY.

TITUS i. 9—"Holding fast the faithful word, as he hath been taught, that he may be able, by sound doctrine, both to exhort and to convince the gainsayers."

A Discourse

DELIVERED ON THE OCCASION OF THE OPENING OF THE LANCASHIRE INDEPENDENT COLLEGE, MANCHESTER, AT THE PREPARATORY SERVICE, ON THE 25TH OF APRIL, 1843.

IN continuation of this morning's service, the course most grateful to my own feelings, Christian friends, would be to select some doctrinal subject, corresponding with those to which your attention has been already directed, and to carry it out to a practical application. But in this I must deny myself. The nature of the occasion which has assembled us —the growing claims of the rising ministry—and the comparative slowness of the Christian Church to meet those claims—remind me that the time has not yet come when a fitting opportunity for advocating an educated ministry can be wisely allowed to pass by unimproved. Such an opportunity is the present. In order to improve it, let me invite your attention to that portion of the word of God which you will find in the first chapter of the Epistle of Paul to Titus, the ninth verse—"Holding fast the faithful word, as he hath been taught, that he may be able, by sound doctrine, both to exhort and to convince the gainsayers." This, according to the apostle, is a part of the qualification and of the duty of a Christian bishop. Instead, however, of strictly confining myself to an exposition of the letter of the text, let me rather fall in with its spirit by attempting, first, to explain the proposition *that the Christian ministry should be educated;* to *state some of the grounds of the importance of such education;* and then *to point out some of the obligations resulting from it.*

I.

First, we have to explain what we mean when we speak of an educated ministry; and, while doing this, we shall, if I mistake not, be incidentally furnishing a sufficient reply to the principal objections of those who not only deny its importance, but even deprecate it as an evil. For you can hardly need to be informed, that in all ages of the Church such persons have existed. As early as the second century of the Christian era a party arose who, confounding the *use* of learning with its *abuse,* denied its compatibility with the spirit of piety. In the third century the controversy raged with considerable violence; and although, owing to the efforts of the Alexandrian school, especially of Clement and Origen, the cause of letters and philosophy gradually triumphed, its opponents have not wanted for reinforcements in any subsequent age. Fortunately, as most of their prejudices originate in ignorance, however well-meaning, they furnish, unintentionally, the most apposite proof of the value of that knowledge which they condemn; since an explanation of the subject seems all that is necessary to silence their complaints.

1. In offering such an explanation, we may remark, first, that in advocating the education of the ministry, *we presuppose the existence of genuine piety in all who receive it.* For we cannot forget that while the private Christian is to be an example to the world, the Christian minister is to be "an ensample to the flock"—a model of models. His central station and official character invest him with influences which render his every movement an object of interest to superior beings, for it deeply implicates the everlasting wel-

fare of all around him. How important that the whole of that influence should be eminently holy; and how can that be but by issuing from a character eminently pious? On this account we call for evidences of the personal piety of every one seeking admission to our collegiate institutions; we take the opinion of his pastor, and of others likely to form a correct judgment of his character, and we subject the whole to the test of a patient and anxious examination.

If, then, it be objected, that some parties have made learning a substitute for piety in the ministry, and that others have appeared to expect that piety would follow as the effect of learning, we need not retort, in the language of Jerome, that there are those who err as egregiously, on the other side, in "mistaking ignorance for sanctity;" we content ourselves with simply remarking that we have no sympathy with the classes described. But, perhaps, it will be alleged that, though we may and do require piety in the Christian student, we endanger his humility and his sense of insufficiency. We reply, first, in the spirit of Dr Johnson's answer to a similar objection, education can minister to vanity only as long as it is regarded as a distinction; let education be universal, and the distinction arising from it will cease. Or, secondly, we might remind the objector that, if the possible abuse of a thing is to lead to its disuse, we shall be adopting a principle which has originated the most fatal errors. For example, the conjugal state has *its* dangers; on his own principle, therefore, he cannot complain of that Church which requires the celibacy of its clergy. Every sense of the body may prove an inlet to evil; shall it therefore be mutilated? or shall piety retire from social life to the monastery, the hermitage, or the desert? One of these alternatives common consistency requires him to adopt. Or, thirdly, we might reply that whatever the dangers of *knowledge* may be, we have yet to learn the peculiar virtues of *ignorance.* We never found it to be a *certain* security against pride. We have known it to be more vain of some scrap of information on which it had accidentally stumbled, than we ever knew learning to be of all its stores. And, when raised to a station of influence, we have ever found the uneducated man to be in much greater danger of pride than the educated. And then, we may add, in proof of the perfect *compatibility* of learning and piety, that the most distinguished member of the Jewish Church, though "learned in all the wisdom of the Egyptians," was the meekest of men; and that the most distinguished member of the Christian Church, though "brought up at the feet of Gamaliel," was the chief of the apostles, and a pattern of humility.

2. Again; *that* education of the rising ministry whose importance we advocate, *has mental development and discipline for its object,* as well as the attainment of actual knowledge. These objects are distinct. Indeed, it is possible so to communicate knowledge, as to enfeeble and pervert the mind which receives it. In other words, it is possible to be learned without being educated. Instances of this truth are to be found in the "endless genealogies," "the strifes about words," and the "vain janglings," against which the apostle cautions Timothy—in the scholastic sophistry of the twelfth and thirteenth centuries—and, if I do not greatly err, in the writings of the Tractarians and Traditionists of the present day. And to these instances may be added, strange as it may seem, the preaching of many of those who object to an educated ministry, and whose discourses abound in verbal quibbles, laborious trifling, ingenious mistakes, and attempts at second-hand learning in a small way. All these may be regarded as exemplifying what may be called the learning of the uneducated—the learning which narrows the mind instead of enlarging it, which leaves it ignorant of great principles, and unable to find them.

Now if this be the evil of which the objector to an educated ministry complains, he should be informed that he has misnamed it, and that the education we contemplate would prove its powerful and certain corrective. Our object is, not to furnish the student in divinity with high scholastic attainments; this the brevity of his term of study forbids: not to store his *memory* with facts and general information; mere scraps and driblets of miscellaneous knowledge are all that the most diligent collector of facts could take away with him: but to furnish him with that mental training which is necessary to the intelligent and useful discharge of the Gospel ministry. Knowledge, indeed, he *will* be acquiring during the entire process—knowledge of the most useful kind—but that which is more important still is, that he will obtain the power of using it, and of augmenting it indefinitely. His capital in actual knowledge may be comparatively small, but give him the right mental habits, and "his pound" will soon "gain ten pounds" in addition. Shew him the importance of great principles, and give him the power of dealing with them, and you have done more for him than as if you had deposited an encyclopædia of knowledge in his memory. For he who knows the *principle* of a truth has in effect mastered all the facts and phenomena belonging to it. He who knows the principle of a truth, like the angel in the midst of the sun, stands in its centre, and sees to its circumference.

3. Further: *that* education of the ministry which we advocate is meant *to correspond with the state of education generally.* If there are some classes of the community, for example, still comparatively unacquainted with even the rudiments of knowledge, we would not insist that their ministers should receive the *highest* educational advantages. And as such classes *do* exist, we rejoice in the existence of some theological institutions in which men of God are qualified by a comparatively elementary course of training for the spheres they are likely to occupy. But for the very same reason that we would observe this correspondence in *their* case, we would insist on a similar proportion between the education of the ministry, and that of the public generally.

All education is comparative. So true is this, that the light possessed by one age is regarded as twilight, as darkness, by a subsequent age. Now the objector to an educated ministry should know that, if his chosen teacher can barely read and write, even that would have been formerly regarded as a very rare and learned accomplishment. We are, therefore, justified in saying to him, You surely do not deem the power of reading and writing and speaking with propriety a superfluous attainment. You would not think of going in search of a man who knew nothing of this attainment, and of adopting him as your teacher on account of his superior ignorance. But, if you would not, you should remember that there was a time when the simple qualification of reading and writing and speaking correctly was considered to be open to all the objections which you now bring against the education of the ministry; for that was *the education of the time.* And as you now smile at the idea that any one could have ever objected to the simple education of that time, so, rely on it, the time will come when your objections to the education of the present day will be viewed in the same light. You should be reminded also, that if you do not object to the power of reading, writing, and accurate speaking, as a ministerial qualification, you are admitting the *whole of the principle for which we contend.* You are allowing that instruction to some extent is necessary. You are conceding that there ought to be some correspondence between the state of education generally and the instruction of the ministry. The only question at issue between us is, not one of principle, but of *degree*—namely, the extent to which education is to be afforded. And this, *we* repeat, should depend partly on the state of knowledge in the general community.

4. The ministerial education which we advocate is *that which yields to Scriptural theology the chief place; and which treats every other branch of study as auxiliary to it.* Now the most uneducated minister of the present day has

unconsciously adopted the same principle; for he is largely indebted to the learned labours of his predecessors. However slender his mental resources may be, he obtains them only by availing himself of the toils of others. If he can but just read his Bible, and some favourite religious author, he is indolently enjoying the results of prodigious labour and abundant learning. Let him think what has been necessary in order to put that translation of the Bible into his hands—what watching, and weariness, and travail—what studying of languages, revision of copies, and collation of manuscripts—what division of labour, and years of persevering application! Surely it is not for one who is thus living on the learning and labour of others to decry education; for the drone to depreciate the process by which the truth, sweeter than honey or the honey-comb, has been hived and made ready for his use.

If, however, he still urges that the Bible intimates that a knowledge of Scripture alone is sufficient to furnish the man of God for his office, we cheerfully admit the same. But then comes the question, what is to be the amount of that Scriptural knowledge;—shall it be the minimum or the maximum? We are anxious to put all the honour on the Bible we can—to extract from it, if possible, all that it contains—to make *the most* of it as God's instrument for the salvation of the world. "Our great divines," says Coleridge, "were not ashamed of the learned discipline to which they had submitted their minds under Aristotle and Tully, but brought the purified products as sacrificial gifts to Christ; they baptized the logic and manly rhetoric of ancient Greece; they made incursions into every province of learning, and returned laden with the choicest plunder; the scheme of the philosopher, the narrative of the historian, the vision of the poet, were all rendered subservient to the one predominant object of their researches; the gold of idolatrous shrines was transmuted into a purer ore by their spiritual alchemy." And the education we advocate for the man of God is such, and such only, as shall be made subservient to his office as an expositor of the Bible; subservient, either by strengthening and preparing his mind as the instrument to be employed on it; or by furnishing him with the means of developing, illustrating, and communicating its truths.

5. Another explanatory remark we would offer is, that the education we advocate *is meant to be held in entire subordination to the agency of the Holy Spirit.* We believe that his agency is present in the intelligent and faithful ministry of the Gospel; and that it is essential to the success of that ministry; and therefore would we have the education of the man of God of a tendency to harmonize his mind with that Divine agency, and to subordinate to it, not his knowledge merely, but all the powers of his renewed nature. So that, if an opponent to an educated ministry object, that Paul renounced all dependence on learning and eloquence, we reply that we would do so likewise. Like him, we would have both, and, like him, would use both, but, like him, would depend on neither. We would not depend even on alms-giving, nor on prayer itself; and yet we would cultivate both as a duty and a privilege. If he allege, however, and perhaps this is his great objection—if he allege *that because the efficiency of the ministry depends ultimately on the influence of the Spirit, therefore education for the ministry is unnecessary,* we reply that his objection rests on an entirely false assumption. It strangely supposes that because God can do a thing in a certain manner, therefore He will so accomplish it. Entirely losing sight of those wise arrangements in nature, providence, and grace, by which means and ends are linked together, it makes the power of God the only rule of his conduct. Most cheerfully do we admit, that *before* the great constitution of nature and grace was actually set up, it rested entirely with the sovereign will of God whether human instrumentality should be employed or not in any thing. But the question with which we have now to do is,

not what *might* have been, but what *is*—not one of *possibility,* but of *fact.* From the moment of man's creation, it became evident that the constitution which the Infinite Mind had seen fit actually to adopt, was one which required man's instrumentality. The constitution of grace adopted the laws of nature, and employs them. And man's wisdom consists in placing himself in harmony with these laws; for God has been pleased to bring himself under the gracious obligation of a promise to connect His blessing with obedience to these laws.

Now your error, we might say to the objector, your error consists in supposing that, because there was a period when God could, hypothetically speaking, have adopted a constitution of things which should have dispensed with human instrumentality, therefore you are at liberty to act as if He had really adopted such a plan; and in supposing that, because He still retains all His original power, and may choose occasionally to employ it out of the ordinary and appointed way, therefore you are at liberty to take His sovereign *exceptions* as your only *rule* of calculation and conduct. How inconsiderate, not to say daring, your conduct! He *could* teach His servants the knowledge of the alphabet, but you would not have had your minister wait, until that knowledge was supernaturally imparted to him. He *can* make the naked rock, or the seashore sand, spontaneously yield corn; but, we presume, you look for it rather in the adjoining field, nor do you expect to find it even there without cultivation. He *can* make the knowledge of a single evangelical truth the means of salvation; He has even often done it; but you would not, on that account, limit your knowledge of the Bible to a single text. You do not make what He *can* do the rule of what He *will* do, in any other department of the Divine conduct—why do you look for it here? Besides, do you not see that, if this rule is to be adopted, it bears equally against an uneducated ministry; that if—to use the language of South—"if God hath no need of our learning, He can have still less of your ignorance;" that absolutely considered, He has no *need* even of your existence? And surely you will not adopt this rule of conduct under the notion of *honouring* God. You surely do not expect that He will distinguish you in the last day as having pre-eminently proved your concern for the progress of His gospel, by having been pre-eminently unconcerned about the qualifications of the instruments you employed. Rely on it, true humility on this subject consists not in neglecting the attainment of knowledge, but in estimating it at its proper worth; in feeling, like Newton, after sounding and navigating the ocean of science, as if one were only a child, sporting on its margin, and collecting its shells. And the Spirit of God is honoured, not by our coming into His presence empty-handed, but by imitating the Apostle Paul, and, after laying out all our resources in His service, feeling that our sufficiency is of God.

Let it be borne in mind, then, that the ministerial education we advocate *presupposes personal piety; has mental development and discipline for its special object; is meant to correspond with the state of education generally; yields to Scriptural theology the chief place; and places itself in entire subordination to the agency of the Holy Spirit.* Now I am not aware of any plausible objection to the education of the ministry, which one or other of these explanatory remarks does not legitimately answer; and, with the subject thus explained, we are prepared to proceed, *secondly, to assign some of the grounds of our conviction of its importance.*

II.

1. And, first, let me remark that the desirableness of ministerial education is *predetermined by the natural activity of the human mind, and by the tendency of the Gospel to excite that activity.* A variety of circumstances may concur to repress the active tendencies of the mind; but let the Gospel obtain admission into it, and, from that moment, the most torpid specimen of humanity is quickened

into a new mental as well as moral life. Even the mind which was previously alive and vigorous becomes conscious of a new impulse to activity, and of a new sphere in which to spend it. In finding a God, he finds the centre of all things; and henceforth the tendency of his mind is ever to harmonize the discordant, to arrange the displaced, and to assign to everything its right position in the great circle which surrounds the Deity. In finding "the truth," he finds an infallible standard by which everything is to be tested; henceforth he would fain try every pretension, weigh every claim, by its relation to this standard, and estimate everything accordingly. And, as the volume of nature is written in illuminated characters and pictured forms, purposely to awaken early curiosity, and to excite the inquiry, "What meaneth this?"—so the volume of inspiration is constructed expressly to stimulate the activity of the renewed mind. Yes; the Bible is distinguished from every other book professedly Divine—from the Shasters of the Brahmin and the Koran of Mahomet—by its earnest commendations of knowledge, and by its power of exciting a thirst for it. It at once creates light and courts it. Not only does it extol knowledge as a glory, but commands us to seek for it as a most sacred duty. But, if Christianity thus awakens the mental and moral activity of man, and if the education we advocate consists in sustaining that activity and directing it aright, the desirableness of such education is no longer a doubtful question. It is an adjudged case—a settled question; settled by no arbitration of ours, but by the predeterminate counsel of Him who gave to our mental constitution its activity, and to the Bible the power of arousing that activity. Unless, therefore, you do violence to the mind, and repress its activity, education, to some extent, becomes a religious necessity. And if education be thus desirable for *every* inquiring Christian mind, how much more important must it be for the man of God who in his public ministry is, in effect, to aid in directing the religious education of others.

2. The importance of the education we advocate arises, secondly, *from the nature and contents of the Bible, and from the relation which the Christian minister sustains to it.* Revealed theology comes to us in a volume consisting of a number of ancient books in the Hebrew and Greek languages. Is it anything more than an act of ordinary propriety for its professed expounder to endeavour to make himself acquainted with all that it contains? Then, to say nothing of Biblical Criticism and Interpretation, he must be able to read it in the original tongues.

The Bible insists on the doctrine of human depravity and ruin. The history of the ancient world is one unbroken record of facts illustrative of this doctrine. An acquaintance with that history gives a depth to the meaning of the apostle in that sketch of the monster-man in his first chapter to the Romans, which no one ignorant of the ancient world can ever perceive; shews that man, so far from ameliorating his moral condition, exhibited an invariable tendency to become worse and worse; that the highest point of the world's civilization was the lowest point of its morality; that so far from reason or philosophy leading men to God, the religion which it constructed and decorated for them uniformly proved their greatest curse; that Christianity came into the midst of the world's systems, with all the freshness and originality of a Divine conception, direct from heaven; that the character of Christ took the world by surprise, as the pure and perfect incarnation of infinite excellence; that his advent was almost as necessary to save the world from temporal, as from eternal ruin. And shall all this remain unknown to the man of God? Give him an opportunity of acquiring the learned languages; and you furnish him with a key to the knowledge of the whole.

The study of language, indeed, *has* a value of its own. When pursued into its philosophy, it is both a mental discipline, an invigorating logical exercise, and is the study of mind itself. And on this independent ground alone, even were it devoid of all other advantage, we should be justified in urging the cultivation of the study. But when it is remembered that the knowledge of the Hebrew, Greek, and Latin languages, besides giving the student access to the original Scriptures, opens to him the temples of ancient philosophy and worship, enabling him to see for himself the necessity, the evidence, and the influence of Divine revelation; places before him the writings of the Greek and Latin fathers—that armoury of the Traditionists—with the power of extracting the useful, and of rejecting the vile; that it enables him to consult the valuable, the *invaluable* theological treatises to be found in the Latin works of foreign divines who have flourished since the Reformation; and that these are only *some* of its advantages—who does not feel the great importance of linguistic studies for the future expounder of the Word of God?

The Bible abounds with *prophecies* relative to the monarchies of the ancient world, and to the Church of God. These prophecies were recorded, of course, that, when they came to pass, we might believe. Many of them have come to pass; and the question arises, shall their fulfilment be known? Shall this part of the temple of Truth be shut up and useless; or shall it be opened, admired, and worshipped in? Here is an important branch of *evidence* for the truth of Divine Revelation; shall it lie waste and useless? shall God have spoken in vain? or shall His voice be heard? But if the man of God is to hear it, he must know something of ancient and modern history, that, by comparing the prophecy with the event, he may perceive its completion.

The Church of God also has a history of *its* own. That part of its history recorded in the Bible is written for our instruction. But the record of its history did not end with what is there written; it has been continuously carried on in laws and monuments, medals and inscriptions, memorials and documents of all kinds; and is replete with interest and instruction down to the present moment. Shall the whole exist in vain? Shall the past heresies and errors of the Church afford no warning? Shall its sins and apostacies excite no penitence? its Divine preservation in the flames of persecution no gratitude? its gradual corruption no illustration of the New Testament prophecies concerning the man of sin? Shall its reformation excite no sense of obligation? or the Divine interpositions for its deliverances, its purification, and enlargement, no trust and zeal for the future? But all this, if it is to be turned to a profitable account, supposes a knowledge of *ecclesiastical* history.

To say that *natural history and philosophy* may be made highly subservient to Christian theology, is only to say, in other words, that the God of nature is also the God of grace. Nature, with all her myriad voices, is ever lecturing on the existence, the providence, and the agency of God. All that has ever been written on the subject, from the writings of Aristotle to the Bridgewater Treatises, is only a comment on the sublime address of the Deity himself in the concluding portion of the Book of Job. We believe, indeed, that all nature and providence are in strict analogy to religion—that all the works and ways of God are His own exposition of His Word. What an important use has Butler made of this idea in his well-known Analogy! And we believe that hereafter it will be seen that the universe was only a vast temple with the cross standing in the centre, and that to that centre every object and event was related and subordinated; that it never moved, but all things fell into its train; never stood, but they all bowed down before it; never spoke, but they all echoed its voice; and that the sight, when beheld in the light of eternity, will fill all heaven with adoration. But we would have the preacher of the cross to see something of it *now;* and hence we would have him to be so far acquainted with the constitution and course of nature, as to feel the eminence on which he stands, and to be able, as he looks down from that eminence, to point out, with holy triumph, how all things are doing homage to the Gospel *now.*

3. The importance of the education we advocate appears, thirdly, *from the official relation which the minister sustains to the mind of his flock, as the expounder of the Bible, and the enforcer of its truths.* We have just seen the importance of his possessing a certain *kind and amount* of knowledge; now we have to regard his qualifications for *imparting that knowledge to others.* In his relation to the Bible, on the one side, he may be perfect; but in vain will be all his Biblical acquisitions, unless, in harmony with his relation to the minds of his people, on the other side, he has the power of clearly and efficiently communicating his knowledge.

For example: as the Christian minister has to address a mixed audience repeatedly every week, it is obviously important that *he should be acquainted with the rules and the capabilities of the language in which he addresses them.* To deny this, would be to affirm, in effect, that the most unintelligible jargon which folly ever uttered was as well adapted for religious usefulness as the reasoning of an Edwards, or the eloquence of a Whitefield.

Again: considering how desultory and vagrant the early mental habits of many of our students must have been, and how indispensable a power of patient, consecutive, and concentrated thinking is, not only to the pursuit of knowledge, but to the arrangement and employment of it when attained, *we cannot but regard that study as beyond all price which at once corrects that parent evil, and confers this master power.* Such a tendency we believe the *pure mathematics* pre-eminently to possess. "In these," says Lord Bacon, "I can report no deficience, except it be that men do not sufficiently understand their excellent use, in that they do remedy and cure many defects in the wit and faculties intellectual. For, if the wit be too dull, they sharpen it; if too wandering, they fix it; if too inherent in the sense, they abstract it." And why are such studies so favourable to intellectual vigour? Simply because, by descending to the foundations of truth, they require the whole mind in perfect abstraction to descend along with it; by tracing the relations of truth, they exercise the faculty of comparison, and the power of reasoning; by exacting definitions, they teach precision; by dealing with principles, they make us feel that truth, *all* truth, is a most substantial and solemn thing—a thing to die for; and, by pointing to its grand results, they lead to careful calculation of consequences, and to far-sighted and comprehensive views.

But besides this mental discipline, and this acquaintance with the powers of the language which he employs, *ought not the future minister to know something of the intellectual and moral constitution of the minds on which he is to operate?* There are but two substances in the universe—matter and spirit. If he had to work in matter, he would be expected to know something of *its* properties. Is spirit so much more simple in its manifestations, and so much more yielding to the touch, that ignorance can deal with it as advantageously as knowledge? Vast and varied as are the phenomena of the material universe, *the mind* is made to respond to every part and property—made to respond to the phenomena of *other worlds, and nobler systems;* and the Word of God, like a piece of heavenly music, is set for, and adapted to, the whole of man's complex nature; shall the hand which is weekly to essay the mighty instrument know nothing of its stops and keys? If he is not to confound emotion with principle, and impulse with habit; if he is not to mistake the natural instincts for virtues, nor the disinterested affections for selfish passions; if human responsibility and Divine sovereignty are not to oppose and neutralize each other; if the pathology of the deceitful heart is to be skilfully treated, and a partial alleviation of threatening symptoms is not to be mistaken for a perfect cure, then must the man of God obtain an insight *into the mental and moral philosophy of human nature.*

Nor must he be left ignorant *of the right methods of placing himself in felt contact with other minds.* Who has not often admired the versatility of the Apostle Paul in this respect? As the Christian philosopher on Mars' Hill, you would hardly have recognised him for the same man as the ardent preacher of the Thessalonian synagogue, where he had been shewing, from the Scriptures, that Jesus is the Christ: and how different again from the strain of the philosopher and the preacher is the method of the same man, when, as the dignified apologist and champion of the Christian faith, he makes a Felix tremble, and an Agrippa "almost a Christian!" And is there nothing in this example worthy of imitation? Ought not the Christian advocate of the present day to understand the principles of argumentation—or logic as an art—for the purpose of informing and convincing the judgment; of persuasion—or rhetoric—for the purpose of moving the passions; of the evidence of testimony, to induce the right degree of respect for authority, and no more? For example, owing to the influence of vicious causes, some men are led to question the claims of the Bible. God has graciously supplied a variety of evidence—prophetic and miraculous, moral and historical—expressly adapted for the conviction of such men. But this very evidence *may* be so exhibited, and often *has* been, as to excite their ridicule and confirm their unbelief. Is it not important that those who profess to exhibit and enforce it, should themselves see its connexion, feel its convincing reasonableness, and be acquainted with the most useful modes of its application? Hence, we claim for the man of God, who is placed, among other things, for "the *defence* of the Gospel," *an acquaintance with the philosophy of evidence.*

4. But the Christian minister is not related to his particular church merely; the importance of the education we advocate will appear if you consider, fourthly, *his relation to the age in which he lives.* The office of the ministry will be generally found to include three classes—men *behind* their day; men *before* their day; and men *of* their day. Those *behind* their day are always preaching to a former

age; are conscious of alarm at every onward movement; and feel as little sympathy with their times as their times feel with them. Those who are *before* their day are generally but few in number; nor is it perhaps desirable that they should be numerous, though the office they fill is something like that of the ancient prophet, pointing to the future, and preparing the Church for its arrival. Standing on a loftier eminence than their contemporaries, their eye sweeps an ampler horizon; and though the distant speck, no larger than a man's hand, enables them to speak of subjects which sound strange to the multitude, their voice never ceases to echo in the Church, correcting its views, animating its activity, and enlarging its expectations.

The men *of* their day are those who, marking its peculiarities, and falling in with its movements, accelerate its progress towards a better state of things. A considerable number of such the Church contains at present. They know, for instance, that it is their duty to assist in enlightening and directing public opinion; and, marking the mighty influence of the press for this end, they contribute what they can to the moral and religious literature of the day. Would that the number of such were greater, and that your college may help to increase them! Is the education of the masses becoming the *question of questions?* Aware how little the science is understood, and how powerful an engine it may be made for evil or for good, they are sensitively alive to the mode of its application; but this of course presupposes, to a certain extent, their own education. Are they placed for the defence of the Gospel? Then they need to know that Popery, on the one hand, is no longer, in its outward policy and tactics, the Popery of the sixteenth century; and that Infidelity, on the other, is no longer the infidelity of Spinoza and the Pantheists, of Bayle and the Sceptics, of Hume, and Gibbon, and Voltaire, but a practical infidelity, with utilitarian science for its god, and the deification of man for its end; and they need skilfully to select and employ their weapons accordingly. Are they to shew themselves the Philanthropists of the day? then, if many around them are seeking, from sincere but mistaken motives, to benefit the world by human expedients alone, they, so far from contenting themselves with merely decrying such expedients, must seek to surpass them by the strenuous application of God's remedy. If other sections of the Church than that to which they belong are abroad in the field of conflict, they are to mark *their* movements, not to envy, but to emulate their activity, and to share in their success. If the world of Paganism is crying for instruction and spiritual help, they should know something of the places to be occupied, and of the facilities for taking possession. And as the demand on the resources of the Church goes on increasing, they should be prepared to bring forth the strong reasons of the Gospel for entire self-consecration. And in thus saying that a ministry to be effective must be adapted to its age, and that this supposes education, what are we saying after all, but that God is conducting the affairs of His kingdom on a plan—that in every age that plan advances—that His ministers are to mark that advance, and to fall in with it; and that, in proportion as they adjust their movements to His—link themselves on to His plans, and keep pace with His progress, they move with the force of Omnipotence, simply by moving in a line and in harmony with it?

5. The importance of the education we advocate will appear if you consider, next, *that a firm and* ENLIGHTENED *confidence in the sufficiency of the Gospel, and in its ultimate and universal triumph, is an essential element of an effective ministry.* Our last particular contemplated the minister in his relation to the *present;* here, we regard him rather as related to the *future.* A conflict is before him—a conflict of opinion, not only with foes without the pale of the visible Church, but with foes within. Shall he advance to it timidly, or full of heart and hope? Leave him in doubt respecting the sufficiency of the Gospel as a remedy

for the world's misery, and you impart feebleness to his ministry, and indifference to the diffusion of the truth ; you dispose him to seek for aid from that very world it is appointed instrumentally to save ; you fill his mind with alarm at every new test to which the discoveries of science may subject the Gospel ; and thus you invite some modern Celsus to repeat one of the oldest charges alleged against it, *that it fears the light of science ;* and you encourage the attacks of a world which it was intended to lead in glorious triumph. But let him see the homage which the truth has invariably received from science ; let him see how the comparative study of languages, which was at one time deemed inimical to the Mosaic history of the dispersion, is now tending to corroborate that history, and causing men, in this respect, "with one mind and one mouth to glorify God ;" how, the farther the physiology of man has been examined, the more evident has become the common parentage of the human race ; how monumental history, once summoned from the cavern temples and tombs of India and Egypt to contradict the Mosaic chronology, has shamed its advocates, and confessed itself of comparatively modern date ; how, when the famed zodiacs were brought from Egypt, and astronomy itself was supposed to be enlisted against the Bible, they turned out to be mere monuments of astrological folly, and the very stars in their courses fought against the infidel attempt ; and how, when geology was invoked to the conflict with the cosmogony of Moses, "the earth literally disclosed her dead"—the fossil remains of successive creations proclaiming the fact that miracles, so far from being impossible, have ever belonged to the course and constitution of nature, viewed on a comprehensive scale ;—let the student of revelation know these facts, and, like the servant of the prophet, his eyes will be opened to behold that the object of his solicitude is surrounded as with horses and chariots of fire. Let him know that the believers in Divine revelation have never had to engage in its defence but they have returned from the conflict laden with fresh spoil; that many, once known as its bitter foes, abandoning the arms wherein they trusted, have swelled the ranks of its enlightened friends; that, however threatening the aspect of a discovery on its first appearance, sooner or later it has uniformly given in its adhesion to the claims of Christianity, and has inscribed its name on the mountain monument of her evidences; that archæology, bringing its medals and inscriptions in profusion, and literature its rolls and documents, and stores of critical science, have poured them like gold and frankincense and myrrh at her feet;—and he will see that every thing has "turned out rather for the furtherance of the Gospel."

Would you augment his confidence in it still further? Shew him how perfectly it is adapted to the nature of man, and to the progress of society—how full it is of principles; how thickly sown with the seeds of things; how suggestive and fertile of good; so that no truly benevolent society or effort is known to us, however original and novel it at first appeared, the principle of which the Bible had not anticipated, and been always enforcing. And, convinced of this, will he not cherish the assurance that many an unthought of agency for good lies slumbering *yet* in its hallowed page?—that many a verse, familiar in appearance as the humble pebble which encloses a precious gem, conceals the type and principle of future agencies destined to scatter their blessings over the earth?—and that every such agency is, in the hand of God, as certain of fulfilling its course, and answering its end, as if it came visibly accredited with the seal of Omnipotence; that we ourselves are not borne through the regions of space by virtue of our union with the globe we inhabit more certainly than such instrumentality is destined to succeed, by virtue of its union with that Divine plan which is ever in progress—ever moving steadily and majestically towards the high throne of God, and bearing the world along with it. An enlightened confidence in the Divine adaptation and sufficiency of the Gospel will render the man of God independent of every other aid—thoroughly furnished for every emergency and every duty; while the firm persuasion of its ultimate triumph will impart an ardour to his activity, and a moral dignity to his onward step, eminently conducive, through God, to the efficiency of his labours.

6. With our views of the importance of an educated ministry thus sustained, are we not warranted to expect, sixthly, *that its importance will be borne out by a reference to history, ancient and modern, sacred and ecclesiastical?* And, here, need I remind you that Moses, "God's first pen," as Lord Bacon calls him, and the instrumental founder of the Jewish economy, was rich in all the lore of Egypt; and that from the time of Samuel, with only one exception so far as we know—that of Amos—the prophets and great public teachers of the people were taken by God from the schools of the prophets, where they had been taught the learning of the country and of the day? Descending to the opening of the Christian economy, need I remind you that the apostles, after enjoying for three years the instructions of the Great Teacher himself, were then made learned by miracle?—that he who was last called—the most useful of them all, and who filled the Roman empire with the sound of salvation—was the scholar and philosopher Paul?—and that he, in condemning, as he did, a false philosophy, was in effect pronouncing a commendation of the true? Need I refer to the high estimate in which education was held by the ancient fathers of the Church, by reminding you of the fact that they deprecated the edict of the emperor Julian—forbidding Christians to lecture in the public schools of science and literature—as more destructive to the Christian faith, than all the sanguinary persecutions inflicted by his predecessors? And why *did* that philosopher of persecution adopt such a measure—but because he well knew the wounds which learning in the hands of Christian apologists had inflicted on Paganism; and that, as Waddington remarks, it was com-

paratively useless to oppress the Christians by bodily coercion, or even by civil degradation, unless he could at the same time degrade their minds by ignorance.

The time, alas! arrived when they began to choose that ignorance for themselves. At the close of the sixth century, Gregory the Great rejected from the service of religion that learning of which he himself was destitute. How appropriate, that the man who first authoritatively extinguished the light of secular knowledge should have been the first potentate in the new kingdom of Popish darkness; for he it was who, finding the various elements of that great system of imposture ready to his hand, organized them into that gigantic structure of evil which for so many ages stood erect with its foot on the neck of the civilized world. How suggestive the fact that he who said, in effect, "let there be mental darkness," and he who said, "let the man of sin arise and triumph," should have been one and the same individual!

Let it not be supposed, indeed, that we attach any spiritual value to *mere* knowledge. We are even free to admit that Germany, the nation perhaps the most profoundly learned, has long been the most prolific of infidelity. But much even of that scepticism is only the natural reaction of the mental darkness and depression in which ignorance so long detained the nations. Yes, ignorance has had her millennium—a long and dreary period during which not merely learning became extinct, but almost the curiosity and desire to learn; the Bible became a book comparatively lost and unknown; and the feeble glimmering of knowledge which remained in the hands of a few was employed, not to enlighten but to delude the people; and proved sufficient to hold the enfeebled mind of Christendom in the most servile subjugation.

With what signal effect the weapon of sanctified learning may be wielded, let the history of the Reformation from that fearful condition of the Church attest. Would you know the opinion of the Reformers themselves on the subject? "If we lose the learned languages by our neglect," said Luther, "we shall lose the gospel." An unlearned theology," said Melancthon, "is an Iliad of evils;"—a sentiment often reiterated by Calvin also. Need I remind you that our Puritan and Nonconformist forefathers—the champions of truth and liberty in their day—and whose standard theology continues to nourish the piety of the Church, were learned divines? Need I add, further, that among the most useful men of modern days, have been a Doddridge and a Watts, a Wesley and a Whitefield, of England; and, of America, an Edwards, a Bellamy, and a Dwight; and that, besides being educated themselves, they advocated the collegiate preparation of others for the ministry—some of them actually presiding in such institutions?

Far be it from us to deny that God has greatly blessed the preaching of some uneducated ministers. "We therein do rejoice, yea, and will rejoice." He did not bless them, however, *on account* of their ignorance, but *in spite* of it. It was not their ignorance which he blessed; but certain other qualities which they possessed in common with the educated man of God—qualities which a wise education would have aided to develope and direct—zeal and devotedness to the glory of God. On the other hand, could we take you to listen to *some* of this class, you would feel at once that their preaching—in which distinctions are made without differences, assertions are mistaken for arguments, and illustrations of truth substituted for doctrines—is of a character to limit their usefulness to a single class of hearers, and to disparage them in the eyes even of some of that class. And how many a minister of this description, could you address him on the subject, would feelingly deplore his own want of early education, and set forth the disadvantages under which he consequently labours! And thus you might easily obtain, from your own observation, an illustration of the same truth, which history in all ages so abundantly confirms, that there exists a relation between religion and an educated ministry, and that, where the latter is wanting, the former invariably tends to superstition, fanaticism, or extinction.

And now, what, after all, is the summary of the various arguments in support of an educated ministry, but simply this—that ignorance is imperfection; and that, in the case of the man of God, we are anxious to lessen that imperfection as much as possible? What is it but saying that, as sin is the parent of all *voluntary* ignorance, and as the gospel is the great remedy for sin, we believe it was meant, directly or indirectly, to remedy such ignorance as well as every other evil; and that we are anxious that the man of God should be an instance of its remedial influence in this, as well as in every other respect? What is it but saying, that, if he speak for God, he should speak according to the rules of language; that, if he attempt to reason for God, he should not do it irrationally, but according to the rules of reasoning; that, if he profess to be an interpreter of the Bible, he should spare no pains necessary to render himself a correct expositor—"an able minister of the New Testament." In a word, what is it but saying that the man of God should be made as acceptable an offering to the Head of the Church, and as efficient an agent for the diffusion of the Gospel, as his own endeavours and the endeavours of the Church, combined with the prayers of both for the impartation of the Holy Spirit, can possibly render him?

III.

Such being some of the grounds of the importance of an educated ministry, I might enlarge, thirdly, on some of the consequent *obligations.* The nature of the occasion, however, which has now assembled us, reminds me that you are already alive to those obligations, and allows me to be as brief as the subject will permit. I will only remind you, therefore, that as your sense of the importance of an educated ministry committed you to the erection of a college, so now the erection of that college commits you to a series of corresponding duties. By selecting the more capable and intelligent, as well as pious, among the youthful members of your churches, to enjoy its advantages; by fairly estimating its pecuniary wants and contributing liberally to its support; by allowing its students the full enjoyment of its entire course, instead of hastily terminating their studies, and hurrying them into the ministry unprepared; and by giving the preference, when called to choose a pastor, not to one of ignorant, but of intelligent piety;—by these means, you cannot fail, under God, to secure an intelligent ministry. And by placing these means in your power, the Head of the Church is leaving you to say whether he shall be served by an illiterate, or by an educated ministry.

Brethren, friends of our collegiate institutions, you are committed to a great work. Bear with me while, in few words, I exhort you to view it *chiefly* in the highest light. View the support of our colleges, if you please, as a service rendered to your respective Christian denominations; and, as such, it richly deserves their practical thanks. But regard it *chiefly* as belonging to that great system of agencies by which God is subduing all things unto himself. Contemplate it *chiefly* in that only light in which it can be invested with enduring importance—as included in that infinite plan which subordinates all our movements to its own designs, and which, while it demands the strenuous activity of every agent in the universe, yet absolutely stands in need of none; and thus regarded, you will feel ennobled while rendering it the humblest service.

Think of the support of our colleges, if you please, as a duty called for by the circumstances of the times—as a work for the day. But fail not, in your holiest moments, to regard it as touching the past eternity and the future—as associated with that ministry of reconciliation which was determined on before the foundation of the world, and with that perfecting of the saints, that edifying of the body of Christ, which is to be the theme of grateful admiration in the eternity to come. Think of our colleges as a means which God will employ for preparing himself agents in days to come—days when nobler services shall be rendered to His cause than we have ever attempted, and when lofter motives shall inspire their performance. Thus regarding them, you will feel that, in sustaining them, you are living for the *future* as well as for the present—that you are setting and keeping in motion trains of ever-augmenting influence, which, deriving their efficacy from heaven, shall hasten the completion of the kingdom of God.

Cherish the conviction, if you please, that *this* institution, combining with other and similar means, will raise the educational character of the Christian ministry, and thus increase its usefulness ; and that, on this account, it will deserve the suffrages of all its friends. But oh ! if you would prove its best friends, place it under the guidance, and at the disposal, of Him " for whom are all things, and by whom all things consist," and you will have secured for it a patronage which can bring good for it even out of evil, and make it subservient to the highest end. Place it, by earnest prayer, in the light of His countenance, and its highest prosperity is secured for ever. Link it as a humble instrumentality to the cross of Christ; and what though no royal munificence endows it, " the Highest himself shall establish it;" what though no lofty pretensions to apostolic succession are made for its sons, the Spirit himself, the Spirit of apostles and prophets, shall descend to anoint them to their office; and " God, even our own God," shall ratify and accept the work of our hands.

SERMON XIII.

RELIGIOUS EDUCATION.

PROV. xxii. 6.—"Train up a child in the way he should go; and when he is old he will not depart from it."

THIS is a familiar text for an occasion like the present. But its very commonness implies its appropriateness; and its appropriateness implies a fulness of meaning—a fulness not yet measured, nor likely to be soon exhausted. It implies, for instance, that, from the earliest childhood, we begin to *walk in some way*—that there is a way in which from childhood we *ought* to walk—that children require to be *trained* to walk in this way—that they are *capable* of this training—that it is the duty of parents, and of those who are themselves walking in this way, to train them—and that, if thus trained to walk in the right way, they will never depart from it.

I.

By childhood, here, we understand all that portion of life which precedes early manhood: and we say the text implies, first, that *from early childhood we begin to walk in some way.* Who shall say at how early a point of our existence our character begins to form and consolidate for eternity? I do not ask at how early a period our moral responsibility begins:—*that,* of course, does not commence till we are capable of distinguishing between good and evil. But the character which *then* becomes accountable, has, long before that, been assuming its peculiar complexion—how early the process began who shall say? Did it begin when the parental ear was delighted with the lisping of the first word? Long before that:—for there is a language earlier than speech, and which speech can never express—the language of looks—the communion of *sympathy* between the world without and the world within. Did it begin the first time its untrained foot touched the earth? Long before that: by that time many a step had been taken, involving future consequences of infinite importance. Did it begin with the first smile that dimpled its cheek, and beamed in its eye? Earlier than that—so early that, in after years, its memory can never go far enough back to date its commencement. Earlier than the moment of the first maternal smile and embrace—for these only contributed to promote it. Earlier, *in some sense,* earlier even than the hour of birth;—for, behold, it was shapen in iniquity, and in sin was it conceived. And all the impressions which it received from that period—and probably it does receive impressions through every subsequent moment—all these are a part of the materials out of which its future character is to be formed—all these are vital seeds, some of which will be bearing their appropriate fruit ten thousand ages hence.

Oh, treat the new-born infant with respect! Hang over its helpless form with reverential awe! It is the most sacred trust which ever came into your hands. In your situation, the Son of God would take it into His hands and bless it. Ponder its vast and mysterious capabilities; and then say, would you stand with awe near the crater of Etna if you heard the subterranean thunder, and knew, by ominous signs, that an ocean of fire was then forcing its way from an unknown depth, heaving and surging on to desolate the country for leagues around? With how much profounder an awe should you contemplate that little one when you think of all the possibilities of his being. Tell me not of the fearful terrors of an active volcano—that infant breast is heaving with infinite possibilities; that pulse is throbbing for eternity. When the mountain shall have burnt out, and its crater be filled with verdure, that child will be a seraph before the throne above, or a fiend in perdition. When the earth itself shall be burnt up, he will have only attained a loftier point of glory, or have sunk to a lower depth of suffering. Ponder the solemnity of its present position; and then say, would you look with interest on an expedition about to navigate unknown seas and to encounter unknown dangers? —that little human bark has just commenced its voyage for eternity. The ocean of being on which it has launched is boundless. One shore it has left, but will never reach another. Young as the infant traveller may be, he is already in motion—on the road some ground has been gone over. How immensely important that his first steps should be right; otherwise, every subsequent step will but take him further into error. How important that, where there are so many wrong roads, some one should point out the right one!

II.

For, secondly, the text implies that *there is a way in which, from earliest childhood, we ought to walk.* There is a right and a wrong concerning everything which relates to moral character. And if, as we have seen, everything is calculated in some way to affect our character, then, from earliest childhood, everything viewed in relation to character is right or wrong. The most obtuse parents sometimes come to see this. Indulgences which they once considered perfectly harmless for their children come to be productive of the most grievous results. Things which they once laughed at in their children as trifles, they come to weep over as of fatal consequence. Painful experience convinces them, too late, that nothing relating to childhood is absolutely indifferent—that everything is right or wrong—that concerning every way in which they walk it may be said, "they *ought* to walk in it, or they ought not."

1. Now, to speak on this part of the subject in broad and

general terms, we might say, first, that the way of *knowledge*, in opposition to that of ignorance, *is right.* For, "that the soul be without knowledge is not good;" that the eye be without light is not good; that the appetite be without food is not good; and as little is it good that the soul be without knowledge; for the soul and knowledge were made for each other, as much as light and the eye, appetite and food. Unless the two are brought together therefore, the ordination of nature is frustrated; the soul is defrauded of its right—some of its noblest powers remain undeveloped and unused, and nothing but evil can ensue. Besides, God has so placed His works before us as to excite inquiry, and to awaken in the young an ardent thirst for knowledge. The great design of the ancient Israelites, in erecting pillars of memorial in different spots, was to excite the curiosity of their children to inquire, "What mean ye by these stones?" that then they might receive an answer which should instruct them in the ways of the Lord. Just so, God may be said to have everywhere set up memorials of His power, and wisdom, and goodness—to have so disposed the objects of nature and the events of providence, as to excite the inquiries of the young—to have strewed their early path with such awakening mementos as should impel them to inquire, "What means this?" and thus to furnish the parent, or the instructor, with an opportunity of leading their youthful feet in the way of salutary knowledge.

2. And, next, the way of *religious truth,* in opposition to that of error, is right. This way leads direct to the Bible. We have remarked that in the fields of nature and providence God has so disposed of things as to raise a spirit of inquiry in the young. And has He done so less in the field of revelation? There is no book so attractive to childhood as the Bible. God himself has designedly—I had almost said *studiously*—made it so. Would *you* not make for your children, were it in your power, a book full of interesting instruction? And has God less of parental love than you

have? Oh, "if ye, being evil, know how to give good things to your children, how much more will God give them?" And one of the best things He *has* bestowed on them is His blessed Word. Here they learn that they have a Father who is in heaven; here they are initiated into a Divine philosophy teaching by example. What pictured beauty in its parables! What graphic and enchaining interest in its narratives! And yet here the attractive is only a means to an end, for it is subordinated to their highest instruction. Here the voice which addresses them speaks to their conscience in the calm tones of unbending authority—the eye which is turned on them appeals to their hearts, for it is felt to be beaming with tenderness, and yet to be fixed upon them in an unslumbering gaze—the hand that is extended full of blessings towards them is seen to be the hand which was nailed to the cross—the heaven of glory which He has here thrown open to their view is arrayed in Divine attractions to invite their approach. Here, if *any* thing be felt, they are made to feel that the depraved heart which it describes is actually in their own bosoms—that the cross which it unveils is their only hope—that the new heart which it promises is the best gift they can receive—that the throne of grace to which it would lead them is the place where that best gift can be obtained—that the future judgment, with all its solemn array on the right hand and on the left, is intended to awaken their dread of hell, and to enkindle their noblest aspirations after heaven. "Lord, wherewithal shall a young man cleanse his way, but by taking heed thereto according to thy word?" Other knowledge may be *useful*, but this is *saving*. Other knowledge may be useful, but this will increase its usefulness—is profitable for the life that now is as well as for that which is to come. Other knowledge, *without* this, *may* be useless, hurtful, the means of arming its possessors with a mightier power of depravity; but, with this, the tendency of the evil heart to pervert knowledge is restrained—knowledge itself is sanctified—converted into wisdom—and rendered conducive to the highest ends. For, "this is life eternal; to know thee the only true God, and Jesus Christ whom thou hast sent."

And, then, the way of holy obedience, in opposition to the way of transgression, is right. And this, we think, is the way especially intended in the text—the cherishing of right tendencies — the implantation of correct principles — the formation of good habits. The impartation of mere knowledge is, as we have shewn, a good: and the communication of religious truth a still greater good. But, important as they are, they are only means to an end—and that end is the production of a right state of mind in relation to God. For "the fear of the Lord, *that* is wisdom; and to depart from evil is understanding."

Now, in the present day, when more is thought of *means* than of *ends*—when everything is to be made *easy*, whatever may become of its *usefulness*—when he who does a thing *quickest*, even in education, is therefore supposed to do it best—there is ground to fear that the way spoken of in the text is too much lost sight of. There is reason to apprehend that, by many, the *intellect* of the young is cultivated to the neglect of the *heart*—that the *amount* of knowledge and of truth which the child can imbibe, is thought far more of than the use he is likely to make of it. On this account, we think highly of the well-conducted infant school, or of the school of any name, where, however small the amount of information imparted, valuable habits are formed —habits of cleanliness, punctuality, order, attention, and obedience. On the same account, we think highly of that family training—not where the heart is indulged and spoiled, as a reward for a little exercise of the head—not where the child is allowed to be self-willed and capricious, as a reward for being clever;—but where filial obedience is taught as a primary duty;—and parental authority is exercised as a sacred trust from God—and where the fear of the Lord is taught as the beginning of wisdom. And for the same reason, we must think most highly of the Sunday-school, where the *chief* object is—not to teach to read—to read even the Bible---or to commit portions of it to memory, but where, without neglecting the mechanical parts of instruction, the knowledge imparted is sought to be *applied*—where the great aim is to reach the heart of the child, and to impress it with a sacred regard for truth—a filial love to its parents—a reverence for the name of God—a desire for the return of the Sabbath—a love for the Bible, and an affection for its teacher as the minister of God to it for good. To attempt this may leave but little time for reading and repeating lessons; *but*, the teacher will have the satisfaction of knowing that he has given himself *principally* to the *principal* object; and should he, by God's blessing, succeed in that object, he will find that but little time is *necessary* for other objects—that the formation of such habits is the soil in which every excellence may speedily take root and flourish. The child thus taught may take away with him a much smaller amount of *religious information* than another child whose time has been wholly occupied in exercises of reading and memory. But the difference between the two will be just that between the thorn-covered ground spoken of in the parable—in which the best seed the sower could cast, however greedily devoured, was soon choked and destroyed—and the prepared ground, in which all the seed that fell brought forth fruit a hundred fold. In the case supposed, we would say to the teacher, you have prepared a soil for the Great Husbandman to sow. You have done more than stored the child's memory with *facts*—with an encyclopædia of facts—you have planted his heart with *principles.* You have placed a grand object before him—the welfare of his moral nature—the salvation of his soul; and it will not be so necessary for you to particularize and prescribe details of duty. For he who is led to devote himself to a great object is a law to himself; he who acts on a high and holy principle lifts his whole nature at once;—he who aims at an exalted end is more than resolving on good acts or even good habits, he is actually producing them;—he who lives for a noble purpose is keeping all laws at once without feeling that he is subjected to any. You have done more for him than to give him verbal directions about the way in which he should go—you have taken him to it—trained him in it—so that now the young traveller for eternity has only to hold on his way, in order to reach the mount of God above.

III.

But then, thirdly, the text intimates that *in order to walk in this way the child requires to be trained.* He is not *born in* it—he must be led to it. He will not take to it *instinctively.* Other ways there are in which he should not go; but in which, if left to follow the influence of evil example, and the bent of his own heart, he will be sure to go. Nay more: his moral history will soon be stained with the record of a first sin—a personal fall. How affecting a consideration is this! We are accustomed to speak, and truly, of the first sin of Adam as the fall of man:—as an event whose fatal consequences can never be fathomed. But has not every man his own fall? Each of us has had his *first* sin; though probably it was committed so early in life that we do not remember it. Yet, in the book of God's remembrance, there stands recorded against us a first sin. The record of *that* sin was the record of our personal fall—"another fall of man." Had either of you never sinned till to-day—had you contracted pollution to-day for the first time, what an era in your existence would it have been!—what a fearful fall!—what a subject for mourning, lamentation, and woe! Alas, for man, that his daily falls, and his years of accumulated guilt, should leave him to sleep as soundly as if his first sin had not yet been committed! And, alas for the infant, slumbering sweetly in utter unconsciousness of actual guilt, that the hour of its personal fall should be at hand! But so it is—the moment when a sense of evil will first cloud its brow, and remorse plant its first arrow in the soul. And that first sin, trifling though it may seem in the eye of man, will contain in it the same fearful elements of guilt as did the first sin of Adam—its first act of disobedience will involve an insult to the entire law of God. As soon as it begins to *go,* it will, like its first parents, begin to go *astray;* and all its subsequent course, if left unrestrained, and undirected by the grace of God, will be but a continuation of that first devious step. You can expect to see it brought into the right way, only as the result of a religious training. This the first transgressors required; and each of all their posterity requires the same.

IV.

Now, fourthly, the text implies that *children are capable of being trained in the way they should go.* All children may not be equally pliable in the hands of the trainer—may not present the same facilities for moral cultivation. But all admit of improvement. There is no fruit known to the horticulturist which was not once a wildling of the field or of the forest. But, by cultivation, the most tasteless has received a flavour—the most nauseous has been made palatable—and many of the most unpromising productions of nature turned into articles of cost and luxury. Would that equal skill and care had always been bestowed on the cultivation of the human plant! How much more precious would be the fruit!—how much more rich and ample the repayment!

And see what facilities God has provided for their training! Would it facilitate the process, could you commence it before their hearts become preoccupied with evil? God affords the parent *this* opportunity. We have no sympathy, indeed, with the theory which represents the human mind as being at first pure and spotless as a sheet of unwritten paper; and as being stained only by *subsequent* impressions. Rather, it resembles the paper which is covered with the secret writing of an invisible ink, and which only requires to be placed near the fire in order to bring out, and make visible, all the characters. But then, parents and friends of the young, it comes to you before it has been placed near the fire, and in order that you may keep it from the exciting influence of evil. It comes to you, free from the blots and stains of *actual* transgression, to be preoccupied as quickly and fully as possible with the writing and signature of heaven—to be made an "epistle of Christ, known and read of all men."

Would a state of *great susceptibility to impression* facilitate their training? The age of childhood is the age of impression; and God commits them to you in that impressible state, that they may receive, through your instrumentality, the imprint of His own image.

Would it conduce to their training, could you find them not inclined to dispute your testimony—not requiring you logically to prove everything—but disposed readily to believe your word? Now you enjoy this advantage. God has so constituted the human mind that, at first, it easily believes all that it is told. Belief is natural to it. It has to learn *not* to believe—and often is it a painful effort. Alas, that the falsehood and deception of those around it should ever drive it to the hard necessity! But, prior to this, belief is natural to it. It asks not for evidence—waits not for proof—but believes on the simple testimony of those it loves. In allusion to this ready and unquestioning faith of children, it was, probably, that our Lord pronounced a blessing on those who should receive the kingdom of God as a little child.

Would it add to your probability of success in training them for the right way, were it so ordered that they should remain for a considerable time in this impressible and improvable state? God has so wisely ordered it that the young of the human kind should remain in a state of comparative helplessness longer than the young of any other kind. The poet of ancient scepticism sang of this long period of infantine dependence as a state of supposed inferiority to the young of the brute creation, and therefore as a proof that there is no Providence. He saw not that it supplies one of the strongest proofs of the contrary. Had the child remained dependent on its parents only as long as the brood remains with the parent bird, the endearing names of *father* and *mother* would have been empty sounds, and justly might the parents have pleaded that the brevity of the term afforded them no opportunity of training their offspring for heaven. But, graciously ordered as it is, they have not only an opportunity of inscribing on their children's heart the first impressions which it receives—and of moulding their character while it is in its most impressible state—but of continuing to retouch and deepen their best impressions for a succession of years.

These are some of the *natural* facilities we possess for training children for God. The *moral* facilities correspond with them. They consist, as we have seen, in the hallowed nature of the knowledge which God has entrusted us to impart to them—and in the attractive manner in which He has conveyed it—in the institution of the Sabbath—in the power of prayer—and in all the appointed means of grace—means, which if rightly employed, cannot fail to render the way in which they should go a way of pleasantness, and a path of peace. Training them for good or for evil, we always are; for, whether we will or not, everything we do and say affects them. And equally certain is it that if we avail ourselves of the facilities we have named, we shall train them in the right way. To this truth, the experience not of a Samuel and a Timothy merely, but of a number in every age can bear testimony, whose youthful feet have trod the path of life; and the experience probably of some present—for, to the prayers and counsels of a pious father, and to the tender and transforming example of a pious mother—or to the efforts of a Christian teacher—they owe it that they are now walking in the way to heaven.

V.

And hence the text implies, in the next place, that *it is the duty of parents, and of those who are themselves walking in the way they should go, to train the young to accompany them.* And, indeed, for what but for holy purposes were the primary and principal relations of life designed at first? For "did He not make one," asks the prophet:—"Yet had He the residue of the Spirit"—that is, He might have made more—"and wherefore one? that He might seek a godly seed"—that every house might be a church—a nursery for heaven. So that in exercising his influence for religious purposes, the Christian parent is but restoring it to the purpose from which sin had diverted it. So mighty is that influence, that the influence which the mightiest monarch ever swayed over his subjects is not to be compared with it. His voice is the first music which his children hear—his smiles their bliss—his authority the image and substitute of the Divine authority. So absolute is the law which impels them to believe his every word—to imitate his every tone, gesture, and action—and to receive the ineffaceable impressions of his character, that his every movement drops a seed into the virgin soil of their hearts to germinate there for eternity. His influence, by blending itself with their early conceptions, and incorporating with the very elements of their being, and by the constancy, subtlety, variety, and power of its operation, gives him a command over their character and destiny, which renders it the most appropriate emblem on earth of the influence of God himself. All this influence he is bound to employ for their highest welfare. It was given him on purpose. As if they had been sent down to him from heaven, with a Divine command to train them for Christ, he is to shed on them nothing but hallowed influence. Their first lispings are to be of Christ—their first imaginings of His love—their first steps to His footstool. The influence of the parent—of *his* Christian character—is to surround them like the atmosphere of a temple; that, by being breathed into and mingled with their earliest being, it may become an elementary part of *their* character. But, though this is the duty of the *parent primarily*—a duty which he can never discharge by proxy—a duty for which no school instruction is an adequate substitute—a duty from which *nothing* can ever release him—yet, it is not his duty *exclusively.* Wherever the Christian may be, he is in the centre of a large circle of duties—to every class of persons included in that circle he owes duties of some kind, and therefore to the young. And when he perceives—as in every neighbourhood—numbers of the young swarming around him—and knows their comparative destitution of religious instruction—and thinks of the important position they hold in society—of the influence which they will exercise in this world—and of their solemn relations to the world to come—is it strange that he should be impelled to say, with a holy yearning for their souls, as his Lord did, "Suffer them to come unto me, and forbid them not?" Is he not under a sacred obligation to do all he can to train them to sing, like the children of old, "Hosanna! blessed is he that cometh in the name of the Lord!" and to do it, in the hope of preparing them to join in the hosannas of the temple above?

VI.

And this is the encouraging prospect which the text holds out to him. For, sixthly, it intimates, that *if children are trained in the way they should go, they will continue to walk in it.* Now, we are free to avow our deep conviction that this is not so much the language of a promise, as the statement of a grand principle of the domestic and social constitution. We think that it is a law so general that it includes many other laws—laws of the mental and moral constitution of man; and we think that it is a law so uniform in its operation, that in the last great day it will be found that it has never known a single exception.

Well am I aware, indeed, of the ready objection which starts to the lips of some on hearing this proposition. They tell us of what they consider painful exceptions to its truth in the circle of their own acquaintance. And to place the fact beyond a doubt, they will, perhaps, name an instance in which the child of an excellent Christian man or minister forced his way to destruction in spite of parental prayers, example, and instruction. Now, it is an ungracious task to have to meet and negative a specified case of this description; for it cannot be done without appearing to bring an accusation against the pious parents; whereas, perhaps, these parents, who have had to mourn over the evil end of their child, actually laboured more to train him aright than another parent has done to train *his* children who yet are all walking in the path of life. But yet, delicate and difficult as the task may be, we must charge their training with some defect; for the truth of God must be vindicated—and that truth affirms that a child trained in the way he should go shall not depart from it when he is old.

Besides, do you not see that a denial of this proposition involves this grave and startling consequence—that here there is no connexion between means and ends—that causes may be put into operation without any corresponding effects being produced—that though, in every other department of human agency, God has graciously pledged himself that if certain things be done certain results shall follow, yet that in this particular department the rule is departed from. Now, one would be justified in demanding *why* this anomaly here? What is it which can induce the Divine Being to depart in *this* single class of cases from the whole tenor of his conduct in every other department—which can induce him to say to the parent, in effect, "though you adopt all the right means, and employ them in the right manner, yet here you must not calculate on any corresponding results?" No; this be far from God!

Brethren, when failure ensues in any other department of

duty, do we rashly conclude that the connexion between means and ends, which has existed since the creation of the world, has at length ceased? Our common sense protects us from such a folly. We rightly conclude that there has been something faulty in the employment of the means. This *alone* is sufficient to account for the failure in every other class of duties; and so it is in this. We say not, indeed, that the failure of parental training, in any given instance, furnishes a looker-on with any ground for concluding that but little has been done for the child's welfare. Comparatively much may have been done; more even than usual. No human eye might be keen enough to detect a fault in it; no human being be justified in pronouncing censure. But, still, we *must* believe that *something* was wanting; or else we must impeach the faithfulness and the grace of God. We must believe that the training was not commenced early enough—or, if it was, that it was not continued long enough—or, if it was, that it suffered interruptions—or, if it did not, that there was too much reliance on other means to the neglect of prayer—or, if prayer was not neglected, that it was not properly combined with the use of other means—or else, that certain parts of the training were not pursued in the right spirit—or else, that parental *example* did not, in some particular, enforce parental precept—or that the influence of one parent neutralized that of the other—or, if not, that the influence of some other party did—or, that indulgence and severity so alternated as to destroy parental authority—that there was a want of adaptation in the training to the peculiar character of the child—or else, a want of holy *earnestness* pervading the whole. Yes, we *must* believe that where nothing is wanting in the means employed, nothing is ever wanting in the end obtained. We do not forget, indeed, that the child himself is a free agent; and that much depends on his own dispositions. This it is which renders the training of a child an art, a science the most sacred—next to that of a parent's own salvation, the most *momentous* occupation in which he can be engaged. But then we must, and do, believe also, that in the day of final account it will appear that every child rightly trained in the way to heaven will certainly be found there.

Oh, what an encouraging consideration is this for the parent and the teacher, who are sincerely seeking the salvation of their children. The language of our subject to you is—aim at the highest results, and expect the most glorious consequences.

1. Would you train up the children committed to your care in the way they should go? Then aim at the highest result—the salvation of their souls. Everything short of this is only a means to that end. Aim at *that* end. Expect it, and it will impart a unity and a power to all you do for them. Expect it—and so far from being surprised at attaining it, you will be restless and dissatisfied till you find that you are in the way of attaining it. Two reasons may be assigned for the frequent failure of religious training in securing the conversion of the young. One is, that their salvation is but very slightly expected, and is therefore but very vaguely aimed at; and thus failure is invited. No good is done, because the *greatest* good was not aimed at. And the other is, that the course of training is so generally abandoned, or suspended, at the very season when it is *most* important—at the critical point when childhood passes into youth—when the world is standing with open arms, and with a thousand carefully prepared snares, to receive and ruin them—and just at the crisis, therefore, when their training should be more than ever vigorous, as it becomes more than ever vital to their welfare. Oh, what multitudes of children are thus lost to the Church and to God! But aim at their highest welfare, and you will *lessen* the evil, if you cannot quite remedy it; for you will not speedily lose sight of them —you will follow them with your prayers and entreaties—you will feel as if you could not let them go till you have brought them to Christ. Expect it—and not only will it

give a directness to your appeals, and a holy energy to your efforts—not only will it keep alive your tenderest sympathies for the souls of the dear children—often will it take you to the throne of grace—for you will feel your entire dependence on the Spirit of God—and there will you wrestle for the success you desire. Look for it—the Saviour will—He comes amongst you seeking fruit—the precious, precious fruit of the travail of His soul. And will not *you* travail in birth again till Christ is formed in the hearts of the children? Nothing less than their conversion—their salvation—will satisfy Him; let nothing less satisfy you.

2. And while aiming at such a result, you are entitled to anticipate the most glorious consequences. Think of the happy results which, by God's blessing, may flow from your instrumentality, both in this world, and in that which is to come. *You are training a new generation for carrying on the cause of knowledge—of philanthropy—of God upon earth.* When you look upon those who are now children, you are to remember that in a few years hence they will have come into the possession of the world, with all its offices and influence—and of the Church, with all its hallowed privileges and momentous duties. What a distinguished honour is yours in having to train them for their posts. Only imagine —if *we* were the first generation of men—if, having come into existence at the beginning of the world, we had lived through all the ages of time, down to the present moment—and if we had just received an intimation from God that our centuries of life were drawing to a close—and that in a few short years the children now around us would be left alone to occupy our places—with what yearning solicitude should we look on them! How anxiously should we prepare them for the eventful change! What father ever warned, and counselled, and imparted his soul to his son with a deeper concern than that with which we should labour to infuse into them the result of all our long experience, and to impress them with the vast responsibility of their position. And if

we selected any of our number to instruct and prepare them for it, how anxiously should we select the holiest, wisest, best, and feel that we were committing to them the most honourable and sacred trust they ever received. Now, such, friends—such, in effect, is your office. For, though we are only one generation of many who have passed over the face of the earth, on us have descended all the influence, advantages, and responsibilities of the past, and on us it devolves to pass on the whole to those who come after us. And your office it is to prepare them to receive it. Soon will the ark of God have to be borne by them—what an honour is yours to train them to carry it! Soon they will have to take the standard of the Lord from your hand—what a distinction to have been employed by the Captain of Salvation to enrol them in His ranks. Those you are now training in the way they should go will then be employed in training others. Who can say how much your knowledge of that fact will enhance your happiness in heaven?

But more—you are training them for a nobler service, and a more distant future—for a state of eternal blessedness above. You are praying for it—are you not? Humble as that childish form may be, it enshrines immortality. Peaceful though its features may be—feelings and passions are folded up in its bosom which require infinity and eternity for their full development—and you are anxious that they may be developed, not in hell, but in heaven. Unmeaning as its countenance may sometimes seem, *you* know that thoughts and capabilities are at this moment sleeping in its frame, some of which will slumber on to the close of life—and you are concerned that they should find scope and expansion in a nobler sphere of existence. And have you been the means of training his dispositions Godward?—you have given him impressions which shall go with him into eternity. Have you taught him the fear of the Lord?—the Christian truth which he has learned at your feet will find a response among angels and archangels—the sacred praise which he has learned at your lips will pour itself forth in perfected tones to a seraph's harp—the Christian charity which he is learning from your example will expand, and be at home in *His* immediate presence who has pronounced himself the "God of Love." Have you trained—are you now training—are you assisting others to train—one of these little ones in the way he should go? Ten thousand ages hence he will be still advancing in the same way, "high in salvation and the climes of bliss;" and as he looks back from the heights he has attained, and as he casts his crown before the throne of God and the Lamb, he will gratefully refer to that instrumentality which taught him to take the first step towards it. "Therefore, my beloved brethren, be ye steadfast, unmovable; always abounding in the work of the Lord; *knowing* that your labour is not in vain in the Lord."

SERMON XIV.

CHRIST PRECIOUS TO THE BELIEVER.

1 PETER ii. 7.—"Unto you, therefore, which believe, he is precious."

On the Death of a Minister of Christ.

A PECULIAR excellence of the Sacred Scriptures is, that they direct our attention to those things only which are truly precious. If they advert for a moment to objects of an inferior or a worthless description, it is only to point out their worthlessness and the danger of loving them—and thus to prepare the way for leading our affections to objects of a higher character and of substantial worth. They propose to impart to us a wisdom more precious than rubies—the science of salvation—the excellent knowledge of Christ Jesus our Lord. They speak of a most precious faith, and of the trial of that faith being much more precious than gold. They tell us of the precious blood of Christ, and give to us promises exceedingly great and precious.

But it would be easy to shew that the value of each of these arises from its relation to Christ; so that in speaking of Him we are speaking of an object from which everything else derives its value. Now, if a tree be more valuable than any one of its fruits singly, or even than all its fruits of a single season, then the Saviour must be regarded as incomparably more precious than any of those things to which he imparts a value. Now, it is He who is here presented to our attention. He is spoken of in the context—which is a quotation from the book of Isaiah—as a living stone, chosen of God and precious; and as a corner-stone, elect, precious—while

His supreme value is spoken of in the text as a truth corroborated by the experience of all who rely on Him; "to them who believe He is precious"—or rather He is preciousness—the very abstract of excellence—the essence of satisfaction and delight. Let it be borne in mind, then, that our attention is now to be occupied by an object whose value transcends to an infinite amount everything else, however valuable, which can be brought into comparison with it. And while our attention is thus employed, may He whose office it is to commend the Saviour to the soul, endear Him to our hearts, and raise our affections from earth to heaven.

In illustrating the excellence of Christ we propose to shew that, tried by every test by which the value of any object can be ascertained, He is supremely precious.

I.

And, first, we remark that *many things are esteemed precious on account of their extreme rareness.* We could specify many things which it was once deemed an honour and a distinction to possess, but which the progress of science has so multiplied that they have now ceased to be sought or valued. And many an object still, to possess which scarcely any price would be thought too costly, or any sacrifice too great, depends for its value on its scarceness alone; multiply it indefinitely and its charm would be gone, its value extinct. Now, by this test, the Saviour is precious; for not only is there no other Saviour—there never *can* be. "Other foundation can no man lay than that is laid, which is Jesus Christ." "Neither is there salvation in any other; for there is none other name under heaven given among men whereby we can be saved." However numerous the ways to destruction may be, there is but one way of escape—but one Mediator between God and man, the man Christ Jesus. However numerous the false refuges we may have devised, He comes forth in His Gospel amidst them all, and proclaims, "I am the Lord; and besides me there is no Saviour." On this account, "to them that believe he is precious." He is the only centre around which their hopes can revolve—the only object to which their hearts can cleave. They have no other name but His to plead for acceptance with the Father—no other robe to wear in the presence of God but that which His righteousness supplies. They feel that to look away from Him in the question of their salvation would be to look away from their light and their life—that to build for eternity on any other basis than that of His perfect mediation would be to build their house upon the sand—that to forsake Him would be to step from the only ark provided for a perishing world into the wide and wasteful ocean of despair. Cleaving to His cross, as to their only hope, they revolt from the idea of forsaking Him, as from the sight of a bottomless gulf—of certain destruction—while they exclaim, "Lord to whom shall we go? thou hast the words of eternal life!"

II.

Secondly, *An object is accounted precious when it has availed us in danger, and procured for us deliverance and security.* Now, tried by this test, the Saviour is precious—tried by this test, He will be found to occupy a rank which nothing can approach within an infinite distance. Others may have saved us from temporal dangers, and ministered to our temporal relief. Others may have broken the chains of the slave—have rescued a people from the fangs of tyranny—have assuaged the sufferings of disease—and, by their painstaking labours and discoveries, have multiplied the enjoyments of mankind. And were there no hereafter—were there no sin to be punished in that hereafter—these would be services of the first importance. But when we look away from this world into eternity, and think at the same time of our sin—how insignificant does every benefit we can receive from man appear, compared with deliverance from sin! There is no shame independently of sin—there is no bondage apart from sin. Take away sin—and the gloomiest dungeon becomes a palace—and death itself becomes stingless—and the undying worm loses its power to torment—and the flames of perdition expire. Now Jesus delivers His people from their sins—and, in saving them from these, He rescues them from every evil; not merely from the evils peculiar to the present life, but from those which would otherwise cleave to them through eternity. And more than this—He has taken their nature into union with His own, and having thus honoured it in His own person, He has borne it into the presence of God, and has placed it on the loftiest seat in the heavenly state—a pledge that He has rescued it from every foe, and secured to it an immortality of life and bliss. As a foretaste of what He proposes to do for them hereafter, He calls them *now* to stand in the light of the Divine countenance—takes them into the sacred embraces of His own friendship—infuses into them His own spirit—and bestows on them the most endearing titles, the most distinguished privileges. And still more, at this moment He is engaged in their behalf—He is preparing mansions for their reception—occupying the throne for them—officiating at the altar of incense for them—and conducting them onwards to that point where the blessings of redemption are to be all unveiled—where the treasures of His grace are to be all displayed before their admiring eyes, and their felicity is to be completed in the enjoyment of more than eye hath seen, or heart hath ever conceived. On this account, to them that believe He is precious. They love Him because He first loved them—and because He has demonstrated His love by delivering them from an evil, and securing to them a good, the amount of which eternity alone can fully display.

III.

Again: *An object is esteemed precious when it has inherent worth, intrinsic excellence,* even though it has never benefited us: but if, in addition to its having been of great advantage to us, it proves also to be valuable in itself, this enhances its worth in our esteem. Now, tried by this test, the Saviour is precious. He has not only laid us under infinite obligation by what He has achieved for us, but the manner in which He has achieved it proves that He is a Being of inherent excellence, of transcendent dignity and perfection. In working out our redemption He has developed His character; and in that character we behold an assemblage of the highest qualities—of qualities which angels admire, and imitate, and adore.

Now it is the spiritual perception of these qualities, as disclosed in the history of our redemption, which wins our confidence and excites our joy. It is not enough that the Being who offers to redeem us be able to do only *almost* everything—that His power be nearly unlimited—He must clearly be able to accomplish everything, or that which He is unable to do may be something which is essential to our salvation. It is not enough that He be compassionate merely, His compassion must be unlimited, or we may be the very sinners who have passed beyond the limits of His grace. He must be willing to pardon every description of sin, every amount of guilt, or we should be constantly harassed with the fear that He had no grace for us. It would satisfy us but little to be assured that He was *all but* free from sin—that He was *nearly* perfect—He must be entirely free from every taint of sin—pure as God himself—or we could not be sure that God would accept Him—or would accept of us for the sake of Him. And it would satisfy us but little to know that He was all this, if at the same time He was liable to change. He must be essentially immutable—otherwise He might change in His conduct towards us—and change, too, at the very moment when it was most important to our happiness that He should not change.

Now the Redeemer is all this—realizes the loftiest conceptions we can form of a perfect Saviour. In power He is omnipotent, able to save unto the uttermost all that come unto God by Him. In purity He is spotless, the perfect image of the invisible God. In compassion He knows no limits, takes no exceptions—whosoever will may come to Him—His blood cleanseth from all sin. Every attribute He possesses, and every office He sustains, are made to pour their fulness into the treasury of His Church, and to contribute to the happiness of His people. While whatever He is at present, He will continue to be to all future time. "the same yesterday, to-day, and for ever."

Who that approaches and contemplates the transcendent excellence of Christ, can for a moment withhold his admiration or restrain his joy? We implore to be saved from impending destruction, and He meets the request by pouring out His blood, enduring our penalty, and procuring for us a right to the tree of life. We admire the surpassing beauty and Divine perfection of His character—and He offers to change us into the same image, to renovate and conform us to the same glorious model. We gaze on the glory by which He is surrounded, and muse on the boundless happiness He enjoys, and while we are lost in the delightful meditation, He offers to share His splendours with us, and declares that we shall sit down with Him upon His own throne! "How great is His goodness, and how great is His beauty." Well may the believer, delighted with the contemplation of them, exclaim, "How precious are Thy thoughts unto me, O God! how great is the sum of them!"

IV.

Fourthly, In order to estimate the value of a thing, we sometimes *compare it with others of the same kind;* and on instituting this test, we not unfrequently find that what we had before undervalued proves to be exceedingly precious. Now, tried by this test, the Saviour is precious. When the Almighty beheld His ancient people engaged in the monstrous occupation of modelling an idol image of Himself, He is represented as inquiring, with a mixture of indignation and pity, "To whom will ye liken me, and make me equal, and compare me, saith the Lord?" The Redeemer may be regarded as uttering the same language in the capacity of Mediator—"To whom will ye liken me, and make me equal?" To whom can we compare Him, in the condescension to which He stooped? Others may have mingled condescension with their kindness towards us, but no other being has descended from heaven to assume our nature as He did, and if there had, that other being would not have had to leave the bosom of the Father as He did, and never having equalled Him in height by an infinite amount, could never have stooped so low as He did by an infinite distance. To what can we compare the value of His atoning blood? It is degraded by bringing it into comparison with anything else. If the sacrifice of a broken and a contrite heart be of greater value in the Divine estimation than the flaming sacrifice of the whole material world, then what must be the value of the precious blood of Christ, who through the Eternal Spirit offered himself up without spot unto God! To what can we compare His divine mediation? or what, were it possible for that mediation to be proved in the slightest degree defective—what could complete it? It stands on a height to which nothing could aspire: it is in its nature so essentially distinct from everything else of the nature of merit, and infinitely superior to it, that nothing could be joined with it.

Now it is the deep conviction of His incomparable worth which endears Him to His people. To behold the perfection of His work, is to behold a description of merit which makes them forget every other ground of trust. To be awakened to a sight of His transcendent worth, is to become acquainted with an order of excellence which eclipses every other. It introduces into the soul a principle of affiance in Christ which admits of no competition—which expels every other ground of hope—which lays every other confidence in the dust—and which places the Saviour in triumph on the throne of the heart.

V.

Fifthly—In order to estimate the value of a thing, we sometimes *consult the opinion of a competent judge;* and on resorting to this test, we not unfrequently find that what we had before but little valued turns out to be highly precious. In forming an opinion of moral and spiritual worth, it is of the greatest importance that we should consult a higher judgment than our own, since this is a department in which we are especially liable to error; for even the Saviour himself informs us here, that that which is highly esteemed among men is often an abomination in the sight of God. But what competent judgment can we consult when the worth of Christ is the question to be determined? what but the infallible estimate, the unerring judgment of the great God himself? Now tried by this test, you need not be informed the Saviour is found to be incalculably precious.

It was owing to His entire fitness to become our Saviour that the Eternal Father elected him to the office, and in the presence of the universe poured on Him expressions of ineffable delight. Passing by all the ranks and orders of created excellence, His complacency found an object only in the person of the Son. To inspire the ancient Church with a measure of that same complacency, the Father announced Him beforehand as *His* elect, in whom His soul delighted. As the architect of that spiritual temple which is to be built of living stones, He invites the admiration of all to the foundation He has chosen. When He laid the foundation of the earth, the morning stars sang together, and all the sons of God shouted for joy. But on laying the basis of human redemption in Christ, the great Builder himself could not survey His work without enlarging complacently on its merits, and uttering the language of exultation and joy, "Behold, saith he, I lay in Zion for a foundation—a stone, a tried stone, a precious corner-stone, a sure foundation." Having followed the Incarnate Saviour with His eye through every part of His earthly progress, and having derived from the contemplation an unmeasured fulness of delight, He raised Him from the dead, and crowned Him with glory and honour. He placed Him at His own right hand, and, summoning around Him the hosts and hierarchies of heaven, proclaimed, "Let all the angels of God worship Him." That nothing might be wanting to demonstrate the infinite extent of His paternal satisfaction, He even resigned the sceptre of authority into His hands. Having adorned the eternal throne with all the emblems of power, and suspended on it all the prerogatives of Deity, He virtually resigned it to His anointed Son, "For the Father loveth the Son, and hath given all things into His hands." And even this, though the highest expression of love He could bestow, is not to be regarded as the last. For, henceforth, this is His commandment, the commandment which His own lips have issued, and made permanent and binding on every human being—the command which takes precedence of every other, and which forms the essence of His revealed will, "that we should believe in the name of His Son Jesus Christ." To love the Saviour, then, and regard Him as precious, is to follow the judgment of God himself; it is to sympathise with the Supreme Mind, and to fall in with the purpose which is the nearest to His heart.

VI.

But there is another test, differing in some respects from each of those we have already named—the test of *experience;* and, on resorting to this, we not unfrequently find that we had entertained an erroneous opinion of the object tried. Now, examined by this test, many of you need not to be informed that the Saviour is incalculably precious—"for unto you that believe he is precious"—you have made the experiment for yourselves, and are prepared to attest His worth.

And, here, are we asked why it is that faith is necessary in order to be convinced of the preciousness of Christ? Not from any arbitrary appointment on the part of God; but from the nature and necessity of the case. You ascertain the value of different objects in modes differing according to the respective natures of the objects. In order to determine the nature of some of the precious metals, you try them by fire. Gems and precious stones you try by weighing, or subject them to a chemical test. But in order to make trial of *moral* worth—faith, confidence, belief is indispensable. Before you can take a single step towards determining the worth of a person, you must, for instance, believe that he exists. And, then, if that person professes kindness to you, how can you prove his sincerity unless you so far believe his word as to put his professions to the test? And if he undertake to extricate you out of some difficulty, or to relieve you in distress, how can you prove his willingness or his power to make good his offers, unless you so far believe in him as to place yourself in that particular in his hands? And having reposed so much faith in him as to place yourself and your affairs at his disposal—and having found that he then made good his promises, and even exceeded them—you would feel constrained to acknowledge his kindness and his worth. Now, had he made the same offer to another in your situation—and had that other doubted his word, and discredited his professions, and refused to avail himself of his offers—the great difference between you and that other would be, that you believed on him and that he did not. And the consequence would be that while to you who had believed on him he was inexpressibly dear, the other, who had not confided in him, would know nothing experimentally of his worth.

Now the application of all this to believing in Christ is easy. The Christian, believing in the fact of His existence, has applied to Him—relying on His promise, has trusted in Him—availing himself of His offered grace—has confided his soul into His hands. And having found Him faithful to His promise—mighty to save, and as gracious as He is mighty—to *all* such He is—He *must* be precious.

The *recollection* of the Saviour is associated in the minds of His people with all that is attractive, and excellent, and divine. It is connected in their thoughts with recollections of what they once were, and of what they would still have been but for the riches of His grace. It is hallowed—it is embalmed in their hearts, with feelings of the deepest gratitude for the past—hopes of the tenderest care and support in the hour of death, and with cheering anticipations of soon beholding Him as He is. They think of Him in sorrow, and are solaced—for they remember that He himself was a man of sorrows, and that He is sympathetically touched with the feeling of their infirmities. They think of Him in affliction, and their afflictions appear light and but for a moment—for they remember that He bare their sins and carried their sorrows—and that still in their afflictions He is afflicted. In the hour of temptation the recollection of Him reinforces their holy principles, and makes them proof against sin. In the path of duty, it quickens their diligence, and inspires their zeal. At the footstool of mercy, it imparts fervour and faith to their supplications. In the prospect of death, it inspires them with a hope full of immortality. When everything else had lost its influence over the expiring saint, how often has even the sound of the Saviour's name lighted up his countenance, and beamed in his closing eye. When dying, the sound of that name has often recalled him as from the gates of death, and enabled him to exclaim, "O death, where is thy sting? O grave, where is thy victory?" It was so effectually bound up with his existence—so wrought into his soul—that the hand of time could not raze it from his memory—nor the hand of disease efface it from his heart—nor the last enemy prevent him from uttering it in death. For to them that believe, His very *name* is precious.

And now, brethren, another emphatic testimony to the infinite preciousness of Christ has been added by the dying experience of a beloved pastor of this church. Often had you heard him expatiate with delight in this sacred desk on the offices and excellences of Christ. Often, as he here led your devotions, and clasped the footstool of mercy in prayer, have you heard him plead the Redeemer's merits, and avow his entire reliance on them for salvation. Often had you marked how he gloried in the cross of Christ as he called you to join him in commemorating the body and the blood of Christ. And often had those of you who knew him best, admired the traces which his character exhibited of the mind of Christ, and "glorified God in him." What remained to complete his testimony to the worth of Christ—if, indeed, anything was wanting—but the experience of his dying hour? Let me, then, conduct you thither for a moment. . . . . . "Christ," said he—it was the last sentiment which lingered on his lips—"Christ is precious to all believers."

Brethren, could *you* ask, or could *he* hope for more than this? It was as if he had said—"Precious as the Saviour is at this moment to me, my experience only accords with the experience of all who have confided in Him, and of all who shall—'that unto them that believe He is precious.' Tell my people this—tell them that now, when everything else has lost its value, Christ is dearer to me than ever—that now, when flesh and heart faileth, Christ is the strength of my heart, and my portion for ever. And tell them, that precious as He is to me, He will be as precious to them—that dear as He is to me, He is only acting in harmony with a principle from which He never departs—and in fulfilment of a promise which He never violates." Yes, brethren, the Bible invites us to mark the perfect man, and to behold the upright, for it declares that the end of that man is peace. It announces beforehand that his end shall answer to his previous course; and when he arrives at his end, it sends us to his sick-chamber to mark the closing scene—to see whether or not it makes good its promise. Having engaged that his end shall be peace, it does not dread the result—it challenges inspection—it would have all the world to go and witness the issue of the important experiment. In the instance of our beloved brother, that result was all that the Gospel promises, and all that the Christian can desire. "His God brought glory to his dying hour—his dying hour brought glory to his God." Here was a peace passing all understanding; not that peace of insensibility which refuses to think, and which reflection would destroy; but that intelligent and conscious peace which can take a calm and comprehensive survey of the approaching conflict, and yet retain on its face the smile and glow of serene satisfaction; that pure peace which mirrors and reflects from its unruffled bosom the light of the Divine countenance. Suffering could not impair it; even the approach of the last enemy could not give it a momentary alarm. Having led him into the chamber of death, the Saviour drew nearer to his soul than ever—administered to the dying saint an anodyne such as no human chemistry can prepare—cheered him with a cordial distilled from the fruits of the tree of life—poured into his spirit a draught prepared by His own hand of love, prepared expressly for the dying saint—kept for each Christian's final hour—the last he needs on earth—a foretaste of the new wine he is soon to drink above, and intended to strengthen him for his upward flight, and enabling him, as his spirit spreads its wing, to testify to the sufficiency and preciousness of Christ.

And oh! were it not vain to attempt a description of the moment after death, might we not tell you of a robe of glory cast over the disembodied spirit by the Saviour's hand of love? Were it allowed us to trace his radiant ascent—to follow him within the veil—to behold his approach before the throne of the Lamb that was slain—to gaze on the scene which then transpires—the Saviour's looks of love on him, and his looks of adoring gratitude in return—the welcome which he received from Christ, and the prostrate homage which Christ received from him—and had we been empowered to bring back from our departed friend a message to the saints below, would it not in substance be this—"Tell them that the half has not been told them—tell them that precious as the Saviour is to them that *believe*, to them that *behold* Him He is incomparably more precious still. Tell them that inexpressibly dear as He is to them at times, and in some of their more clear and vigorous exercises of faith—the *vision* of His face—the *heaven* of His unveiled and immediate presence, is more than it hath entered into the heart of man to conceive!"

And is it so, brethren? What, then, is the temper of mind in which we should contemplate our brother's removal? That the event should have diffused sorrow through the circle in which he moved and was known is natural; and to indulge with moderation the emotion of grief is allowable and proper. But let us not be so selfishly engrossed by the gloom of the event, as to overlook the glory. Let us not be sullenly insensible even to those causes for gratitude which arise from the temporal abatements and mitigations of the event. Is it nothing that he was exempted at last from the sufferings of a lingering, wasting, and painful disease? that death should have come to him, not as the king of terrors, but as an angel of mercy? that his death should have had all the happiness of sudden dissolution, unaccompanied by its surprise? that no mortal struggle, no agonizing convulsion, should have marked the moment of the soul's departure? that it should have been on the wing, and far above the toils and dangers of mortality, almost before attendant friends had discovered even its preparations for flight?

True, his sun is gone down before night—he is cut off in the vigour of life; but he is gone to take possession of a higher order of life—of that which alone is worthy the name of life. He is dismissed from a station of great usefulness—but it is that he might occupy a higher sphere of service and of honour. Many hopes may have died with him, and much excellence have perished from the earth—

but if lost by the Church below, it is gained by the Church above—heaven is the richer for it. He no longer *lives* for us; but is there not a sense in which he has died for us? teaching us how to die—illustrating for us the sufficiency and value of the gospel—increasing our interest in the heaven whither he has gone—and quickening our progress to reach it. Our loss, however great, can be estimated; but his gain is too vast to admit of computation. Our loss is but for a season—for we also must soon go hence; but his gain is eternal—an eternal weight of glory.

Nothing is left us, then, but to seek to profit by the event. Christian brethren, members of this bereaved Church, were an apostle now addressing you, he would probably say—"Remember them who have had the rule over you—who have spoken unto you the word of God; whose faith follow; considering the end of their conversation—Jesus Christ, the same yesterday, to-day, and for ever." As if he should say, "Their course is finished; but though all your intercourse with them is for the present cut off—forget not the faith they displayed—the truths they taught—the example they set you. Reflect on the happy manner in which they quitted this transitory life—on the support they found in their latest moments from that Saviour they had proclaimed to others—and on that heroic resolution with which many of them were animated to meet even martyrdom itself in His sacred name. And, oh, let it further encourage you to reflect, that though *they* may be removed from among you, yet Christ himself, the Great Shepherd—the Founder of the Church—the Guardian of His people—is the same yesterday, and to-day, and for ever—and therefore your support is certain, your salvation is secure."

Think, brethren, of the proof which He has given of His tenderness and unchangeableness in the history of His Church already. He has already conducted it through fires that have been kindled to consume it—through rivers of blood drained from the veins of its martyred members—

through storms of persecution raised by the powers of darkness to overwhelm it. I ask for its early enemies, when the world seemed leagued against it, and I am shewn their graves. I ask for its friends—and, "lo, a great multitude, which no man can number, of all nations, and kindreds, and peoples, and tongues, before the throne and before the Lamb, clothed with white robes, and palms in their hands." I ask for the Leader of this innumerable host—and am answered by a universal shout from heaven and earth—"blessing, and honour, and glory, and power, be unto Him that sitteth upon the throne, and unto the Lamb for ever." I ask how it is that, while other systems decay, and other kingdoms vanish, the kingdom of Christ should not only survive, but grow stronger by age, and more glorious by conflict—and I am told that it is because He is the same yesterday, to-day, and for ever—and because He stamps His own immutability on everything which belongs to Him.

Let this bereavement, then, endear to you the presence and the promises of Him whose glory it is that He changeth not. Is He dear to you? You will confide in Him all the more entirely for the supporting grace which He afforded to your departed pastor. You will remember that whatever you saw in him to admire was derived from Christ. Is the Saviour dear to you? You will evince it at the present crisis, by cherishing a supreme anxiety for the welfare of His cause here—consulting His will in every step you take respecting it—and placing it more entirely than ever under His immediate guidance.

There are those who deeply share in the sympathy of this assembly—the bereaved widow, and the mourning children of the departed. And I would say to them, whether they are present or absent—Jesus wept. And there is a sense in which even now He mingles His tears with yours. Oh, let His sympathy assuage your sorrow—and His Gospel blend it with hope. Your husband, your father, is not dead, but sleepeth—and the day will come when your Lord will say,

"I go that I may awake him out of sleep." "Believest thou this?" Then your separation is not final—your union is only for a time suspended. At the coming of the Lord you shall again be gathered together unto Him—and together you shall approach the throne of the Lamb—and together cast down your crowns at His feet. And so shall you ever be with the Lord.

But let me not conclude without addressing a remark to the members of this congregation generally. Ask yourselves, I entreat you—ask yourselves with the seriousness of men that know they must give an account—What has been the effect of all the instructions and hallowing influences which have been brought to bear upon you while enjoying the labours of your departed minister? No more shall you hear the voice which has so often and earnestly invited you to Christ, and warned you to flee from the wrath to come. He is gone. Do you realize the fact? He is gone! For the last time he has besought you in Christ's stead to be reconciled to God. No more will you hear him plead for you at a throne of grace. But at another throne you will meet him. Think what a meeting that will be, if you be found still careless and impenitent, after all his warnings, exhortations, and entreaties! What! shall your faithful, and earnest, and affectionate pastor, rise up in the judgment to condemn you? Shall he who has often pleaded your cause with God, and even with yourselves, but pleaded it in vain, appear at that awful day against you, to silence every entreaty for forgiveness—every appeal to mercy—by reminding you how you were commanded, and besought, and threatened, and invited with every form of persuasion and of argument—but were bent on your ruin, and refused to turn unto God? My fellow-sinner, your death may supply the next warning to this congregation. Oh, may the death of your minister do what his instructions never effected—awaken you to a deep concern for the salvation of your soul! How many a conviction have you stifled—how many a purpose and solemn vow, which his entreaties had led you to form, have you broken—frustrating his best efforts, and blasting his fondest expectations! Will you grieve, too, the Spirit of the living God? Will you provoke Him to depart from you? God grant that the death of your minister may prove the occasion of your life.

Finally, brethren, let this event remind us that an unchanging Saviour is the only appropriate refuge for the immortal soul. Everything else is in a state of fluctuation and change. Time?—with our dear departed brother, time is gone for ever. Friends?—his death reminds us that their breath is in their nostrils, and that the tie which binds them to us will soon be dissolved. The world—and its riches, honours, pleasures—are they not incessantly changing hands?—is not mutability inscribed on them all? But why do I speak of change on so small a scale? It is a small thing that our brief days are speeding away. Where are now the years before the flood—the men whose lives stretched out through centuries? It is a small thing even that thrones, and dynasties, and empires pass away from the page of history—even the works of God around us, and above us, evince the same symptoms of decay, the same tendency to dissolution. "For the heavens shall pass away with a great noise, and the elements shall melt with fervent heat—the earth also, and all the works that are therein, shall be burnt up." Amidst this universal ruin is there nothing permanent, nothing immutable? Yes, He who made them all—"Jesus Christ, the same yesterday, to-day, and for ever." "Thou, Lord, in the beginning hast laid the foundation of the earth, and the heavens are the works of thy hands: they shall perish, but thou remainest; and they all shall wax old as doth a garment, and as a vesture shalt thou fold them up; and they shall be changed; but thou art the same, and thy years shall not fail." And is it true also of us, who are surrounded by those fading and passing worlds, that our years will not fail, our duration will not end? Ten thousand ages after this earth has been consumed, and these heavens have been dissolved, shall we be alive—still in need of a refuge, a habitation, and a home? "Lord, thou hast been the dwelling-place of thy people in all generations! Lord, to whom shall we go but unto thee? thou only hast the words of eternal life." And Thou art gone to prepare a place for us. There, all that is great is imperishable, all that is lovely blooms without decay. Around the throne which He occupies, bands of the blessed have already collected. Our fathers and our brethren are there. And as they prove anew the preciousness of Christ, they beckon us to follow. Oh, be followers of them "who, through faith and patience have inherited the promises." Fight the good fight, finish your course, keep the faith, and a crown shall be bestowed upon you in that day, and not upon you only, but upon all them also that love His appearing. Commit your soul into His hands, and it will be as safe as Omnipotence can make it. Take refuge in His grace, and temptation shall not overcome, sin shall not destroy, death itself shall not injure you. Join yourselves to Him, and nothing shall be able to separate you from the love of Christ. You shall know in whom you have trusted, and feel persuaded of your safety. You shall be enabled to await the approach of death with tranquillity; and to anticipate with joy the blessed day when your bodies shall be raised and fashioned like unto your Saviour's glorious body; and when, with all the sainted friends who have gone before you into eternity, you shall approach together the throne of the Lamb, and together cast down your crowns at His feet. Oh, to be so interested in Christ! so filled with the hopes and consolations of the Gospel! Blessed Jesus, these are the gifts of Thy grace; let these precious hopes and consolations be ours! Amen.

SERMON XV.

JACOB'S DREAM.

GENESIS xxviii. 16, 17.—"And Jacob awaked out of his sleep, and he said, Surely the Lord is in this place, and I knew it not. And he was afraid, and said, How dreadful is this place! this is none other but the house of God, and this is the gate of heaven."

THE narrative of which this language forms a part is doubtless familiar to you all. Jacob had just quitted his father's tent at Beer-sheba, to journey to distant Padan-aram, to his mother's father. Having obtained the birth-right by stealth, he had departed hastily to avoid the murderous anger of Esau his brother. Dark and pungent must have been his reflections as he pursued his solitary way—his only possession the staff in his hand—an exile from the land his anxiety to obtain which had involved him in the treachery that now compelled him to quit it. His first day's journey, of about forty miles, had come to a close. The setting sun found him in a solitude far from city or tent. As the stars came forth, he selected a spot, and—as probably in that soft climate he had often done before—collected and placed a few stones, against which he might recline and sleep.

"And he dreamed, and, behold"—not a vague, shadowy, ordinary dream, but a vision clear, significant, sublime, preternatural—"a ladder set up on the earth, and the top of it reached to heaven; and, behold, the angels of God ascending and descending on it. And, behold, the Lord stood above it," and addressed him. By the ladder, I apprehend, we are not to understand the ordinary structure which that name denotes. The idea would be mean, and on many accounts incongruous. When the patriarch speaks here of "the *house* of God" we understand him to mean, not a building, but *a place* of peculiar Divine manifestation; and when he speaks of "the *gate* of heaven" we understand him to mean *the entrance* to heaven; and so by the term "ladder" we may understand him to mean a direct *medium* of communication by stairs or steps. The Hebrew term denotes an elevation—a mound, or pile, cast up. A mountain on the north of Ptolemais was called *the ladder of the Tyrians.* And the fact that the elevation in question, while requiring nothing itself to rest against, presented to the eye of the dreamer the Lord himself *stationed* properly—not standing, but *stationed, dwelling*—at the top of it, plainly indicates a mountain-elevation. This mountain-pile—set up on the earth, or springing direct out of the plain where the dreamer slept—towered towards heaven. Angelic beings scaled and descended its precipitous sides. On its lofty summit reposed the Shekinah—the symbol of the manifested God, the future Messiah; thus antedating, by a thousand years, one of Isaiah's visions; "and the mountain of the Lord's house shall be established on the top of the mountains." And forth from this symbolic glory proceeded the voice of God, renewing to Jacob the great promise already made to Abraham and to Isaac.

So powerfully was the patriarch affected by the vision that he awoke. The desert around him seemed peopled with spiritual beings. He had been sleeping at the gate of heaven. Light from the throne of God seemed still to fall on him. He was standing in the awful Presence. How dreadful is the place! His first involuntary exclamation denotes awful surprise; surprise, remark, not that God had found *him* there, but that *he* had found *God* there. "Surely the Lord is in *this* place;" or, as the Chaldee paraphrases it, "the glory of the Lord dwelleth in this place, and I knew it not." But why this profound surprise? Had he forgotten the doctrine of the Divine Omnipresence? Or did he suppose that all Divine manifestations were confined to his father's tent and altar at Beersheba? that in leaving those hallowed precincts he was leaving behind him the circle sacred to the Divine worship and presence? or, did he expect to be apprised of the Divine presence before he had laid himself down, by some peculiar tokens of consecration—by monumental signs already set up—or by audible voices from invisible beings? Whatever the occasion of his surprise may have been, it was evidently founded in misapprehension. The event demonstrated that God *was* there; there, in a sense, in which, at that moment, He was nowhere else in the universe; and that where He is, there is the gate of heaven.

The misapprehension of the patriarch belongs to a large class of errors on the same subject—errors always rife, but never more so than at present. We propose, therefore, as a topic suited in general to the passing day, and to this occasion in particular, to consider *the proneness of the human mind to mistake the method, and to limit the conditions of the Divine manifestations.* May the tendency of our remarks lead us to desire, and prepare us to receive, such sacred manifestations during this service!

First, let me notice the principal of these errors as at present existing.

1. *Polytheism* has *its* errors on the subject. Mistaking the various *manifestations* of God in nature for so many *gods*, it assigns to each of its "lords many and gods many" his own district and his own mode of operation. *Beyond* his own territorial limits the god is not expected to act, and even *within* that boundary he is not expected to act, except in his own peculiar *manner*. Parts of the world are thus left unoccupied by any god—wide spaces which no deity owns or inhabits—and certain modes of agency are quite unprovided for. To meet with any Divine manifestation in such places, and of such kinds, would overwhelm the discoverer with awful surprise. And was there nothing of this emotion in the exclamation of the patriarch? To find the God of

Beersheba in the desert—to find that although he was so far from his father's tent, he had not yet wandered beyond the domain of the God of Abraham—the discovery amazed him—enlarged his views of the Divine dominions. How different the awful strain of the Psalmist—"Whither shall I go from thy spirit? or whither shall I flee from thy presence? If I ascend up into heaven, thou art there; if I make my bed in Hades, behold thou art there. If I take the wings of the morning, and dwell in the uttermost parts of the sea, even there shall thy hand lead me, and thy right hand shall hold me. If I say, Surely the darkness shall cover me; even the night shall be light about me!" Here is a recognition of the unity, the spirituality, and the omnipresence of God, in the light of which polytheism expires. And yet what other view is suited to the truth and magnitude of the subject? Behold, heaven and the heaven of heavens cannot contain Him, but He himself contains, and is the place of all being. We ourselves are moving among the stars, are we not? careering through space; but though perpetually changing our place in the universe, ever surrounded by His presence, and enclosed by His essence. And could we speed our way to scenes beyond all that eye hath explored, or even thought has reached, what should surprise us there to behold creations in process, new worlds taking their appointed place, sudden manifestations of the present God!

But even the limits of the created universe are no limits to Him. There, where no wing has yet sped, no creative fiat yet taken effect, where all is silence, solitude, and awful gloom, God is already present. And could we, like the patriarch in the lone desert, imagine ourselves to be even there, what should it surprise us to behold some token of the Shekinah—some vision of the present God? Infinite space is but the dark background on which He is ever inscribing His unfinished and unutterable name in characters of living light. Immensity is but His temple, and at any moment He could fill and flood the whole with His glory.

2. The *materialism* of the day has its creed on the subject. According to it, the world may have been indebted for its *origin* to the will of God; but everything ever since has proceeded according to law and natural development. According to it, all that we behold is only the result of an impulse given far back in eternity, by a Being ever since far off in space. According to it, creation is now independent of its Creator! For aught it knows or cares, He may even have ceased to exist: it can do without Him. In a word, it denies His providential government; as if, forsooth, we could conceive of a self-sustained universe, any more than we can of a self-originated creation. It pretends to a concern for the Divine dignity and ease, as if the infinite God were a being like ourselves, whose distinction may consist in doing nothing; or as if it would be a degradation for Him to *sustain* a world which it was yet His glory to create. It pleads the regularity of nature as a proof that all is resolvable into law; as if, forsooth, law had any meaning apart from mind, or as if God would govern in any way except by law. It represents the Omniscient as if He saw nothing, the Omnipotent as doing nothing, the Omnipresent as universally absent, the All-sufficient as the author of a universe which excludes His own activity.

Far different is the doctrine of Scripture. It teaches me to combine the doctrine of His *original* appointment with that of His ever *present* agency. Everything has the ground of its existence, from moment to moment, in the will of God. Every law in nature is a mode of His working, and a proclamation of His order. Every atom has its holy of holies which He inhabits. He underlies every surface on which our eye may rest, and is enshrined in every material object we admire. Physically, He is present with every part of my system; and present with every different part in a different respect. With my *organisation*, He is present as life, and even with my *will*, not indeed to move it, but to sustain it in the power of self-motion. In the *spiritual kingdom*, every ordinance is an instrument of which He is the power; every institution, a form of which He is the essence; every Christian soul, a moving temple of Him the Infinite. I am not alone with my Spirit. He himself inhabits my consciousness. So near is He, that a desire reveals Him as not only present, but as present and working. And, as in some passages of Scripture it is difficult to determine whether the phrase "the love of God" means His love to us, or ours to Him, so in some states of the mind it is not easy to decide (happy perplexity!) whether the flame of holy love of which we are conscious burns from Him to us, or the converse. "He that dwelleth in love, dwelleth in God, and God in him."

Beyond this, the Bible draws aside the veil which hides the spiritual world from our view, and, behold, a vast scheme of providence administered by God himself; a scheme in which every want of His people is noticed; every object numbered; every being moving in the direct gaze of Omniscience. Every human pang is seen vibrating to the throne of God. Lines of relation are seen to be established between every sanctified trial on earth and the blessedness of the remotest future. Angels are seen speeding on His service in every direction. Horses and chariots of fire encompass the endangered servant of God. And even the solitary and benighted pilgrim, apparently alone on the desert, is in reality reposing at the very gate of heaven.

3. *Pantheism*—the pantheism of the day—has its creed on the subject of the Divine manifestation. It goes to the opposite extreme of materialism. It *professes* to find God everywhere. Every sound is His voice, not poetically but literally; every object is an aspect of Him, not sentimentally but really; every change is but His substance entering into a new relation. Mind and matter, in all their boundless varieties, are but modifications of Him. Materialism gives us a universe without a God, here is, properly, a God without a universe; for the universe itself is God. "In Him," says Scripture, "we live, and move, and have our being;" no, says pantheism, we are Him; portions of His very essence.

And multitudes are smitten with the pretended sublimity of the notion. It even exceeds the first promise of the tempter himself, "Ye shall be *as* gods;" it assures them that they *are* God; and again man awakes from the sweet intoxication —if indeed he does awake—to find that it has cheated him out of everything worth believing and hoping for. It even outstrips polytheism and materialism in the career of error. Like *polytheism,* it mistakes the manifestations of God for God; and hence, while, in its *philosophic* moods, it despises polytheism, in its eastern home where it is popularised and made acceptable to three hundred millions of mankind, it boasts about the same number of divinities. And like the *materialism* of which we have spoken, it ignores all idea of a providence, for its God is a being who has no will of his own—who does whatever he does necessarily—who is himself the victim of an iron fate. Strictly speaking, therefore, it outstrips both these forms of error, in denying to God any true personal existence. His activity is not the result of choice, for he has no choice. The mechanical laws are not His *appointments,* but *himself.* Creation, revelation, providential interposition—all these are impossible, for *they* suppose a free will—a benevolent disposition—and a Divine purpose; whereas will, disposition, and purpose, are words for which pantheism has no use. It proceeds even to the length of affirming that man has less need of God than God has of man; for on the principle, that it is a *necessity* in the Deity to be ever projecting existence and absorbing it again, it follows that He is more indebted to His creatures than His creatures are to Him.

And having thus denied to God a free personal existence, and degraded Him to a state of dependence, it proceeds to reduce man to a corresponding level. While pretending to exalt him to God, it really degrades him below the level of a man. He believes himself to be a free moral agent; but it assures him that he is only a machine—that when he fancies he is performing his own act, he is only an instrument developing a concealed necessity. He is conscious of a sense of responsibility; but it reminds him that he *cannot* sin; that moral evil has no existence, since that would suppose the existence of a free accountable will, which there is not. He deems himself called to aim at virtue; it derides the idea, and assures him that lust in all its foulness, and vice in all its varieties, are equally essential to his self-development as what he calls virtue. And myriads of its Hindoo votaries, to say nothing of others elsewhere, act out the revolting imposture. He aspires after immortality; but it tells him that he must be content to be re-absorbed into the Divine essence of which he is an eternal part—to fall back at death like a drop into the ocean from which for a moment he had been exhaled—and to lose for ever his individual consciousness, and separate existence. Even the *dream* of the patriarch was a Divine revelation, a sublime reality, but here it is a system—one of the fashions of the day—which assures its devotees that our most vivid waking realities are only dreams—that the universe around us, substantial as it may seem, is only an empty fiction, an aggregate of deceptive appearances.

4. This, too, is a subject on which the custom-bound *formalist* has *his* creed. Forms, indeed, of some kind, man must employ even for his most spiritual conceptions. They are the words which clothe his thoughts; the body which gives visibility and instrumentality to his spirit. But the error of the mere ritualist lies in coming to think more of the letter than of the spirit—in attaching greater importance to the means than to the end—in being so satisfied with the streams as to forget the fountain—and, at length, so satisfied even with the channels as to forget the very streams themselves. He would read with pity of the ancient Tyrians chaining their god to his altar, during an invasion, lest he should pass over to the side of the enemy; and yet he virtually re-enacts the folly, for his rites are chains, and to lose *them* would be, in his eyes, to lose his God. He

would eschew with pious horror the errors of the polytheist, the materialist, and the pantheist, as at hostile variance with the Word of God; but, while accepting with unquestioning confidence the *facts* of Holy Scriptures, all the *lessons* which the facts were meant to convey are lost on him, and wellnigh all the doctrines too. Christianity is eminently non-ritual; for "where the Spirit of the Lord is there is liberty;" but the formalist indites a book of Leviticus for himself, and cannot conceive even of the Infinite Presence as sanctioning any party less respectable, or of revealing itself in any observances less ancient or customary, than his own. Having dug certain little trenches in his own garden, he forgets that the rivulets which trickle through are not the river itself, and that even he would be passed by unvisited and unrefreshed if the river did not generously overflow its banks to reach him. Everything of a Divine nature is reduced with him to the measure of his own little circle of experiences; and to expect or to report anything greater, he would deem enthusiasm or credulity.

II.

From this notice of prevailing errors on the subject of Divine manifestation, let us pass, secondly, to a few scriptural illustrations. Under the former dispensation—who that had been sent to the Old Testament to select one of the most Divine passages which it contained, would have fixed, unless by a kind of spiritual instinct, on the apparently vague and unpretending language of the first promise? Yet the evolutions of time have proved that in that brief sentence a scheme of mercy was enwrapped; that under that humble guise was concealed more than the gate of heaven. Surely God was there in promise, and the gospel in the germ—the Shekinah at the gates of revelation—and men, generally, knew it not!

At the period of the text, if it had been known that a

Divine manifestation was about to take place, how certainly would man have selected, had it been left to his option, some school of Indian philosophy, or some Egyptian temple, and have assembled the great and learned of the day, and have looked for the disclosure of a sublime theory of existence and human destiny. But on the Syrian desert, with a stone for his pillow, and the earth for his bed, there lies a lone wanderer; and instead of coming to a palace, the very palace of heaven comes to that solitary man; and there, in the silence of night, is made to him a promise so brief and simple, as to seem almost entirely personal, and yet so far-reaching and full as to enclose a blessing for all the families of the earth.

In process of time, and not far from that memorable spot, a magnificent temple is reared, reared in obedience to a Divine command, after a Divine model, and expressly as the scene of Divine manifestation. There the victim ever bleeds, the incense ever ascends, and the place of the oracle is ever accessible. Surely the mode and the scene of Divine intercourse with man is now ascertained and *secured.* On the contrary, from the moment *that* thought came to prevail, it was time for the temple to be abolished. From the moment men came to be proud of their temple—came to rely on it as if it must needs be an attraction to the blessed God—came to feel as if God had allowed himself to be there built in, localized, and engrossed—leaving all the world without unhallowed and unvisited—from that moment it was high time to disabuse them, to shew them that the temple was meant for *their* convenience, not for *His*—that His temple is everywhere, and that the *chosen* scene of His manifestation is in the humble and contrite heart. "Thus saith the Lord, The heaven is my throne, and the earth is my footstool: where is the house that ye build unto me? and where is the place of my rest?" "Thus saith the high and lofty One that inhabiteth eternity, whose name is Holy; I dwell in the high and holy place, with him also that is of a contrite and humble spirit." With him also! In that height, and in that depth! Far above all angelic thrones, and with that man—lowly and broken-hearted—seated in the dust. For what knows the Divine omnipresence of local transition! What difference to Infinite Greatness whether He dwell here or there! "The Lord looketh at the heart." How pitiable the folly of supposing that the favour of infinite excellence could be propitiated by material gifts, or the presence of the Omnipresent be limited to any circle that we could draw!

Another period elapsed, and the fulness of time hath come; a thousand predictions are to be fulfilled; man's redemption is to be accomplished; God is to be manifest in the flesh! Who can foresee (it might have been said) the splendours of His advent! What preternatural pomp will invest Him! Surely the princes of this world will know Him. The temple will first receive Him. His kingdom will come with observation.

Was this expected? For that very reason, if for no other, it was necessary that the reality should be in contrast to all this. One object of His coming was to disabuse the human mind respecting what *is* greatness—to introduce a new order of greatness—greatness which an earthly diadem could not enhance, nor a crown of thorns diminish; which a real sceptre could not increase, nor a mock sceptre degrade.

But "can any good thing come out of *Nazareth?*" And "his brethren, are they not with us?" And "have any of the rulers believed on him?" Such were the questions of the day. And had we lived at the time, He had "no form or comeliness" by which *we* should have recognized Him; and when we saw Him, "there was no beauty that we should have desired Him." Had we met Him on the world's highway with our mind preoccupied, there was no visible sign to arrest our attention, and point Him out. Had we passed Him in the streets of Jerusalem, no supernatural thrill would have made us conscious that we were in an unearthly presence. Yet surely God was in that human form—the "fulness of the Godhead"—though men knew it not. It was He whom Jacob beheld in vision as Jehovah, seated high up on the summit of glory, now come down to tabernacle on earth; and hence He was heard to say, at the opening of His ministry, " Hereafter *ye* shall see heaven open, and the angels of God ascending and descending upon the Son of man." Occasional glimpses of irrepressible glory revealed Him to the few, but the world knew Him not. He was transfigured; but it was before the eyes of a few of His humble disciples. He spake as never man spake, but it was to the common people who heard Him gladly. He appeared in the temple, but it was to drive from it those who had turned it into a den of thieves. If you would behold Him *at home,* you must repair to the domestic circle at Bethany. He announced the nature of His kingdom; but it was—how divinely simple and affecting the symbol—by taking a little child—a little child—and setting it in the midst of His disciples—a spectacle more truly sublime even than that which Jacob beheld in vision—do you not see it?—an act by which He said emphatically, Surely God is in this child, and you know it not. Become like it, and " the kingdom of God is within you." He laid the foundations of His kingdom; but it was by means the world had never seen employed—by *humbling himself,* by becoming obedient unto death, even the death of the cross. Ask you what signs announced that His death was the commencement of a kingdom? Portents there were, stupendous signs, which shewed that His death drew to itself the attention, and, in some sense, involved the interests of the universe. Gross signs of physical struggle there were not. Power itself is not a thing to be seen. The magnitude of a contest cannot be estimated by its noise. Whole nations had often fought and fallen; but the deadly shock had settled no question, originated no new impulse, turned back no current of fate; while inferior contests—waged on a scale too small to be heeded at the time—had often constituted important epochs in the history of the race. A great principle was involved, and they changed the face of the world.

But here, here was a concentration of all the interests of time. Here all law looked for vindication—all government, for sanction—and a world perishing, for rescue. The crisis was too great to be signalized by gross material conflict—too unearthly and spiritual to be apprehended by mortal sense. But the conflict was real, *because* it was moral. "He blotted out the handwriting that was against us, that was contrary to us, and took it out of the way, nailing it to his cross: and having spoiled principalities and powers, he made a show of them openly, triumphing over them *in it.*" To the eye of sense, no handwriting was visible, but the superscription of His supposed offence; no engine of destruction, but the cross; no foe, but such as the gates of Jerusalem had poured forth. Yet that was "the hour and power of darkness." A crowded field, impalpable to human eye, stretched around Him. And a concussion of powers, inaudible to human ear, went vibrating through the universe.

Surely God *was* in that place, yet men *knew it not.* In the absence of all *their* vulgar signs of greatness *they knew it not.* He had asked for no territory on which to plant an ensign; and as they could not conceive of an empire whose seat is the soul, they *knew it not.* He had unfurled no standard to rally an army; and as they could not conceive of an assault on spiritual foes, they *knew it not.* Even His disciples—disappointed of the godlike displays of power they had looked for on that occasion, *knew it not.* But soon, like Jacob starting from his dream, they awoke to find that there, where they had seen him die, they had beheld the pang and the travail of infinite Love; that on that cross they had seen the Son of God; that in the Being who hung there, they had seen Divinity and humanity brought into the close embrace and union of one Person; that in that act He had honoured the very law which man had ruined himself by resisting—that He had thus made the pardon of the sinner more compatible with justice, more glorious to God, than even his punishment would be; that henceforth the open heart of infinite love might freely discharge its transforming power on the heart of the world. They lifted up their eyes, and, behold, on a height loftier than that scaled by the angels in Jacob's vision, they saw that "God also had highly exalted him, and given to him a name which is above every name"—given Him a right to the homage of every being in heaven, and to the love of every heart on earth!

And now (you will be ready to say), "assuredly now the danger is past. The scenes of Calvary must for ever prevent men from again associating Divine manifestations with worldly greatness and show. Henceforth men will look rather to the simple, the humble, and unostentatious, and be quick to apprehend the signs of the spiritual *wherever* they may appear." Alas, for such calculations! The history of Christianity from the first presents an unbroken repetition of the same errors. "The Jews required a sign"—a grand outburst of national glory, which should bring the nations in homage to their feet. "The Greeks sought after wisdom"—sublime speculations on the Divine nature, new theories of the universe. And the Roman, he could not conceive of any distinguished claim apart from a display of martial power—an unfurled banner and a conquering legion. True, here was a new thing in the earth—a kingdom not of this world, and yet mastering the world—a kingdom growing even by the martyrdom of its subjects. Hearts were changed by an invisible power. A doctrine—the doctrine of the Cross—was transforming everything. Society, like a skin shed and shrivelled, might retain something of its outward form; but here was a new society, all elasticity and spirit. The old religions might retain for awhile their deserted temples and their empty rites; but here was a religion without a temple, and almost without a rite, yet making converts by thousands, and every convert a living temple. With no weapons but those of truth and love, what victories it achieved, what kingdoms won! Surely God was in it. Silently as the light it came, and the darkness of ages fled before it. With the majesty of law it came, and the anarchy of evil subsided into order and peace. It came in the calmness of a Divine power, bringing to each of its subjects self-restoration, and restoration to God, and an undying zeal for the restoration of others. Surely, here was evidence enough that God was in it, yet men knew it not. But they looked for the signs of human greatness, and the means of human success—oratory, wealth, arms, rank, custom, authority—and not finding these, they professed to find nothing. Because *man* was not in it in these accustomed forms, they could not believe that GOD was in it. They forgot that even their own religion must once have had a beginning—and that at its commencement it must have been a strange novelty. They forgot that though God is the God of order, He is not restricted to the employment of the same unvarying class of means; that the very fact that He has honoured one class for a time, may be a sufficient reason for calling into existence another—"that no flesh should glory in his presence." The very fact that the foolish things of the world were seen confounding the wise, and the weak things of the world confounding the things which were mighty, ought to have led men to ask whether God was not in it of a truth. But they construed this—the very *evidence* of His *presence* into the proof of His absence.

III.

If such are some of the existing forms of the spirit in question, and some of the historical evils resulting from it, *let us glance, thirdly, at some of its evil effects at present, and among ourselves.* For example, does it not prevent us from looking for God in the *present*, as compared with what we believe respecting His manifestations in the past and the future? Undeniably He has been in portions of the past, and will be in the future, as we are not justified to look for Him in the present. Looking back, we behold Him introducing a new dispensation. Miracle, prophecy, inspiration are there—a reality eclipsing the vision which Jacob saw—an incarnate Saviour, and a descending Spirit. We do not expect a repetition of such scenes. Looking forwards, we believe the future to be stored with preternatural events. There lie the mystic occurrences portended by the last vials of apocalyptic vision. And there, in the dark background, are seen to loom the awful grandeurs of the second coming. But who does not know that many a Christian is relying so confidently on what that future will achieve, and calculating so nicely on the year of the occurrence, as to ignore the present, and to refer everything great and good to that future time? We, indeed, may pity and disown the error in this excessive form, but let us not hastily conclude that we have therefore escaped it altogether. Are we not living on our faith in the past and the future, rather than on our faith in a present God? Like the servants in the parable whose lord had gone away into a far country, have we not the feeling that our Lord is, in some sense, absent from us? and have we not practically adjusted and resigned ourselves to that idea?

If asked for further proof, I would refer to the existence of that antagonistic error—that pantheism which insists that God is *more* present now than ever—that the past is as nothing—that the present is the true age of inspiration—that man himself is now more evidently than ever divine. For it may be laid down as an axiom in history, that every error calls into existence its opposite. If the world therefore is making too much of the present, it is an almost infallible indication that the Church is, in *some* respects, making too little of it. If they are idolizing man as the god of the present, it is a sign that we are worshipping *too* exclusively the God of the past and the future.

Besides which, is it not a historical fact, that God has never proved himself present, by "reviving His work in the midst of the years," without taking the Church by surprise? Prior to such revival, Christians would doubtless have resented the charge that they did not sufficiently believe

Him present, as *we* may now be disposed to resent it. But no sooner did the manifestation take place—at the Reformation, for example; or in the middle of the last century, in the labours of Wesley and Whitfield—than the Church turned uneasily in its slumbers—awoke slowly and full of suspicion to the clear perception of the fact—and took some years before it could bring itself heartily to exclaim, "Surely God is in this work, and we knew it not!"

Let me not be supposed to imply that we make too much of the historical past, or of the prophetic future; the complaint is that we make too little of the actual present. Let me not be thought to allege that *we* are doing nothing—the praiseworthy activity of individuals and of societies would disprove the charge; the complaint is that we are not looking for *God* to do much. Let me not be imagined to mean that we do not recognize the hand of God in every instance of individual conversion and of spiritual prosperity; the complaint is that we do not feel that He is present in such changes, as much and as really as He was present on Sinai or on the day of Pentecost—that such changes admit of indefinite multiplication—that God is present and waiting to effect them—present to raise and invest the passing day with all the spiritual interest of the most splendid eras in the past and the future. The complaint is, not that we make too much of the facts recorded in the Bible; but that we make too little of certain facts which are not recorded there, and because they are not recorded there. Admitted that the Church has an inspired history in the Bible—it has an uninspired history also. And was not God as really present in the facts of the uninspired, as of the inspired history? Are not *some* of the facts of the uninspired history more important to us than some of the facts of the inspired—the Protestant Reformation, for instance, as compared with some of the superficial and short-lived reformations recorded of the ancient Jewish Church; the translation and universal circulation of the Sacred Scriptures, as compared with the fact that Josiah caused the Hebrew Scriptures to be read and explained to the people; the great fact of modern Christian missions into all the world, as compared with the fact that teaching Levites were sent through the small district of Israel. Supposing the canon of Scripture were not yet closed, may we not conclude the Divine Spirit would cause many of these facts to be placed on inspired record? The complaint is, not that we make too much of any one part of the Bible, but that there are some parts of it of which we do not make enough; not that we make too much of its history of the past, or of its predictions of the future, but that we too much slight its promises made to the present. God *has been* in the history, He *will be* in the prophecy; but He *is* in the promise—a God near at hand and not afar off. The history and the prophecy are only for limited times—the promise is for all time—large as the heart of God, and the fullest utterance of it. The history tells me only what God *has* done, and the prophecy what he *will* do; but the promise tells me what he *might* do—do, if the restraints which our want of prayer and faith impose were all cast off—do, if He might but "make bare His arm"—do, if we would but accept the challenge of His grace, "Prove me now herewith." Yes, while we are wondering at the past, He is saying to us, "Ye shall see greater works than these; greater works than these shall *ye* do." Surely God is in these promises, though we act as if we knew it not!

Another and a kindred evil is, that we are in danger of looking for God only in specific times and places. We wonder at the folly of the polytheist, in restricting his notion of the presence of his gods to the hill or the valley, the stream or the grove. Yet how prone are we ourselves to regard the worship of God as entirely an affair of times and places! The error is, not that we look for Him too confidently on the Lord's Day, and in the sanctuary, but that we look for Him too *exclusively* then and there. And the consequence is, that religion, with numbers, is restricted to small and separate portions of life—is fenced off within little enclosures of time; that, instead of consisting of habits, it consists only of occasional acts; and that, instead of living with the man, and leavening him, and becoming one with him, he and it come together only at set times, and by particular appointment.

We wonder at the impiety of the materialist, in supposing that God absents himself from the world which He has made. Yet how prone are we ourselves to look for Him in the great events of providence—that is, in what we deem the great—rather than in the little; and in the smallest *external* events, rather than in the quiet and unseen movements of the mind within. The error is, not that we look for Him *there* too much, but that we look for Him *here* too little. We look for His glory in the stars, and omit to notice His footprints in the dust. We listen for Him in the thunder, but the small still voice is almost unheeded. Who would not have looked for Him the week after the crucifixion and resurrection amidst the solemn rites of the temple? and yet it was in "the upper room" that He shewed to His disciples His hands and His feet. And when the day of Pentecost was fully come, it was not the place of sacrifice, or the holiest of all, that was shaken by the descending Spirit, but the humble house in which the disciples had met with one accord.

He *may be* in the elaborate and gorgeous ritual, not, indeed, because of its elaboration, often in spite of it; but He *is* where two or three are devoutly met together in His name. He *may be* in the former, and surely Satan *may be* there, in that place, though those assembled think not of it. Let your minds wander to some of the most splendid ecclesiastical edifices of Christendom, and when you think of the uses to which they *have* been put, to which they *are* put, and of the vast system of superstition they help to uphold, you will exclaim, Surely the power of darkness is there; there to cheat the intellect by charming the senses; there to blunt the conscience by occupying the imagination; there to intercept and appropriate whatever should ascend to God, and to make *His* absence unfelt by crowding into the vacuum a host of priests, and martyrs, and saints, impiously invested with His prerogatives! Meanwhile, wherever the Bible is devoutly read, and the Gospel preached, wherever the prayer of faith ascends, and the sacrifice of the broken heart is offered, surely God in Christ is there, though they know it not.

IV.

What, then, fourthly, are the means of attracting and recognizing the Divine Presence amongst us? Tell me, if you can, a more important inquiry than this. Were our men of science to be assured that the atmosphere here, in this place, contained some subtle element nowhere else to be found, an element unique, mysterious, capable of the most extensive application, and certain of immortalizing whoever might succeed in discovering it, what untiring efforts would be made to elicit it! No number of failures would induce them to desist. No apparatus would be deemed too costly to insure success. To develope, to analyze, and to apply it, would be the cheerful occupation of their life. Or, were there some one spot on this wide earth where the Divine Presence was manifested visibly—the earth's holiest of all—where, whoever entered, heard the voice of God, saw corruscations of His glory, slept only to have visions of angels ascending and descending, and awoke only to feel that all around was instinct with a Divine Presence, who would not make a pilgrimage thither, though it should be far as the Syrian desert where the patriarch slept, and what a profound satisfaction would be felt, though life should be half spent in reaching it!

Brethren, that pilgrimage would end only in disappointment, if the sacred precincts were entered with an *unprepared* heart; and with a prepared heart the pilgrimage is unnecessary. The presence we seek "is not hidden from us, neither is it far off." It is not in heaven that we should say, Who shall go up for us unto heaven, and bring it unto us. Neither is it beyond the sea that we should say, Who shall go over the sea for us, and bring it unto us. It is very nigh unto us. It is close to us. It is here! Without the heart to desire it, and the eye to perceive it, it might indeed as well be far off, at the very outskirts of the universe. There are chemical experiments in which, if a certain condition be wanting, the element sought for cannot be elicited. It is present, waiting, ready to leap into activity the moment the condition is present. But as long as that is wanting, the element is imprisoned, separated by an impassable barrier—and might almost be said to be non-existent. Similarly, the preoccupied mind might sleep at the very gate of heaven; no celestial dreams would visit it. The worldly mind might find itself in the house of God; in the holiest of all; but the skirts of the Divine glory would sweep by it unnoticed. A mind keen after earthly objects, and engrossed by the interests of time, might live here threescore years and ten—with "the powers of the world to come" all the time surrounding it, soliciting it, pressing in upon it—and yet never once recognize a single indication of the Divine Presence. And he who finds nothing of heaven on earth would find nothing but earth even in heaven. "The pure in heart shall see God;" this is the condition even of the beatific vision. The pure in heart behold Him here; the impure could not see Him even there. Fancy not, then, that change of place would remedy the evil; all observatories are alike to the blind. Complain not of the conditions of your being, as unfavourable to the perception and sense of the Divine Presence; the Psalmist thought not so; he felt himself beset behind and before; haunted by the Omniscient eye; and, if not oppressed, yet consciously surrounded by the living God.

The manifestation, then, of the Divine Presence in any

place, or to any person, depends on certain spiritual conditions; and the ordinances of religion are designed to produce those conditions. As the Lord, the Spirit, He is present in our meetings for prayer—present to impart and infuse a Divine life;—let Him see every high thought and imagination cast down—and find us panting, languishing for His aid, as those who feel they must perish without it—and He will manifest himself unto us as He does not unto the world—filling us with His own life. As the great source of all spiritual usefulness, He is present in all our religious societies and organizations—present to see if He can *trust us* with success, or if we are ready to appropriate the honour of success to ourselves, and thus rob Him of the glory. Let Him see us, on every fresh instance of prosperity, taking it to His footstool—hastening to cast it as a crown at His feet—casting ourselves there, and exclaiming, "Not unto us, O God, not unto us, but unto thy name be the glory"—let Him see this, and He will not merely manifest His power *to* us, He will make us the manifestations of His power to the world. He is present as often as His Word is read, and His Gospel is pressed home on the hearer—present to mark if the proud heart is humbled—if the hard and insensible heart begins to quiver with sensibility—let His Gospel be thus honoured, and, in the language of the apostle, the unbeliever himself, "finding the secrets of his heart made manifest, will fall down on his face to worship God, and will report that God is in you of a truth."

And is He not present here as the Lord of the house? "Behold," saith He, "I stand at the door and knock." Who can imagine the scene of His entrance here without deep emotion? Suppose, then, that something like it were now to take place—that now, while we are thus assembled, meditating on the subject of the Divine manifestation, the Divine Redeemer were to approach, and by some undoubted sign, were to signify His arrival, and His desire to enter. How should we prepare to receive Him? Would the patriarch have been able to sleep had he foreseen the vision which awaited him? And what searchings of heart would there be with us! What looks of anxiety would be exchanged!

Prayerless, unconverted man, what could we say to you, but beseech you, in few and fervid accents, to be reconciled to God? And what could you do, but fall down and cry for mercy? Or, if your heart were too hard even for that, what could you do but complain of its hardness; and entreat that it might be broken, bruised, changed into a heart of flesh?

And you who seem to be passing from death unto life—and have long seemed to be passing—what could you do but lament your indecision—and place your trembling heart before Him—and cry, "Create within me a clean heart, O God, and renew within me a right spirit?"

And you who have done this already, what could you do but receive Him in the attitude of devout and humble prostration? What an attractive spectacle would such an assembly present! How effectually would it be prepared for His admission! With what Divine complacency would His eye survey the blessed scene! And, as it glanced from one to another—saw that each breast was bared for His inspection—each heart a bleeding sacrifice—each soul a living temple inviting Him to enter and take possession—and as His countenance beamed and brightened with love—who would not feel that the windows of heaven were about to be opened—that a time of refreshing had come, the happy results of which it was impossible to foretell! Surely this would be none other than the house of God; this would be the gate of heaven! Scenes which kings, and prophets, and righteous men desired to see—visions transcending that which Jacob saw—would stand disclosed to us! No angel's wing might fan our brow; but I say unto you, there would be joy among the angels in the presence of God; and that God himself would be present! The gates of the celestial city might not brighten to our eye, nor the music of its harps fall on our ear. But the reality would be here without the imagery; the Spirit, without the rushing mighty wind; Pentecost, in its converting and transforming results; Truth, in the calmness of its power; Love, in its purifying flame; the kingdom of heaven in the soul.

CHARGES

DELIVERED AT ORDINATIONS.

CHARGE I.

THE SERVANT OF JESUS CHRIST.

ROM. i. 1.—"A servant of Jesus Christ."

MY Christian brother, how many the moral stages which, in the short course of your religious career, you have necessarily passed through already—how momentous the stage which you have now reached—and, if seasonable advice was important at each of those preceding stages, how responsible is the office of him who undertakes to give you counsel now!

There was the moment when in feeling, if not in words, your prevailing inquiry was, "What must I do to be saved?" How much depended on the answer which you then received—an ambiguous, unscriptural reply might, humanly speaking, have led to the loss of your soul. There was the hour when you sat in deep solicitude, anxious to hear, yet trembling when told, that you were received into communion with a Christian church. And the solemn hour when, with agitated hand, you first took the memorials of the body and the blood of Christ—how full of interest and influence was every word which then fell on your ear! There was the season when you first stood up, fearful, yet desirous, of speaking to others in the name of Christ. And again, when the subject of your preparing for the office of the ministry was first broached, how much depended, under God, on the propriety of what was then said to you. There was the hour, when you found yourself crossing the threshold of the institution in which you were to prepare for the office. And again, (can you ever forget it?) when your heart first thrilled with wonder and gratitude at the information that God had blessed your preaching to the conversion of a soul. If, in reference to each of these occasions, it might be said, "a word in season, how good it is! how full of influence it is at the moment! how laden with consequences for all the future! then, who shall calculate the importance of the words addressed to you at the solemn stage which you have now reached! all the past has been only preparatory to this. Numerous and eventful as the previous stages of your moral history may have been, all their influence meets and is summed up in this stage. This is the crisis to which the prayers, desires, and endeavours of years have been tending —and from this central, this culminating point, the future, with you, may take its moral complexion for eternity! With you? perhaps with numbers! For if you take heed to yourself, and to the doctrine, and continue in it, you will both save yourself and those that hear you. True, my brother, the office on which you are entering has, no doubt, so much engaged your serious consideration already, that possibly nothing which I can advance will much add to your knowledge of its duties and details. But when I remember that it behoves me to address you, as if none of these duties had yet presented itself to your notice—and that not only your own welfare, but the endless wellbeing of others, may more or less depend on the way in which the duty is discharged,—"Who is sufficient for these things?" God grant that whatever my insufficiency may be, you, as a man of God, deriving your instructions direct from the Bible, may be perfect, thoroughly furnished unto all good works.

The passage of Holy Scripture which has presented itself to my mind, as suggestive of a train of remark appropriate to the occasion, you will find in the first chapter of the Romans, first verse, "A servant of Jesus Christ." Independently of the general adaptation of this clause to the nature of your new official relation to Christ, and to His Church, I have been induced to select and detach it from the context, partly that, through its brevity, simplicity, and forcibleness, it may the more easily and permanently secure a place in your memory. Often may it serve to recall the hallowed solemnities and obligations of the day; and, though every observation now addressed to you by the speaker should be forgotten, may the text be remembered—and, as often as it is remembered, may it bring back with it a recollection of the good confession which you have now publicly made—the solemn vows you have recorded—the earnest and united prayers offered by your fathers and brethren in the ministry in your behalf—the Christian sympathies of this congregation, including, as it does, members of many of the neighbouring churches—and the hallowed impressions of which, I doubt not, your heart has been deeply conscious. In moments of depression, may the recollection cheer and sustain you; and in seasons of difficulty, or of approaching indifference, may it arouse and excite you to vigorous effort, like the blast of a trumpet! Take it, then, as your motto—inscribe it on your official banner, and let your own private meditations on it supply the deficiencies which may attend my endeavour to illustrate and apply it.

I.

Let me remind you, that in order to comprehend your present position as a servant of Christ, it is important that you should bear in mind, first, *The origin of the relationship*—how it is that He is a Master, and that you are His servant. There was a time when Christ himself was a servant—but, oh, in how peculiar and sublime a sense—He "who, being in the form of God, thought it not robbery to be equal with God; but made himself of no reputation, and took upon him the form of a servant, and was made in the likeness of men; and being found in fashion as a man, humbled himself, and became obedient unto death, even the death of the cross." You know "the work which was then given him to do"—a work for the Godhead—a service voluntarily undertaken—a service which no other being in the universe could have rendered—a service which involved a sacrifice such as can never be repeated. Well may the apostle linger on it as he does—dividing it into parts—as if the immensity of the stoop which the Saviour made were too vast to be comprehended at once—tracing it from point to point—and following Him downwards from stage to stage, till He has reached the lowest depths of His humiliation. But amazing as was that ever-deepening series of condescending acts—and costly beyond all compensation as was the sacrifice in which they ended—never did the Saviour cease voluntarily to serve and to suffer, till He could lift up His eyes to heaven, and say, "I have finished the work which thou gavest me to do." I have magnified the law—expiated human guilt—demonstrated that God is Love. It is finished! Then closed His servitude. *He dieth no more;* death hath no more dominion over Him. *He is a servant no more.* His service has been rewarded by investiture with authority. *He is a master now.* "Wherefore God also hath highly exalted him, and hath given to him a name which is above every name." *He has a throne now;* for "when he had by himself expiated our sins, he sat down at the right hand of the majesty on high." *He has servants of His own now;* "all power is his in heaven and on earth." "For, for this cause Christ both died, and rose, and revived, that he might be Lord both of the dead and of the living."

This, then, accounts for His being a Divine Master—"a Son over his own house." How, and in what sense, have you become His servant? The term is used in Scripture in two senses—or in reference to two classes of persons. Private Christians, whatever their stations may be, are reminded that they "serve the Lord Christ"—that, whatever the stations assigned to them by the providence of God, they are never for a moment to forget that they are the servants of Christ, and are to discharge all their diversified duties, "as to the Lord, and not to men." Now, in this sense, you are a servant of Christ, in common with all the community of the faithful. And the way in which you have been brought under special obligation to serve Him, as a Christian man, should ever be present to your mind. "You are bought with a price." You were not always in His service. Once you were the bond-slave of Satan; but Christ hath redeemed you—redeemed you with His own most precious blood—laid all your nature under obligation—bought all your powers—and, therefore, as an emancipated, pardoned sinner, and an accepted believer, you can say with the Psalmist, "O Lord, I am thy servant; I am thy servant; thou hast loosed my bonds."

But there is another kind of service to be rendered to Christ than that which we owe to Him in our several stations as Christian men—a service relating more directly to *Himself,* to His *Church,* and to the *diffusion of His Gospel* through the world. Having finished His work of obedience and atonement on earth, He is exalted and empowered to apply it, and to reap its fruits in the salvation of all them that believe. He who on the cross "obtained eternal redemption" for sinners, is now on the throne to bestow it; and, for this end, He employs the agency of some of those who have themselves received it. "Wherefore, when he ascended up on high, he led captivity captive, and gave gifts unto men. And he gave some, apostles; and some, prophets; and some, evangelists; and some, pastors and teachers; for the perfecting of the saints, for the work of the ministry, for the edifying of the body of Christ." "He gave some, apostles;" concerning whom He said, in solemn prayer to the Father, "As thou hast sent me into the world, even so have I also sent them into the world." Accordingly, they devoted themselves to the work of the Christian ministry. As apostles, indeed—companions of Christ during His earthly sojourn, and witnesses of His resurrection, their office was peculiar, beginning and ending with themselves. But, as preachers of the Gospel, they stood not alone; for the same Supreme authority which gave apostles, gave also evangelists, pastors, and teachers. Nay, the proclamation of redemption through Christ was the *chief* occupation even of the apostles; and hence they were heard on one occasion to say, "We will give ourselves continually to prayer, and to the ministry of the Word;" and hence, too, they called themselves apostles and servants of Jesus Christ. And as others, constrained by the love of Christ, were proclaiming the Gospel as successfully as themselves, they spoke of them as co-workers, and as fellow-servants. They could not hear of Christian men who were "apt to teach and well-reported of by the brethren" becoming Christian ministers, without emotions of delight. Knowing as they did the magnitude of the work implied in preaching the Gospel to every creature, and the glorious results depending on its performance, they hailed every faithful and devoted minister of the Gospel as a fellow-servant in Christ.

Now in this high, holy, and official sense, you, my brother, have this day become a publicly-recognized servant of Christ, and a fellow-servant with apostles. In this manner, and in this sense, you succeed them—devote yourself to the same kind of work—serve the same Master, and aim at the same ends.

And here let me remind you that, from the view we have taken of the manner in which Christ has become a Master, it is evident that if you are His servant, His will must be your only law. You are to yield to no other will—to obey no other law—to have no will even of your own. Had you just terminated a course of training for some worldly station, your friends would be congratulating you that you had become your own master now; but by assuming the office of the Christian ministry, "One is your Master, even Christ." Were you just entering on a course of servitude to an earthly master, his will must be obeyed only in subordination to that of the Master who is in heaven. If the two wills were at variance, the unalterable law of Christian morals is this,

"We must obey God rather than man." But in entering on the service of the Lord Christ, you have no intermediate will to consult—your constant appeal must be to His volume of directions—your habitual inquiry, "What saith the Master?" In crossing the threshold of the Church of Christ as one of His ministers, you enter a circle in which every object is sacred to His name, and sprinkled with His blood—every doctrine you are to preach is already prescribed—every duty you are to perform is already set down—a circle in which no will but His is to be thought of; you enter a sphere in which the eternal Father himself has no will distinct from that of Christ—in which "He hath given all things into the hands" of Christ, and in which the infinite and holy Spirit fulfils the office of glorifying Christ. Seek the promised aid of that Spirit, my brother, that you may rightly understand the will of your Master, and that your only concern may be to perform it. Think how duty is simplified by such a course—how the sources of perplexity are dried up—how, when you can say, "Let whatever consequences may result, I am following the will of my Master"—how the heart is lightened of care, and the spirit cheered as with sunshine from the face of God. The time may come, my brother, when this reflection may be your only source of consolation. May you never be without it! May you ever be able to adopt the language of one of your Master's most faithful servants, and say, "For we are not as many, who corrupt the word of God, but as of sincerity, but as of God; in the sight of God speak we in Christ"—"not walking in craftiness, nor handling the Word of God deceitfully; but by manifestation of the truth commending ourselves to every man's conscience in the sight of God."

2. And then, from the sense and the manner in which you have become his servant, let me remind you that the love of Christ must be your motive and principle of action—that is, the love of moral complacency and delight in all the inherent excellences of his character, and the love of

deep, deep gratitude for the rich wonders of His redeeming grace. This He requires from all His followers, but specially from His ministers. "Lovest thou me?" is the question, my brother, which at this moment the Master is proposing to you. *We* have asked you other questions, and have listened to your replies with profit and delight. But the Master has one question more to put, "Lovest thou me?" and again he repeats it, for it includes every other, and therefore he saith unto you the third time, "Lovest thou me?" We anticipate the reply which is ready to start to your lips. We believe you *do* love Him. But the particular to which I would respectfully point your attention is, that it is only as you are prepared to appeal and reply to Him in the affirmative, that he adds, "Feed my lambs," and "Feed my sheep"—that He calls you to work for Him, or accepts of your service. On this point He is jealous. If served at all, He must be served from love. All that *He* has done for the glory of God, and for the redemption of man, He has done from love. It is this which renders His mediatorial service acceptable to God, and melting and constraining in its influence upon His people—"He loved us, and gave himself for us." And of all that is done for Him love must be the impulsive principle also. And oh! who in the universe so worthy of our love? Whom shall we love, if not Him, whom the Father himself accounts infinitely lovely? Whom shall we love, if not Him, who, though He was rich, for our sakes became poor, that we, through His poverty, might be rich—rich in that favour which we share with the cherubim—rich in a throne which we are to share with Christ himself. Think of this, my brother; daily renew your contemplation of the theme, and you will love Him as the Saviour of sinners, whom you are appointed to invite to Him; you will love Him as the great Shepherd of the sheep you are appointed to feed; you will love Him as your own Saviour—as Him who hath bought you with His blood, and hath then counted you faithful, putting you into the ministry.

Yes, the fact that He has so honoured you as to call you into His special service will often fill you with holy amazement and adoring gratitude. The love of Christ will constrain you, and your chief concern will be, that the entire dedication of your all to His service should so inadequately express your sense of obligation.

II.

Now, bearing in mind the origin of the relationship implied in the text—or, how it is that Christ is a Master, and that you are His servant—you will understand, secondly, *the nature of your work.* Did your Master acquire His official authority *as the Saviour of sinners?* Then, His servants are to find occupation in carrying out the purposes of His atoning death. Is the Master exalted as a Prince and a Saviour to give repentance and the remission of sins? Then, the only reason why He employs servants is, that they may instrumentally make converts to His grace, and build up His people in their most holy faith.

Had you come here, my brother, to address a people entirely ignorant of the Gospel, your first object would have been to beseech them, in Christ's stead, to be reconciled to God. And having succeeded, through "the power of God," in the conversion of some of them, your next duty would have been to collect them into a Christian Church, that they might celebrate the death of Christ, observe all His ordinances, and "follow the Lord fully." And when you had thus become the pastor of a Christian Church, you would then have proceeded to shew them how they could aid you in your endeavour to serve Christ on a still larger scale, by adding their prayers and efforts to yours for the salvation of others. Now, true it is that you do not come here to begin the first of these stages of work—you find converts already made; nor to begin the second of these stages—here is a church already planted; nor even to commence the third stage—"others have laboured, and in these respects, you are entering into their labours."

But, still, your duty is as simple and as straightforward as if you had to lay the first stone of the spiritual edifice, and then to rear the building. For, what though some are converted? As long as one of your hearers remains unconverted, you, as a servant of Christ, have to watch for that soul as one of those that must give an account. Is there more than one? The responsibility increases. Do they amount to tens, to twenties, to fifties, to hundreds? Oh, how the field of labour enlarges! Ignorance is to be instructed—inquiry directed—prejudice disarmed—insensibility aroused—mistakes corrected—uncertainties resolved—the erring conscience enlightened—the gay and thoughtless reminded of the instability of earthly enjoyments—and the self-righteous drawn from their refuges of lies—and all this, O servant of Christ, you are to do in the name of your Master, and with a view of bringing them in penitence to His feet.

And what though a Church be planted here, your business is to aim at its enlargement. And for this end, the wavering purpose is to be fixed—backsliders reclaimed—wanderers restored—the young allured and enlisted—the sick visited in their affliction—and those who have given themselves unto the Lord urged to give themselves unto His people according to His will. And all this, O servant of Christ, you are to do, remembering that it is *His* Church you are enlarging, and *His* glory you are promoting.

And what though you succeed (God helping you) in enlarging the Church here, your ministry, to be effective, must be calculated to develope all the resources of the Church, and to bring them into actual operation. A servant of Christ is not the servant of the Church in the sense of having to perform its work. He has *his* work; and each several member has *his*. But the work peculiarly his—as far as they are concerned—consists in exciting their diligence, encouraging their liberality, directing their activity, stimulating their zeal, and multiplying their agencies. The holder of the five talents, you remember, was to increase them, not by trading without them, but with them. And the servant of Christ, when put in trust with the ministry of a particular church, is to look on each of its members as a talent concerning which the Great Proprietor is saying, "Occupy till I come—employ them all to the best advantage—that each may be the means of winning another, and that My Church of five or of fifty may be the means of gaining five or fifty more." My brother, a ministry which begins and ends with itself, however pious, intelligent, and attractive it may be, is, after all, the ministry of only one man; and, even that, neutralized, counteracted, and rendered worse than useless in its effects on the world, by the slumbering and selfish inactivity of the hearers. But a ministry which sets and keeps in useful motion an entire Church, becomes, in effect, the ministry of all its members, and thus proves an instrumentality of the widest influence, and of the greatest efficiency. Aim at this high object, my brother, in relation to this Church, aim at it under the solemn conviction that never till the entire Church is thus stirred in all its depths, and all its resources put into actual requisition, will the full value of the Christian ministry be seen; for never till then will it answer the high end of its Divine appointment in recovering the world to Christ.

Such, then, is the nature of your work as a servant of Christ—to convert sinners to Christ, to enlarge the Church of Christ, to excite its members to zeal and devotedness in His service. My brother, this is why He himself performed the transcendently sublime service of "obedience unto death;" this is why He is now a Master and chooses to employ servants. And because this is and ever has been His object, therefore it is that you are to preach His death, for it is the sinner's only means of atonement; and His righteousness, for it is the sinner's only ground of justification; and His resurrection, for, as the seal of heaven to His work, it is the sinner's only hope. Therefore it is that Christ is to be the grand theme of your ministry—that you are to preach His fulness of grace, for it is His people's only treasury; His promises, for it is their only encouragement; His example, for it is the only perfect pattern of obedience; His approbation, as their highest reward; His indwelling Spirit, as their only earnest of future glory. My brother, the work of the Spirit himself is of the same nature as yours, and tends to the same end. Not more truly did Christ once become the servant of the Father, than the Spirit is now acting as the servant of Christ—glorifying Christ—convincing men of sin and bringing men to Christ. For this the ministry, the Church, the world, the universe, exists; for this Christ is on His throne, and His angels on the wing; for this the Father, the Son, and the Holy Spirit combine their offices and influences infinite, and point them all in one direction; and for this, (oh, distinguishing honour!) for this you are to live and to labour as a servant of Christ.

III.

Now, if such be the nature of the work, let me invite your attention, thirdly, to *the spirit and manner in which it should be performed.* And, first, let me impress you with the importance of *sympathy with your Divine Master in His compassion for the souls of men.* My brother, it is well for us that we are made responsible only for our work—not for the success of our work. But that is a state of mind which I trust you will never be able to understand, which can be content *without* success. Paul could not; he agonized for it—was ready to become a curse for it. And you know that his Master and yours travailed in soul—actually became a curse for it. Try, oh, try to look at perishing men with His eyes. Try to view them from the same points, and in the same solemn lights, in which He viewed them. As you stand where I now stand, and look around on your hearers, remember that you are looking on some who are yet unsaved—that the sermons which have proved to some a savour of life unto life, have proved to them a savour of death unto death—that mercy has often wept over them in vain. Can you conceive of any beings more deserving of your deep commiseration? Think of your having to appear as a witness against them. Can you conceive of any prospect more appalling? Look forwards, in imagination, to the end of their course—listen to the pronouncement of their doom—behold the pit open to receive them—and hear, by anticipation, their hopeless cries for deliverance—and your deep anxiety to pluck the firebrands from the flames will impart fresh tenderness to your expostulations, and unwearied earnestness to your solicitude for their salvation. Oh, look at them, in imagination, till your eyes fill with tears—till your heart fills with pity—and you not only beseech *them*, but beseech God also in their behalf.

Cultivate this tender solicitude for the souls of your hearers, and it will serve in the stead of a thousand cautions and maxims to regulate your conduct. It will preserve you, for example, from confounding philosophizing with preaching; from pandering to the morbid curiosity of any when you should be ministering to their spiritual health; from accepting any of the shallow novelties of the day in exchange for the faith once delivered to the saints. It will save you from that languor and indifference in your work, which the regularity and constancy of its recurrence is in danger of begetting. Never may you come to discharge your sacred functions with that cold professional unconcern which is the certain death of all usefulness! Never may you give any class of your hearers just ground to doubt your desire for their conversion! Regard them as in danger of perishing under your eye—and you will not. It will impart that freshness and fervour to your spirit which will demonstrate your own sympathy with the work, and which is essential to excite and secure the sympathy of others. Cherish an habitual concern for their salvation; and there will be nothing from which you will shrink with a more sensitive dread than the saying or the doing of anything calculated even to *delay* the attainment of that object. For their souls' sake, you will, when in their society, "set a watch over the door of your lips, that you sin not with your tongue." Remembering how easily your usefulness may be impaired —that the bright mirror of ministerial character may be stained by a breath, you will, for their souls' sake, abstain from all appearance of evil—you will look well to your goings—ponder the path of your feet—aim to be an example, even to the believers, in conversation, in charity, in spirit, in faith, in purity—you will aspire to walk even as Christ walked.

2. Let me remind you next of the dignity of your employment. I know, my brother, I need not caution you against the danger of transferring to yourself that importance which belongs alone to your work. You will not erroneously suppose that you are vindicating the importance of your office, by an obtrusive self-importance. This be far from you—and it is far from you. You can well distinguish between the service and the servant. You have looked at the service—have you not, my brother?—till the perception of its magnitude has made *you* shrink and dwindle into insignificance—till, in the sight of its glory, you have disappeared, and, for awhile, have forgotten your own existence. Often return and resume the contemplation. Compare the dignity of *your* work with that of the ministers of an earthly sovereign—and yet they are proud, though they have titles and coronets of their own—proud to call themselves "her majesty's servants"—and talk of the time since they "have had the honour to serve her;"—you "serve the Lord Christ"—the Prince of the kings of the earth. Ask a Paul his estimate of the ministerial office—or rather infer what it was, when, with a celestial crown and a throne in his view, he could yet say, "I am in a strait, I wot not what to choose." Had it been to sway the sceptre of a province, he would have felt no strait—he would have counted that a comparative waste of existence. The diadems of earth would have pos-

sessed no attractions for him—for *there*, full before him were the open portals of the New Jerusalem—and its unfading glories streamed on his view—and its glad acclamations reached his ear—and there (he distinctly saw it), there was his own Redeemer, holding up to his view a crown of life. And is it possible that aught on earth could detain him from hasting at once to possess it? Yes, though he desired to depart—and was all but on the wing—he thought of his work as a servant of Christ, and such was his estimate of its importance, that his seraphic soul returned to it—and in the next moment you might have seen him writing himself "a servant of Christ," as one of the highest titles—writing it with a greater sense of its dignity than he would have felt in ascending the steps of a throne, and putting on a crown.

And you know why he felt thus—why others have felt the same? You know that in becoming a servant of Christ, you fall into, and form part of a train, in which the prophets and apostles, the martyrs and confessors, the reformers, worthies, and saints, of all ages, have formed a part—a procession of which the front ranks have long been mingling with the radiance of the ineffable Glory—a train which still reaches from earth to heaven. Ye know that, in becoming a servant of Christ, you become a fellow-servant with angels—who, were it permitted them, would gladly resign for awhile their heavenly seats, might they only wield your influence, and sustain your ministerial office. Oh, rise, rise, my brother, to a full sense of the dignity of your work. You have not to do, like others, with shadows and surfaces—but with essences, with the sublime, the imperishable, and the eternal—you have to do with the merit of an Infinite Sacrifice—the purposes of an Infinite Mind—the agencies of an Infinite Spirit—the everlasting destinies of souls. The earth itself exists only as a stage for carrying on the great work to which you are committed; then, bid every inferior interest to stand aside that you may see your work;—command every minor object to leave your path that you may press right on. Clothe yourself with a sense of the importance of your work as with a robe; recollect that many things which might be pardonable in others would be debasing, trifling in you, and silence every voice that would divert you from your work, by saying, "I am about a great work and cannot come down."

3. But, then, let me remind you next, that as is the dignity and importance of the work, so is the responsibility. It would not be difficult, my brother, to present your responsibility as a minister of Christ in a light which it would be painful, impossible, long to bear. But I have no desire to make the attempt. You have thought much of the subject already, till you have, no doubt, often trembled. You know that, *in some sense*, every soul here is committed into your hands—that there is established between you and every one of your hearers a relation, the fruits of which will certainly form a subject of separate and solemn examination in the final day—the results of which will reach through eternity. You know that all those offices of civil and social life, which imply unusual trust, are selected and employed in Scripture to denote ministerial responsibility—the builder laying the foundation of a building; whose strength involves the life of those who will enter it—the steward, on whom it devolves to provide for the wants of a numerous household—the sentinel, on whose vigilant guardianship of the city walls the security of thousands depends—the ambassador, to whose negotiations and entreaties has been committed the reconciliation of a rebellious province. You know that in your office all these elements of responsibility are included, and infinitely exceeded. And you know that the weight of the responsibility is such, that it pressed from the apostle Paul an exclamation which the faithful servant of Christ in every subsequent age has often and feelingly repeated, "Who is sufficient for these things!"

Oh! my brother, labour to keep alive your sense of ministerial responsibility: it will operate advantageously for your own personal piety. You will take heed unto yourself, and to the ministry, that you fulfil it—watching over yourself with a godly jealousy—jealous lest any thing in your character should counteract the effect of your ministry—jealous lest, while dispensing to others the heavenly manna, your own relish for it should diminish, and you should begin to distribute it with a careless hand—lest, in composing your sermon, you should be drawing up your own indictment—lest, after having preached to others, you yourself should be a castaway. Maintain a sense of your responsibility, and your service will be marked by unceasing diligence—not terminating with the Sabbath—not ending when you descend from the pulpit—but pausing in one form and in one direction only to be resumed in another—ceasing in public only to be taken up before God in private. Cherish the conviction of your official responsibility, and your social intercourse with the unconverted part of your hearers will never contradict your public ministrations. You will not regard your Master's enemies as if they were His friends, after solemnly assuring them from the pulpit that, as children of disobedience, they are children of wrath, exposed to destruction; you will not lead them to infer that they need be under no concern about it, by shewing that you are under no concern yourself—that from the time you closed the Bible, there was an end of the matter. You will occasionally resume the subject with them in private. This may be a delicate and a difficult task; but the difficulty, I imagine, lies very much in our own apprehension, and would hardly be felt at all if we set ourselves to perform the duty from the first. On this, at least, you may confidently rely, that where our unconverted hearers are once surprised at our addressing them religiously, they are ten times surprised at our silence—that you cannot easily be more faithful to them than they expect you to be. Oh! maintain, then, a deep sense of your ministerial responsibility—maintain it as carefully as you would have fed and kept alive the sacred fire in the Jewish temple. It will save you from being satisfied with any thing short of the souls of your hearers. If your ministry prove acceptable to them, you will be thankful to God for it; but you will regard it only as means to an end —and that end their salvation. You will be grateful for their kindness, and their hospitality you will value—but you will not accept it as a compromise for their souls. No complimentary conduct, no amount of pecuniary remuneration, would be received by you as a substitute for their souls. Claim souls for your hire, and set your standard of responsibility so high, as to claim them all. Yes, aim at the salvation of the whole—taking for your motto the language of the apostle, "warning every man, and teaching every man in all wisdom; that we may present every man perfect in Christ Jesus. Whereunto I also labour, striving according to his working, which worketh in me mightily." And that you may maintain this sense of your ministerial responsibility, let me counsel you to familiarize your mind, if you have not already, with the biography of the more eminent of the servants of Christ, who have left their example as a precious legacy to the Christian Church—with the lives and memoirs of such men as Neff and Oberlin, Martyn and Brainard, Eliot and Payson, Flavel and Halyburton, Owen and Doddridge and Baxter. Let me remind you, as a further incentive to fidelity, that the eye of the Master is never withdrawn from you. The servants of earthly masters are admonished by the apostle against mere eye service—service which is relaxed or suspended as soon as the eye of the master is withdrawn. My brother, you serve a Master whose eye, from the first moment of your ministry to the last, will never cease to be fixed on you *as a flame of fire.* Were it to be withdrawn from every other object in the universe, on His ministers it would still continue to be fastened, so that at any moment of your course He could say to you, as He did to the ministers of certain other churches—"I know thy works"—and could proceed to recount every item of your service. And most materially would it tend to keep alive your sense of ministerial responsibility, were you to keep steadily in view, not merely the solemnity of the *final* account, but to be continually rendering to God your account *now*. In the sixth chapter of Mark we read, "And the apostles gathered themselves together unto Jesus, and told him all things, both what they had done, and what they had taught." And when the apostle Paul says of certain Christian teachers, "they watch for souls as they that must give account"—the reference appears to be to an account which they were in the *habit* of rendering to God. My brother, you could not go into the presence of God from time to time for this purpose, without leaving, like the high priest when he came forth from within the mysterious veil, with a profounder sense of your official responsibility.

4. And need I remind you, under this head, that your work is to be performed in a spirit of devout *dependence?* My brother, cultivate the other states of mind which I have specified, and they will all infallibly lead to this. Sympathize with your Master in His compassion for souls, and you will wrestle in prayer as He did—keep in view the dignity of your work, and you will feel, with an ever deepening conviction, that your "sufficiency is of God" alone—cherish the sense of your responsibility, and you will lean your entire weight upon the arm of God. Besides, intercession is a part of your *official* work; and a spirit of ministerial prayer is quite as necessary to form your character as a pastor, as a spirit of personal prayer is to form your character as a Christian. Yes, my brother, you have entered on the cultivation of a field in which whoever sows, though it be a Paul, and whoever waters, though it be an Apollos, the Spirit of God alone can give the increase. Honour the Spirit by your humble dependence and earnest prayers, and He will honour you with a harvest of usefulness.

IV.

Thus have I directed your attention to the origin of your relationship as a servant of Christ—to the nature of your work—and to the spirit in which it should be performed. And now, fourthly, let me briefly remind you of *the gracious reward which awaits the faithful servant of Christ at the end of his course.* "Wherefore, we labour," saith the apostle, "that whether present or absent (whether in the body or absent from it) we may be accepted of him." What was it that cheered his spirit in the anticipation of his Master's coming? It was the thought of having been instrumental, notwithstanding all his conscious deficiencies and unworthiness, in saving many souls, and thus contributing to the glory of Christ. "For what is our hope, or joy, or crown of rejoicing? are not even ye, in the presence of our Lord Jesus Christ at his coming? For ye are our glory and joy." And what is the encouragement which he holds forth to his son Timothy, when exhorting him to "watch in all things, to endure afflictions, to do the work of an evangelist, to make full proof of his ministry?" It is drawn from his own confident anticipations of that day—"For I am now ready to be offered, and the time of my departure is at hand. I have fought a good fight, I have finished my course, I have kept the faith. Henceforth there is laid up for me a crown of righteousness which the Lord the righteous judge shall give unto me at that day; and not to me only, but to all them also that love his appearing." Oh, the transcendent happiness that day will bring to the faithful servant of Christ! My brother, the sun in the firmament is lighted up partly as an emblem of the glory which awaits him then—"for they that turn many to righteousness shall shine as the brightness of the firmament, and as the sun, for ever and ever in the kingdom of their Father." Yes, and one reason why there is a day of universal assembling appointed is—that the faithful servants of the Cross may have a fitting reception—that the fruits of their labour may be presented—and their honours be distributed by the hand of Grace before a fitting assembly. Think you that number without number will be convened to hear what armies fought—what wealth was gained by commerce—or what fame ambition won? Worldly conflicts and wealth, and honours, are subjects which will not then be mentioned. The only triumphs recounted then will be those of holiness over sin—of the good soldier of Christ over the powers of darkness; the only wealth allowed to be brought into the presence of Christ will be the spoils won from the kingdom of Satan—the precious wealth of immortal souls; the only honours recognized and conferred will be the crown and the palm awarded by the hand of Sovereign Grace. Live, and labour, my brother, for that day. Never till then will your ministry be consummated, for not till then will all its fruit be reaped. Then may you appear with a goodly number of rejoicing converts—then may your labours be forgotten in rest—your conscious unworthiness in the joys of Divine acceptance—your conflicts in perfect and glorious triumph! Now you receive the affectionate and prayerful sympathies of your fellow Christians, and fellow servants in Christ; then may you receive the "well done, good and faithful servant," of the Great Master himself! Now you are girding yourself for His service; then may you know the meaning of that wondrous declaration to His faithful servants, "Verily, I say unto you, that the Master shall gird himself, and make them sit down to meat, and will come forth and serve them!"

"O man of God, fight the good fight of faith, lay hold on eternal life—whereunto thou art also called—and hast professed a good profession before many witnesses. I give thee charge in the sight of God, who quickeneth all things, and before Christ Jesus, who before Pontius Pilate witnessed a good confession, that thou keep this commandment (as far as it agrees with the word of God) unrebukable, until the appearing of our Lord Jesus Christ." Amen!

CHARGE II.

THE IDEA AND AIM OF THE CHRISTIAN MINISTRY.

COL. i. 28, 29.—"Whom we preach, warning every man, and teaching every man in all wisdom; that we may present every man perfect in Christ Jesus; whereunto I also labour, striving according to his working, which worketh in me mightily."

HERE are the inspired idea and the ultimate aim of the Christian ministry. In exhibiting them, I would call your attention to these remarks—that the Christian minister has to do with Divine ideals suggestive of the highest aim and end—that the preaching of Christ is essential to the attainment of this end—that, in order to success, even this preaching requires wise adaptation—and that the attainment of such an end deserves and calls for a Divine energy in the employment of the means.

I.

First, The Christian minister has to do with Divine ideals suggestive of the highest aims. Christianity is distinguished from every system of human origin in this—that it brings before the mind the true and only standard of spiritual excellence, and concerns itself only with realizing it. GOD—God is a name which, with us, stands for all imaginable excellence—for excellence unimaginable—unlimited. "Our conception of God," remarks Robert Hall—and perhaps there is no sentence of his more frequently quoted—"our conception of God is continually receiving fresh accessions by attracting to itself as a centre whatever bears the impress of dignity, order, and happiness. It borrows splendour from all that is fair, subordinates to itself all that is great, and sits enthroned on the riches of the universe." In itself the sentence is harmonious—grand. But the heart of its grandeur lies in its truth. The idea of God was originally let down from heaven, that it might take man back on its wings.

"And God made man in his own image." Here, again, is the realization of a Divine idea. "God," we are told, "because He could swear by no greater, sware by himself;" and because He could work after no higher model, He made man in His own image, after His own likeness. This is not merely stated; but, in the opening of Genesis, the fact gradually reports itself in the ascending scale of the creating process. At each rising step you see a prophecy of something nobler yet to come, till at length there comes forth from under the Divine hand, and stands erect, the very image of the Creator. At each rising step you read, "And it was so"—the effect produced, that is, exactly answered to a Divine conception, and was therefore *good.* But at length you come to God's own conception of himself; and it is not until He has embodied that idea, that He desists and rests. And what is the grand distinction of this human model of the Divine? Why, that as man answered to the Divine idea of created perfection, so he is conscious of ideas of uncreated perfection to which God alone answers. Man is constituted to feel that no excellence can exist in himself of which the counterpart does not exist in God. By a rebound of his mind from all the limits of his own nature, he thinks of the same excellences in God as unlimited—infinite. His conception of God is the only one which can satisfy his idea of absolute perfection. His other conceptions of excellence he may often feel as if he were close on the verge of realizing. But this ever towers above him—rises as he rises—yet ever calls him higher.

But what if man should not like to retain God in his knowledge—should so lose the idea of God? Will he not then become a god to himself? A god—an ideal standard of some kind he must have. He cannot go on thinking without it. And as he himself is the highest being he knows after God, is he not likely to settle down on the idea of himself? This, as you know, is his literal history. He who had been made in the image of God began to make gods in his own image. He who had been made the best and brightest symbol of God began to make symbols of himself—of his passions and vices—and to worship them. And this is heathenism.

But while this debasing process was yet going on, there was a small number, even among the heathen, haunted with the conviction that they had lost the true idea of God. Mournfully said one of them, "Man only paints himself in his gods." Truly said another, "Man degrades the gods to himself, instead of elevating himself to the gods." And another taught that the archetype of everything true and good is and must be in the Divine mind. But the *moral* character of the Divine Being himself they knew not. Having willingly lost it, man had morally incapacitated himself for recovering it. It towered above his horizon. Could such minds as Socrates and Plato have been disabused of all the influences of heathenism, and have been then suddenly put in possession of the Scriptural idea of God, I imagine they would have been conscious of adoring awe such as we expect to feel if permitted to stand before the vision of God above.

When the fulness of the time had come for recalling and restoring man to the lost image of God, what was the course pursued but to place before his eyes the Divine archetype to which humanity was to be conformed—CHRIST? Here was the archetype of the first man himself—the archetype which never had been, never could be, absent from the mind of God. The first Adam himself had been but the type of Him that was to come. Indeed, here strictly was the first Adam—the only true and proper head of humanity—He, without whom the Adam of the Fall would never have existed—He, of whom the fallen Adam might justly say, like John the Baptist, "He is preferred before me, for He was before me"—He who from eternity had existed as the archetype of humanity inhabited by Deity—the brightness of the Father's glory—the express image of His person.

But now, how is this living manifestation of God to become a transforming power? Here is the Divine archetype—how is this world of moral deformities to be brought back to His image? Why, He is to set before them another model; in His own person He is to expound the perfect, the infinite love of God. Illustrations of that love had been already given. But they had not been carried out and up to the Divine idea and standard. They might have astonished other orders of beings; but they did not satisfy the Divine conception of what man needed—nor the Divine consciousness of its own ocean-like love. They announced the *existence* of that love, but they did not measure its fulness—did not prove it to be immeasurable. God—if I may so say—could not rest in them. The new creation-week had come—and, as it was in the successive days of the old creation, so now, He cannot rest, cannot enjoy a Sabbath, until He beholds the very image of His love—beholds Him making a sacrifice beyond which it cannot go—to which nothing can be added. In this consummation He can rest. It is His own conception of His own love realized—His heart on a cross. He can call the attention of the world to it, assured of the result. And as generation after generation comes up and gazes—one bows in admiration, and exclaims, "God *so* loved the world." Another looks through His tears, and says, "Herein *is* love!" And another trembles with delight as he sings, "God is love"—the sublime indefiniteness of the language proving that they feel themselves in the presence of a love which passeth knowledge.

Then, again, what is the nature of the change which this Divine power is to produce? Why, man is to be conformed to this Divine ideal. It is not said, coldly and feebly, that man is to be made good, better, excellent. No, every thing good has an ideal to which it is an approach—and man is to be "renewed after the image of Him that created him" —to be brought back again to the original archetype. From the first renovating touch of the Holy Spirit, through all the successive changes which Christians undergo—there is a Divine model after which He works, and to which they are ever approaching—they are predestinated to be conformed to the image of Christ—predestinated—the purpose dates from the past eternity, and the great archetype towers in the future—and the whole time-interval is to be occupied in bringing the saved up to that standard. Still more strikingly and spiritually in our context—the great mystery hid from generations is said to be the Gospel—and the heart of the Gospel, Christ—and Christ himself the heart —the innermost life of the Christian—"Christ in you the hope of glory." Spiritually, the Divine archetype himself is there—there as the hope of glory—there as the Divine ideal of character *within*, yearning after a Divine ideal of condition *without*—glory—the inner life of a piece with the outer state. He is there, not dimly, vaguely, and as an abstraction—but as a Divine personifying energy—there, to awaken a diviner consciousness. The Christian life is a Christ-forming process.

Then, again, the Church—the society of all those who are thus being brought back again to the Divine image—that has its model in the Divine mind. The Jewish temple was its visible symbol. And even that, you know, was not set up at random, or left to human taste. Its model came down from God. It was built after the pattern of heavenly things. But, spiritually, here is its archetype: "till we all come in the unity of the faith, and of the knowledge of the Son of God, unto a perfect man, unto the measure of the stature of the fulness of Christ." Here is the Divine architype of the Christian Church; and the ministry exists to conform the Church to it. The Christian Pastorate is to continue till the

Church attains its highest point of development—to the full stature of Christ. The growth is not fanciful, but is to result from His imparted fulness. Nor is the standard imaginary; for its spiritual height and symmetry are to resemble the divine humanity of Christ.

But if this was the design of God in instituting the ministry—this the Divine ideal and standard to which the ministry is to bring the Church—what should be the aim and model ever present to the mind of the ministers of Christ?—"whom we preach, warning every man, and teaching every man, that we may present every man perfect in Christ Jesus." That was a sublime view of a great artist, which represented the sculptor as seeing, in the yet unshaped block of marble, the future statue. That is a sublimer view, which not only foresees the angel, or the spirit of the just man made perfect, in the yet ignorant and unrenewed hearer, but which already places a congregation of such in grand perspective around the throne of God. And yet the apostle did this and more. He aspired to present *all* he addressed, "every man perfect before God."

Godlike anticipation this! Not, indeed, that the Christian minister is answerable for success. Not that his non-attainment of visible success, even in a single instance, would be a proof of absolute failure. Ends of vast importance might be gained short of the great and final one. That for which you *are* answerable is the height of your aim, and the employment of the means for attaining it. That, however, is a state of mind which I trust you will never be able to understand, which can be content without success—with merely aiming high. Paul could not; he agonized for it—was ready to become a curse for it. And you know that his Master and yours travailed in soul—actually became a curse for it.

II.

This leads to our second remark—that the preaching of

Christ is essential to the attainment of this high end—"*whom we preach*, in order that we may present every man perfect in Christ Jesus,"—implying that the two things are connected as cause and effect, condition and consequence, means and end. It is not the good man of Plato, nor the virtuous man of the Stoic, nor the perfect man of any vague ideal that men may set up in their own minds, that you are to aim at, but the perfection of Christ—the reproduction of his image. If our copies are to be Christ-like, our model must be Christ.

Perhaps there is a tendency in some of the preaching of the day, not, indeed, to aim at something else than perfection of character, but to forget that the only perfection we know of is Christ-like perfection. Having become familiar with the idea of moral excellence, we are in danger of forgetting the original from which we have all derived it. The various steps in this process of forgetfulness appear to be these: At a time of general awakening (like that by Whitfield and Wesley), men emphatically preach Christ. They find themselves standing close to Him—see nothing but Him—feel that the awakening comes directly from *Him*. They speak not of "evangelical principles" so much as of "the person of Christ;" nor of the atonement as a "doctrine," but of the atoning death of Christ; nor of the force of duty, but of the constraining love of Christ. After a while, they or their successors begin to think more of the results of their preaching—of presenting every man perfect in Christ. For where is the use of preaching if it does not lead to this? Hence Christian character comes to be more and more insisted on, and the duty of individual obligation more and more enforced. This is the second stage of the process. And if the Apostolic balance could be preserved between the two—preaching Christ as the *means*, to secure Christian perfection as the *end*—that would be the perfection of preaching. But the scale gradually turns in favour of the latter—Christian character. Argument takes the place of testimony—the head is appealed to rather than the heart—the reasonableness of Christianity is preached rather than Christianity itself—and the advantages and excellence of the character at which it aims, rather than the means which it supplies for producing it. And this prepares the way for the third stage of the process. What man can do, and ought to be—an ideal of human duty and perfection—comes next too much to engross the minds of many; but an ideal which is in danger, owing to the very fact that it does so engross them, of being cut off on the one side from the only means which can produce perfection—the preaching of Christ—and on the other, from the only model of perfection which the Gospel recognises—the image of Christ. And thus comes in a great element of legality, of unaided, unsanctified human effort, ending in shams and semblances of the Christian life, but with little of its spring, and heartiness, and joyous reality; in failure and prostration, but without any accompanying humility—in man-preaching instead of Christ-preaching—a state calling aloud for another day of awakening. And thus the cycle goes round.

Observe, I do not say that the preacher is always to abide, to live and to die, in the first stage. I do not say that the preaching suited to that first state of things is therefore equally suited to a succeeding state of things. I have already intimated that the perfection of preaching is that which combines in due proportion the exposition alike of the *means*, and of the end to be aimed at. And, indeed, if we could always go on with the same hearers, and the same only—hearers on whom the means had taken Divine effect—we might then enlarge more and more on the *end*, without much of the danger to which I have adverted. But such is not the case. And we must not suppose, because we ourselves have grown familiar with "the truth as it is in Jesus," that therefore others need not be made familiar with it. We must not suppose, when we hear a chain of reasoning respecting human perfectibility, that because we can supply the missing links out of our own Christian experience—can, by a kind of Divine instinct, link it on to the cross from which we have just come—that therefore others will do the same who have never been taken to the cross, and who have no experience to draw from. We must remember that a new generation is ever rising up around us, that unconverted adults are listening to us, and that if we would edify them, build up their character, that is, into a Christian edifice, we must first lay a foundation; and "other foundation can no man lay than that is laid, which is Jesus Christ." Who thinks of learning to read while skipping the alphabet? or of teaching the science of astronomy without referring to the stars? or of expatiating on bodily health, and growth, and perfection, apart from air, and food, and exercise? Christian perfection is only the reproduction of Christ in the man—the expansion of the life of Christ in the Church. And never can you nourish and develop that life more effectually than by preaching Christ. That alone which first begets the Christian life can bring it to maturity.

My brother, take this problem—given two Christian ministers—one of whom occupies two-thirds of his preaching with the means—Christ, and one-third with the end—*duty;* the other, occupying two-thirds of his with man and duty, and only one-third with Christ; which of the two (all other things being equal) will secure most of the end—Christian conversion, Christian training, Christian perfection? Observe, neither of them neglects wholly either the means or the end; but they attend to each respectively in different proportions—the proportions of two to one. And which, I ask, Christ-preaching, or man-and-duty preaching, is likely to draw the other after it most certainly? Is the Christ-preacher more likely to secure the performance of duty, or the duty-preacher to lead to Christ? Which of the two falls in more with the strain of the Apostolic preaching? which of the two is more likely to lead to a state of things needing a revival? which of the two, if a revival became necessary, would be most likely to produce it? I will take your reply for granted. You have not so learned Christ as to hesitate.

Then let this distinction determine you in the choice of your subjects. Would you see the young eye glisten, and the young bosom heave? win them into the presence of Christ that He may lay His hands upon them, and bless them? Would you smite the heart of rock, and see the stream of penitence gush forth? Let "Jesus Christ be evidently set forth crucified before their eyes." Would you sway a sceptre here over human wills? speak as from the throne of a living loving Christ.

Let it determine you, not merely in the *choice* of your subjects, but in the treatment of them when you have chosen them. Be as original as you please in the illustration of your great theme—for everything in the universe is meant to do it homage. Be as varied as you please in its statement—for it deserves the utmost exercise of the human mind. It endows you with all large-hearted truths—includes all that is great in the character of God—all that is holy in His government—all that is loving in His heart. Your ministry may have a vast circumference of instruction and admonition, of duty and motive; but thus preach, and every part and point of the circumference will be seen running back to Christ the centre, or springing directly from Him. This is a line of truth reaching from the heart of God to the heart of man—the line along which the Spirit of God delights to move and to which the heart of man first vibrates. If the Word of God, as a whole, be the sword of the Spirit, this is its soul-subduing edge. Let others blunt or polish it away if they will, be it yours to wield it with effect as a good soldier of Jesus Christ.

III.

But, thirdly, in order to success, even the preacher of Christ requires wise adaptation:—"warning every man, and teaching every man in all wisdom." This does not mean so much *warning of danger*—though that is a part of the preacher's duty—as *admonishing* all of the claims of the Gospel. Here are the two classes into which your hearers may be divided—those who need to be brought to believe, and those who, believing, need instruction and Christian development. Rather, here are the two stages through which you are to aim at conducting your hearers—first across the line which brings them into "the kingdom of God's dear Son," and then over the lengths and breadths of that kingdom.

So in the generalization of the last day, all mankind will be divided into two classes—the righteous and the wicked. But, oh, how great the diversity of character included in each! And yet then it will be made to appear that there was some portion or aspect of Divine truth which had been minutely adapted to each diversity. Let that adaptation be apparent in your ministry. Let none of your hearers escape through a vague generality of address. Let each heart feel your searching hand in turn. Reason patiently with the backslider. Unmask the hypocrite. Track the self-deceiver through the labyrinth in which he lives, and bring him forth. Rebuke the trifler in religion—let him come here to see the gulf yawn, and the flames burst forth at his feet—to see worlds contending for his soul. The worldling will come here—come with the world in his heart; let him see you weigh it against the loss of his soul—kindle it into a fire to alarm him; let him see it burn to ashes in his embrace, but leaving behind it, in his inmost soul, a fire never to be quenched. The undecided and procrastinating will come—recall their solemn impressions, interpret their fears, surround them with the realities of "the world to come." "Knowing the terrors of the Lord, *persuade* men." Could you concentrate all those terrors into a focus—into one fiery point—still you must so hold it over the heart, as that it shall only melt, not burn. Never forget that you are the minister of Divine pity.

On the other hand, you are to teach—not producing the

mere speculatist in religion by an undue exhibition of doctrinal truth, nor catering to a morbid sentimentalism by mere emotional preaching, nor, by mere practical preaching, surrounding yourself with a crowd of formalists. Aim to exhibit the truth in its *evidence*, that it may be believed; in its *excellence*, that it may be felt; and in its *practical claims*, that it may be obeyed. By caring for the young, comforting the feeble-minded, and rightly dividing the word of truth, commend yourself to every man's conscience in the sight of God, and so aim to present every man perfect in Christ Jesus. And here is your encouragement, that every man has that in him to which you may confidently appeal with the hope of a response; that, as the believer has that in him which awaits your *teaching*, so the non-believer has that within him which awaits your *admonition*—which starts up at it as at the old and familiar voice of an injured friend—sides with you against himself. Bad as a man may be, yet evil, as evil, has no witness for itself in his breast. *Passion* may plead for it; his judgment and conscience are against it. They who would persuade him to error, can succeed only by giving to it the semblance of truth; and they who would seduce him to evil, must give it the appearance of good—a proof that he was made *for* truth and *for* goodness. And you may be certain that in every man there is some one point that will echo back your voice in their behalf.

And here is another encouraging fact, that every man in your congregation so far resembles every other man, that, in addressing one class, you may be benefitting all. Touch *one* key in an organ and the whole instrument vibrates. Aye, and not unfrequently, the class most benefitted is the one you thought not of. You call for conversion, and the advanced Christian is quickened. You enlarge on Christian experience, and the dead in sin is awakened: the truth being, that every man has both parties within him—saint and sinner. You will not misconceive me, as if I meant that there is no essential difference in character—but simply that as the best man is not all angel, so the worst man is not all fiend; and consequently the arrow you aimed at the one may quiver in the breast of the other—your admonitions may teach, and your teaching admonish. Observe, from first to last you address (if I may so say) an ideal hearer—the man that *ought* or that *is* to be. In calling the unbeliever—"awake thou that sleepest"—you address the man that *ought* to be, but is not yet. In exhorting the believer, "Be perfect, even as your Father in heaven is perfect," you address the man that is to be—call on him to realize his own idea of perfection. And in addressing each, you are to point to Christ as the source and the standard of life to both, to all. Of this high aim you can never safely lose sight. Look even at the true artist—he does not aim merely to interest—he would scorn that—he interests only that he may reach a higher point—may excite reflection, contemplation, call up ideas of perfection. You are both to interest and to awaken this idea, that you may reach a yet higher point—may conduct your hearers to Him who is the living model of that perfection, and who will enable them to realize it. My brother, if your object were the lowest, merely to keep a congregation together, you could not act more wisely than to preach as if you were really aiming at the highest. But believing, as I do, that your aim is thus high and ultimate, you have no alternative. Here is your motto, "Whom we preach, warning every man, and teaching every man, in all wisdom, that we may present every man perfect in Christ Jesus."

V.

And, then, fourthly, the attainment of such an end deserves and calls for a Divine energy in the employment of the means "whereunto I also labour, striving according to his working, which worketh in me mightily."

I have not gone into detail respecting such topics as the preservation of your health—the husbanding of your time—the arrangement of your various pastoral duties—and the thousand ways in which your character may have the effect of neutralizing the influence of your preaching, or be made to increase and enforce it. And I have abstained from this ground chiefly from the conviction, that if you aim *not* at the high end set before you, no amount of exhortation on these points would be of any avail; but that if you do—that aim itself will supply the place of a thousand laws—by consecrating your whole nature to its attainment, and filling you with a kind of Divine instinct in adopting the necessary means. Aim at this end; and what a society do you join! "Whom *we* preach!" Preach Christ, as the apostles did, and you join them—you succeed them. They kindled the lamp you carry. Their feet wore the paths you tread. You pass to your work through their bending ranks. "Other men have laboured, and we have entered into their labours." But we inherit the past only as we *employ* it, and that we *may* employ it. Aim at this end; and with what sacred models will it surround you! The artist surrounds himself in his studio with the purest and the noblest models of antiquity. His aim is, that by ever working in their presence, he may make nearer and nearer approaches to perfection. The choicest specimens of sanctified humanity offer themselves to your acceptance—men who were smit with the passion—consumed with the Divine ambition of saving souls. Study their biography, that you may imbibe their spirit. You could not indulge in more pleasant and profitable reading.

Aim at this end; and you will form such a conception of the magnitude of your office, and of your need of Christian co-operation, that you will deem your own duty to consist very much in enlisting the agency of others, in developing, organizing, and employing the resources of the Church. The mainspring in a piece of machinery implies subordinate springs and parts, and fulfils its office, not by superseding, but by giving impulse and direction to them all. The value of your agency will be more than doubled by its putting or keeping in motion the activities of the Church. Much as his ministry may call for gratitude, who saves a soul from death, still more does his, who, having done this, then puts that saved soul in the way of saving others. The one may make *proof* of his ministry, the other makes *full* proof. The one may make proof of his ministry to the *Church*, the other, besides doing this, adds the ministry of the Church to his own, and makes full proof of it to the world.

Aim at the high end described in the text, and you will so see the magnitude of your office that you will call in more than human aid. You will not merely and humanly strive —agonize — but agonize according to a Divine energy. Observe, you are not merely to be occupied with a Divine work, and to be impelled by Divine motives, but to be conscious of a Divine co-working—of being the medium and agent of a Divine power. You are not merely to work with the government of God, and to move in a line with His purposes; others may do this unconsciously, but you yourself are to be the conductor of a Divine energy. You are not to pray merely for ordinary aid, nor merely to intercede for your people, though intercession is to be an habitual part of your official work, as it is of your Master's; but you are to calculate on the real living conjunction, in your own person, of Divine and human forces! And all this, just because it is God's own work, and not yours. You have but just heard of it—caught a glimpse of it—adopted it. He is the creator of it—the author of the entire plan—the originator of all its means—has had even to incline you to take part in it.

What inspiration should there be for you in this fact—that this is God's house—not so much your working place as His—that, come here when you may, He is here before you —that, ask whatever energy you may, He is ready to give you more—to fill you up to the measure of your capacity—that strive as you may, He is striving still more, not only in you, but with you! Why it is as if the racer in the Grecian games—which the apostle had probably in his eye—as if the racer, with the goal before him, should be stimulated not merely by the cheers of the myriads of excited spectators, but should feel as if they had all suddenly transferred and infused into Him all their own muscular energy. You are to regard yourself as labouring here in an atmosphere of Divine power.

Finally, aim at the end the apostle proposed, and what a reward awaits you! The same in *kind* as that which awaits your Lord himself. For why did He agonize—die? "That he might *present it to himself a glorious church.*" "This was the joy set before him, and for which he endured the cross." This is the object which now, on His throne, He is "henceforth expecting"—the ideal is ever present to His mind—the prospect ever stretched out before His gaze. Of what a mighty cycle will that be the completion! The new-creation week is still in process. The sixth concluding day is yet to come—when the self-destroyed creature shall be seen brought back again to the image of God in the perfected Church. Yes; that Divine ideal will yet be realized—will be seen standing erect, temple-like, and complete—a glorious Church.

Live and labour, my brother, for that day. Erect no inferior standard. Aim to save all you address—to present them perfect in Christ Jesus. How shall we picture the joy of the faithful minister of Christ in that day! To meet alike the embrace of those who were the means of saving him, and of all who were saved by him. How Divine the delight of finding themselves all in the presence of the great Master—receiving His approbation—entering into His joy—sharing it with Him—rejoicing with Him in the harmony and welfare of all sanctified spiritual being, in the attainment of which He allowed them the honour to participate.

Live and labour, I say, for that day. And may the joy of the Lord be your strength. And may the Christian sympathies and congratulations of this evening be the prophecy and prelude of the well-done, good and faithful servant of that day. Amen.

CHARGE III.

THE CAPABILITIES OF THE CHRISTIAN MINISTRY.

2 TIMOTHY iv. 5.—"Make full proof of thy ministry."

I HAVE the pleasure of addressing you, for the first time, not now as a student, but as "a brother beloved;" *called* by a voice, of which the call of the Church is but the echo; *ordained* by the imposition of a hand, of which ours is but the symbol and recognition. "Grace be to you, my brother, and mercy, and peace, from God the Father, and the Lord Jesus Christ, our Saviour."

As my business at this moment is exclusively with yourself—with no theory to propound, no argument to sustain, no multitude to move—with nothing to excite interest but the weight or worth of the remarks appropriate to your new position—let me hope that that attention may be *voluntarily* accorded, which I might not otherwise be able to secure. I wish to address you on *the capabilities of the Christian ministry.* The basis of my remarks you will find in 2 Tim. iv. 5, "Make full proof of thy ministry." Similar to this is the language of the same apostle in his Epistle to the Colossians, "Say to Archippus, Take heed to the ministry which thou hast received of the Lord, that thou *fulfil* it." Only in the text there is a shade of greater urgency and stress. Indeed, the gist and force of all the apostolic charges to ministers—to Timothy, Titus, Archippus, and the elders at Ephesus, is this, Discharge *all* your duties to the *utmost;* make the *most* of your office.

I.

Now before we can see *how* this is to be done, or point to the *motives* for doing it, we must glance first at the *nature* of the ministry itself, and your connexion with it. A limb, a foot, or a wing, can be understood only in connexion with the body to which it belongs. And the text, simple and self-evident as it may seem, is part of a system, and derives all its significance from connexion with that system. Now the moment we lift up our eyes from the text to survey the great horizon of truth which surrounds it, we are everywhere met with one sight—the cross. We are conscious of a universal presence—Christ. As if you had suddenly woke up in the Jewish temple on the morning of the great day of atonement—the altar, the high priest, the veil—everything speaks of sacrifice, propitiation, and acceptance. Now *your* ministry points back to *His*. "You know the grace of our Lord Jesus Christ, how, though He was rich, for our sakes He became poor." *He* was a minister then—made full proof of *His* ministry—but in how peculiar and sublime a sense! You know the work which was then given him to do—a work for the Godhead—a service which no other being in the universe could have performed—a sacrifice such as can never be repeated. But, amazing as were the ever-deepening stages of His humiliation, never did He cease to serve and to suffer, till, lifting up His eyes to heaven, He could say, "Father, I have finished the work which Thou gavest me to do. I have magnified law; expiated guilt; demonstrated that Thou art love; laboured, agonized, to fulfil my commission. And now it is finished. Father, glorify Thy Son." Then closed His servitude. He dieth no more. He is a servant no more. He is a *master* now. He has a *throne*, He has servants of *His own* now. "For, for this cause Christ both died, and rose, and lives again, that He might be Lord both of the dead and of the living." He has ministers of His own now, and *you* profess to be among them.

But what does this imply? Christianity is one thing; your connexion with it is another. And yet your position this morning implies the *vitality* of your connexion with it. Christianity does not exist for you as something at a distance—something standing outside your nature. The atmosphere not merely encompasses you, it passes into you, colours your blood, and sustains your life. And these gospel facts have passed from without into your nature. In their spirit and meaning, they have become a part of you. They belong to your experience. They have brought you a divine life; and you find yourself in the possession of it. Life itself—ordinary human life—was meant to be a great discovery—a series of surprises. With most, indeed, it is little more than a series of postponements—disappointments—or a state of somnambulism. But, as every morning awakens us afresh, life was meant to be a succession of awakenings and wonders. All the principles of external nature are lodged in us, and invite discovery. To the natural is added the supernatural—principles and powers which mere material nature could neither enclose nor express; and they are in us expressly that we may find them, feel them, live in the consciousness of them. But when Christ came, higher principles still were embodied in Him—principles which till then had been at large in the universe; dim and diffuse, as the poet represents the light, till it was collected and put into the sun. But "in Him dwelt all the fulness of the Godhead bodily"—power which no obstacle can limit—holiness no law can transcend—love incarnate—the heart of God beating and bleeding for man's recovery.

Now, in the presence of God thus "manifest in the flesh," you have found not only a new *capacity* for life, but capacity for *a new life, and the means of living it.* How often does a man, placed in a new position, find emotion, capacity, and aspiration which he never knew before! You have been lifted by a Divine hand into the visions of God. The character of Christ has flashed a new light on your own character. You have made the discovery, that your nature is not a mere organization for animal enjoyment, nor a house for domestic ends, nor a laboratory for scientific investigation, nor a hall for social purposes, but a temple for God. "Know ye not that your body is the temple of the Holy Ghost?" You have discovered, within, the ruins of an altar; and a sacred recess—the very *sanctum sanctorum*—disused, and in danger of being for ever shut up; and pollution everywhere, calling for the blood of sprinkling and reconsecration. And then the fact that God himself should have come down, and come near to you, with all the means and appliances in order to your temple-restoration—that He should have redeemed you with the precious blood of Christ—*this* it is which makes you feel that you are not your own. As if you had been present at His death—had witnessed the great transaction—you feel, in common with every servant of Christ, that He has laid all your nature under obligation, bought all your powers; and therefore it is that you have placed yourself at His sovereign disposal.

And here begin your spiritual qualifications for the ministry. You have this discovery of the love of Christ to make known. You have this great experience to make use of. The Mohammedans have a legend, that what made Enoch so faithful as a preacher of righteousness was, that he had asked and obtained permission first to go down and see the lost in perdition. You occupy a more advantageous position. "The word is nigh thee, even in thy mouth, and in thy heart." The mediation of Christ has given you a longer line for sounding the depths of evil—a truer rate and standard for computing the worth of the soul—the deepest insight into the love of God. You come here not from the prison-house of justice, but from beholding what manner of love the Father hath bestowed on us. A benigner impulse moves you. "Knowing the terrors of the Lord, *you persuade* men." You stand near the cross. And you cannot but speak the things which you have seen and heard. Your preaching cannot be a feeble stream of words. Like the waters of prophetic vision, it must bring with it the medicinal virtues of the soil whence it comes. Your every sermon will be, more or less, a portion of yourself—a testimony of the things which you have tasted, and felt, and handled of the Word of Life.

And here you see the *nature* of the ministry, and the *reason* of its urgency. God has a message of mercy to man; and you, having yourself believed it, are called to deliver it to others. God is now on a throne of grace; and you, having yourself bowed before it, have offered to unveil that throne in the eyes of the guilty. God is now waiting to save; and you have stepped forth from the ranks of ordinary Christian activity, and have volunteered to "pray men, in Christ's stead, to be reconciled to God." You might be a mere *playfellow* with the laws of nature, as many are who amuse themselves with science. But you have to do with laws which God himself could not expound except by an infinite sacrifice—and with these you are to be a "co-worker"—a "true yokefellow." You are appointed by God to represent them. Your preaching is to stand for them. Your ministry is to be of a piece with them. You are not to be a mere dangling pendant to the office, but a living expression of the laws which have led to it. Your preaching, so far from ending in words, is to flow forth in acts—in the organization and vitality of a Church—a body for expressing, and working, and diffusing the light, and love, and life of the same laws. Let this be your conception of your office; and you will find that all nature does but symbolize it, and all providence celebrates and is one with it.

II.

Secondly, *how* is such a ministry to be made the most of? Not, certainly, by *ritualizing* it, and so, in effect, transferring to yourself the importance which belongs alone to your office, but by viewing it as *a living moral agency.* There are those who fancy they are magnifying their office by pretending to a sacerdotal sanctity and a special investiture; by mystifying the two simple rites of Christianity; by pompously decorating and dramatizing the spiritual worship of God; by arrogating for their office a mystic influence, and an authority so vast as almost to engross the government of the Church on earth, and to leave the Redeemer nothing but a naked throne and a nominal Headship.

But this is to absorb the *office* instead of letting the office absorb them. This is to stand *before* it—*outside* of it, as if it were a piece of machinery, instead of entering into it, and becoming one with it, as a living agency. The text implies that it is not an *opus operatum,* independent of the character of him who fills it—a wheel independent of everything but the hand that turns it—operating rigidly and necessarily like a law of nature; but that it admits of experiment, and of *degrees* of fulfilment, rising from the point of utter failure up to the point of full proof or complete accomplishment. Having to do with rational and emotional beings, influenced by motives and example, you cannot be said to exercise *any* ministry, except as you reason with them, and appeal to them, and move them by your character, and according to the *degree* in which you do all this. Under God, your ministry will be what you make it. As much of the Christian element as there is in you, so much will there be in your ministry, and no more. I am not now speaking of your *success.* That will depend not only on the character of your ministry, but also on the character of those among whom you minister. Given, the character of a minister, and the character of the people ministered to, and the result is likely to be in the proportion of these two conditions combined. But taking your ministry by itself, it will be just what you are. In the mechanical world there are what are called testing-houses for ascertaining what weight a beam will carry, what stress a spring will bear, what explosive power a gun will resist. And were man a machine, or the ministry amenable to mechanical laws, we might determine what is its full proof by measure and number. But as a moral agency, this is a question for the adjudication of the agent alone. Need I say that for you, my brother, it is *the* question? There is indeed one law or fact in mechanics that analogically applies—the fact that the strength of a machine is as its *weakest* part. A man of great physical energy may fancy that he is making full proof of his ministry by physically exhausting himself. He whose forte lies in reasoning may suppose that he is doing the same by taxing his logic to the utmost; and he of strong emotions may think that he is doing it by expending himself in pathos and appeal. But each is strong only in one respect; and in that one respect his ministry may be of the highest efficacy to an individual here and there; in relation to the mass, its worth must be estimated from its weakest, and not from its strongest point. If either would make full proof of his ministry, he must develop and strengthen its weaker parts. It is only an entire ministry that can make itself be felt by an entire people.

2. Clearly, the text would not be complied with by going to the opposite extreme of the ritualist, and *secularizing* the ministry, but by making the most of it as a *distinctive spiritual* function. If *he* secularizes the ministry who would abrogate it as a distinct office, and place its work on a level with that of ordinary philanthropy, still more does he debase it who, while insisting on its distinctiveness, treats it merely as a profession—as *one* of the professions—acts as if its claims could be easily satisfied, and even exceeded, and who, accordingly, finds leisure for occupations alien to its spirit. "But did not Paul labour with his hands?" Undoubtedly; not, however, because he thought *so little* but *so much* of the ministry—because under exceptional and very peculiar circumstances he sought to preserve the high sanctity of the office, as a spiritual function, unstained. "And would you not employ lay agency and co-operation?" To the utmost. In many instances, I would even measure the success of the ministry by the *amount* of such agency which it called forth. But in all this I only see the ministry multiplying its powers

—not descending to a lower level, but drawing up other agencies to its own height—confessing its own inadequacy for the greatness of its charge. "And are you not limiting the work of the ministry to the mere function of preaching?" Far from it. Paul himself did not. *He* taught from house to house—travelled from region to region—appealed from one court of justice to another—sent letters to individuals and to churches—thought of the wants of the Church in the future as well as for the present—wept, prayed, agonized much in private as well as in public—was "in labours more abundant;" but one aim gave unity to the whole—that he might make full proof of his ministry by doing his utmost for the Church of Christ. "But *he* was an Apostle." He was. But let me beg you to remark that, with him, the *minister* generally eclipsed the *apostle;* he seems often to have forgotten the apostle, the minister never. His claims to the apostolate he asserts only when writing officially to the Churches, or when, by its being called in question, his ministerial usefulness was endangered. Ordinarily, he speaks and acts only as the preacher, the minister, the missionary, the fellow-labourer of non-apostolic men, charged with the task of saving souls from death. But as he raised his eye to the height of this aim, and saw how far below it his utmost efforts fell, no one could more feelingly exclaim, "Who is sufficient for these things!" or more frequently hasten away to God, and take refuge in His abounding mercy.

My brother, we have read of men who always seemed greater than their greatest deeds, who seemed to have more power latent than they had ever put forth, who stood among their fellows like a great reserved force, whose mere presence acted without any means. I fancy Paul was such a man. But whether we believe this of *Paul* or not, we know that *he* believed this indefinable grandeur of the ministry. And do you not see that, by thus avowing that he could never equal his own conceptions of the office, he was most effectually exalting it? It is easy to exceed the *legitimate* claims of any secular office. But here is an office which defies such exaggeration, which enlarges the mind it employs, and employs all the powers which it enlarges. And in the Apostle we behold a man who, having made, if ever man did make, the grand experiment of weighing its claims, reported that he could find nothing weighty enough with which to compare it—nothing vast enough with which to measure it—that its limits are nowhere to be found.

My brother, form the same high estimate of your new, your spiritual vocation, and you will feel that all your powers are due—that your very position consecrates you to the loftiest service. You may not *profess* great things, but you will *live* them. Your faith will not be a feeling of self-sufficiency, but of humble dependence on God. Your confidence will not consist in an affected superiority to the opinions of others, but in the deep conviction that God is working with you. Your activity will not make you regardless of heavenly aid, but will only render you more concerned to obtain it. Your earnestness will not impel you to attempt the *impossible*, or even the *extravagant*, but it will impel you to make full proof of your ministry.

3. Nor can the charge in the text be obeyed by making the ministry an occasion for mere *philosophizing*, and indulging in *speculative novelties*, but by *testifying repentance towards God and faith in our Lord Jesus Christ.* The cross, indeed, has a philosophy of its own—the true *prima philosophia*—destined to subordinate and imbue every other. Expatiate on this as much as you please, for it includes all that is great in the character of God, all that is holy in His government, all that is loving in His heart. It endows you with all large-hearted truths, and for analogies and illustrations, it makes you free of the universe. Far be it from you to exhibit the cross as a root out of a dry ground, though others may so esteem it. In your hand let it bud, and blossom, and become a fruit-bearing tree of life.

That which we denounce is the attempt to carve the cross

into a new shape—to convert it into the philosopher's chair—to place over it a new superscription—and all this under the idea of consulting the taste of the age. Some, indeed, would go further, and dispense with everything *peculiar* to the Gospel. According to them, the millennium of philosophy is just ahead. As if it were the easiest thing in the world to write Bibles, and to introduce new dispensations, they are ready to disclaim all connexion with the past, and to begin anew. This very idea of theirs, indeed, is a stolen one, and it augurs badly for the originality of an era which begins in a plagiarism from antiquity. And is it not a suspicious thing when the *past* must be disparaged as the first step towards magnifying the present? Is it not more than suspicious when a man must burn the Alexandrian library as the only chance of getting his own book read; or must burn down the temple at Ephesus as the only means of saving his name from oblivion; or must extinguish the race, in order to be a first man? As if, forsooth, a truly great and formative period ever did thus decry the past, or prate about "inaugurating a new period," about "interpreting the age," about its "mission," about a "coming man." Like nature itself, it is too great for words, utters itself in deeds, perfects its great tasks in silence. As if, too, separation from the past were *possible*, even if *desirable;* as if the river *could be any other* than the continuation of the stream, or the man any other than the child developed, or to-day any other than the offspring of yesterday. As if, too, such detachment from the past were *desirable*, even if possible. Get rid, if you please, of all that is worthless in the past. But let us remember that the proportion of chaff to the wheat is as great in the present day, in the departments of philosophy and theology, as in any past day. True greatness has no relation to time or place, is never past, never superannuated, never distant—is always present, and of to-day. Of such greatness the Bible is the temple, and you are to serve at its altars. In an age enamoured of *little things*, you are to lead in all that is glorious in *the past*, and to bring it to bear on the present, with a view to all the future. In an age enamoured of *itself*, you are to shew that we have come into the midst of all that is ennobling and Divine—"to Mount Sion, to the city of the living God, the heavenly Jerusalem, to the general assembly and church of the first-born, to the spirits of just men made perfect, and to Jesus the mediator of the new covenant." In an age smitten and disheartened with the spirit of uncertainty, you have to testify on subjects always seasonable, infallibly certain, and of Divine authority.

In an early period of the Christian Church it became the custom, at the ordination of a bishop, to place an open Bible on his head, and then to give it into his hands, to denote that he was constantly to consult it as his guide and authority. While dispensing with the *sign*, we exhort you, my brother, to retain the thing signified. You have now passed within that veil where God is jealous for His glory. You have entered a circle in which every object is sacred to His name, and sprinkled with blood—every doctrine you are to preach is already prescribed—every principle from which you are to act, already set down—a circle in which no will but His is to be thought of. God manifest for man's salvation is to be the one theme of your ministry. God giving himself *for* man that He might give himself *to* man; this is a line of truth reaching from the heart of God to the heart of man—*the* line along which the Spirit of God delights to operate, and to which the heart of sinful man first vibrates. Know nothing but this—glory in this—and you will make full proof of your ministry.

4. This is to be done, not by *isolating* the office from the Church, and by *monopolizing and performing* the duties of the Church, but by *developing, organizing,* and *employing all its resources.* The *mainspring* in a piece of machinery implies *subordinate* springs and parts, and fulfils its office, not by superseding, but by giving impulse and direction to them all. The duties of the minister and the Church are

reciprocal. If a people would have their minister devoted to his office—a man of *one* object—it follows that they are to aim at the same singleness of purpose; for where is the propriety of a minister devoted to one object in a Church devoted to *none?* They can never consistently complain of his inactivity, without meaning to say, "We ourselves are impatient to *give* more, *pray* more, *labour* more for God." He alone is not the Church, and it is by the Church that the world is to be instrumentally benefited. His preaching alone is not to effect it; but his preaching illustrated by their holy living, and followed up and enforced by their prayers and self-denying efforts.

As the minister of a Christian Church, you become the centre and mainspring of an organization for usefulness, not merely to the Church itself, but to a circle beyond. Its sick are to be visited—its ignorant instructed—its children trained in the ways of God—its widows, and fatherless, and destitute visited in the times of their affliction—the whole of its area filled with appropriate works of faith and labours of love. Hence all your means—the mite of the widow, and the wealth of the affluent—the leisure of one, and the influence of another—the ardour of the young, the wisdom of the aged—the resources of all, are to be combined and employed. Here the motto of each is to be, "None of us liveth to himself;" each one is to be assigned a form of duty; the influence of each, by union with all, is made to be felt; and as often as others are added to the number, you are to regard your strength as proportionally increased, only as the means of increased activity.

My brother, the corruption of Christianity by Popery is twofold: it blinds man to a sense of his *individual personal* accountableness as a *sinner*, and to a sense of his duty to his fellow-men as a *Christian*—and it does this by undertaking to do everything for him. The Reformation rescued us from one half of the evil—from that part which blinded men to a sense of their personal concern in the affair of *their own* salvation. But while the Protestant wonders at the infatuation of the Papist in imagining that anything can exempt him from the necessity of personal diligence in seeking his own salvation, are we not too willing to retain the other half of the evil, and to act as if we *could devolve* it almost entirely on ministers to seek the salvation of others? Each is alike essential Popery; and glorious as the Reformation was for the *Church,* in making each member feel the necessity of personal faith and personal holiness, as glorious will that reformation be for the world (and thank God it is in progress) which shall make each one feel his responsibility to God for personal activity in the work of human salvation. And much as *his* ministry may call for gratitude who saves a soul from death, still more does his who, having done this, then puts that saved soul in the way of saving others. The one may make *proof* of his ministry; the other makes *full proof.* The one may make proof of his ministry to the *Church;* the other, besides doing this, adds the ministry of the Church to his own, and makes full proof of it to the world.

III.

Passing by other modes of complying with the injunction in the text, let me advert, thirdly, to some of the *considerations* which should move you to make the most of the ministry.

1. I might urge it, first, if only for the sake of vindicating the office from the tendency of many to disparage it. It *has* been "mighty through God." It has regenerated communities — subdued kingdoms — wrought righteousness — turned to flight the armies of the aliens. It has graven its history on the face of society. Nor is there any reason in the institution itself why it should not still be a power—a great transforming power. It only requires to be made full proof of in order to justify itself as the highest appointment of Heaven upon earth.

2. But throughout his pastoral epistles—and, indeed, in all his scattered references to the Christian ministry—the prevailing motive of the apostle is the *sacred* and *spiritual* greatness of the office. Imagine what his estimate of it must have been, when, with a celestial crown in view, he could yet say, "I am in a strait; I wot not which to choose." Had it been to rule a kingdom, or to wear the purple, he would have felt no strait. How *could* the diadems of earth possess attractions for him, when *there*—full before him—were the open portals of the New Jerusalem, and its unfading glories streamed on his view, and its glad hosannahs reached his ear, and there (he distinctly saw it) his own Redeemer held up to view a crown of life. And is it possible that aught on earth can prevent him from hasting at once to possess it? Yes, though he desired to depart, and was all but on the wing, he thought of his work as a minister of Christ; and such was his estimate of its importance, that his seraphic soul returned to it, and in the next moment you might have seen him writing himself, "Paul, a minister of Christ," as one of the highest titles—writing it with a greater sense of its dignity than he would have felt at ascending the steps of a throne and putting on a crown.

Rise, my brother, to a conception of the dignity of your office. You are an agent of heaven. All holy motives move you—motives which have made a Saviour, which have developed new features in the character of the blessed God. All spiritual forces meet you to-day at the threshold of your office, and offer to join you—the Spirit himself. All lofty themes gather around you—the highest among them are to be your ordinary topics. Think, your *ordinary* themes transcend the sublimest themes of the ancient philosophers. Socrates in his last hour could only lisp and guess on subjects on which you can fluently expatiate and authoritatively pronounce. Plato and Pythagoras sit at your feet. In your every discourse, *you* can produce a sublimer "Phædo," or become the teacher of Cicero on the "Nature of the gods."

You are a steward of the mysteries of God—a confidant of the heart of God. They only saw the shadows behind *a veil*, which you are permitted to raise, and within which you are called to officiate. You have not to do with shadows and with surfaces, but with essences—with the sublime, the imperishable, and the eternal. You have to do with the merit of an infinite sacrifice—the purposes of an infinite mind—the agencies of an infinite Spirit—the everlasting destinies of souls. The earth itself exists only as a stage for carrying on the great work to which you are committed. Then bid every inferior interest to stand aside, that you may see your work—to quit your path, that you may press right on. Gaze at it, till you see nothing else. Weigh it, measure it, walk around it, and you will be secure against vanity, from a perpetual consciousness of defect; and against indolence, from mere incapacity of finding rest otherwise than in labouring to fulfil it; and against defeat, for you will see that the glory of God is bound up with its triumph.

3. Remember, too, the noble succession in which you stand. To this motive the apostle appeals, "Make full proof of thy ministry; *for I* am now ready to be offered, and the time of *my* departure is at hand." In becoming a minister of Christ, you fall into a train in which the prophets and apostles, the martyrs and confessors, the reformers and missionaries, the worthies and saints of all ages have formed a part—a procession of which the front ranks have long been mingling with the radiance of the ineffable glory—a train which still reaches from earth to heaven. You are encompassed by a great cloud of witnesses. You pass to your work through their bending ranks. A part of their joy consists in seeing you prosecuting their work and emulating their example. They kindled the lamps we carry. Their feet wore the paths we tread—paths which were not seldom watered with tears—soddened with blood. We inherit their experience. "Other men have laboured, and we have entered into their labours." But we cannot live

on the past. We inherit it only as we *employ* it, and only that we *may* employ it. Their labours did not leave the world as they found it; and we *enter* into their labours only as we *carry them forwards,* and make full proof of our ministry.

4. And then glance at the glorious *issue* of such a service. Of this the apostle never seems to have lost sight. As in the context, as often as he lifted up his eyes, *there* was suspended the crown of life. My brother, we must not *so* think of the solemnity and responsibility of our work as to forget its *joyfulness.* I do not think that, generally speaking, enough of *this* element enters into our preaching. True, it is a tender, grave, affecting work. But it began in love, and ends in joy. Our theme is *gospel.* It was announced from heaven in song. Every step it takes is part of a triumphal march. Every truly Christian sermon is a rehearsal for the final chorus—is, in effect, already set to music. Every truly Christian ministry is a perpetual feast of the Epiphany—a constant *manifestation* of a living, glorified, triumphant Saviour. Every Christian minister works with the government of God—moves in a line with His purposes. Every hallowed aim takes an angel-shape. Every lofty aspiration enters into a bright imperishable form. There is nothing good which it does not bless—nothing great which does not bless it, and join it. That was a sublime view of a great artist which represented the sculptor as seeing, in the yet unshaped block of marble, the future statue. That is a sublimer view which not only foresees the angel, or the spirit of the just man made perfect, in the yet ignorant and unrenewed hearer, but which already places a congregation of such in grand perspective around the throne of God. And yet the apostle did this. He aspired to present all he addressed, "every man perfect before God." Blessed anticipation this! The faithful minister of Christ "gathereth fruit unto life eternal." He has operated on *mind*—cultivated *spirit*—sown immortal seed in immortal soil; and he goes

to reap a harvest which will be ever growing under his sickle—to pluck fruit over which time and change have no dominion. And the reward of each is to be enjoyed in fellowship with all; and is thus to be indefinitely enhanced. How shall we picture the joy of spirits, rescued themselves from endless death, meeting alike the embrace of those who were the means of saving them, and of those who were afterwards saved by them? How Divine the delight of finding themselves all in the presence of the great Master—receiving His approbation—entering into His joy—sharing it with Him—rejoicing with Him in the harmony and welfare of all sanctified spiritual being, in the attainment of which He allowed them the honour to participate. In prospect of that day, "the Lord bless you, and keep you; the Lord make his face to shine upon you, and be gracious unto you; the Lord lift up his countenance upon you, and give you peace. Amen."

CHARGE IV.*

THE GOOD SOLDIER OF JESUS CHRIST.

2 TIM. ii. 3, 4—"Thou therefore endure hardness, as a good soldier of Jesus Christ. No man that warreth entangleth himself with the affairs of this life, that he may please him who hath chosen him to be a soldier."

HERE are three things—the character to be aimed at by the Christian minister, the conditions of his success, and the hope which should inspire him in fulfilling those conditions.

I.

The character he is to aim at is that of a good soldier of Jesus Christ. This single simple phrase lays open to view, as by a magic touch, or as when the eyes of the prophet's servant were unsealed, a wide scene of martial conflict, filled with more than horses and chariots of fire. It may take us back in thought to the hour of the Fall; for then the struggle began, and the martial imagery was first employed—"The seed of the woman shall bruise the serpent's head." Through all the long ages of expectation which followed, the promised Deliverer was seen in prophetic vision, "girding His sword upon His thigh," and preparing for the great encounter. And though His arrival was at length announced as "peace on earth;" though that was the great design of His coming, and will be its certain issue; so certainly would the godlike attempt array all the hostility of hell against it, that He himself averred, "I am come," first

* This charge was Dr Harris's last public discourse, delivered, about three weeks before his death, at the recognition of the Rev. —— Macbrair, as minister of Barbican Chapel.

and in fact, "not to send peace on earth," though ultimately and in principle that is my only object, "but a sword."

1. As a soldier of Christ, it is important, first, that the Christian minister bear in mind the spiritual nature of the conquest He came to achieve. No marks of *earthly* greatness distinguished Him; and, therefore, none of the princes of this world knew Him. *Their* purple would have concealed His majesty, and their sceptres have enfeebled His arm. He had come to introduce a higher order of greatness—greatness which an earthly diadem could not enhance, nor a crown of thorns diminish; which a real sceptre could not increase, nor a mock sceptre degrade. Oh! who would not rather read that He stood at Pilate's bar, than that, for a single hour, He shared his throne? Occasional escapes of glory revealed Him to the few; but the world knew Him not. He was a prince in disguise. He asked for no *territory* on which to plant an ensign and develop His plans—the seat of His empire was the human soul. He unfurled no standard to rally an army—the foes He came to assail were spiritual—and the only sword rashly unsheathed in His behalf incurred His rebuke. No clang of trumpets or noisy pageant heralded His course—His ear was filled with other sounds, with the sighs and groans pressed from the suffering heart of sinful man. No willing subjects thronged His path—He had to make them. They are in revolt, and He must subdue them—under condemnation, and, as the champion of law, His first step must be to satisfy the demands of law on their behalf. How *can* he reconcile such benevolence with the claims of offended justice? how with such subjects lay the foundation of a righteous kingdom?

You know the amazing expedient! You know its *grace;* how, though He was in the form of God, and thought it no robbery to be equal with God, He made himself of no reputation, took our nature, assumed our liabilities, and humbled himself so as to become obedient unto death, even the death of the cross. You know its *wisdom;* how the same act which made it consistent for God to be gracious to man, made it impossible for man, when duly acquainted and divinely impressed with it, to resist its attractive and subduing force. You know its *power;* how, as His heart swelled with the consciousness of its moral might, He exclaimed, "Now shall the prince of this world be cast out: and I, if I be lifted up from the earth, will draw all men unto *me.*" Those human passions shall burn for me. Those countless multitudes shall bow to me. My cross shall stand the centre of the recovered world. "And for the joy thus set before him, He endured the cross, despising the shame."

Ask you, what signs announced that His death was the achievement of a triumph? Portents there were—stupendous signs—which shewed that His death drew to itself the attention, and, in some sense, involved the interests of the universe. Gross signs of physical struggle there were not. Power itself, you know, is not a thing to be seen. The magnitude of a contest cannot be estimated by its noise. Whole nations have often fought and fallen; but the deadly shock settled no question, originated no new impulse, turned back no current of fate; while inferior contests, waged on a scale too small to be heeded at the time, have often constituted epochs in the history of the race. Some great principle was involved, and they changed the face of the world. But here, here was a concentration of all the interests of time. Here all law looked for vindication, all government for sanction, and a world perishing for rescue. Here was a crisis too great to be signalized by gross, material conflict; too unearthly and spiritual to be apprehended by mortal sense. But the conflict was real, *because* it was moral. "He blotted out the handwriting that was against us, and took it out of the way, nailing it to His cross. And having spoiled principalities and powers, He made a show of them openly, triumphing over them *in it.*" To the eye of sense, no handwriting was visible but the superscription of His supposed offence; no engine of destruction but the cross;

no foe but such as the gates of Jerusalem had poured forth. Yet that was "*the* hour and power of darkness." An invisible foe confronted Him; a crowded field, impalpable to human eye, stretched around Him; and a concussion of powers, inaudible to human ear, went vibrating through the universe.

That was, indeed, the pang and travail of infinite love. That *He* should have been seen by the universe in a station of obedience; that He should find the highest glory in honouring the very law which man had ruined himself by resisting; that the great controversy respecting the *love* of God should be thus set at rest by the very same act which exalted His justice; that the *pardon* of the penitent should thus be made more compatible with the Divine rectitude —more glorious to God than his punishment would be; that Divinity and humanity should thus have been brought into the close embrace and union of one person—the open heart of infinite love discharge its transforming power on the heart of the world!—here, indeed, were elements of triumph! This was, indeed, to secure the means for converting this sin-worn world into a loyal province of the King of kings. "Wherefore God also hath highly exalted Him, and hath given to Him a name which is above every name" —hath given Him a right to the homage of every knee and the love of every heart; and hath given to Him the agency of the Holy Spirit to enforce that right, and so to recover the world to God.

2. Next, a soldier of Christ is one who, besides taking right views of the official triumph achieved by the Captain of our salvation, has himself been the subject of a spiritual conflict, and has so shared in the fruits of his Leader's triumph. The world is too apt to fancy that the only wars are those which involve the shock of arms; and hence human history has reported little more than "the confused noise of the battle of the warrior, and garments rolled in blood." During the middle ages, to be a soldier of the cross was to go to the

Holy Land to fight the Saracen. And even in the present day, it is to be feared that many of those who make the noisiest pretensions to a new type of Christianity know but little of any conflicts except conflicts of intellectualism and sentimentalism. The true soldier knows that earth has no battle-fields comparable to those of the human breast; that while every age has had some one country in which the wars of the period have been fought out till the soil was drenched with blood, the human breast is the unchanging battle-field of all periods alike; and that all the contests waged *without* are but mimic shows of the strife within. Tradition tells us that on the eve of certain great battles, armies of shadowy warriors were seen in the air, and the din of conflict heard there, as if in rehearsal for the coming strife. But of this we may rest assured, that all the outward struggles of earth are but the signs and spectres of the strife within. For "whence come wars and fightings among you? come they not from the sinful heart within?" They are but the human heart externalized. They do but repeat and represent the man within. Yes, I recall the expression that the martial language of the first promise, or of any spiritual conflict, is *figurative.* The *outward* conflicts of time are the figures, of which the stern realities are within. Did not the apostle mean this when he said, "We wrestle not against flesh and blood — against palpable, organized, assailable humanity; *that* would be an ordinary contest; but against invisible spirit-foes—against evil in its essence and fountain"?

Now you profess—the apostle might be regarded as saying to the Christian minister—to have entered on this spiritual conflict. You are no longer led captive by Satan at his will. You have burst your fetters, and have taken up arms. Sin had converted you into a rebel against God, and, if left unchecked, would have converted all your members into instruments of unrighteousness—an organization of evil. But a sight of the great love wherewith He hath loved you softened and subdued your spirit. You heard the appealing voice of mercy, and the weapons of hostility fell from your hands. You saw the cross—saw its deep Divine significance as an exponent of the love of God, and the symbol of human redemption—and the sight smote you into penitence, and aroused you to holy activity. You took sides, and began to mingle in the conflict of ages. Your own heart became a seat of war. You looked abroad, indeed, and saw that a struggle was raging without in every direction. But you soon felt that the counterpart of all that strife was within. Your heart was a disputed throne. Your new nature had to struggle for existence. Some of your own powers were doing battle with others—the lower with the higher. You discovered that however admirably some regions are adapted for war as compared with others, there is no region that admits of ambuscades, evolutions, and such various strategy, as the human breast. And you quickly found—did you not? —that in this war you could hope for success only as you were heartened and aided by Him who hath said, "Be of good cheer, I have overcome the world." And here begin your spiritual qualifications for the ministry. You have, first, the knowledge of your Lord's great spiritual war of deliverance to make known; and, next, you have this great experience of your own to make use of. You cannot but speak the things which you have seen, and heard, and felt.

3. And this reminds us, next, that a good soldier of Jesus Christ is one who is not only himself the subject of a spiritual conflict, and is so prepared to understand the nature of the great world-wide and time-long conflict between sin and holiness, but is actually able to take open and public part in it. He is not so engrossed with the defensive but that he can act on the aggressive. He does not so interpret the fact that Christ hath overcome the world, and destroyed the works of the devil, as to leave no world for him to overcome, and no satanic works for him to destroy, but as having made it possible for him to do both, by securing the necessary aids, and by shewing him how to employ them. He knows full

well that it is an entailed war—entailed from age to age. Many *human* conquests, or plans of conquest, have been of this description; that, for example, which the allied powers have just been resisting, is supposed to be part of a scheme of aggression dating ages back and looking ages forward. In such a case, the death of a leader or of a sovereign matters little. Hopes of peace may be excited for the moment, but the object is hereditary—conquest, an entailed obligation; and if the struggle pauses in one quarter, sooner or later it will be resumed with greater vigour in another. *Here* is an entailed war made necessary by an entailed rebellion—a war of deliverance—a war waged for human souls, and for the establishment of a kingdom of life and peace.

To this war *all* the subjects of Christ are summoned, in one capacity or another. To the Christian minister it may be said, You have volunteered to take arms, and go to the field. You have looked at man's spiritual thraldom, till you burn to do something for his release. You have thought of your Saviour's rights—for "the heathen are His inheritance, and the uttermost parts of the earth His promised possession" —and you are stirred to aid in asserting and recovering His rights. To you, therefore, the language of the apostle, "Put on the whole armour of God," comes like the martial shout, "To arms"—rings like a trumpet-blast on the field. "Put on the panoply of God, in order that you may be able to stand against the stratagems of the devil." *His*, remember, is a war of stratagems, ambuscades, and surprises. And let me remind you, that one of his most ordinary devices, in situations like yours, is to withdraw attention from the care due to your own soul; to induce you to lay aside your defensive armour; to make you feel as if your official position were a sufficient guarantee for your personal safety. "Wherefore," says the apostle, "put on the whole armour—girdle and breastplate, sandals and shield, helmet and sword—leave not a part exposed." And let it be *divine*—forged on no earthly anvil—tempered by no human skill—the whole armour *of*

God. The girdle of truth—the consciousness that you believe, and that it is God's truth which you believe. This gives the combatant alertness and buoyancy in the battle. The breastplate of righteousness—the cuirass of a higher, a diviner righteousness than your own, repelling every thrust aimed at your peace on the ground of your own conscious unworthiness and guilt. Your feet shod with the preparedness of the gospel of peace—giving alacrity and spontaneousness to your movements; for joy wings the feet of him who bears its message, and you are the bearer of gospel—the herald of God's peace. The shield, the great door-like shield, of faith—of unwavering confidence in God—turning aside the blazing arrows of the evil one. And take the helmet of salvation—not the mere hope of it; it is the conscious possession alone that "covers the head in day of battle." And the sword of the Spirit, which is the Word of God. You know how your Lord and Leader used it when He was assailed; and the same keen, bright weapon must flash in your hand. With all prayer and supplication, praying always in the Spirit; here is the state of mind in which the armour should be assumed, the position be taken, the enemy met, and the combat pursued. The order of thought is—make preparation, take the armour, stand, fight, and all the while be praying—praying in the Spirit—panting for His aid, and relying on it.

And if you refer to the passage in the sixth of Ephesians, you will see that the arms and armour enumerated are all for defence; reminding you of these facts, that your power over others must be preceded and prepared for by your conquest of yourself. Personal piety is essential to ministerial usefulness, and is, in many instances, the measure of it; implying, too, that this celestial mail must never be laid aside—your Christian self-vigilance never relaxed. It may be more necessary during the *second* period of your warfare than during the first, and during the third than in the second. At what an advanced period in their history had Athens and Rome to fight their sternest battles. Your Thermopylæ and

Cannæ may be yet to come. And reminding you, further, that if all this armour be necessary for the Christian in his private capacity, how much more may be expected in his public relation as a good soldier of Jesus Christ.

4. Again, in your new capacity, the apostle may be regarded as saying to Timothy, you are to be valiant for the truth. But what is truth? Whatever relates essentially to the remedial provision made by a holy God for the recovery of sinful man. If, for example, there have been some fearful *event* in the history of man which has made a provision of mercy necessary—if there be some one *Being* to whom every antecedent event pointed as the medium of that provision—if there be some one *saying* concerning Him deemed by God himself worthy of all acceptation, and some one *Agent* necessary to give due effect to that saying—and some one glorious *end* to be attained by the whole—then the propositions affirming these truths constitute the gospel; and no preacher can be said to exhibit them who does not make that event, that Being, that saying, that Agent, that end, the scope and end of his teaching. This is to preach Christ. Your ministry may have a vast circumference of instruction and admonition, of duty, motive, and illustration; but thus preach, and every point of the circumference will be seen running back to Christ the centre, or springing from Him. This is a line of truth reaching from the heart of God to the heart of man—the line along which the Spirit of God delights to move, and to which the heart of man first vibrates. If the Word of God, as a whole, be the sword of the Spirit, this is its soul-subduing edge. Let others blunt or polish it away if they will, be it your study to wield it with effect as a good soldier of Jesus Christ.

5. Further, the servant of Christ is to be faithful and urgent in the exhibition and application of the truth. He is not merely to retain his sword unimpaired, but to ply it with vigour. He is to storm that stronghold, the human will. And hence, in Scripture, the soldier in actual

conflict, the strife and agony of the wrestler, the eager swiftness of the racer, are all wrought into a vivid imagery to represent the work of salvation. "Agonize to enter in at the strait gate." "Lay hold on eternal life." "Work out your salvation with fear and trembling." "We pray you, in Christ's stead, be ye reconciled to God." Such is the living language of Scripture addressed to the human will. Minister of Christ, you cannot be more fervid than the Word of God—you cannot be more earnest than the occasion requires, nor more faithful, even in conversation, than your hearers expect you to be. Only let your ardour be tempered with love. "Knowing the terrors of the Lord, we persuade men." Could you concentrate all the awful terrors of God into a focus, into one fiery point, still you must so hold it over the heart as that it shall melt, not burn.

6. And, then, a good soldier knows that he must obey a guiding will. An army is a vast human organization with a single will. This chiefly distinguishes it from a mob. The soldier of the cross cannot doubt his relation to the Divine will. Minister of Christ, you have sworn *allegiance* to Christ. You have passed within that veil where God is jealous for His glory. You have entered a circle in which everything is sacred to His name, and sprinkled with blood. Every doctrine you are to preach is already prescribed—every principle from which you are to act already set down—a circle in which no will but His is to be thought of. Consult it, honour it, and it will deliver you from these three dangers. You will avoid getting into contests of your own—wasting in private and personal collisions resources which ought to be given to the great Christian cause—confounding your own affairs with zeal for your Leader.

You will not attempt, nor even connive at, a compromise with the foe. This—whether in relation to truth or holiness—whether in the pulpit or the parlour—is treason in the camp. And, then, think how duty is simplified by such a course—how the sources of perplexity are dried up—how, when you can say, "Well, let whatever consequences may result, I am obeying the will of my Divine Leader," how the heart is lightened of care, and the spirit cheered as with sunshine from the face of God. Never may *you* be destitute of that consolation!

II.

But, secondly, in order to be a good soldier of Christ, two conditions are here specified. "No man that warreth entangleth himself with the affairs of this life." In other words, he must be characterized by *singleness of aim*. It is something to have an aim—any aim—in life. In proportion as that aim is high, it deserves, and is likely to require concentration—to require that one thing after another shall be dropped, abandoned, left behind, as so much impediment-baggage, in order to attain it. Here is the highest aim—relating to the diffusion of the life of God—and therefore requiring that the alien affairs of this life should be subordinated to it. You, fellow-soldier, have doubtless read the rules of war on this subject prescribed to the Roman soldier. Evidently the apostle had read them—probably while he was a prisoner in the Prætorium. The rules of the Christian war are not less stringent. And, by your position, fellow-soldier of the cross, you subscribe them. Like the Roman soldier, you take your *sacramentum*, your oath of obedience and fidelity. Here is your motto—"One thing I do." Not that your activity will be restricted to one form of duty—to the mere function of preaching. The apostle's was not. His labours were diversified without end. But one aim gave unity to the whole—that he might do his utmost for the Church of Christ.

You go forth, not merely to do the work of an evangelist, but to assist as a tutor in the literary training of students for the ministry. Only let that training be discharged with a view to *their* ministry, as well as in subordination to *your own;* only remember that the training is a means of which the ministry of the gospel is the end, and your work will still be one. Relaxation you must have in the prosecution of your work, and in order to it—but only in order to it. Taste must be indulged only sparingly. Works of imagination resorted to seldom or not at all. Even the claims of classical literature—though belonging to your office—must be conscientiously adjusted, and not exceeded. You know that just so much friction as takes place in the internal working of a piece of machinery is so much power lost to the application of the machine. A good soldier of the cross is a man internally united and self-governed. No part of his nature is wanting—no part exercising a counter-influence. The whole man is bound and braced up for duty. One thing he feels, and one thing he does. He is an agent of heaven. For to him to live is Christ. Necessity is laid upon him.

2. The second condition is, that he "endure hardness,"—that is, that he lay his account with a certain amount of trial. Had other human beings been living at the time, one can easily imagine how they would have envied the happy dwellers in Eden; how, as they approached the sacred enclosure, or looked through its gates, or gazed on its golden fruits and verdant foliage, they would have thought only of immortal food, and celestial visitants, and holy security, and have sighed to share the blessedness of the place. Did the result justify such a desire? Perhaps the very spot which would have most intently fixed their gaze was that which concealed the serpent, and the tree whose fruit would have waved most pleasantly to the eye was the tree of the knowledge of good and evil. And because your office, man of God, places you near to the tree of life, the inconsiderate may fancy that you are exempt from every danger, and may envy your security. But is it so? You know that change of station is only change of danger—that every new relation is only a new form of trial.

Your duties, as I have just intimated, are diverse; shall the inferior prove a snare—absorbing your attention and diverting your spirit from the superior—the exhibition and enforcement of Christian truth? You will assume your duties far removed from those whose opinion at present you may chiefly value; but shall you on that account act inconsiderately, and not rather feel yourself referred all the more to your Christian principles? As an agent of an institution, you will have to act much in concert with others; shall you be chargeable with an unconciliatory spirit? That be far from you; and I believe it will be far from you. Your duties are of regular recurrence; shall that regularity in public lead to irregularity in private? shall the fire of the sanctuary be kept bright and burning by fuel stolen from the altar of the closet? or shall your exhaustion in public only send you more eagerly back to the fountain of life, there to renew your spiritual strength? Your office will invest you with influence, and secure you respect; shall that respect beget self-importance? or shall it not lead you to gaze at the magnitude of your work, till in the sight of *its* glory *you* disappear? Should you find the discharge of your duties grow easy by habit, shall it be followed by indolence and self-dependence? or shall it lead you to enlarge the sphere of your activity for God?

To *dangers* may be added *trials.* You would smile at hearing of a recruit bargaining at his enlistment, that he should not be subjected to fatiguing marches, or coarseness of fare, to privations, dangers, or to anything incompatible with his personal comfort. The sufferings of the Crimean campaign fearfully contrast with such a notion of service. Man of God, you did not enter the ministry on such terms; although it is to be feared there are some who would not enter it on any other. You know that self-denial, endurance, is a law of Christian discipleship—"If any man will come after me, let him deny himself, take up *his* cross, and follow me." True; the world's *redemption* required *the mediatorial* cross. But not the less true is it, that the world's salvation requires from each Christian a *moral* cross—cannot be effected without. What meant the apostle *but* this, when he tells us that he panted to "fill up that which is behind of the afflictions of Christ for his body's sake, which is the Church." It is not enough that we glory in the cross as the symbol of our own salvation. We must take up our own cross in the work of saving others. The Church exists only *while* struggling, and *by* struggling. She is not a palace, but an encampment on the field. And you are in the field. "Endure hardness as a good soldier of Jesus Christ."

III.

But why should he act thus? The text suggests, thirdly, the motive or hope which should inspire him—that he may please Him that hath chosen him to be a soldier; and if the followers of an earthly standard find inspiration in their leader, how much more should he!

Remember, servant of Christ, that He you serve is not an abstraction. He is a Person. Imagine Him present with you—you cannot make a loftier use of your imagination. Believe Him present—your faith cannot know a sublimer exercise. He is a Person with affections. He hath *loved* you. He, the Infinite, hath loved you, and chosen you to be a soldier of the cross. Let that sentiment lie upon your heart to melt it; and you will daily resort to Him—consult Him—converse with Him—appeal to Him—study to please Him.

You would please Him by steadily keeping in view the solemnity of your *final* account, but still more by continually rendering to Him your account *now*. We read in the sixth of Mark, "And the apostles gathered themselves together unto Jesus, and told him all things, both what they had done and what they had taught." And when Paul says of certain Christian teachers, "They watch for your souls as they that must give account," the reference appears to be to an account which they were in the *habit* of giving. My brother soldier, you could not go into the presence of your Lord from time to time for this purpose, without being conscious, like the High Priest when he came forth from within the veil, of a profounder sense of your official responsibility.

Earthly commanders and sovereigns repair to the seat of war to inspirit their armies by their presence. Your Commander is there before you—never quits the field—" Lo, I am with you always." From the first moment of your ministry to the last, His eye will never cease to be fixed on you as a flame of fire. Were it to be withdrawn from every other object in the universe, on His minister it would still continue to be fastened; so that at any moment of your course He could say to you, as He did to the ministers of certain other churches, " I know thy works," and could proceed to recount every item of your service.

Servant of Christ, study to please the Captain of your salvation, and you will not need particular rules and minute prescriptions; you will be a law to yourself—you will be obeying all laws at once, without feeling that you are subjected to any. Approve yourself to Him, and the very attempt will lift your whole nature at once out of the ranks of ordinary piety, above the level of ordinary activity, and place you on a summit perpetually lighted up with the beams of the Divine countenance. Approve yourself to Him, and everything excellent will approve itself unto you. You will carry along with you the sympathy and influence of everything moving in the same direction. Approve yourself unto God, and what a society do you join! The most distinguished saint could not receive a higher testimony than this, that he pleased God. Your Lord himself said, and felt that He was uttering His highest vindication in saying it, " I always do the things that please Him."

Happy, exalted condition of service this! The highest archangel, as he speeds his way on some high and heavenly mission, knows no loftier motive than this—" that he is pleasing Him" " whose favour is life." And yet this is to be your prevailing motive—the happy nature of your entire service. True, it is a tender, grave, affecting work; but it began in love, and ends in joy. It was announced from heaven in song. Every step it takes is part of a triumphal march. Every Christian soldier joins—not a band called immortal (like that of Alexander's) by a mere poetic figure, but Christ's true immortal band, for he quits the field *here* only to join a world of conquerors *there.* Every truly Christian sermon is a rehearsal for the final chorus—is, in effect, already set to music. Every truly Christian ministry is a perpetual proclamation of a living, glorified, and triumphant Saviour. Every life of Christian usefulness—every instance of success—is a prelude of the final song—the TE DEUM of the universe. Live and labour, my brother soldier, for that day, as if the light of its dawn already fell on your path. The only triumphs recounted then will be those of holiness over sin—of the good soldier of Christ over the powers of darkness. The only honours distributed then will be the crown and the palm awarded by the hand of Sovereign Grace. May your hand, now wielding the sword, then bear the palm—and the brow that now wears the helmet be then crowned with the garland—and the heart that now receives the sympathy of his fellow-soldiers of the cross, then receive the "WELL DONE" of the Divine Commander himself. "O man of God, fight the good fight of faith;" be "a good soldier of Jesus Christ." And the Lord bless you, and keep you. The Lord make His face to shine upon you, and be gracious unto you! The Lord lift up His countenance upon you, and give you peace! Amen!

VALUABLE WORKS PUBLISHED BY GOULD & LINCOLN, BOSTON.

CYCLOPÆDIA OF ANECDOTES OF LITERATURE AND THE FINE ARTS.

A choice selection of Anecdotes of the various forms of Literature, of the Arts, of Architecture, Engravings, Music, Poetry, Painting and Sculpture, and of the most celebrated Literary Characters and Artists of different Countries and Ages, &c. By KAZLITT ARVINE, A. M. With numerous Illustrations. 725 pages, octavo, cloth, $3.00.

This is unquestionably the choicest collection of ANECDOTES ever published. It contains THREE THOUSAND AND FORTY ANECDOTES, and more than ONE HUNDRED AND FIFTY ILLUSTRATIONS. It is admirably adapted to literary and scientific men, to artists, mechanics, and others, as a DICTIONARY FOR REFERENCE, in relation to facts on the numberless subjects and characters introduced.

KITTO'S POPULAR CYCLOPÆDIA OF BIBLICAL LITERATURE.

Condensed from the larger work, by the author, JOHN KITTO, D. D. Assisted by JAMES TAYLOR, D. D. With *over* 500 *Illustrations*. Octavo, 812 pp., cloth, $3.00.

This work answers the purpose of a commentary, while at the same time it furnishes a complete DICTIONARY OF THE BIBLE, embodying the products of the best and most recent researches in biblical literature, in which the scholars of Europe and America have been engaged. It is not only intended for ministers and theological students, but is also particularly adapted to parents, Sabbath-school teachers, and the great body of the religious public.

HISTORY OF PALESTINE.

With the Geography and Natural History of the Country, the Customs and Institutions of the Hebrews, etc. By JOHN KITTO, D. D. With upwards of 200 Illustrations. 12mo, cloth, $1.25.

Beyond all dispute this is the best historical compendium of the Holy Land, from the days of Abraham to those of the late Pasha of Egypt, Mehemet Ali. — [Edinburgh Review.

☞ In the numerous notices and reviews, the work has been strongly recommended, as not only admirably adapted to the FAMILY, but also as a text-book for SABBATH and WEEK DAY SCHOOLS.

CHAMBERS'S CYCLOPÆDIA OF ENGLISH LITERATURE.

Two large imperial octavo volumes of 1400 pages; with upwards of 300 elegant Illustrations. By ROBERT CHAMBERS. Embossed cloth, $5.00.

This work embraces about ONE THOUSAND AUTHORS, chronologically arranged and classed as Poets, Historians, Dramatists, Philosophers, Metaphysicians, Divines, etc., with choice selections from their writings, connected by a Biographical, Historical, and Critical Narrative; thus presenting a complete view of English literature from the earliest to the present time. Let the reader open where he will, he cannot fail to find matter for profit and delight. The selections are gems — infinite riches in a little room; in the language of another, "A WHOLE ENGLISH LIBRARY FUSED DOWN INTO ONE CHEAP BOOK!"

CHAMBERS'S MISCELLANY OF USEFUL AND ENTERTAINING KNOWLEDGE.

By WILLIAM CHAMBERS. With Illustrations. Ten vols., 16mo, cloth, $7.00.

CHAMBERS'S HOME BOOK AND POCKET MISCELLANY.

A choice Selection of Interesting and Instructive Reading for the Old and the Young. Six vols. 16mo, cloth, $3.00.

This work is fully equal, if not superior, to either of the Chambers's other works in interest, containing a vast fund of valuable information, furnishing ample variety for every class of readers.

CHAMBERS'S REPOSITORY OF INSTRUCTIVE AND AMUSING PAPERS.

With Illustrations. 16mo, cloth, bound. 4 vols. in two, $1.75; and 4 vols. in one, $1.50.

SACRED RHETORIC;

Or, Composition and Delivery of Sermons. By HENRY J. RIPLEY, Professor in Newton Theological Institution. Including Professor Ware's Hints on Extemporaneous Preaching. 12mo, 75 cts.

THE PREACHER AND THE KING;

Or, Bourdaloue in the Court of Louis XIV. An Account of that distinguished Era, Translated from the French of L. F. BUNGENER. With an Introduction by the Rev. GEORGE POTTS, D. D. New edition, with a fine Likeness, and a Sketch of the Author's Life. 12mo, cloth, $1.25.

It combines substantial history with the highest charm of romance. Its attractions are so various that it can hardly fail to find readers of almost every description. — [Puritan Recorder.

THE PRIEST AND THE HUGUENOT;

Or, Persecution in the Age of Louis XV. Translated from the French of L. F. BUNGENER. 2 vols., 12mo, cloth, $2.25.

☞ This is truly a masterly production, full of interest, and may be set down as one of the greatest Protestant works of the age.

FOOTSTEPS OF OUR FOREFATHERS.

What they Suffered and what they Sought. Describing Localities and portraying Personages and Events conspicuous in the Struggles for Religious Liberty. By JAMES G. MIALL. Thirty-six fine Illustrations. 12mo, $1.00.

An exceedingly entertaining work. The reader soon becomes so deeply entertained that he finds it difficult to lay aside the book till finished. — [Ch. Parlor Mag.

A work absorbingly interesting, and very instructive. — [Western Lit. Magazine.

MEMORIALS OF EARLY CHRISTIANITY.

Presenting, in a graphic, compact, and popular form, Memorable Events of Early Ecclesiastical History, etc. By JAMES G. MIALL. With numerous elegant Illustrations. 12mo, cloth, $1.00.

☞ This, like the "Footsteps of our Forefathers," will be found a work of uncommon interest.

WORKS BY JOHN HARRIS, D. D.

THE PRE-ADAMITE EARTH. Contributions to Theological Science. 12mo, cloth, $1.00.

MAN PRIMEVAL; or, the Constitution and Primitive Condition of the Human Being. With a fine Portrait of the Author. 12mo, cloth, $1.25.

PATRIARCHY; or, THE FAMILY. Its Constitution and Probation; being the *third* volume of "Contributions to Theological Science." $1.25.

THE GREAT TEACHER; or, Characteristics of our Lord's Ministry. With an Introductory Essay. By H. HUMPHREY, D. D. 12mo, cloth, 85 cts.

THE GREAT COMMISSION; or, the Christian Church constituted and charged to convey the Gospel to the World. Introductory Essay by W. R. WILLIAMS, D. D. 12mo, cloth, $1.00.

ZEBULON; Or, the Moral Claims of Seamen. 18mo, cloth, 25 cts.

PHILIP DODDRIDGE.

His Life and Labors. By JOHN STOUGHTON, D. D., with beautiful Illuminated Title-page and Frontispiece. 16mo, cloth, 60 cents.

THE EVIDENCES OF CHRISTIANITY,

As exhibited in the writings of its apologists, down to Augustine. By W. J. BOLTON, of Gonville and Caius College, Cambridge. 12mo, cloth, 80 cents.

WORKS BY DR. TWEEDIE.

GLAD TIDINGS; or, The Gospel of Peace. A series of Daily Meditations for Christian Disciples. By Rev. W. K. TWEEDIE, D. D. With elegant Illustrated Title-page. 16mo, cloth, 63 cts.

THE MORN OF LIFE; or, Examples of Female Excellence. A Book for Young Ladies. 16mo, cloth. *In press.*

A LAMP TO THE PATH; or, the Bible in the Heart, the Home, and the Market Place. With an elegant Illustrated Title-page. 16mo, cloth, 63 cts.

SEED TIME AND HARVEST; or, Sow Well and Reap Well. A Book for the Young. With an elegant Illustrated Title-page. 16mo, cloth, 63 cts.

☞ The above works, by Dr. Tweedie, are of uniform size and style. They are most charming, pious, and instructive works, beautifully gotten up, and well adapted for "gift-books."

WORKS BY JOHN ANGELL JAMES.

THE CHURCH MEMBER'S GUIDE; Edited by J. O. CHOULES, D D. New edition. With an Introductory Essay by Rev. HUBBARD WINSLOW. Cloth, 33c.

CHRISTIAN PROGRESS. A Sequel to the Anxious Inquirer. 18mo, cloth, 31c.

☞ one of the best and most useful works of this popular author.

THE CHURCH IN EARNEST. Seventh thousand. 18mo, cloth, 40 cents

MOTHERS OF THE WISE AND GOOD.

By JABEZ BURNS, D. D. 16mo, cloth, 75 cents.

We wish it were in every family, and read by every mother in the land.—[Lutheran Observer.

MY MOTHER;

Or, Recollections of Maternal Influence. By a New England Clergyman. With a beautiful Frontispiece. 12mo, cloth, 75 cents.

This is one of the most charming books that have issued from the press for a long period. "It is," says a distinguished author, "one of those rare pictures painted from life with the exquisite skill of one of the 'Old Masters,' which so seldom present themselves to the amateur."

THE EXCELLENT WOMAN.

With an Introduction by Rev. W. B. SPRAGUE, D.D. Containing twenty-four splendid Illustrations. 12mo, cloth, $1.00; cloth, gilt, $1.75; extra Turkey, $2.50.

☞ This elegant volume is an appropriate and valuable "gift book" for the husband to present the wife, or the child the mother.

MEMORIES OF A GRANDMOTHER.

By a Lady of Massachusetts. 16mo, cloth, 50 cents,

THE MARRIAGE RING;

Or, How to make Home Happy. By JOHN ANGELL JAMES. Beautiful illustrated edition 16mo, cloth, gilt, 75 cents.

A beautiful volume, and a very suitable present to a newly-married couple.—[N. Y. Christian Intelligencer.

WORKS BY WILLIAM R. WILLIAMS, D. D.

RELIGIOUS PROGRESS; Discourses on the Development of the Christian Character. 12mo, cloth, 85 cts.

This work is from the pen of one of the brightest lights of the American pulpit. We scarcely know of any living writer who has a finer command of powerful thought and glowing, impressive language than he.—[DR. SPRAGUE, Alb. Atl.

LECTURES ON THE LORD'S PRAYER Third edition. 12mo, cloth, 85 cts.

Their breadth of view, strength of logic, and stirring eloquence place them among the very best homilitical efforts of the age. Every page is full of suggestions as well as eloquence.—Ch. Parlor Mag.

MISCELLANIES. New improved edition. *Price reduced.* 12mo, $1 25.

THE CRUISE OF THE NORTH STAR;

A Narrative of the Excursion of Mr. Vanderbilt's Party, in her Voyage to England, Russia, Denmark, France, Spain, Italy, Malta, Turkey, Madeira, etc. By Rev. JOHN OVERTON CHOULES, D. D. With elegant Illustrations, etc. 12mo, cloth, gilt back and sides, $1.50.

VISITS TO EUROPEAN CELEBRITIES.

By the Rev. WILLIAM B. SPRAGUE, D.D. 12mo, cloth, $1.00.

A series of graphic and life-like Personal Sketches of many of the most distinguished men and women of Europe, with whom the author became acquainted in the course of several European tours, where he saw them in their own homes and under the most advantageous circumstances. "It was my uniform custom, after every such interview, to take copious memoranda of the conversation, including an account of the individual's appearance and manners; in short, defining, as well as I could, the whole impression which his physical, intellectual, and moral man had made upon me." From the memoranda thus made, the material for the present instructive and exceedingly interesting volume is derived. Besides these "pen and ink" sketches, the work contains the novel attraction of a FAC SIMILE OF THE SIGNATURE of each of the persons introduced.

PILGRIMAGE TO EGYPT; EXPLORATIONS OF THE NILE.

With Observations, illustrative of the Manners, Customs, etc. By Hon. J. V. C. SMITH, M. D. With numerous elegant Engravings. 12mo, cloth, $1.25.

THE STORY OF THE CAMPAIGN.

A complete Narrative of the War in Southern Russia. Written in a Tent in the Crimea. By Major E. BRUCE HAMLEY, author of "Lady Lee's Widowhood." With a new and complete Map of the Seat of War. 12mo, paper covers, 37½ cts.

POETICAL WORKS.

MILTON'S POETICAL WORKS. With Life and Elegant Illustrations. 16mo, cloth, $1.00; fine cloth, gilt, $1.25.

POETICAL WORKS OF SIR WALTER SCOTT. With Life, and Illustrations on Steel. 16mo, cl., $1; fine cl., gilt, $1.25.

COMPLETE POETICAL WORKS OF WILLIAM COWPER. With a Life, and Critical Notices of his Writings. With new and elegant Illustrations on Steel. 16mo, cloth, $1.00; fine cloth, gilt, $1.25.

☞ The above Poetical Works, by standard authors, are all of uniform size and style, printed on fine paper, from clear, distinct type, with new and elegant illustrations, richly bound in full gilt, and plain; thus rendering them, in connection with the exceedingly LOW PRICE at which they are offered, the cheapest and most desirable of any of the numerous editions of these author's works now in the market.

LIFE AND CORRESPONDENCE OF JOHN FOSTER.

Edited by J. E. RYLAND, with Notices of Mr. Foster as a Preacher and a Companion. By JOHN SHEPPARD. Two volumes in one, 700 pages. 12mo, cloth, $1.25.

In simplicity of language, in majesty of conception, in the eloquence of that conciseness which conveys in a short sentence more meaning than the mind dares at once admit, — his writings are unmatched. — [North British Review.

GUIDO AND JULIUS.

The Doctrine of Sin and the Propitiator; or, the True Consecration of the Doubter. Exhibited in the Correspondence of two Friends. By FREDERICK AUGUSTUS O. THOLUCH, D. D. Translated by JONATHAN EDWARDS RYLAND. With an Introduction by JOHN PYE SMITH, D. D. 16mo, cloth, 60 cents.

NEW AND COMPLETE CONDENSED CONCORDANCE

To the Holy Scriptures. By ALEXANDER CRUDEN. Revised and re-edited by Rev. DAVID KING, L.L. D. Octavo, cloth backs, $1.25; sheep, $1.50.

GOULD AND LINCOLN,

59 WASHINGTON STREET, BOSTON,

Would call particular attention to the following valuable works described in their Catalogue of Publications, viz.:

Hugh Miller's Works.

Baync's Works. Walker's Works. Miall's Works. Bungener's Work.

Annual of Scientific Discovery. Knight's Knowledge is Power.

Krummacher's Suffering Saviour,

Banvard's American Histories. The Aimwell Stories.

Newcomb's Works. Tweedie's Works. Chambers's Works. Harris' Works.

Kitto's Cyclopædia of Biblical Literature.

Mrs. Knight's Life of Montgomery. Kitto's History of Palestin

Wheewell's Work. Wayland's Works. Agassiz's Works.

William's Works. Guyot's Works.

Thompson's Better Land. Kimball's Heaven. Valuable Works on Missions.

Haven's Mental Philosophy. Buchanan's Modern Atheism.

Cruden's Condensed Concordance. Eadie's Analytical Concordance.

The Psalmist: a Collection of Hymns.

Valuable School Books. Works for Sabbath Schools.

Memoir of Amos Lawrence.

Poetical Works of Milton, Cowper, Scott. Elegant Miniature Volumes.

Arvine's Cyclopædia of Anecdotes.

Ripley's Notes on Gospels, Acts, and Romans.

Sprague's European Celebrities. Marsh's Camel and the Hallig.

Roget's Thesaurus of English Words.

Hackett's Notes on Acts. M'Whorter's Yahveh Christ.

Siebold and Stannius's Comparative Anatomy. Marco's Geological Map, U. S.

Religious and Miscellaneous Works.

Works in the various Departments of Literature, Science and Art.

www.ingramcontent.com/pod-product-compliance
Lightning Source LLC
LaVergne TN
LVHW020106110826
845151LV00001B/75